Safe Passage

Safe Passage

SAFE PASSAGE

A Global Spiritual Sourcebook for Care at the End of Life

Edited by

Mark Lazenby, MA, MSN, PhD

Assistant Professor of Nursing & Divinity
Core Faculty, Council on Middle East Studies
Yale University
New Haven, Connecticut

Ruth McCorkle, PhD, RN, FAAN

Florence S. Wald Professor of Nursing
* and Professor of Epidemiology*
School of Nursing and School of Public Health
Yale University
Director of Psychosocial Research
Yale Comprehensive Cancer Center
Yale University
New Haven, Connecticut

Daniel P. Sulmasy, MD, PhD

Kilbride-Clinton Professor of Medicine and Ethics,
The Department of Medicine and Divinity School
Associate Director, MacLean Center for Clinical Medical Ethics
Co-Director, Program on Medicine and Religion
The University of Chicago
Chicago, Illinois

OXFORD
UNIVERSITY PRESS

OXFORD
UNIVERSITY PRESS

Oxford University Press is a department of the University of Oxford.
It furthers the University's objective of excellence in research, scholarship,
and education by publishing worldwide.

Oxford   New York
Auckland   Cape Town   Dar es Salaam   Hong Kong   Karachi
Kuala Lumpur   Madrid   Melbourne   Mexico City   Nairobi
New Delhi   Shanghai   Taipei   Toronto

With offices in
Argentina   Austria   Brazil   Chile   Czech Republic   France   Greece
Guatemala   Hungary   Italy   Japan   Poland   Portugal   Singapore
South Korea   Switzerland   Thailand   Turkey   Ukraine   Vietnam

Oxford is a registered trademark of Oxford University Press
in the UK and certain other countries.

Published in the United States of America by
Oxford University Press
198 Madison Avenue, New York, NY 10016

Library of Congress Cataloging-in-Publication Data
Safe passage (Oxford University Press)
Safe passage : a global spiritual sourcebook for care at the end of life / edited by Mark Lazenby, Ruth
McCorkle, Daniel P. Sulmasy.
    p. ; cm.
Includes bibliographical references and index.
ISBN 978-0-19-991463-0 (alk. paper)
I. Lazenby, Mark, editor.   II. McCorkle, Ruth, 1941– editor.   III. Sulmasy, Daniel P.,
1956– editor.   IV. Title.
[DNLM: 1. Terminal Care—psychology.   2. Attitude to Death—ethnology.
3. Cross-Cultural Comparison.   4. Spirituality.   5. Terminal Care—history. WB 310]
R726.8
616.02'9—dc23   2013021648

9 8 7 6 5 4 3
Printed in the United States of America
on acid-free paper

For Jodi, for your love and patience, advice and strength—on you I constantly rely; and
For Ethan, for your gentle presence and preternatural wisdom—you assure me of the beauty of life and the reality of the spirit. (ML)

℅

For the many young men in Vietnam who started me on my journey to improve the care of the dying,
To Cicely Saunders who taught me the importance of being present with people and their families,
To Jeanne Benoliel who taught me how to study people who are dying and their families,
To my children who give me the strength and joy in everyday living,
And to my mother and father who taught me the values of family, culture, and faith are all encompassing in life and death. (RM)

℅

For Lois—our journey to new life began in our thinking together about death. You are my inspiration. You are my *vita nuova*. (DPS)

A NOTE ABOUT HOW TO READ THIS BOOK

This book is not linear. It should not be read linearly, either. It is a sourcebook. How might one read a sourcebook? Imagine that it is an app on your handheld device or tablet. Imagine that this app is about the spiritual decisions you face with respect to the end of life—for your loved ones, your patients, the people in your community (whether it be a spiritual or civic community), or even regarding your own life. Search on this app for the particular decision you or those near you face. Or "click" on your or another particular spiritual tradition, or on the region of the world from which you or they come or live. Read what comes up. Parts of this book are scholarly. Academics, students, clergy, and health care professionals may find interest in reading these parts linearly, particularly the first unit. Ethicists and scholars of religion may wish to read the second unit straight through—to hunt for similarities and differences among spiritual traditions. However one reads it, though, one should still think of it as an app—a tool that can be arranged and rearranged according to one's spiritual, clinical, or personal questions.

CONTENTS

IV. Coda
 Mark Lazenby, Ruth McCorkle, Daniel P. Sulmasy

FOREWORD

Major traditions of religion and spirituality have endured in large part because they have had something to say in response to the deepest questions in people's lives. These questions surely include our searches for meaning in experiences of suffering, of illness, of dying; and they include our discernment of responsibilities one to another in the face of such human experiences. We perhaps know more about these experiences today than ever before, but they also generate new and more complex questions. The contexts—medical, familial, social, political, economic—in which we make choices in response to such experiences have changed, and so have our options. Resolutions of dilemmas, conflicts, even uncertainties about otherwise reasonable actions, do not come so easily anymore. This is especially true in situations where we, or ones we care for, face decisions as we approach our dying.

This volume is framed with the underlying assumption that religious and spiritual traditions can, at least for many people, shed light on our concrete situations, as well as "make sense" of our hopes and fears, our desires and decisions. Although it is true that diverse traditions can offer quite different (even opposing) answers to fundamental human questions, this may not detract from their importance in discerning truthful responses to the challenge of human experiences. Most of us no longer live in cultures or spiritual traditions that are isolated from one another. We find ourselves in medical contexts, for example, where there may be already shared perspectives, values, and goals, but there may also be profoundly diverse worldviews, yielding divergent or convergent interpretations of illness, pain, or threats to physical and spiritual life. We have therefore come to realize the importance of understanding our own traditions, but not only our own. For it is in learning about other traditions that we may come to a better knowledge of our own; it is in understanding other traditions that we may come to better care for those who stand within them.

Religious and spiritual insights need not do violence to empirical data and ordinary logic; they may illuminate and be illuminated by them. This particular volume is an extraordinary treasure and gift, since it gives us access to all of these sources of insight. It fits our time and our needs, providing avenues to mutual respect, honor, compassion and care. It offers us methods and tools, knowledge and wisdom. Multidisciplinary, cross-cultural, and interreligious, its goals are eminently practical. At the same time, it may take us to the springs of our beliefs and our hopes, and thereby lead us—caring and cared for—to the rivers of action.

Margaret Farley, PhD, RSM
Gilbert L. Stark Professor Emerita of Christian Ethics
Yale University Divinity School
New Haven, Connecticut
USA

ACKNOWLEDGMENTS

We acknowledge the work of the Marshall Islands Research Focus Group: Maria Kabua Fowler (traditional leader and activist), Brenda Mellon (Customary Law and Language Commission), Lydia Tibon (*Kijle*, an NGO for women's health), Miram deBrum (*Wutmii*, Women United Together—Marshall Islands), Marcelle Badock (Marshall Islands Cancer Survivors), Camilla Ingram (Marshall Islands Cancer Survivors), Rosina Korean (College of the Marshall Islands), Brooke Takala Abraham, Terse Timothy, Susan Jieta, and Yolanda McKay (University of the South Pacific). We also acknowledge Abby Gross, Andrea Seils, and Rebecca Suzan at Oxford University Press; their dedication, guidance, and technical support have made this book a reality.

CONTRIBUTORS

Ramaswamy Akileswaran, MD
CEO and Medical Director
HCA Hospice Care
Chairman, Singapore Hospice
    Council
Singapore, Singapore

Elizabeth Alexander, PhD
Thomas E. Donnelley Professor of
    African American Studies
Professor American Studies & English
Yale University
New Haven, Connecticut

Mohammad Zafir Al-Shahri, MD
Consultant, Palliative Medicine
Director, Palliative Medicine
    Fellowship Program
King Faisal Specialist Hospital &
    Research Center
Riyadh, Saudi Arabia

**Canon James Nathaniel Amanze,
    PhD**
Professor, Theology & Religious
    Studies
Department of Theology & Religious
    Studies
University of Botswana
Gaborone, Botswana

Norshisham Bin Main, MD
Consultant in Geriatric Medicine
Khoo Teck Puat Hospital
Singapore, Singapore

Rabbi Herbert Brockman, PhD
Congregation Mishkan Israel
Lecturer, Supervised Ministries
Yale Divinity School
New Haven, Connecticut

Eduardo Bruera, MD
Professor
Department of Palliative Care and
    Rehabilitation Medicine
University of Texas MD Anderson
    Cancer Center
Houston, Texas

Ira Byock, MD
Palliative Care Physician
Professor of Medicine
Geisel School of Medicine
    at Dartmouth
Lebanon, New Hampshire

Daniel Callahan, PhD
Senior Research Scholar and
    President Emeritus
The Hastings Center
Garrison, New York

Arthur Caplan, PhD
Drs. William F. and Virginia
  Connolly Mitty Chair
Director, Division of Medical
  Ethics
NYU Langome Medical Center
New York, New York

Carlos Centeno, MD, PhD
Assistant Professor of Palliative
  Medicine
ATLANTES Research Program
Institute for Culture and Society (ICS)
University of Navarra
Pamplona, Spain

Surjeet Kaur Chahal, PhD
Professor of Philosophy
Head of the Department of
  Philosophy
University of Pune
Pune, India

**Santosh K. Chaturvedi, MD,
  FRCPsych**
Professor of Psychiatry
National Institute of Mental Health
  & Neurosciences
Bangalore, India

David Clark, PhD
Professor
School of Interdisciplinary
  Studies
University of Glasgow
Scotland, United Kingdom

Anne J. Davis, RN, PhD, FAAN
Professor Emerita of Nursing
University of California San
  Francisco
San Francisco, California

Marvin Omar Delgado-Guay, MD
Assistant Professor
Department of Palliative Care and
  Rehabilitation Medicine
The University of Texas MD
  Anderson Cancer Center
Houston, Texas

Ruiping Fan, PhD
Professor of Philosophy
Department of Public & Social
  Administration
City University of Hong Kong
Hong Kong, China

**Betty Ferrell, RN, PhD,
  FAAN, FPCN**
Professor
Nursing Research and Education
City of Hope
Duarte, California

Kathleen M. Foley, MD
The Society of Memorial
  Sloan-Kettering Cancer
  Center Chair
Memorial Sloan-Kettering
  Cancer Center
New York, New York

**Reverend David Galimaka-
  Kabalega, BD, DipTh**
Head of Pastoral Care,
  Mildmay Uganda
Kampala, Uganda

Cynthia, Goh, MD
Associate Professor
Senior Consultant in Palliative
  Medicine
National Cancer Centre
Chairman, Asia Pacific Hospice
  Palliative Care Network
Singapore, Singapore

John K. Graham, MD, DMin
President, Institute for Spirituality
and Health
Texas Medical Center
Houston, Texas

Reverend M. Jan Holton, PhD
Associate Professor of Pastoral Care
and Counseling
Yale University Divinity School
New Haven, Connecticut

Soraj Hongladarom, PhD
Director
Center for Ethics of Science and
Technology
Professor of Philosophy
Department of Philosophy
Faculty of Arts
Chulalongkorn University
Bangkok, Thailand

Najmeh Jafari, MD
Community Medicine Specialist
Post-doc Scientist
George Washington Institute for
Spirituality and Health
George Washington University
School of Medicine
Washington, District of Columbia

**David Albert Jones, MA (Cantab),
MA, MSt, DPhil (Oxon.)**
Director, The Anscombe
Bioethics Centre
Research Fellow, Blackfriars Hall
University of Oxford, Oxford, United
Kingdom
Visiting Professor, St Mary's
University College
Twickenham, United Kingdom

**David Kissane, MD, MPH,
FRANZCP, FRAChPM**
Professor and Head of Psychiatry
Monash University
Melbourne, Australia

Margaret E. Mohrmann, MD, PhD
Emily Davie and Joseph S. Kornfeld
Foundation Professor of
Biomedical Ethics
Director, Program of Biomedical
Ethics, Center for Biomedical
Ethics and Humanities
Professor of Pediatrics and Medical
Education
Professor of Religious Studies
University of Virginia
Charlottesville, Virginia

R. Sean Morrison, MD
Hermin Merkin Professor of
Palliative Care
Director, Hertzberg Palliative Care
Institute
Brookdale Department of Geriatrics
and Palliative Medicine
Mount Sinai School of Medicine
New York, New York

Uma Mysorekar, MD, FACOG
President
The Hindu Temple Society of North
America
Flushing, New York

Reverend Jan K. Nielsen, JD, MDiv
Senior Minister
The Universalist Church
West Hartford, Connecticut

Richard A. Powell, BA, MA, MSc
Formerly Director of Learning and
  Research
African Palliative Care Association,
Kampala, Uganda
Currently Deputy Director of Research
HealthCare Chaplaincy
New York, New York

Christina Puchalski, MD, MS, FACP
Professor of Medicine and Health
  Sciences
Director, George Washington
  Institute for Spirituality
  and Health
George Washington University
  School of Medicine
Washington, District of Columbia

Tariq Ramadan, PhD
Professor of Contemporary Islamic
  Studies
University of Oxford
Oxford, United Kingdom

Ashley E. Shreves, MD
Assistant Professor
Department of Emergency
  Medicine
Brookdale Department of Geriatrics
  and Palliative Medicine
Mount Sinai School of Medicine
New York, New York

Nagesh Simha, MS(GS), FICS,
  MSc Pall Med (Cardiff),
  FRCP Lon (Hon)
Chairman and Medical
  Director, *Karunashraya*
President, Indian Association of
  Palliative Care
Bangalore, India

Lucy Selman, BA, MPhil, PhD
Research Associate
Department of Palliative Care,
  Policy and Rehabilitation
King's College London
Cicely Saunders Institute
London, United Kingdom

Irene Taafaki, EdD
Director
University of the South Pacific
Majuro
Marshall Islands

Carol Taylor, PhD, RN
Professor of Nursing
Kennedy Institute of Ethics Scholar
Georgetown University School of
  Nursing and Health Studies
Washington, DC

Charles F. von Gunten, MD, PhD
Vice President, Medical Affairs
Hospice and Palliative Care
  OhioHealth
Columbus, Ohio

Mary Vachon, RN, PhD
Professor, Dalla Lana School of
  Public Health
Professor, Department of Psychiatry
University of Toronto
Psychotherapist in private practice
Toronto, Canada

I

Poem

Autumn Passage

ELIZABETH ALEXANDER

On suffering, which is real.
On the mouth that never closes,
the air that dries the mouth.

On the miraculous dying body,
its greens and purples.
On the beauty of hair itself.

On the dazzling toddler:
"Like eggplant," he says,
when you say "Vegetable,"

"Chrysanthemum" to "Flower."
On his grandmother's suffering, larger
than vanished skyscrapers,

September zucchini,
other things too big. For her glory
that goes along with it,

glory of grown children's vigil,
communal fealty, glory
of the body that operates

even as it falls apart, the body
that can no longer even make fever
but nonetheless burns

florid and bright and magnificent
as it dims, as it shrinks,
as it turns to something else.

Palliative and End-of-Life Care for Safe Passage

Introduction: On Safe Passage

MARK LAZENBY, RUTH McCORKLE, DANIEL P. SULMASY

Death, it has been said, is not an event in life; and because death is not an event in life, some have argued that there is nothing to say about it.[1] Such a view shuts down all talk of death. This book moves against that view. Death comes to all of us—in all our lives. In the moments when it comes, we are moved, whether we expected it or not. We are moved sometimes to silence, but at other times, to talk. We have to talk about death. We have decisions to make about it, safe passages to negotiate for those in our care. And after death claims our loved ones, we have lives to lead. We must talk about death, and when we do, we talk about it in accordance with our beliefs and practices. That is what this book is about—talking about death in accordance with our various beliefs and practices.

This book talks about death from the perspectives of the world's most prevalent belief systems. That fact alone, however, could not make this book universal. This book is for all of us because death comes to all of us—in our lives. This book is for people living with life-limiting diseases who, negotiating the end of life, may herein find possibilities for themselves in the ideas explored, stories told, and beliefs shared as they—indeed, as we all—prepare for death. This book is for the families and friends who countenance death's coming to their loved ones. It is for the clinicians—the chaplains, funeral directors, home-care providers, medical assistants, nurses, physicians, psychologists, social workers, and volunteers—who care for the dying and the families and friends of the dying; for the ministers and spiritual advisors who stand side-by-side with us in these events in our lives; for those who teach us, in our professional schools and in our daily lives, how to be human when death comes. This book is for all of us.

This book is for all of us because, when death comes, we all have decisions to make and, amid and after its coming, lives to go on leading. The need to make decisions about our own deaths or the deaths of those near to us and the need to go on living our lives can, as William James noted over a century ago, cause us to "become the prey of a pathological melancholy."[2] Yet, as James also noted, exploring our sensitivity and susceptibility to death's melancholy may, in fact, free us from its pathological grip. James himself looked to spiritual experiences as a way of overcoming these pathological melancholies.

Our book—this book—arose out of our desire to explore our sensitivities and susceptibilities to death's sometimes paralyzing and, at other times, pathological grip. As with James, we conduct our explorations from within the frame of the spiritual beliefs and practices that give our lives meaning. This, then, is the purpose of this book: to explore death—and its deep and profound effects on our lives—from within the varieties of spiritual experiences, as a way of walking through its melancholy to arrive at a place in our minds and hearts in which we can go on living.

The first unit of this book explores the clinical and spiritual care available to the dying and the loved ones of the dying across broad geographical regions of the world. This global tour describes the historical perspectives of end-of-life care across the United States, Africa, Europe, the Indian subcontinent, Latin America, the Middle East, and Pacific Asia. These essays outline the history of end-of-life care in each region. They then describe both the current state of the region's end-of-life care and how families' beliefs and practices intersect with the delivery of that care. They tell us where we have come from, but also where we are and where we need to go with palliative care that embraces the varieties of cultural and spiritual beliefs and practices. It should be noted that these regional essays are far from exhaustive; for example, the care of the dying in Canada and New Zealand are missing. However, we have included an essay that describes both the systems of delivery of end-of-life care and the people who deliver it, and an essay that describes the clinical spiritual care of the dying and their loved ones.

After this global tour comes the second unit of the book, which explores situations in which death poses difficult decisions for us—decisions that may, without the guidance of our beliefs and practices, paralyze us. The second unit presents a series of case studies. We ask clinicians and ethicists to explain why, clinically and ethically, the events are just so paralyzing. Then we turn to thinkers from among the world's thirteen most prevalent spiritual traditions. These thinkers use their spiritual beliefs and practices to guide us, as if we were among that tradition's faithful, through death's valley. They use their beliefs and practices as a map to lead us to the land where the faithful may go on living. And they teach us how, from within their beliefs and practices, to care for those who have difficult decisions to make; and how, after these decisions and after their loved ones' deaths, to lead the bereaved on the journey back to everyday life.

A common theme among these essays, particularly those in the first unit, is the legacy of Dame Cicely Saunders, one of the founders of the modern hospice movement. Dame Cicely founded St Christopher's Hospice in London in 1967. One of us (RM) knew Dame Cicely, worked alongside her, and learned from her in the 1970s. Dame Cicely's view of end-of-life care arose out of her own spiritual beliefs and practices. In the 1950s, advances in medicine meant longer life; but with these advances came a view that death was a failure of treatment—a view that, some may say, persists today. The care of the dying, Dame Cicely noticed, was too often secondary to the goal of curing. As a result, the dying experienced pain. She recognized that this pain was not only physical: it was also psychological and spiritual. Friends and family felt pain, too. She believed that one way to improve the care of the dying and to address the complex nature of the pain dying people and their loved ones felt was to provide hospice care. Saunders chose this word "hospice" deliberately. Hospices in the Middle Ages were places where religious pilgrims could find rest and sustenance on their journeys. Hospices were, in Saunders's view, a stopping off place for pilgrims on death's journey—and for those who accompanied them on their journeys. They were places where the pain of the dying and their families could be attended to—the whole of their pain—their physical, psychological, social, and spiritual pain. People at the end of life are still people whose whole selves need rest and sustenance. And hospices were to be, in Saunders's view, a place to help each other walk the mile and bear the load.

Dame Cicely was not alone, of course. Elizabeth Kübler-Ross, an American psychiatrist, had been bringing the holistic needs of the dying to public attention.[3] Another American psychiatrist, Avery Weisman, spoke of the need to provide safe passage to people while on their journeys toward death. He did this out of an understanding of the vulnerabilities of people at end of their lives.[4,5] People with life-limiting illnesses learn to cope with disability. Amid this coping, they learn to maintain their morale. And finally when death draws nigh, they search for meaning. Along the way, we all walk with them. We love them. We are loyal, faithful, and honest with them. We attend to their needs, ameliorate their pain, and salve their wounds, whether they be physical, psychological, or spiritual. Through our journeying with them during their vulnerabilities, we provide them safe passage.

We can provide safe passage in the simplest of ways, including creating a safe environment in which to die. Saunders believed that most patients, at the end of life, will draw upon their own strengths and resources and reach a resolution of their inner pain—if they have the space. The physical environment at St Christopher's was deliberately set up to be a sanctuary—a safe place for patients and families and for staff. The safety of the space permitted all those involved—families and staff—to have the resources to journey with patients; to offer them safe passage.

Safe passage, of course, begins early in the diagnosis of a life-limiting disease, by offering the care and environment people need in order to reach a resolution of their inner pain. Balfour Mount, a Canadian oncologic surgeon, visited Saunders in London and, upon his return to the Royal Victoria Hospital in Montreal, created a palliative care unit. It was the first dedicated palliative care unit within a hospital, and some attribute the modern usage of the term "palliative care" to him.[6] In addition to Mount's notion of a safe place within a hospital, indigenous peoples such as the Maoris in New Zealand teach us the importance of dying in the place preferred by the beliefs and practices of culture—for them, home.[7] Wherever that safe place is, it is there that we can find within ourselves the strength to resolve our own inner pain and to accept death.

In the first essay on the history of palliative and end-of-life care, Kathleen Foley describes the origins of palliative care in the United States as the concern of a civil society. And although concerns over funding and differing philosophical approaches to care delivery persist, Foley clearly argues that a civil society attends to the pain and suffering of those with life-limiting illnesses, and does so within its religiously multicultural frame.

Following Foley's essay, Richard Powell, Lucy Selman, and David Galimaka-Kabalega tell the now thirty-year-long effort to bring palliative care to Africa. Still today, however, the need far outstrips the resources available, though valiant training efforts exist and, notably, the African Palliative Care Association leads the way. The essay talks of the cultural view among sub-Saharan Africans that we are all interconnected. Through this view of our complete and total interconnectedness, we offer safe passage for the dying.

David Clark and Carlos Centeno sketch the influence of Dame Cicely Saunders on the springing up of palliative care and hospice services throughout Europe in the 1970s, 80s, and 90s. They, as Foley, describe the drive to make such services available as arising out of the concerns of a civil society. Part of this civility is rooted deeply in European religious sensibilities. Although many people in Europe may have left the institutional church behind, they have not traded in their religious understanding that the universal human—and spiritual—needs of all dying people include love and meaning; forgiveness and reconciliation; peace and transcendence. Palliative and hospice care may have originated in institutional religious settings in some instances, but the fact that Europe is moving away from institutional religion does not imply that it is not moving away from the profound spiritual belief and practice of providing safe passage.

In Latin America, according to Eduardo Bruera and Marvin Omar Delgado-Guay, the challenges of a civil society focus health care on disease prevention, prenatal care, and, in some cases, the basic needs of everyday life. With palliative and hospice care coming to Latin America only in the mid-1980s, Bruera and Delgado-Guay sketch the outlines of a movement spreading throughout the region to provide palliative care for all. They also limn the importance of a spirituality rooted in faith and family that sustains Latinos and Latinas when well and provides strength for their final journeys.

Mohammad Zafir Al-Shahri begins his essay on the Middle East and North Africa with the stark picture of the need. People with life-limiting diseases such as cancer present late in the course of disease, so late that their first and only need is often for palliative and hospice care. First introduced into Arab society in the 1990s as a home-based service in Saudi Arabia, palliative care has now spread to other countries of the region, though the gap between need and services available is still great. In Islam, the most prevalent religion in the Arabic-speaking region, the notion of suffering as redemptive may help some people to cope with the psychological impact of life-limiting illnesses, Al-Shahri explains. Yet others may view suffering at the end of life as God's punishment of them. Because of this, the palliative and hospice care of Muslims, Al-Shahri notes, needs to have a spiritual component. Al-Shahri attached case studies to his essay, which we have placed in the Appendix.

Ramaswamy Akileswaran, Norshisham Bin Main, and Cynthia Goh show how, in Pacific Asia, Buddhism, Christianity, Hinduism, and Islam have different views on, say, the care of the body after death. However, what holds these differing religious views together is the importance of people's religious and spiritual practices at the end of life. Palliative and hospice care workers, they suggest, need to elicit the help of spiritual guides or religious masters in order to provide the right kind of safe passage for the dying, depending on their religious point of view.

Santosh Chaturvedi and Nagesh Simha, in their chapter on palliative care in the Indian subcontinent, rightly challenge us: "Palliative care," they write, "is a Western phenomenon." Death, dying, and suffering are as old as time. And before the advent of modern health care, palliative and end-of-life care was the provenance of local spiritual and religious customs. It was largely provided in the home and in accordance with traditional rituals. In their description of the move to provide adequate pain and symptom management for people dying of life-limiting diseases, they show the importance of not separating the spiritual care of people from the need to treat their pain with opioids.

These essays on the state of palliative and end-of-life care region by region highlight the centrality of spiritual beliefs and practices in our lives when we talk about death. When it comes to death—what we believe about it, and how we provide care to those who are dying—we do what we do because of where we are. Thus, the type of palliative and end-of-life care that is available by region is deeply influenced by spiritual values. These essays, when considered as a whole, show us that the question for palliative and end-of-life care today—in global context—is not just how to increase worldwide the availability of opioid medications for end-of-life pain relief. Nor is it just the question merely how to increase the availability of clinicians trained in palliative care. The question includes how to create a safe environment in which people can avail themselves of the spiritual resources that will allow them to find resolution to their lives at the time of death. This larger question includes the question of how to provide safe passage for someone whose spiritual traditions at the end of life may differ from our own. In this day and age, when interconnectedness means that we may be caring for someone whose spiritual traditions come from a faraway land, this is an important question. What are the tasks of providing safe passage? What must be done with the body at the time of death? Who washes it? Who sits with it—and for how long? What are the rituals that provide meaning as death draws nigh and at the time of its final appearance? This book addresses such questions.

The first unit of the book ends with two chapters on the delivery of palliative and hospice care. Charles von Gunten provides an overview of palliative and end-of-life care health care delivery. Throughout this overview runs an argument that the training of palliative care workforce reinforces a view that the body is separate from the soul. Clinicians have historically been trained to care for the body. Von Gunten, however, argues against such separation, and reclaims the spiritual domain as a part of the care of the dying as important as the physical. Christina Puchalski, in the final chapter in the unit, describes how clinicians in large hospital settings can assess the spiritual needs of their patients and provide them with appropriate spiritual care. Her essay is a how-to guide for conducting spiritual histories and assessments.

Appropriate spiritual care differs tradition by tradition, region by region, and, ultimately, person by person. What does not differ, however, is the fundamental need to talk about our spiritual beliefs and practices surrounding death. If death is not an event we can talk about, then we rule out of hand the very idea of providing our loved ones and ourselves the safety of our beliefs and practices at the time of death. Only a few of these essays speak directly of language—of being bounded by language. What seems to hold them together is the view that we need to speak about important matters of life and death, that we need to reflect with people on those beliefs and practices that the dying hold dear and that will, at the time of death, provide them safe passage. Providing palliative and end-of-life care is as much an exploration into people's spiritual beliefs and practices as it is the provision of technical, high-end medical care. The importance of family waxes and wanes by region and tradition. Some regions seem to have what contemporary Westerners might consider a paternalistic stance toward the dying and their families. The acceptance and importance of non-Western approaches to health care—such as traditional medicine and healing—differ too. What does not differ, however, is that talk of how to provide safe passage at the time of death is itself part of providing palliative care to the dying and to the loved ones of the dying. What does not differ is that we must talk about death's melancholy grip, and that, to provide safe passage through it, we must draw upon our beliefs and practices and therein find strength for the journey.

Dame Cicely Saunders was, in her time, a founding saint for palliative and hospice care. Some of her protégés have written essays for this book. But now, as her protégés themselves move into retirement, we have to take up from them her mantle. That mantle includes embracing the continuity of our spiritual beliefs and practices around death. We have to embrace this continuity not just for ourselves—for our own continuity with those who have gone before us—but for our children, so they too may be at one with the beliefs and practices that define us in life and in death.

REFERENCES

1. Wittgenstein L. *Tractatus logico-philosophicus*. London; New York: Routledge & Paul; Humanities Press; 1961:166.
2. James W. *The varieties of religious experience: A study in human nature*. ed. ME Marty. Harmondsworth, Middlesex, England; New York, N.Y.: Penguin Books; 1982:534.
3. Kübler-Ross E. *On death and dying*. New York: Macmillan; 1969:260.
4. Weisman AD, Worden JW. The existential plight in cancer: Significance of the first 100 days. *Int J Psychiatry Med*. 1976;7(1):1–15.
5. Weisman AD. *On dying and denying: A psychiatric study of terminality*. New York: Behavioral Publications; 1972:247.
6. Duffy A. A moral force: The story of Dr. Balfour Mount. *Ottawa Citizen*. April 15, 2005 2005. Available from: http://www.canada.com/ottawacitizen/story.html?id=896d005a-fedd-4f50-a2d9-83a95fc56464. Accessed March 8, 2013.
7. Schwass M. *Last words: Approaches to death in New Zealand*. Wellington, New Zealand: Bridget Williams Books; 2005.

CHAPTER 1

Historical Perspectives on End-of-life Care in Global Context

United States

KATHLEEN FOLEY

INTRODUCTION

The history of palliative care in the United States reflects the growing desire of a civil society to improve the care of the dying. This social trend began first as an advocacy movement focused on both the over-medicalization of death and its institutionalization. In 1975, the first free-standing hospice opened in Connecticut, modeled after St Christopher's Hospice in London and based on the principles of care so charismatically described by Dame Cicely Saunders.

The movement was initially nursing driven but soon engaged a wide range of health care professionals as well as the public, who started philanthropically supporting community-based hospice programs to care for those dying, with an emphasis on home deaths. This grassroots effort operated outside the traditional, US-hospital–based health care system and served as a parallel program of community-based care focused on the terminally ill patient with cancer. The emphasis of care was on the family unit; symptom control and psychological and spiritual support were the focus of the work of volunteer professionals who visited patients at home and delivered a range of services, including pain management, treatment of nausea and vomiting, and distress, grief, and bereavement support to surviving family members.

The US hospice movement leadership in the 1970s and 80s understood the need for government support for the movement to be sustainable, and by 1982, they had sufficient credibility and political support to lobby Congress to pass the Medicare Hospice Benefit, which exists today.

The Medicare Hospice Benefit is an entitlement program for patients over 65 who have a prognosis of less than six months. To be eligible for treatment, patients must agree to forego active therapies like chemotherapy, but this requirement is evolving as palliative care services have developed. The benefit states that 80% of the care must be delivered in the home and provides a multidisciplinary team of nurses, social workers, and counselors, supervised by a physician who provides expert pain and symptom management, psychological support, and bereavement follow up to surviving family members. In special circumstances, respite care and inpatient admission for emergency stabilization is possible for limited periods. For patients under 65, private insurance plans and state Medicaid programs provide similar but variable coverage. Because the number of children's deaths is small, pediatric hospice services initially were often integrated into adult programs, with few freestanding pediatric hospice units. There now are a growing number of pediatric hospice and palliative care programs associated with children's hospitals, reflecting the growing expertise and interest in pediatric services. This expansion has been encouraged by changes in US health care legislation that, as of 2010, required state Medicaid programs to pay for both curative and hospice services for children under the age of 21 who qualified. This new legislation allowing access to hospice services for a broader number of children with complex chronic illness recognizes that palliative care for children needs to start at the time of diagnosis and be delivered concurrently in a program that is community based and integrated with the multiple services available for children with complex health needs. Although the data is limited, it is estimated that upwards of 1,000,000 children in the United States experience a complex, chronic medical illness in which palliative care services could improve their quality of life. California's leading coalition, called the Children's Hospice and Palliative Care Coalition (CHPCC), successfully changed its state health law to ensure the best quality of care for children with complex illnesses by advocating both for payment systems that cover care costs and for research to build the case for community-based care.

Starting in the 1990s and driven by escalating Medicare costs that showed that the 23% of Medicare patients with more than four chronic conditions account for 68% of all Medicare spending and that 70% of Medicare payments are in the last six months of life, concern for the costs of the care of the dying added an impetus to the concerns about the quality and appropriateness of their care. Numerous data described that care for such patients with chronic and progressive medical illness was inadequate and expensive and that significant barriers to providing humane, appropriate, and competent care were evident. These issues were clearly delineated in the pivotal Study to Understand Prognoses and Preferences for Outcomes and Risks of Treatment (SUPPORT).[1] This two-phase study of seriously ill patients in hospitals, which was supported by the Robert Wood Johnson Foundation, demonstrated that patient and family communication with health care professionals was poor, the cost of care exhausted many families' life savings, and 50% of patients experienced moderate to severe pain in the last three days of life. More than 200 papers resulted from this major research effort and provided the evidence base for why care was so compromised. This study together with many smaller studies identified numerous factors hindering appropriate care at the end of life. They included: deficiencies in our health care system; serious weaknesses in our education of health care professionals; and major inadequacies in our knowledge about the course, treatment, and outcomes for dying patients and their families. A further confounding aspect at this time was a growing "right to die" movement, with debates on euthanasia, physician-assisted suicide, autonomy, and an expansion of bioethics adding to the level of interest and engagement in public discourse on policies influencing end-of- life care.

At about the same time, in 1994, the Project on Death in America began as a nine-year, 45 million-dollar philanthropic effort to improve the care of the dying by providing funding for programs and individuals to address these barriers through research and model systems of care. Numerous other foundations including the Robert Wood Johnson Foundation, the Kornfeld Foundation, and many others committed more than 350 million dollars to improve care at the end of life over the ensuing 15 years.[2,3]

These philanthropic efforts catalyzed a wide range of stakeholders to develop innovative activities that resulted in building the field of palliative care in the United States. This confluence of events, from the identified need to address this public health problem, to the wide range of influential stakeholders ready to offer solutions, to the philanthropic support available, led to the rapid growth of the field of palliative care and the expansion of hospice care for both cancer and non-cancer patients.

One of these efforts was to develop the epidemiologic and sociologic data on dying in the United States, as a first step in improving care. Three seminal reports developed and published by the Institute of Medicine (IOM) of the National Academy of Sciences from 1997 to 2001, "Approaching Death," "When Children Die," and "Improving Palliative Care for Cancer," defined the issues and challenges and offered recommendations decision makers could use to address the multiple deficiencies in end-of-life care for adults and children.[4-6] All three reports provided a comprehensive review of the problem, and all indicted health care professionals' lack of education and knowledge as one of the major barriers to improving end-of-life care.

Creating national standards. In 2001, a national leadership conference in palliative care served as the springboard for the development of a national consensus process for the establishment of clinical practice guidelines for quality palliative care in the United States. This initiative became the National Consensus Project (NCP); this group served as a task force of the National Coalition of Hospice and Palliative Care Organizations and included the

American Academy of Hospice and Palliative Medicine (AAHPM), the Center to Advance Palliative Care (CAPC), Hospice and Palliative Nurses Association (HPNA), and the National Palliative Care Research Center (NPCRC). The Guidelines for Quality Palliative Care were first published in 2004 and were subsequently revised in 2010. The National Quality Forum then endorsed these guidelines and created a National Framework and Preferred Practices for Palliative and Hospice Care Quality, identifying 38 preferred practices.[7,8] From these initiatives, the Joint Commission on Hospital Accreditation created an Advanced Certification Program in Palliative Care and published its own Palliative Care Certification Manual. This consensus process formalized the delivery of palliative care within the US health care setting and served as both a model and an advocacy strategy to grow the field.

Developing educational programs. In 2001, to address the need identified in the IOM reports for physician education, a major national training program supported by the American Medical Association entitled EPEC—Educating Physicians in End-of-life Care—was started. Through train-the-trainer programs and an extensive national educational effort, hundreds of thousands of American physicians increased their knowledge about palliative care. There are now more than eight adaptations of this program that include curricula on pediatrics, geriatrics, veterans' care, emergency medicine, and cancer, as well as a full-service website and continuing educational programs. Seeing a need to address the special concerns of African Americans who, based on survey data, viewed palliative and hospice care as second-class care and another way for the established society to marginalize their access to tertiary medical-care centers, a special curriculum named APPEAL (A Progressive Palliative Care Educational Curriculum for Care of African Americans at Life's End) was developed to educate physicians who cared for African Americans, providing not only technical expertise but insights into the barriers and challenges to palliative care delivery for this population. A specialized cancer curriculum called Education in Palliative and End-of-Life Care for Oncology (EPEC-O) was supported by the National Cancer Institute, who has made all the educational materials available free online or in CD format. A similar national effort called the End-of-Life Nursing Education Consortium (ELNEC), developed by the American Association of Colleges of Nursing, created a comprehensive training program for nurses with train-the-trainer programs, a range of curricula adapted to special populations including children and veterans, and a major, international, outreach effort, with curricula translated into more than eight languages. These major, mass-educational efforts have had a significant impact on the education of American health care professionals. They are also widely used internationally, in over 60 countries, to teach about the principles and practices of palliative care.

As of 2007, Palliative Medicine has medical subspecialty status in the United States, with more than 3000 certified physicians and more that 73 training-fellowship programs. As of 2012, to become board-certified in palliative care, a physician will need to take a one-year fellowship program and pass the subspecialty board exam. Fellowship programs for nurses, social workers, and chaplains are also developing and growing. There are more than 5000 nurses who are certified in hospice and palliative care. There are now certification programs for hospice directors and social workers, as well as for chaplains. Subspecialty status, combined with the growth of palliative care programs in hospitals and major medical centers associated with medical schools, has enabled the creation of numerous endowed chairs in palliative care, supporting both physicians and nurses at leading medical schools and universities

Setting a research agenda. Several research initiatives have been developed to support palliative care. Based on a review of National Institutes of Health (NIH) funding, less than 1%–2% of NIH research funds support work in palliative care; however, two State of the Science conferences and a NIH Summit Meeting, in which there were clear recommendations supporting priorities for palliative care research, seem to have had an impact, with increased funding in the years 2006–2010.[9] Because the monies from the NIH have been limited, the NPCRC was created with philanthropic support to fund pilot studies and junior faculty research awards with a generous grant from the Kornfeld Foundation. This philanthropically supported imitative directed by Dr. Sean Morrison has played a key role in advancing palliative care research in the United States in the last ten years. The American Cancer Society has committed 500,000 dollars a year to palliative care research and, working in collaboration with NPCRC, holds a joint yearly conference to showcase the work of these young investigators and to network them with senior researchers. There are now a series of US studies which demonstrate improved quality of care, cost effectiveness, increased patient and provider satisfaction, and earlier referral to hospice and which have led to the recognition of palliative care as a clear standard of care for patients with cancer and for seriously ill patients with complex medical illnesses. For example, a major breakthrough is that the American Society of Clinical Oncology has developed a clear, palliative, cancer care strategy and is now advocating for the full integration of that strategy into medical oncology practice with quality standards.[10,11]

Building the field. Field building in medicine requires technical support to develop innovative programs and policies in medical institutions and health care facilities. The CAPC was a brilliant strategic initiative to help hospitals and health care institutions create the necessary infrastructure, protocols, guidelines, and business plans to support expansion into this new field of clinical care. The CAPC now serves as the lead organization in providing technical support, education, and innovation to health care institutions to develop palliative care programs. Through conferences, webinars, model programs, and a host of educational approaches, it provides critically useful tools to develop hospital-, home-, and community-based palliative care programs within the current and changing structure of the US health care system. It enables programs to be compared to other programs in a benchmarking process, and it releases regular report cards on US palliative care efforts.

Supporting professional organizations. With the growth of palliative care has come a range of professional organizations to sustain, educate, and advocate for the health care professionals, the providers, and the public whom they serve. Emphasizing the professional status of the field of palliative care, the AAHPM now boosts over 5000 members, 90% of whom are physicians, with a journal and a range of programs to advance education and research in the field. The HPNA has over 11,000 members publishes a journal, and cosponsors a yearly conference with AAHPM and a range of educational programs. The National Hospice and Palliative Care Organization (NHPCO), with over 49,000 members, 3,880 provider members, and 48 state organizations, represents hospice and palliative care providers. These three organizations drive much of the education, advocacy, and quality care agenda for palliative care in the United States.

CURRENT STATUS OF HOSPICE AND PALLIATIVE CARE

Based on mortality data from 2012, there were 2,513,000 deaths in the United States, of which 1,059,000 were hospice deaths. The NHPCO estimates that 1.65 million patients received hospice services, and 44.6% of all deaths were under the care of a hospice program. There are now more than 5300 hospice programs in the United States, with an increasing number of patients without cancer receiving hospice care. Depending on the community in which patients live, 50% to 90% of patients with cancer receive hospice care before they die. The non-cancer population entering hospice is the largest growing number, with twice as many people dying in hospice care than in a hospital or nursing home, as compared with a decade ago. Yet, of concern, data from 2009 show that a quarter of hospice care was for three days or less, with 40% of those late referrals following a hospitalization with an intensive care stay.[12] These data continue to reflect the late referral to hospice care in the United States, which, in part, reflects the fact that patients and their families see turning to hospice care as "giving up". The increased efforts to develop bridging programs between palliative care programs and hospice services and the efforts in cancer care to develop concurrent palliative care service delivery models will hopefully reduce these challenges to providing appropriate care. As of 2012, the number of hospitals with a palliative care team increased from 658 (24.5%) to 1635 (65.7%), an increase of 148.5% from 2000–2010. The largest growth has been in the Northeast and South. Nearly 90% (87.9%) of hospitals with 300 or more beds have a palliative care team (see Figure 1.1). These show the growth of palliative care in US hospitals, as published in CAPC's 2012 Report Card.[13]

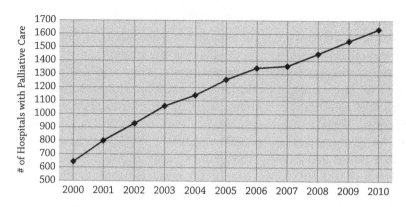

Figure 1.1: Growth of Palliative Care in the United States.

Whereas the growth has been steady, there are a series of major challenges facing the expansion of palliative care services for those with life-limiting illnesses that might benefit from such care. One major challenge is the limited workforce capacity of health care professionals trained and certified to care for the growing population of the elderly. A second challenge is educating the public about palliative care as a continuum of care, clarifying that it is care that matches treatment with patients' goals and that it is not just focused on end-of-life care or hospice services. A third challenge is a growing concern that palliative care services may reduce rather than expand referrals to hospice care. Competition between palliative care programs and hospice programs is starting to pit one against the other and could derail both movements that could only benefit from each other's expertise and advocacy for comprehensive appropriate care. Perhaps the greatest challenge is making palliative care available to all who need it. That implies that Americans know what palliative care is and demand it. Yet national surveys show that Americans do not know what palliative care is and confuse it with hospice care. In the recent debates on health care reform it was clear that Americans do not want limits placed on their choices for care when they have a serious, life-limiting illness. However, a real discussion of choices for care at the end of life was hijacked by rhetoric about "death panels," which, it was suggested, would limit care to Medicare recipients. This attempt to provide a physician reimbursement framework for discussing end-of-life care was dropped from the legislation. In contrast, a series of innovative efforts to encourage conversations about the care they would like to receive as they face a terminal illness has engaged many Americans and has encouraged them to use living wills, advance directives, and health care proxies to honor their wishes when they are incompetent. These efforts are working, as evidenced by studies that show that patients with such advance directives are more likely to die at home rather than in an intensive care unit and to enter hospice programs earlier. Yet, the multicultural aspects of American society play a major role in how Americans come to terms with serious, life-limiting illnesses. There is no one perspective but an array of views formed by culture, religion, tradition, experience, and language that is now changing as discussions about death and dying are becoming part of the fabric of national conversations.

DEFINING RELIGIOUS AND SPIRITUAL ASPECTS OF PALLIATIVE CARE

Hospice and palliative care services in the United States have from their early beginnings emphasized the need to be culturally competent and provide approaches to address patients' and families' religious and spiritual needs. The origins of many hospice programs were as outgrowths of faith-based community services for the sick. A 1997 Gallup Poll survey about dying revealed that Americans were afraid of dying in pain and alone, and wanted to have the opportunity to say goodbye to loved ones and to make peace with their maker. Numerous other US-based studies about dying patients' perceptions of religion and spirituality suggest that up to 40% of patients report spiritual concerns.[14,15] This research and survey data has led to a robust field of clinical and research work to define the role of religious and spiritual beliefs in palliative care. The George Washington Institute for Spirituality and Care has been the leader in developing clinical assessment tools to evaluate patients' spiritual concerns and in sponsoring a national consensus conference that set forth recommendations on how the spiritual and religious concerns of patients could be incorporated into the National Guidelines for Quality Palliative Care and the National Quality Forum Framework. Philanthropic efforts by several foundations, including the Templeton Foundation, have supported studies to assess the role of chaplains and clinical pastoral care workers and their impact on improving the care of patients who express spiritual distress; and these foundations have also supported medical school educational programs focused on integrating spiritual care in medical curricula. By opening up the opportunity to better understand the religious and spiritual domains of the lived experience of serious illness and dying, scholars are providing those who care for patients and families with greater insight into the dimensions of suffering and existential distress, as well as with potential ways to address and comfort those in need. At the same time, clinicians are assessing the spiritual concerns of their patients as an approach to providing holistic care.

Palliative and hospice care are now an integral part of the US health care system, yet they face significant challenges as they propose an innovative and comprehensive approach to the seriously ill. The trajectory of growth over the last 25 years suggests that the system they have been implementing resonates with those in need; but further growth will require adopting the philosophy of care and the current practices to the economic and cultural constraints of the day.

REFERENCES

1. A controlled trial to improve care for seriously ill hospitalized patients. The study to understand prognoses and preferences for outcomes and risks of treatments (SUPPORT). The SUPPORT principal investigators. *JAMA.* 1995;274(20):1591–1598.
2. Clark D. *Transforming the culture of dying? A history of the project on death in America.* New York, NY: Oxford University Press; in press.
3. Meier DE, Isaacs SL, Hughes RG. *Palliative care: Transforming the care of serious illness.* 1st ed. San Francisco: Jossey-Bass; 2010:452.
4. Field MJ, Cassel CK, Institute of Medicine. Committee on Care at the End of Life. *Approaching death: Improving care at the end of life.* Washington, D.C.: National Academy Press; 1997:437.
5. Field MJ, Behrman RE, Institute of Medicine. Committee on Palliative and End-of-Life Care for Children and Their Families. *When children die: Improving palliative and end-of-life care for children and their families.* Washington, D.C.: Institute of Medicine, National Academies Press; 2003:690.
6. Foley KM, Gelband H, eds. *Improving Palliative Care for Cancer.* Washington, D.C.: Institute of Medicine, National Academies Press; 2001:64.
7. Dahlin, C, ed. *The National Consensus Project for Quality Palliative Care Clinical Practice Guidelines for Quality Palliative Care.* 3rd ed. Pittsburgh, PA: National Consensus Project for Quality Palliative Care; 2013. http://www.nationalconsensusproject.org/Guidelines_Download2.aspx. Accessed July 17, 2013.
8. National Quality Forum. Palliative and hospital care: Framework and practice. http://www.qualityforum.org/Home.aspx. Updated 2013. Accessed February 18, 2013.
9. Gelfman LP, Du Q, Morrison RS. An update: NIH research funding for palliative medicine 2006 to 2010. *J Palliat Med.* 2013;16(2):125–129. doi: 10.1089/jpm.2012.0427; 10.1089/jpm.2012.0427.
10. Ferris FD, Bruera E, Cherny N, et al. Palliative cancer care a decade later: Accomplishments, the need, next steps—from the American Society of Clinical Oncology. *J Clin Oncol.* 2009;27(18):3052–3058. doi: 10.1200/JCO.2008.20.1558; 10.1200/JCO.2008.20.1558.
11. Smith TJ, Temin S, Alesi ER, et al. American Society of Clinical Oncology provisional clinical opinion: The integration of palliative care into standard oncology care. *J Clin Oncol.* 2012;30(8):880–887. doi: 10.1200/JCO.2011.38.5161; 10.1200/JCO.2011.38.5161.
12. Morden NE, Chang CH, Jacobson JO, et al. End-of-life care for Medicare beneficiaries with cancer is highly intensive overall and varies widely. *Health Aff (Millwood).* 2012;31(4):786–796. doi: 10.1377/hlthaff.2011.0650; 10.1377/hlthaff.2011.0650.
13. Morrison RS, Augustin R, Souvanna P, Meier DE. America's care of serious illness: A state-by-state report card on access to palliative care in our nation's

hospitals. *J Palliat Med.* 2011;*14*(10):1094–1096. doi: 10.1089/jpm.2011.9634; 10.1089/jpm.2011.9634.

14. Puchalski CM, Dorff RE, Hendi IY. Spirituality, religion, and healing in palliative care. *Clin Geriatr Med.* 2004;*20*(4):689–714, vi–vii. doi: 10.1016/j.cger.2004.07.004.

15. Otis-Green S, Ferrell B, Borneman T, Puchalski C, Uman G, Garcia A. Integrating spiritual care within palliative care: An overview of nine demonstration projects. *J Palliat Med.* 2012;*15*(2):154–162. doi: 10.1089/jpm.2011.0211; 10.1089/jpm.2011.0211.

CHAPTER 2

Historial Perspectives on End-of-life Care in Global Context

Africa

RICHARD POWELL, LUCY SELMAN,
DAVID GALIMAKA-KABALEGA

INTRODUCTION

Africa is characterised by a significant burden of communicable and noncommunicable diseases. By 2009, 22.5 million people in sub-Saharan Africa were
living with HIV/AIDS (in North Africa and the Middle East the number is com-
parably only 470,000). Africa shoulders 68% of the global disease burden, with
1.9 million new infections reported in that year alone.[1] Antiretroviral therapy
(ART) has heralded improved prognoses and extended life expectancy, transforming HIV into a manageable, chronic illness for those infected, if they can
access the treatment.[2] However, treatment failure for some ART patients, and
increasingly limited access to third-line combination regimens in a stagnating
HIV-funding environment,[3] means increasing demand for noncurative care.
Additionally, in 2010, Africa accounted for nine of the 22 countries that com-
prised 80% of the 8.8 million incident cases of tuberculosis (TB) and, importantly, 82% of the estimated number of HIV-positive new TB cases.[4]

Moreover, just as noncommunicable diseases are significant sources of
morbidity and mortality globally,[5] regionally, cancer is an emerging public
health problem.[6] In 2008, there were 715,000 new cancer cases and 542,000
cancer-related deaths in Africa,[7] with cancer rates on the continent expected
to grow by 400% over the next 50 years.[8] Approximately 36% of cancers in
Africa are infection-related, twice the global average,[9] reflecting the challenge
of infectious diseases generally and the fact that many patients with cancer

Figure. 2.1: Map of the African continent.

have an HIV comorbidity. There is also a growing concern that, as Africans' lifestyles change and nutritional preferences and non-sedentary work patterns also change, Africa may experience an increase in the incidence of chronic, life-limiting diseases.[10] Consequently, and based upon WHO[11] estimates, approximately 10 million people directly (excluding family members) need palliative care for these and other life-limiting illnesses across Africa.

HISTORY AND CURRENT STATUS OF PALLIATIVE CARE

Evolution and key players. Palliative care in Africa originated in the late 1970s, when the Island Hospice and Bereavement Service was founded in Harare, Zimbabwe. Subsequent hospice initiatives were established in Johannesburg, Port Elizabeth, Cape Town, and Durban in South Africa.[12] More than 30 years later, there were an estimated 136 hospice and palliative care organizations operating in 15 African countries, and capacity building present in 11 others.[12] The year 1993 saw the foundation of Hospice Africa Uganda (HAU), a service that has been depicted as a model for palliative care provision in resource-poor settings,[13] supplemented five years later by Mobile Hospice Mbarara and Little Hospice Hoima. Often initiated by highly motivated, charismatic individuals with minimal financial resources, these NGOs were, and remain for the vast majority, located outside existing public health systems, with limited geographic service coverage.

Many funding and partner agencies have contributed critically to the development of palliative care on the continent, primarily in response to the HIV/AIDS epidemic. The most significant players have been: the Virginia-based Foundation for Hospices in Sub-Saharan Africa (FHSSA); the London-based Diana, Princess of Wales Memorial Fund (Diana Fund); the US government's (USG) President's Emergency Plan for AIDS Relief (PEPFAR); and the African Palliative Care Association (APCA).

FHSSA is a nonprofit organization established in 1999, originally conceived as a means to provide direct financial and technical assistance to African hospice and palliative care organizations. Based on a foundation of partnering, FHSSA aims to promote mutually beneficial relationships between US- and Africa-based service providers.[14]

Since 2001, expanding palliative care for people with life-limiting illnesses in sub-Saharan Africa, under its Palliative Care Initiative, has been one of the Diana Fund's four major objectives. As well as funding projects across a range of thematic areas (e.g., advocacy, education, training, and research) in its focus countries, in November 2002, the Diana Fund supported a meeting in Cape Town of 28 African palliative care trainers from five countries to develop a strategy for the systematic development of palliative care on the continent. The resulting Cape Town Declaration[15] stated that palliative care is the right of every adult and child with a life-limiting illness; the control of pain and other symptoms is a human right, making access to essential medicines critical; all health care providers need appropriate training in palliative care; and such care should be delivered at all levels of care delivery—primary, secondary, and tertiary.

Two years later, PEPFAR, a landmark global health initiative, was launched. Targeting HIV/AIDS interventions at 15 prioritized countries worldwide, 12 of which were located in sub-Saharan Africa, 15% of its initial 15 billion–US-dollar budget was allocated to palliative care. The preliminary successes of the program's capacity building and service development outcomes were reported one year later: Of the 5,400 USG-funded outlets and programs providing palliative care in the 15 focus countries, 99% were in sub-Saharan Africa; of the 36,700 individuals trained to provide palliative care, 96% were based on the continent; and of the 854,800 HIV-infected individuals receiving palliative care, approximately 96% were in sub-Saharan Africa.[16]

However, caution was expressed at the time in interpreting these ostensibly significant service developments in African palliative care. Critical to PEPFAR's numerical achievements was its broadening of the inclusivity parameters of the traditional, WHO definition of palliative care. As Wright and Clark (p. 9)[12] remarked, the classificatory amendments were so all-embracing that: "In fact, it appear[ed] that every HIV-infected person receiving any form of treatment from US Government-supported outlets [was] designated as being in receipt of palliative care."

In 2005, with seed funding received from PEPFAR, an organization that was conceptualized at the Cape Town meeting was operationalized: the APCA. APCA's vision is to ensure access to palliative care for all in need across Africa, with broad external objectives.

Partly as a consequence of APCA's work, a number of national palliative care associations have been formed, especially in eastern and southern Africa, to spearhead and act as focal points for in-country palliative care development.

Public health approach Palliative care services in Africa have followed the WHO's public (and, subsequently, enhanced public) health approach.[17] This approach is founded upon: 1) appropriate government policies, including a national health policy, an essential medicines policy, and education policies; 2) on the adequate availability of medicines; 3) on the education of health professionals; and 4) on integration of palliative care at all levels in national health care systems.[18] Against a backdrop of health systems deficits, contracted hospital inpatient stays, and scarce programmatic resources, palliative care providers in Africa have developed a home-based care (HBC) model to implement this public health approach. The HBC model is based on a tripartite framework of care delivery comprising trained health professionals, community-based volunteers, and family carers, who are often the primary caregivers.

Current status and areas for improvement. Over the 30 years since the formation of services in Zimbabwe, improvements in palliative care provision in Africa have been evident across a range of metrics, including the extent and quality of clinical coverage. This section discusses the current status of palliative care provision, highlighting particular gaps in relation to pediatric care and exploring the growing field of palliative care research.

Current status. From 2004 to 2005, a global study of hospice and palliative care services was conducted that used a four-part typology to depict levels of service development by country:[19]

Group 1: No known hospice/palliative care activity
Group 2: Capacity-building activity
Group 3: Localized hospice/palliative care provision, and
Group 4: Countries where hospice/palliative care services were reaching a measure of integration with the mainstream health care system.

The study reported not only that 21 of 47 African countries surveyed had no identified hospice or palliative care activity, but also that just four of the 47

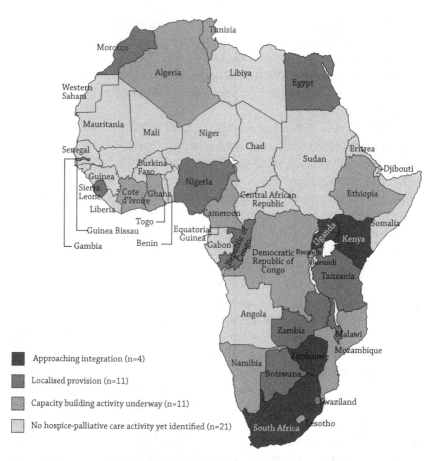

Figure. 2.2: Hospice/palliative care service development in the countries of Africa. Reprinted with permission from Wright and Clark.[12]

could be classified as having services approaching some measure of integration with mainstream service providers.

Five years later, and employing a slightly modified ranking system, follow-up research by the World Palliative Care Alliance[20] noted a number of significant advances against this baseline data. Nine countries progressed from no known activity/capacity building (groups 1/2), to isolated provision (group 3a), while four countries moved from group 3 to group 4a (preliminary integration into mainstream service provision). Uganda was the only African country ranked as 4b (advanced integration into mainstream service provision), equivalent to industrialized countries such as Australia, the United Kingdom, and the United States of America.

However, given methodological limitations in the study—for example, the existence of a national palliative care association is graded equally to comprehensive provision of all types of palliative care by multiple service providers—the grading is unlikely to reflect the extent to which services have been "mainstreamed" clinically. Despite the undoubted progress made in advancing service provision in Africa,[21] palliative care coverage on the continent remains deficient.[22,23] Indeed, for the vast majority of Africans with progressive, life-limiting illnesses, access to culturally appropriate, holistic palliative care remains at best limited, and at worst, nonexistent.[24] Furthermore, where it is available, it is primarily provided by NGOs with limited service coverage, rather than embedded within mainstream public health systems.

There is a growing consensus that, if palliative care is to reach all in need, service development should focus on embedding models of care within mainstream health care systems. An example of how this can be achieved is evident in Kenya, where 220 health professionals are being trained to integrate palliative care into 11 major public and provincial government hospitals.[25] Moreover, palliative care should link with services providing care for other life-limiting illnesses, with the recent prioritization of the noncommunicable disease agenda by the United Nations creating a possible strategic opportunity.

Pediatric services. The overwhelming majority of children in the world living with HIV—about nine in every 10—are located in sub-Saharan Africa.[26] Indeed, in 2007, an estimated 1.8 million children under the age of 15 in sub-Saharan Africa were living with HIV/AIDS, with an average of 240,000 dying in that year alone.[27]

As for adults, cancer is a growing problem for children, with a review of childhood cancer treatment highlighting that the high cure rates seen in developed countries are impossible in Africa due to resource deficits, poor treatment compliance, and late presentations.[28]

Despite the evident need for noncurative interventions, palliative care for children has remained a neglected part of service provision. In a systematic review to map children's palliative care services worldwide, Knapp et al.[29] found that among the 53 African countries, 43 were ranked at level 1 (no known activities), and only one at level 4 (provision reaching mainstream). Indeed, South Africa is presently the only country in the region with a pediatric portfolio within their national palliative care association.

Pediatric palliative care is a critical element of service development that needs to be planned for simultaneously with the mainstreaming of adult clinical services. Some of the key areas to be addressed include: access to pediatric medical formulations; improved understanding of the disease process in children; improved access to affordable and accessible chemotherapy and ART services; challenging societal myths concerning children's perception of pain; integrating pediatric palliative care into generalist palliative care trainings so nurses operating in rural areas can provide essential care; and improved networking and collaboration between organizations involved in pediatric palliative care.

Palliative care research. Despite care providers' recognition of the need for a local evidence base, the research evidence that underpins much of current palliative care service provision on the continent remains inadequate.[30] A systematic review of research on end-of-life care in sub-Saharan Africa uncovered "a wealth of clinical and academic experience but a dearth of methodologically robust evidence."[24] Whereas the value of research that has been conducted to date should not be underestimated, the growth and development of palliative care research in Africa is limited by several factors, including: the short-term and project-specific commitment of some international partners; inadequate financing; overdependency on key individuals rather than institutions; an overemphasis on north-south partnerships; and a lack of a strategic organizational model to ensure sustainable collaboration.[31]

Researchers working in Africa have up to now largely failed to take advantage of the potential for comparative analyses of a range of differing service models and settings, patient populations, ages and diagnoses, and sociocultural contexts. To address this limitation in strategic thinking and architectural infrastructure, APCA recently formed the African Palliative Care Research Network (APCRN), a multicountry collaboration which unites African researchers with those in Europe and North America. The APCRN aims to build a methodologically strong evidence base for palliative care in Africa by:

- Developing and delivering a region-wide, prioritized palliative care research agenda
- Bringing existing researchers together in productive partnerships to generate primary data
- Building research skills and knowledge among health care professionals to generate a critical mass of researchers
- Connecting academic researchers with palliative care clinicians and advocates
- Mobilizing the resources necessary to conduct high-impact research
- Fostering a critical and vibrant research culture within the discipline

The development of a research agenda is a particularly relevant concern given that existing research has predominantly focussed on physical dimensions of care rather than patients' and family members' holistic experience of illness. Few studies have identified, explored, or measured palliative care needs in patients in sub-Saharan Africa.[32,33] A recent systematic review of qualitative evidence relating to end-of-life care in Africa highlighted the fragmented nature of existing research on patient and carer experiences and the neglect of important areas of research.[32] Particularly glaring gaps in the literature are the cultural and spiritual dimensions of health and sickness in Africa, such as the ways in which people find meaning in illness. Evidence in these areas is essential to guide services in the provision of culturally appropriate care that meets patients' needs.[30]

Research into the spiritual and cultural aspects of care is all the more pressing given that the richness and diversity of patients' and family members' spiritual and cultural worldviews is one of the most rewarding and yet challenging aspects of working in African palliative care. The societies of sub-Saharan Africa are predominantly highly religious and committed to their spiritual practices and beliefs. From 2008 to 2009, the Pew Research Center conducted more than 25,000 face-to-face interviews in more than 60 languages or dialects in 19 sub-Saharan African nations and found that between 68% (Botswana) and 98% (Senegal) consider religion to be very important in their lives (by comparison, 57% of adults in the USA say this).[34] A median of 81% of Christians and 87% of Muslims attend religious services weekly or more, and overall 77% pray at least once a day (72% of Christians and 92% of Muslims). Reading religious scriptures, pamphlets, magazines, newspapers, and books, listening to religious radio, and watching religious television programs are also common.

Christianity in Africa. Christianity, as expressed and practiced in the African context, can appear and function very differently from in the industrialized world. Religious acculturation has occurred as traditional religions have encountered Christianity, involving the fusion of elements of the new religion and the old tradition. The resultant forms of religious syncretism form the new religious movement of the African Independent churches, in which "biblical and African world views are combined in meaningful ways to the converts."[35] (See the essays on African Independent and Pentecostal Churches in Chapters 10–14.) Protestantism is therefore quite diverse in sub-Saharan Africa, with each country displaying a unique blend of denominational affiliations, as demonstrated by census results.

Another hallmark of religious practice in Africa is that it often involves intense, personal encounters with God, spirits, and miraculous events.[34] A significant proportion of people in sub-Saharan Africa believe that they are living at a time of momentous religious events, with Christians believing that they will see the return of Jesus to Earth and Muslims expecting the re-establishment of the Islamic caliphate (divinely mandated government). In the Christian community, miraculous events and intense, personal encounters with God are often associated with the Pentecostal movement, which emphasizes the direct intervention of the Holy Spirit in the believer's daily life. Pentecostals place a strong emphasis on the Bible and fundamental doctrines (the deity of Christ, virgin birth, substitutionary atonement by Christ's death, and so on). Among the practices associated with Pentecostalism are speaking in tongues, receiving direct revelations from God, and giving or interpreting prophecies.

However, many of these phenomena are prevalent even among African Christians who are not affiliated with Pentecostal churches. In South Africa and Uganda, for example, 36% and 39% of these respective populations say they have experienced or witnessed the divine healing of an illness or injury.[34] Many of these people are affiliated with "charismatic" churches, an umbrella term used to describe the neo-Pentecostal movement that swept into non-Pentecostal churches in the 1960s and 1970s.

Like Pentecostals, most charismatics define speaking in an unknown tongue as the evidence of being "Baptized by the Spirit", although a few accept any of the described gifts as evidence. Doctrinal beliefs vary widely from conservative to liberal, from separatistic to ecumenical, from Baptist to Roman Catholic and Eastern Orthodox. Charismatics can be found in nearly all denominations. Those from charismatic churches may or may not be evangelical, but, like Pentecostals, are likely to believe in speaking in tongues, seeing visions, and miracle healings.

The Pentecostal movement is also closely associated with the "prosperity gospel," which teaches that health and wealth are promised to those who have sufficient faith. In most sub-Saharan countries, more than half of Christians believe that God will grant wealth and health to believers who have enough faith.[34] These findings also suggest that the impact of Pentecostalism extends well beyond the growth of Pentecostal churches. Beliefs in both divine healing and the prosperity gospel are also likely to have a significant impact on health-related behavior and patients' experience of, and response to, illness.

In the countries of sub-Saharan Africa, religious and political histories are often inextricably linked. For example, regarding South Africa, De Gruchy[36] writes:

> The transformation of Christianity, from a white, European-dominated settler religion, with expatriate missionaries engaged in evangelizing the indigenous people of the country, to a black-majority religion rooted in African culture and engaged in the struggle against white social, political and ecclesial domination, is undoubtedly the most significant development of twentieth-century Christianity in South Africa.

The traditional African worldview. The Pew Forum survey throws light on the complex mix of Christian and traditional belief prevalent in the general African population.[34] In total, the survey included questions about seven beliefs common to traditional African religions (belief in the protective power of certain spiritual people, the power of juju and other sacred objects, the evil eye, witchcraft, evil spirits, the protective power of sacrificial offerings to ancestors, and reincarnation). The survey also included questions on four traditional religious practices (visiting traditional healers, owning sacred objects, participating in ceremonies to honor ancestors, and participating in traditional puberty rituals). These 11 items were combined into a single scale, and high levels of traditional African religious beliefs and practices were defined as believing or participating in six or more of the items. On these criteria, 26%

of the people surveyed exhibited high levels of traditional African religious belief and practice. For example, a median of 27% believed sacrifices to spirits or ancestors can protect them from bad things happening.[34]

In traditional African religion, the ancestors represent a powerful moral sanction that affirms the values upon which society is based.[37] The good deeds of the ancestors spur the living on to good conduct, while the threat of ancestral punishment deters violation of sanctioned mores:

> Ancestral beliefs…underscore certain social ideals: the vibrant reality of the spiritual world or 'an alive universe', the continuity of life and human relationship beyond death, the unbroken bond of obligations and the seamless web of community.[38]

Death may be seen as a "mere passage from the human world to the spirit world,"[38] enhancing spiritual powers and enabling one to operate as a family guardian or protective spirit. Belief in reincarnation is prevalent, with ancestors seen as returning through their children.

Attitudes to illness in Africa are widely influenced by traditional spiritual views of the world and our place within it.[39, 40] The use of traditional and herbal medicine is common,[41] with a survey of palliative care services reporting that 80% of patients seek the advice of traditional healers.[33] The Pew Forum survey found that in 14 of the 19 sub-Saharan countries surveyed, more than three in 10 people said they had consulted traditional healers when someone in their household was sick.[34] The authors suggest that, whereas the recourse to traditional healers may be motivated in part by economic reasons and an absence of health care alternatives, it is also rooted in religious beliefs about the efficacy of this approach.

Another relevant aspect of sub-Saharan African culture is the idea of "*Ubuntu*,"* a philosophy which underpins sub-Saharan social values and ideals of leadership, governance, and justice. Desmond Tutu has described the concept of *Ubuntu* as follows:

> One of the sayings in our country is Ubuntu—the essence of being human. Ubuntu speaks particularly about the fact that you can't exist as a human being in isolation. It speaks about our interconnectedness…We think of ourselves far too frequently as just individuals, separated from one another, whereas you are connected and what you do affects the whole world.[42]

The concept of *Ubuntu* is expressed in the isiZulu maxim *umuntu ngumuntu ngabantu* ("a person is a person through (other) persons"). In other words,

---

* The concept of *Ubuntu* appears in many African languages, e.g., "*ubuntu*"(isiZulu, Kinyarwanda, Kirundi), "*unhu*" (Shona), "*botho*" (Setswana), and "*obuntu*"(Luganda, Runyakitara).

the person one becomes by behaving with humanity is an ancestor worthy of respect or veneration. Those who uphold the principle of *Ubuntu* throughout their lives are considered to achieve, in death, a unity with those still living.[43] *Ubuntu* thus embodies cultural collectivism.[44] The central role of collectivism to people approaching the end of life in Africa is supported by van der Geest's description of a "good death" in Ghana, in which the dying person's relationship with other people is of central importance, and securing peace with others is a fundamental requirement for the patient's own acceptance of their impending death.[45]

Spiritual well-being. There is limited evidence from sub-Saharan Africa regarding the spiritual well-being of patients with incurable, progressive disease, with existing studies from South Africa, Tanzania, Rwanda, Kenya, and Uganda giving conflicting results.[46–51] Several quantitative studies are poorly reported and exhibit methodological limitations, such as the use of unvalidated tools. Murray et al.[52] conducted a comparative qualitative study of patients with incurable cancer and their informal carers in Scotland and Kenya (n = 20 and n = 24 patients, respectively). The authors report that, in contrast to Scottish patients, physical pain and financial worries dominated the lives of Kenyan patients and their carers whereas psychological, social, and spiritual needs were met by patients' families, local community, and religious groups.

However, Selman et al.[50] report that among 285 patients receiving palliative care in South Africa and Uganda, 21% to 58% scored poorly on spiritual well-being as measured by the Spirit 8, a tool with good internal consistency in sub-Saharan Africa. For example, 32% of patients agreed or agreed strongly with the statement "I am unsettled and unprepared to leave this life," 31% with the statement "I have less of a sense of meaning in my life now than I have had in the past," and 23% with "Life has lost all value for me; every day is a burden." Overall, the same patients judged feeling at peace and having a sense of meaning in life to be more important to them than physical comfort,[53] indicating that, in the sub-Saharan context, spiritual distress is likely to have a particularly detrimental effect on quality of life. In studies from the United States, neglect of patients' spiritual needs has been associated with reduced quality of life and satisfaction with care[54–56] and increased health care costs at the end of life.[57]

Spiritual care in an African context. Several misperceptions can color the way that health and social care staff approach caring for African patients toward the end of life. Firstly, it may be thought that, in a religious society, patients' and families' spiritual needs are met by the church community to which they belong. However, discrimination and stigma against those with HIV and their families have been documented in some faith communities in Africa.[58] Patients may feel abandoned or judged by the church and church community, and the difficulty of disclosing a positive HIV status in the face of potential stigma is detrimental to the interpersonal relationships fundamental to spiritual well-being. Among 36 people with HIV in Arusha, Tanzania, for example, personal faith positively influenced patients' experiences of living with HIV, but religious organizations were reported as having neutral or negative influences.[59] Prayer gave patients hope and, for some, supported their adherence to medications. However, few disclosed their HIV status in their religious communities, expressing fear of stigma. Whereas it was common to hear messages about HIV prevention from churches or mosques, few had heard messages about living with HIV. The authors suggest that religious organizations miss opportunities to support people living with HIV.

Secondly, some health and social care staff, as in the general population, may believe that religious teachings and beliefs are universally supportive and beneficial to patients but that traditional beliefs and consultations with traditional healers are not. A recent study from Uganda, for example, suggests that palliative care staff tend to focus on traditional African beliefs as a barrier rather than a facilitator of effective spiritual care and may not recognize the wider existential issues with which traditional healers can help patients.[60] In fact, external structures such as the church, church community, and traditional healers can have both positive and negative influences on patients' lives. For example, a traditional healer might recommend physical extraction of a serpent from the bowels of someone with rectal cancer, whereas a pastor might convince a patient with HIV that he no longer needs to take his antiretroviral medication as the church congregation is praying for him. The same is true for personal beliefs and spiritual practices: conceptions of God and the ancestors, for example, can be supportive and unsupportive depending on their cognitive and emotional content. Simplistic conceptions of either religion or traditional healing as universally negative or positive in its effects should therefore be guarded against.

Finally, in religious societies such as many of those in sub-Saharan Africa, spirituality might be perceived as a universally positive force in patients' and family members' lives. It is important to recognize that not all beliefs and teachings espoused by spiritual leaders are supportive; in fact, some contravene the duty of care that health and social care workers have towards the patient. Patients can be made to feel that their illness must be a result of past sins, not living up to a strict Christian moral code, or failure to fulfill the rituals required upon a relative's death.

Given these possible misperceptions and the complexity of cultural and spiritual beliefs, it is essential that health and social care workers understand spiritual care in a wide sense, as encompassing not solely religious guidance and support but support with wider existential concerns. The assessment of spiritual needs should explore the content of patient and family members' beliefs, rather than simply the source of those beliefs. Care providers are directed to evidence-based spiritual care recommendations for sub-Saharan Africa authored by experts in the field, including two of the coauthors of this chapter.[61] In addition, to improve the quality of spiritual care and ensure patients' needs are met in a way that is effective and resource efficient, the outcomes of spiritual care require monitoring (through clinical audit using the APCA African Palliative Outcome Scale (POS), for example).[62, 63] To ensure that finite resources are allocated optimally, further research is required to evaluate different models of spiritual care provision in sub-Saharan Africa.

REFERENCES

1. Joint United Nations Programme on HIV/AIDS. *Global report: UNAIDS report on the global AIDS epidemic 2010*. Geneva: World Health Organization; 2010.
2. Mills EJ, Bakanda C, Birungi J, et al. Life expectancy of persons receiving combination antiretroviral therapy in low-income countries: A cohort analysis from Uganda. *Ann Intern Med*. 2011;155(4):209–217.
3. Grepin KA. Efficiency considerations of donor fatigue, universal access to ARTs and health systems. *Sex Transm Infect*. 2012;88(2):75–78.
4. World Health Organization. *Global tuberculosis control: WHO report*. Geneva: World Health Organization; 2010.
5. Alwan A. *Global status report on noncommunicable diseases 2010*. Geneva: World Health Organization; 2011.
6. Jemal A, Bray F, Forman D, et al. Cancer burden in Africa and opportunities for prevention. *Cancer*. 2012;118(18):4372–4384.
7. Ferlay J, Shin HR, Bray F, et al. Estimates of worldwide burden of cancer in 2008: GLOBOCAN 2008. *Int J Cancer*. 2010;127(12):2893–2917.
8. Morris K. Cancer? In Africa? *Lancet Oncol*. 2003;4(4).
9. Parkin DM. The global health burden of infection-associated cancers in the year 2002. *Int J Cancer*. 2006;118(12):3030–3044.
10. World Health Organization. *The African regional health report: The health of the people*. Geneva: World Health Organization; 2006.
11. World Health Organization. *A community health approach to palliative care for HIV/AIDS and cancer patients in sub-Saharan Africa*. Geneva: World Health Organization; 2005.
12. Wright M, Clark D, Hunt J, et al. *Hospice and palliative care in Africa: A review of developments and challenges*. Oxford University Press; 2006.
13. Merriman A, Harding R. Pain control in the African context: The Ugandan introduction of affordable morphine to relieve suffering at the end of life. *Philos Ethics Humanit Med*. 2010;5(1).
14. Mastrojohn III J, Smith ENS, DiSorbo P. Partnering for effective HIV/AIDS palliative care in sub-Saharan Africa. *Int J Palliat Nurs*. 2010;15(12):576–578.
15. Sebuyira LM, Mwangi-Powell F, Pereira J, et al. The Cape Town palliative care declaration: Home-grown solutions for sub-Saharan Africa. *J Palliat Med*. 2003;6(3):341–343.
16. Office of the United States Global AIDS Coordinator. *Engendering bold leadership. The President's Emergency Plan for AIDS Relief*. First Annual Report to Congress; 2005. http://www.state.gov/s/gac/rl/c14961.htm. Accessed May 8, 2012.
17. Stjernswärd J, Foley KM, Ferris FD. The public health strategy for palliative care. *J Pain Symptom Manage*. 2007;33(5):486–493.

18. World Health Organization. *Cancer pain relief and palliative care (technical report series 804).*Geneva: World Health Organization; 1990.

19. Clark D, Wright M, Hunt J, et al. Hospice and palliative care development in Africa: A multi-method review of services and experiences. *J Pain Symptom Manage.* 2007;33(6):698–710.

20. World Palliative Care Alliance. *Mapping levels of palliative care development: A global update.* London: World Palliative Care Alliance; 2011.

21. Mwangi-Powell FN, Downing J, Ddungu H, et al. Palliative care in Africa. In: Ferrell BR, Coyle N, eds. *Textbook of palliative nursing.* 3rd ed. New York: Oxford University Press; 2010:1319–1329.

22. Grant L, Downing J, Namukwaya E, et al. Palliative care in Africa since 2005: Good progress, but much further to go. *BMJ Support Palliat Care.* 2011;1(2):118–122.

23. Powell RA, Mwangi-Powell FN, Kiyange F, et al. Palliative care development in Africa: How we can provide enough quality care? *BMJ Support Palliat Care.* 2011;1:113–114.

24. Harding R, Higginson I. Palliative care in sub-Saharan Africa: An appraisal. *Lancet.* 2005;365:1971–1977.

25. Achia G. Palliative care key in cancer management. *Science Africa.* 2011;18:5.

26. WHO, UNAIDS, & UNICEF. *Global HIV/AIDS response: Epidemic update & health sector progress towards universal access. Progress report.* 2011.

27. Joint United Nations Programme on HIV/AIDS. *2008 report on the global AIDS epidemic.* Geneva: World Health Organization; 2008.

28. Krüger C. Childhood cancer treatment in developing countries. *Lancet.* 2005;365(9461):752–753.

29. Knapp C, Woodworth L, Wright M, et al. Paediatric palliative care provision around the world: A systematic review. *Pediatr Blood Cancer.* 2011;57(3):361–368.

30. Harding R, Powell RA, Downing J, et al. Generating an African palliative care evidence base: The context, need, challenges, and strategies. *J Pain Symptom Manage.* 2008;36(3):304–309.

31. Powell RA, Downing J, Radbruch L, et al. Advancing palliative care research in sub-Saharan Africa: From the Venice declaration, to Nairobi and beyond. *Palliat Med.* 2008a;22(8):885–887.

32. Gysels M, Pell C, Straus L, et al. End of life care in sub-Saharan Africa: A systematic review of the qualitative literature. *BMC Palliat Care.* 2011;10(6).

33. Harding R, Stewart K, Marconi K, et al. Current HIV/AIDS end-of-life care in sub-Saharan Africa: A survey of models, services, challenges and priorities. *BMC Public Health.* 2003;3(1):33.

34. Pew Forum on Religion and Public Life. *Tolerance and tension: Islam and Christianity in sub-Saharan Africa.* Washington, USA: The Pew Forum on Religion and Public Life; 2010.

35. Olupona JK. Major issues in the study of African traditional religion. In: Olupona JK, ed. *African traditional religions in contemporary society.* New York: Paragon House; 1991:25–33.

36. De Gruchy JW. Christianity in twentieth-century South Africa. In: Prozesky M, De Gruchy JW, eds. *Living faiths in South Africa.* London: Hurst & Co; 1995:83–115.

37. Opoku KA. *West African traditional religion.* Accra, Ghana: Fep International Private Limited; 1978.

38. Kalu OU. Ancestral spirituality and society in Africa. In: Olupona JK, ed. *African spirituality: Forms, meanings, and expressions*. New York: Herder and Herder; 2000:54–84.

39. Powell RA, Downing J, Mwangi-Powell F, et al. Advancing palliative care research in sub-Saharan Africa: From Venice to Nairobi. *EJPC*. 2008b;15(5):228–233.

40. Furnham A, Akande D, Baguma P. Beliefs about health and illness in three countries: Britain, South Africa and Uganda. *Psychol Health Med*. 1999;4:189–201.

41. Nelms LW, Gorski J. The role of the African traditional healer in women's health. *J Transcult Nurs*. 2006;17(2):184–189.

42. Ubuntu Women Institute USA. Ubuntu women institute USA (UWIU) with SSIWEL as its first south Sudan project. Ubuntu Women Institute, USA. https://www.facebook.com/UbuntuWomenInstituteUsaInc. Accessed July 17, 2013.

43. Samkange S, Samkange TM. *Hunhuism or ubuntuism: A Zimbabwe indigenous political philosophy*. Salisbury: Graham; 1980.

44. Hofstede G. *Culture's consequences: Comparing values, behaviors, institutions and organizations across nations*. Thousand Oaks, CA: Sage Publications; 2001.

45. van der Geest S. Dying peacefully: Considering good death and bad death in Kwahu-Tafo, Ghana. *Soc Sci Med*. 2004;58(5):899–911.

46. Collins K, Harding R. Improving HIV management in sub-Saharan Africa: How much palliative care is needed? *AIDS Care*. 2007;19(10):1304–1306.

47. Sepulveda C, Habiyambere V, Amandua J, et al. Quality care at the end of life in Africa. *BMJ*. 2003;327(7408):209–213.

48. Shawn ER, Campbell L, Mnguni MB, et al. The spectrum of symptoms among rural South Africans with HIV infection. *J Assoc Nurses AIDS Care*. 2005;16(6):12–23.

49. Kikule E. A good death in Uganda: Survey of needs for palliative care for terminally ill people in urban areas. *BMJ*. 2003;327(7408):192–194.

50. Selman L, Siegert RJ, Higginson IJ, et al. The "spirit 8" successfully captured spiritual well-being in African palliative care: Factor and rasch analysis. *J Clin Epidemiol*. 2012;65(4):434–443.

51. Uwimana J, Struthers P. Met and unmet palliative care needs of people living with HIV/AIDS in Rwanda. *SAHARA J*. 2007;4(1):575–585.

52. Murray SA, Grant E, Grant A, et al. Dying from cancer in developed and developing countries: Lessons from two qualitative interview studies of patients and their carers. *BMJ*. 2003;326(7385):368–371.

53. Selman LE, Higginson IJ, Agupio G, et al. Quality of life among patients receiving palliative care in South Africa and Uganda: A multi-centred study. *Health Qual Life Outcomes*. 2011;9:21.

54. Astrow AB, Wexler A, Texeira K, et al. Is failure to meet spiritual needs associated with cancer patients' perceptions of quality of care and their satisfaction with care?.*JCO*. 2007;25(36):5753–5757.

55. Clark PA, Drain M, Malone MP. Addressing patients' emotional and spiritual needs. *Jt Comm J Qual Patient Saf*. 2003;29(12):659–670.

56. Heyland DK, Cook DJ, Rocker GM, et al. Canadian Researchers at the End of Life Network (CARENET). Defining priorities for improving end-of-life care in Canada. *CMAJ*. 2010;182(16):E747–E52.

57. Balboni T, Balboni M, Paulk ME, et al. Support of cancer patients' spiritual needs and associations with medical care costs at the end of life. *Cancer*. 2011;117(23):5383–5391.

58. Cotton S, Tsevat J, Szaflarski M, et al. Changes in religiousness and spirituality attributed to HIV/AIDS: Are there sex and race differences? *J Gen Intern Med.* 2006;*21*(Suppl 5):S14–S20.

59. Watt MH, Maman S, Jacobson M, et al. Missed opportunities for religious organizations to support people living with HIV/AIDS: Findings from Tanzania. *AIDS Patient Care STDS.* 2009;*23*(5):389–394.

60. Kale SS. Perspectives on spiritual care at Hospice Africa Uganda. *Int J Palliat Nurs.* 2011;*17*(4):177–182.

61. Selman L, Harding R, Agupio G, et al. *Spiritual care recommendations for people receiving palliative care in sub-Saharan Africa.* London: Cicely Saunders International / King's College London; 2010.

62. Harding R, Selman L, Agupio G, et al. Validation of a core outcome measure for palliative care in Africa: The APCA African palliative outcome scale. *Health Qual Life Outcomes.* 2010;*8*:10.

63. Powell RA, Downing J, Harding R, et al. Development of the APCA African palliative outcome scale. *J Pain Symptom Manage.* 2007;*33*(2):229–232.

CHAPTER 3

Historical Perspectives on End-of-life Care in Global Context

Europe

DAVID CLARK, CARLOS CENTENO

In this chapter we sketch out the history of palliative care in Europe. We give a brief account of its current development, the patterns and trends that are emerging and the special areas of activity that are being initiated. We explore barriers and achievements and look at ways in which collaborative efforts are seeking to promote the growth of palliative care across the diverse cultures of Europe. We conclude with some thoughts on the role of religion and spirituality in European palliative care and how this might relate to future provision.

HISTORY

The roots of palliative care in Europe can be found in several settings and contexts, some but not all of which are religious. In the late 1950s and early 1960s, Cicely Saunders sought to build on traditions of care for the dying that had developed in both Catholic and Protestant religious orders from the late nineteenth century onwards.[1] She was also influenced by twentieth-century writers who wrote from religious and philosophical perspectives, such as Viktor Frankl, CS Lewis, Norman Autton, and Martin Buber. In addition, she combined these religious and intellectual influences with practical experience drawn from social work, nursing, and medicine and took a keen interest in the phenomenon of pain—seen in its multidimensional aspects. Out of this rich set of inspirations, she forged the modern notion of palliative care—albeit a term introduced to her by the Canadian surgeon Balfour Mount. Her work centered on the development of St Christopher's Hospice in south London, a place that would serve as a beacon of inspiration to many others and that combine excellent clinical care with teaching and research. Almost ten years in development, the hospice opened its doors in 1967.

It was then another decade until the first services began to appear elsewhere in Western Europe: in Sweden (1977), Italy (1980), Germany (1983), Spain (1984), Belgium (1985), and the Netherlands (1991). In the former communist countries of Eastern Europe and Central Asia, there were few palliative care developments in the years of Soviet domination. A volunteer hospice service began in Krakow, Poland as early as 1976. Lakhta Hospice opened in St. Petersburg, Russia in 1990, and a service started in Budapest, Hungary the following year. After that, initiatives got underway in Bulgaria, Romania, the Czech Republic, and Slovenia (1992); Albania, Kyrgyzstan, and Lithuania (1993); Belarus and Croatia (1994); Ukraine (1996); Estonia and Latvia (1997); Azerbaijan, Bosnia, Macedonia, and Moldova (1998); Armenia (1999); Slovakia (1999); Serbia (2000); and Georgia (2001).

In many of these instances, we can find the development of palliative care being driven through the mechanism of civil society, in the form of hospices organized from local support and fundraising, fostered through philanthropy, and heavily reliant on voluntary support, in some cases for "core" medical services as well as for the provision of social and psychological interventions. Very often, the individuals who became involved in such programs were motivated by religious faith and saw their actions as a working through of belief into practice. Priests, nuns, clergy, ministers, and pastors are often present and highly active in the narratives of pioneer hospice and palliative care services in Europe, often working alongside lay people of similar faith and commitment. Religious associations and organizations are also a significant force—providing expertise, finance, resources, and a wider community of support. But there are also narratives of palliative care in some countries that reveal the work of individuals operating within mainstream and largely secular health care systems, and within which the challenge of palliative care was expressed in purely professional terms and framed within discourses of clinical practice, public health, and policy making. In a sense, this is what makes the landscape of palliative care in Europe so rich and diverse. Not only has palliative care in Europe developed across many language groups, geographies, and cultures, it has also done so in ways which give differing emphases to values, beliefs, modes of practice, and models of care.

Clearly, in the United Kingdom, there was an initial emphasis on voluntary inpatient hospices, many of which had Christian origins. Echoes of this model can also been seen elsewhere but are almost always nuanced to the local context and conditions. For example, in Germany, the influences of religion and civil society were strong, and the early hospice services were more likely to be community based, with limited medical involvement. In Romania, the first hospice had many of the attributes of its British equivalents but was adapted to a culture where voluntary engagement was relatively unfamiliar and where religious traditions had been suppressed under a communist dictatorship. In Spain, physicians who pioneered palliative care did so within the public health system and established services in hospitals, major oncological centers, and polyclinics, where their influence could be as wide as possible; when a hospice did emerge, it was one based along British lines and led by British expats.

As one of us has previously observed, modern palliative care history in Europe has three clear phases.[2]

1945–1965: Ideas were forged which drew special attention to care at the end of life. In Western Europe, systems of socialized medicine were being developed; specialization was advancing rapidly; new treatments were proliferating; and there was an increasing emphasis upon cure and rehabilitation. Death in the hospital, rather than at home, was becoming more common, and the dying patient was seen increasingly as a "failure" of medical practice. A death-denying culture was in evidence in which the fact of human mortality was regarded increasingly as a private, rather distasteful matter—even a taboo. But other concerns were emerging—about the *neglect* of the dying within the health care system and the way in which medicine had retreated from the deathbed. In many countries, attention shifted to the growing incidence of cancer and the expanding elderly population. How were the dying and the dying elderly to be cared for in a system designed to cure and to rehabilitate? In the 1950s, for the first time, we begin to see an interest in research about terminal care—undertaken by social workers, psychologists, psychiatrists, and physicians. In London, John Bowlby and Colin Murray Parkes were exploring theoretical ideas about bereavement, and John Hinton was conducting empirical studies with dying patients. Above all, it was Cicely Saunders, who published her first paper on the care of the dying in 1958 and who forged a new philosophy and practice for care at the end of life. A major aspect of her approach was the use of patient narratives—listening carefully to stories of illness, disease, and suffering—and finding within them the concept of "total pain."[3] This view of pain moved beyond the physical, to capture the social, emotional, even spiritual dimensions of suffering—brilliantly summarized by one of Cicely Saunders's patients who told her "all of me is wrong."

1965–1985: The ideas and practices of terminal care, hospice care, and palliative care take hold and spread. We see at this time in several countries a growing concern about the nature of death and bereavement and a new interest in how the dying should be cared for. In France, for example, *thanatology* became a subject for intellectual endeavor. In the clinical setting, ideas about the importance of multidisciplinary teamwork in the care of the dying began to develop, and there was a growing recognition that the individual subjectivity of the patient must be respected. Above all, it was a time for exploring new ways to organize and deliver care. In many countries, the process of innovation and dissemination during this period relied heavily upon charismatic leadership. Individuals such as Lisette Custermans and Sister Leontine, in Belgium; Haline Bortnowska in Poland; Cicely Saunders and Eric Wilkes in the United Kingdom; and Vittoria Ventafridda in Italy are just a few examples. As the developments matured however, the key role for these individuals began to change. Having established the central principles of palliative care and demonstrated how they might work in practice, it would now be necessary to engage with wider questions of policy, funding, and integration within the health care system—in a bid to make palliative care available to all who might need it and not just to those cancer patients who might be fortunate enough to gain access to specialist provision.

1985–Present: In this period, which is ongoing, palliative care has been seeking to gain recognition within mainstream health care provision. In some countries, where palliative care developments occurred earlier, working toward integration was a goal that developed over time. In other places, this challenge came at the outset. Spain is the paradigm in the latter category, with an emphasis on rational planning, needs assessment, and high coverage—all priorities that were identified from the start. Likewise in Sweden, the role of voluntary or religious hospices was very limited. Here it was medically advanced home care—the Motala model pioneered from 1977 by Barbro Beck-Friis—which was the major contribution. Elsewhere, in the poorer countries of Eastern Europe, "integration" with the mainstream health system remains a challenge and a somewhat distant vision. Here we still see small numbers of independently organized hospice and palliative care services acting as beacons for the education and inspiration of others.

One spur to the integration of palliative care within the health care mainstream has been the creation of national and international umbrella bodies to disseminate information, promote public understanding, and lobby governments. Founded in Milan in 1988 by 42 members from nine countries, the European Association for Palliative Care (EAPC) deserves special mention. EAPC has done much to promote public, professional, and governmental understanding of the importance of palliative care and places a strong and growing emphasis on dissemination to politicians and policy makers. The integration of palliative care into the wider policy and health care framework is seen by some as the sine qua non for its success. Only by such means, it is claimed, can high coverage, equity of provision, and an affordable service be provided, particularly to those with diseases other than cancer. Others acknowledge these points, but fear the loss of key values within the culture of palliative care. There is a concern that pain and symptom management may come to predominate, squeezing out spiritual and psychosocial issues. Some bemoan a more interventionist, short-term approach that denies opportunities for long-term care. We see these various concerns as signs of the process of integration. They are typical conditions associated with the maturation of a social movement and a clinical specialty—when debates about future direction, strategy, and priorities come to the fore and sometimes divide the opinions of experts in the field.

DEVELOPMENT

We have previously summarized the various studies that have sought to map the development of palliative care in Europe.[4] Our own work as part of the EAPC Taskforce on the Development of Palliative Care in Europe is also providing unfolding evidence of developments over time. From a survey in 2006, we noted that various models of service delivery have been implemented throughout the countries of Europe.[5] For example, in addition to the United Kingdom, the countries of Germany, Austria, Poland, and Italy all have a well-developed and extensive network of hospices. The model for mobile teams or hospital support teams has been adopted in a number of countries, most notably in France. "Day Centres" are a development that is characteristic of the United Kingdom, with hundreds of these services currently in operation. In 2006, the number of palliative care beds per million inhabitants ranged between 45–75 beds in the most advanced European countries, to only a few beds in others. The countries with the highest development of palliative care in their respective subregions as measured in terms of ratio of services per one million inhabitants were: Western Europe—United Kingdom (15); Central and Eastern Europe—Poland (9); and Commonwealth of Independent States—Armenia (8).

Other findings from the Taskforce have highlighted particular barriers to palliative care development.[6,7] In Western Europe, these consist of: (i) a lack of palliative care education and training programs; (ii) a lack of awareness and recognition of palliative care; (iii) a limited availability of/knowledge about opioid analgesics; (iv) limited funding; (v) a lack of coordination among services; and (vi) uneven palliative care coverage. It appears that barriers to the development of palliative care in Western Europe may differ substantially from each other in both their scope and context and that some may be considered to be of greater significance than others. In countries where palliative care is not integrated into undergraduate and postgraduate education and training programs for medical students and other health professionals, the lack of awareness and recognition of the discipline may continue. This fosters an inability to deliver homogeneous standards of palliative care in a country due to the lack of suitably qualified staff, limited knowledge about opioid analgesics, and a shortage of "product champions" capable of leveraging change and promoting palliative care within national policies for health care.

In Eastern Europe, four significant barriers to the development of palliative care have been identified: (i) financial and material resources; (ii) problems relating to opioid availability; (iii) lack of public awareness and government recognition of palliative care as a field of specialization; and (iv) lack of palliative care education and training programs. Huge variations exist in the levels of provision across Central and Eastern Europe and the Commonwealth of Independent States, and the development of palliative care in many countries continues to remain uneven, uncoordinated, and poorly integrated across wider health care systems, mainly as a result of inadequate investment and limited palliative care service capacity.

There are a number of instances where barriers may intertwine and interconnect with each other. For example, a lack of palliative care education and training, concomitant with a lack of knowledge about the use of opioids, may result in the promulgation of irrational myths and negative stereotypes about the dangers of opioid abuse amongst health professionals. A lack of awareness and recognition of palliative care can result in uneven coverage in countries where services that are promoted as "specialist palliative care" are far removed from established international standards, or where governments think that the palliative care needs of the population are covered by a small number of hospice beds in each area. Within this context, the restricted focus on resources allocated solely for hospices may be a potential barrier to the provision of palliative care for the wider population; for example, in some Western European countries, palliative care is still rarely integrated into hospital departments or nursing and care homes. Lack of government awareness and recognition of palliative care often means that the political will necessary to generate funding is absent or that palliative care does not feature in government financial targets.

Another strand of work that gives a picture of palliative care progression in the European context is the "world map" publications that have appeared in 2008 and 2013.[8,9] The latest of these shows that 23 of the 53 countries that comprise the WHO European Region are in the top two categories of palliative care development of "preliminary" and "advanced" integration (see Table 3.1). In Western Europe, only the small countries such as Andorra, Monaco, and the Holy See (Vatican) are in the lowest categories of development, although British regions such as Guernsey and the Isle of Man have medium levels

Table 3.1. HIGHEST RANKING COUNTRIES FROM WHO EUROPEAN REGION IN THE WORLD MAP OF 2013

"Preliminary integration" (n = 10)	Denmark, Finland, Hungary, Luxembourg, Mongolia, Netherlands, Serbia, Slovakia, Slovenia, Spain
"Advanced integration" (n = 13)	Austria, Belgium, France, Germany, Iceland, Ireland, Italy, Norway, Poland, Romania, Sweden, Switzerland, United Kingdom

of development. In Central and Eastern Europe and the Commonwealth of Independent States, countries such as Turkmenistan and Uzbekistan have no known palliative care capacity—in stark contrast to Poland and Romania, which are in the highest category of development.

See Figure 3.1 for a map depicting levels of development and integration of palliative care across Europe.

Such indicators are less successful at measuring the overall sense of "vitality" of palliative care in the European context. A brief survey of the scene reveals a growing interest in a wide range of topics. The Access to Opioid Medication in Europe (ATOME) collaboration focuses on access to opioid medications in 12 countries. The EAPC also champions a wide range of initiatives and taskforces.[10] There is currently work on the mapping of medical training and physician certification in palliative medicine in Europe and on the EAPC curriculum in palliative care for undergraduate medical education. Nor is medicine the sole focus. One group concentrates on the scope and remit of occupational therapy in palliative care in Europe, another on the diversity of roles, tasks, and education of European palliative care social workers, and a third is examining education for physiotherapists in palliative care. There is interest in the educational curricula for health care professionals working in pediatric palliative care in Europe as well as in aspects of palliative care for people with non-cancer diagnoses. Palliative care in long-term care settings for older people is an object of enquiry, and there is ongoing work on primary palliative care in the community. Mapping studies of various kinds have taken off in

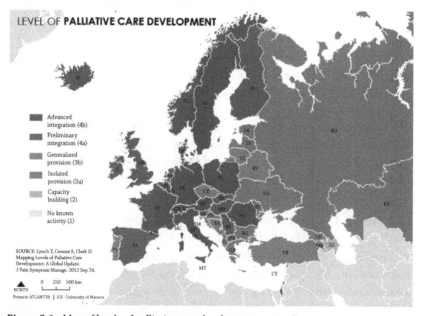

Figure 3.1: Map of levels of palliative care development across Europe.

recent years. The European Palliative Care Research Centre (PRC) was officially launched in October 2009. The PRC seeks to improve palliative care through research, teaching, and implementation of research findings in an international setting. Based in the Faculty of Medicine of the Norwegian University of Science and Technology at Trondheim University Hospital, the PRC was established with recommendations and support from the EAPC. It coordinates research groups and individual researchers across Europe along with others in North America and Australia.[11] Palliative care research across Europe is growing in quantity and quality, as evidenced by the biannual research congresses of the EAPC, which are now global in their reach. European groups are active participants in the World Hospice and Palliative Care Day in October each year and some countries, such as Hungary, Ireland, and the United Kingdom have made notable efforts to raise public awareness of end-of-life issues through mass media campaigns and social marketing. Several European countries have made notable headway in achieving policy recognition for palliative care and some have also seen national initiatives, supported by government, to roll out ambitious strategies for improving palliative and end-of-life care within mainstream services and public health systems.

These examples all evidence the growing vitality of the palliative care scene in Europe, though it remains to be seen if the collective effect of these ventures will be sufficient to meet the volume of need that will emerge as European populations age and the demand for good-quality end-of-life care increases. In the European Union, the number of those aged over 65 years in the total population is projected to increase from 84.6 million in 2008 (17.1%) to 151.5 million by 2060 (30.0%).[12] At the same time, in the European member states, the old-age dependency ratio—defined as the level of support of those over 65 by those between 15 and 64—will be increasing, from a quarter at present to over a half by 2060. In the WHO European Region, of 53 countries and some 900 million people, about nine million die each year, 24% of them from cancer.[13] How are such levels of need to be supported in times of economic austerity and when current levels of expenditure on and resourcing of health and social care will become increasingly difficult to sustain?

Ending life with dignity, with freedom from pain, and with appropriate social and medical support are widely accepted as attributes of palliative care—but the manner in which this can be achieved certainly varies enormously across cultures, jurisdictions, and settings in the European context. Although efforts to extend quality end-of-life care are underway in many European countries, they often lack coverage and are under-resourced. Moreover, we still have limited agreement on just how these efforts might be more successful. There are examples from many societies of the apparent failure to care for older people effectively and adequately as they face death—at home, in hospitals, in care homes, prisons, and other institutional settings. As the effects of population ageing are felt and as the incidence and prevalence of dementia increase, these challenges will grow. Recently there has been debate about whether specialist palliative care can or should be the answer to good end-of-life care in all contexts. Some arguments, particularly from the rich world, propose wider access to assisted dying and the legalization of euthanasia, to extend "choice" at the end of life and promote autonomy. Others seek not elite dying for the few, but palliative care principles embedded across the health and social care system, thereby maximizing benefits for the greatest number. Some positions revolve around the need to build community resilience in the facing of ageing, dying, and death, drawing on perspectives from health promotion and public health to develop strategies for intervention.

It is not uncommon in these debates to come across exhortations to promote care that is "culturally appropriate" or "culturally sensitive." We understand culture to consist of the beliefs, values, behaviors, and dispositions that exist among groups in society. Culture also has a material dimension—in objects, creations, and practical inventions. Through culture, we define who we are, to what extent we conform to shared values, and how we contribute to society. There is, of course, a close link between culture and religion. Although palliative care makes universal and global cultural claims on behalf of all people with life-limiting conditions, there has long been a recognition that it must be rooted in specific cultural contexts if it is to thrive and be effective—and that must include an attention to religious issues. We then begin to move into some challenging questions about the relationship between the practice of palliative care and the religious, spiritual, humanistic, and political orientations of its practitioners. What do we know about the motivations of "palliateurs," and to what extent does religion remain a motivating force for palliative care workers and activists?

THE PLACE OF RELIGION IN EUROPEAN PALLIATIVE CARE

For many years it was common for sociological writers to espouse theories of secularization when making sense of the European religious landscape. The influence of the churches was said to be in decline, religious beliefs were continuing to erode, and the extent of religious participation was falling. More recently, however, there has been interest in the "new" vitality of religion and a clearer recognition of the place of religion, not only within individual-life worlds but also at the social level. How does this relate to the development of palliative care in the European context?

Broeckeart and colleagues[14] observe that in the course of the last four decades, church attendance in Western European countries has declined significantly, whereas, in the same period, palliative care programs have been developed, and palliative care has gradually gained public support. They suggest that the simultaneous decline in church attendance and the growth of palliative care services in Western Europe may seem remarkable, as the founders of the modern palliative care movement clearly drew inspiration from religion in general and Christianity in particular. How, therefore, can palliative care thrive in times during which declining church attendance seems to imply a decrease in interest in religion? They cite the theory of secularization within hospice and palliative care as one possible explanation. According to this position, religious concerns in palliative care have been rethought in a secular manner, and the medical, psychosocial, and educational aspects of palliative care have become more prominent. Thus, palliative care no longer needs a religious society in which to flourish. Recent surveys among the general public point toward another possible explanation for this paradox. These surveys show that religion and, more broadly speaking, worldview, is a multifaceted phenomenon that encompasses much more than just attendance at religious services. So, for example, sociologists talk about the notion of "believing without belonging." In Western Europe, many people have bid the church farewell, yet remain interested in religious issues—and this might include the provision of palliative care.

Another dimension to this is what we refer to as "the spiritual turn" within palliative care. As the hospice and palliative care movement developed in various European settings, it seems that a broader spiritual perspective began to emerge. Although still acknowledging the Christian origins of many hospices, there was growing interest in the needs of those who subscribed to other faiths, or none. Clinical experience appeared to show that nonreligious patients demonstrated similar needs to their religious counterparts: for love, for meaning, for forgiveness, for reconciliation, and for transcendence. Accordingly, a more encompassing concept of spirituality came into being; a concept which seeks to recognize both religious and nonreligious perspectives of personhood.

At the level of clinical care, this has involved a reorientation away from explicitly religious engagement with patients and families towards one which acknowledges the wider spiritual concerns of those who make use of palliative care services. This can encompass broader concerns, such as the quest for meaning in the face of illness and death, attempts to make sense of suffering, a desire to give meaning to life in the face of mortality, and a concern to make interpersonal connections in the face of death. In such ways, it has been possible to observe in the European context a shift in emphasis towards "human dignity" and "quality of life"—and away from religiously invested language relating to "sympathy," "love," and "sanctity of life." But this acknowledgement of a wider, "postmodern" and syncretistic "spirituality" should not be at the expense of overlooking the enduring power of religious culture and experience. Wright makes the point about older people who have long turned away from their religious origins reconnecting with them as they face the end of life: "as medicine runs out of options, as hopes for cure have passed and the old certainties fade away—religious memories resurface to claim a newfound significance of transcendence and hope in the face of death and bereavement."[15]

Revisionist commentators, following the ideas of Max Weber, have been inclined to describe this shift from "religion" to "spirituality" as an unintended, even unwelcome aspect of the "routinization" of hospice and palliative care. Better informed by historical analysis, we may see the shift as a conscious response to changing social circumstances and a necessary adjustment within a changing health care environment. At the same time, religion has been central to early articulations of hospice philosophy, and we might speculate that the transition to an apparently more inclusive model of "spirituality" may have wider ramifications: in patterns of staff recruitment and retention; in public perceptions of the work of hospices and palliative care; and in the experience of patients, particularly those who do endorse a formal religious tradition. Cicely Saunders saw the development of hospice care as a personal calling and located her efforts firmly within the Christian tradition. Yet, as St Christopher's Hospice developed, it became a place that was open to and supportive of those from other faiths. This was in part because, as an organization, it "took religion seriously" (personal communication to DC). At the same time, the concept of "total pain" was one which could be generalized to include religion, spirituality, identity, and personhood—making it peculiarly adaptable across settings. As European societies become more multicultural, the "spiritual turn" in palliative care makes sense as an "inclusive" response. But for many older people, as well as those in rural areas and in specific communities and regions, the power of formal religion should not be underestimated. On the whole, we may say that the churches remain slow to fully engage with palliative care and to seek dialogue and ways to offer support. The European religious landscape is complex and varied. Recent appeals for a better understanding of culture when planning end-of-life services place are well made.[16] Perhaps it is also time for a new consideration of the roles of religion, belief, and spiritual practice in our ordering of palliative care provision for diverse and changing societies.

REFERENCES

1. Clark D. Religion, medicine, and community in the early origins of St Christopher's Hospice. *J Palliat Med.* 2001;4(3):353–360.
2. Clark D. Palliative care history: A ritual process.. *European Journal of Palliative Care.* 2000;7(2):50–55.
3. Clark D. "Total pain", disciplinary power and the body in the work of Cicely Saunders, 1958-1967. *Soc Sci Med.* 1999;49(6):727–736.
4. Clark D, Centeno C. Palliative care in Europe: An emerging approach to comparative analysis. *Clin Med.* 2006;6(2):197–201.

5. Centeno C, Clark D, Lynch T, et al. Facts and indicators on palliative care development in 52 countries of the WHO European Region: Results of an EAPC task force. *Palliat Med.* 2007;21(6):463–471. doi: 10.1177/0269216307081942.
6. Lynch T, Clark D, Centeno C, et al. Barriers to the development of palliative care in the countries of Central and Eastern Europe and the Commonwealth of Independent States. *J Pain Symptom Manage.* 2009;37(3):305–315. doi: 10.1016/j.jpainsymman.2008.03.011.
7. Lynch T, Clark D, Centeno C, et al. Barriers to the development of palliative care in Western Europe. *Palliat Med.* 2010;24(8):812–819. doi: 10.1177/0269216310368578.
8. Wright M, Wood J, Lynch T, et al. Mapping levels of palliative care development: A global view. *J Pain Symptom Manage.* 2008;35(5):469–485. doi: 10.1016/j.jpainsymman.2007.06.006.
9. Worldwide Palliative Care Alliance. Mapping levels of palliative care development. A global update 2011. http://www.thewpca.org/resources/. Updated 2013. Accessed July 17, 2013.
10. EAPC Task Force. About the EAPC. http://www.eapcnet.eu/Corporate/AbouttheEAPC/Projectsandtaskforces/EAPCTaskforces.aspx. Updated 2010. Accessed July 17, 2013.
11. Norwegian University of Science and Technology. European Palliative Care Research Centre—About. http://www.ntnu.edu/prc/about. Accessed July 17, 2013.
12. Cohen J, Deliens L. Applying a public health perspective to end-of-life care. In: Cohen J, Deliens L, eds. *A public health perspective on end of life care.* New York: Oxford University Press; 2012:3–18.
13. WHO Statistical Information System (WHOSIS). WHO statistical information system (WHOSIS). http://www.who.int/gho/en/. Updated 2013. Accessed July 17, 2013.
14. Broeckaert B, Gielen J, Van Iersel T, et al. Palliative care physicians' religious/world view and attitude towards euthanasia: A quantitative study among Flemish palliative care physicians. *Indian J Palliat Care.* 2009;15(1):41–50. doi: 10.4103/0973-1075.53511.
15. Wright M, Clark D. Cicely Saunders and the development of hospice palliative care. In: Coward H, Stajduhar KI, eds. *Religious understandings of a good death in hospice palliative care.* State University of New York Press; 2012:11–28.
16. Clark D. Cultural considerations in planning palliative and end of life care. *Palliat Med.* 2012;26(3):195–196. doi: 10.1177/0269216312440659.

CHAPTER 4

Historical Perspectives on End-of-life Care in Global Context

Indian SubContinent

SANTOSH K. CHATURVEDI, NAGESH SIMHA

INTRODUCTION

Palliative care is a Western phenomenon. It arose out of the need for improving the quality of care and an attempt to reduce suffering in advanced diseases and during terminal stages. It involves pain relief and symptom relief, in order to improve quality of life, especially during end-of-life stages.

Death, dying, and suffering at the end of life is ubiquitous. Traditional palliative care in society has been practiced since ancient times, before the modern medical concepts emerged. In South Asian countries, end-of-life care was provided through home-based spiritual and religious care of the dying according to traditional customs and rituals.[1] With the advent of modern medicine, palliative care is being reformed. A majority of newly diagnosed cancer patients in South Asian developing countries have advanced disease. These patients are usually neglected or often receive futile, expensive anticancer treatments, whereas what they really need is maximum medical management in the form of palliative care and psychosocial support.

HISTORY AND CURRENT STATUS OF PALLIATIVE CARE IN THE INDIAN SUBCONTINENT

Some information is available on the development of palliative care services in the Indian subcontinent.[2] Bangladesh held its first national seminar on palliative care in Dhaka in 2006. Three services were up and running by 2006, the first dating from 1992. Some clinicians from Bangladesh have undertaken training programs in Calicut, India. A new cancer hospital has been developed that has incorporated a dedicated ward for palliative care (see below). In Nepal, the first palliative care service opened in 2000, and, as of 2006, five services were operational; in India, over 138 organizations were known to be providing hospice/palliative care services in 16 states or union territories till 2006. These services are usually concentrated in large cities and regional cancer centers—with the exception of Kerala (a state in southern India), where services are more widespread. This exemplifies the disparity among services in large countries: a state such as Kerala has a highly developed structure for palliative care education and delivery—with up to 90% coverage in some districts; other states have no provision whatsoever. The extent of problems relating to the lack of palliative care, and its implications, is well acknowledged for cancer or nonmalignant diseases.[3] The universal spirituality in the South Asian countries adds to the complex issue of multiple religions in many countries. This gains significance given the importance of religion in death and pre- and postdeath ceremonies.[4]

Shanti Avedana Ashram in Mumbai is perhaps the first hospice in India since the late '80s, followed by its branches in a couple of other cities. The next decade saw a sprouting of small and big hospices, palliative care units, and centers, along with palliative care in patient facilities, around the country. Incidentally, these were located in the metro cities and urban areas. It is difficult to confirm any such centers being available in rural areas, with the community palliative care program in Kerala being a prominent exception. Increasing poverty, patients and families receiving inadequate information about their diagnosis or prognosis, drug availability and costs, and insufficient knowledge by health care providers are obstacles to palliative care in the Indian subcontinent. Palliative home care at many of the centers has been regarded as popular and convenient.

The Indian Association of Palliative Care was founded in 1994, and is modestly active, with annual conferences, periodic meetings, continuing medical education programs, and a popular Medline/PubMed indexed journal, the Indian Journal of Palliative Care.

Current status. Countries in the Indian subcontinent have many systems of alternate and unorthodox medicine, with some links to spirituality. Palliative care and hospice professionals recommend that these are best tried outside the hospice and should be complementary. However, the availability of numerous systems of alternative medicine, and a hope for cure even at a late stage of the disease, means that many patients depend on these as their main form of treatment.[5] Complementary and alternative medicine play key roles in palliative care. They improve the quality of life, somewhat, perhaps because of some overlap or admixture with spirituality; and they have religious overtones as well. For example, yoga and meditation are considered to be Hindu oriented, whereas Unani has a Muslim orientation. The Siddha system of medicine is another traditional system popular in the southern part of India. The fact that there is little scientific research on these complementary or alternative methods casts doubts on their effectiveness, which has not dented their popularity though.[4]

Palliative care in the Indian subcontinent and the South Asian countries has developed gradually over the last couple of decades. Some places have made more advances than others. There have been difficulties mainly because of a lack of trained professionals, a lack of training opportunities within the countries, and the low priority given to palliative care services and education. A formal postgraduate course has started this year, which is recognized by the Medical Council of India. Other South Asian countries do not have this luxury. Many short-term courses and training programs have been held in India for almost a decade.

The main obstacles to cancer-pain relief in low- and middle-income countries are an inadequate supply of opioid drugs because of regulatory and pricing obstacles,[6,7] lack of knowledge and poor attitudes of health staff, and lack of knowledge in the community.[8] The current state of palliative care and areas of improvement in the countries of the Indian subcontinent are discussed here.

India. In India (and other countries in the subcontinent), the availability of oral morphine is often restricted for pain relief because of excessive regulations imposed to prevent misuse and diversion.[9] Thus, on the one hand, opioid availability is seriously limited; on the other hand, there are differing public opinions and attitudes about the use of opiates. Many myths about the treatment of cancer pain and opiates are as prevalent, if not more so, as in other countries. Hence, because of the restrictions and legal hurdles in the opiate availability and dispensing, cancer pain patients end up suffering.[10]

Numerous attempts have been made to increase morphine availability through the courts in India, which have issued directives to improve morphine availability; yet, the majority of Indian cancer patients have poor access to the drug.[10] Recent efforts from the higher courts and an attempt to rationalize the legislation to make oral morphine available for palliative care may bring some respite. The government of India is on the threshold of bringing major changes to the Narcotic Drugs and Psychotropic Substances (NDPS) Act. It is hoped that this will make it easier for patients needing opioids to access them.

Indian society is known for its traditional use of raw opium in the form of *amal* or *doda*, because of the climate and difficult living conditions. The ethnographic information suggests that opium use is, in many ways, integrated into the sociocultural fabric of the local community. Raw opium is used for recreation and within settings that facilitate social bonding. A recent study, however, confirmed that diversion of medical morphine toward recreational use is not really an issue.[9,10] Many inexpensive analgesic drugs are not readily available, and some very expensive drugs are often prescribed, adding to the patients' burden.

Spiritual care is an essential component of palliative care. It is especially important in the developing world, where medical and comfort resources are limited. It is known that patients, at the end of their lives, are vulnerable to suggestions, and counselors need to desist from imposing their own beliefs. In most instances, a sympathetic hearing of spiritual concerns is needed, helping individuals to come to their own conclusions. Many hospices in India provide nursing care through Christian missionaries,[2] who do a tremendous selfless service; but this brings in a conflict with the predominant religious groups of Hindus and Muslims.

A number of NGOs are involved in providing supportive services for palliative care. These NGOs have volunteers and survivors or family members of cancer patients and provide psychosocial support, bereavement support, and family support.

Education, research, and services are all areas that need improvement. Great strides have been made in terms of short-term and certificate-training programs. A postgraduation course in palliative medicine has started. More diploma, masters, and innovative training programs are needed. Services have developed reasonably, and most cancer centers and hospitals have either palliative care services or pain relief centers/pain clinics. Hospices are also starting to be established in different cities. Research is in its childhood, but is gradually picking up.

Pakistan. Palliative care services have started here and are picking up gradually. Pakistan is a country with a high tumor burden. Late presentation of cancer also warrants an essential basic awareness about palliative care, palliative care centers (hospices), and about the availability and judicious use of pain control medications.[11] A survey demonstrated that, despite the fact that most of Pakistan's physicians come in contact with cancer patients, fears and misconceptions about cancer, such as that cancer is contagious and that chemotherapy makes patients miserable, exist even among the physician community, together with an ignorance of the fact that cancer is a major cause of disease burden in Pakistan. Knowledge and availability of pain control medication is limited, as is awareness of the existence of hospices in Pakistan or even an understanding of the term itself: though more than 90% of physicians were aware of palliative care, only 23% of postgraduates and 35% of consultants were aware of hospices and what the term "hospice" meant.

In another survey,[12] 32 physicians (46%) said that pain control was the primary aim of palliative care management and 21(30%) said rehabilitation, whereas 13 physicians (18%) said that counseling was the primary aim. When they were asked whether they had any experience in palliative medicine, 36 physicians (54%) stated that they had been involved, whereas 34 (49%) said that they had never been involved in palliative medicine. When asked whether they felt the bad news of the disease being incurable was conveyed appropriately, 42 physicians (60%) felt that it was; of these, 11 (26%) stated that they conveyed the news to the families and not directly to the patients. When asked about choice of analgesics, 50% did not answer, and only 5% considered oral morphine. The physicians were also asked whether they felt comfortable with any other form of treatment other than allopathic. Forty-seven physicians (67%) stated that they had no objection, whereas 23 (33%) felt uneasy about it; the alternative treatments mentioned by the physicians were spiritual (33%), homeopathic (20%), herbal/hikmat (wisdom; 23%), and acupuncture (9%). Regarding physicians' knowledge about hospices, 40 physicians (57%) said that they had heard about a hospice, although only 19 physicians (27%) had seen one; only one physician had worked in a hospice. When asked about the preferred place of providing terminal care, 49 physicians (70%) chose home, 16 physicians (23%) chose hospital, and 2 physicians (3%) chose hospice.

Complementary medicines still seem to be popular in cancer care and palliative care. There is no evidence that any complementary medicine can provide curative treatment, but techniques like aromatherapy, music therapy, acupuncture, relaxation therapy, and so on have been helpful in managing patients' suffering and mental distress. In Muslim countries, religious coping mechanisms are a well-established source of strength and well-being. This mechanism is also supported in the bereavement phase. In the West, bereavement support is provided by trained counselors, but, on the Indian subcontinent, extended families play an important role. The findings of this survey indicate that majority of the physicians respect the patients' right to complementary medicine.

The cultural and religious beliefs of Pakistani elders often influence their end-of-life decision making. Older patients are likely to prefer family-centered care and decision making rather than autonomous. Suicide is forbidden, so advance directives may be viewed as "giving up," and many patients will not agree to "do not resuscitate" instructions.

All areas of palliative care—services, education, and research—need improvement. Given the strengths of family and social support, supportive services can be organized without too much difficulty. Measures to minimize stigma are needed. Knowledge and perception of palliative care among physicians, nurses, and other health care professionals need attention. Education and knowledge about palliative care will perhaps help in reducing stigma and alter perceptions and help in developing palliative care services.

Bangladesh. There is hardly any information available in the scientific literature about palliative care services in Bangladesh. However, some published research and other information is available about Bangladeshi patients receiving palliative care in other countries. Spruyt[13] described the palliative care experiences of Bangladeshi patients and caregivers in London. Interviews were carried out with bereaved primary caregivers in Sylheti, the Bengali dialect. Though the diagnosis was known by all patients, only 56% of caregivers agreed with disclosure. Fourteen patients died in London; however, 13 were buried in Bangladesh. Caregivers often reported symptoms as being poorly controlled. Pain was said to be severe for most patients, and pain control said to be poor. Family and friends provided most support during the illness and bereavement. Serious financial difficulties occurred in half the families. In conclusion, the study identified ethnospecific needs in this particular community, many of which arise from socioeconomic factors, recent migration, and religious beliefs, and which are highlighted by terminal illness.

In a qualitative study on Bangladeshi patients, Somerville,[14] reported that four themes emerged: caring, support, communication, and home and family. In addition to the demands and stresses caused by their relative's symptoms and the knowledge that they were dying, the Bangladeshi caregivers experienced communication barriers, isolation, and anxieties regarding visas and housing—yet all were uncomplaining about their situation.

Recently, the Palliative Care Centre at Bangabandhu Sheikh Mujib Medical University, which is seen as an historical landmark for palliative care in Bangladesh, has been formally launched. Information about the center is available online from the websites for the Bangladesh Palliative & Supportive Care Foundation (http://www.bdpallcare.com/), the Worldwide Palliative Care Alliance (http://www.thewpca.org/latest-news/palliative-care-in-bangladesh), and the Asia Pacific Hospice Palliative Care Network (http://aphn.wordpress.com/in-the-region/directory-of-services/bangladesh/).

Sri Lanka. Palliative care services seem to be grossly underdeveloped in Sri Lanka. Lack of trained manpower (especially professionals) is the major challenge. At present, there is only one physician in Sri Lanka who is trained in palliative care. However, palliative care in Sri Lanka is at the point of a major development: Demonstration projects on Community Based Palliative care have been set up in three districts;[15] the service is being developed with the help of the Neighbourhood Network in Palliative Care in Kerala[16] working in collaboration with Sri Lanka's National Cancer Control Programme. In addition, with the support of Institute of Palliative Medicine in India, Sri Lanka launched its first-ever course in palliative care for professionals, for up to 50 physicians, in November 2012. Moreover, the Karapitiya branch of the Cancer Care Association has initiated a "Home-based Palliative Care Service" for the first time in Sri Lanka, for needy, terminally ill patients, initially in the Galle district, with the intention of expanding to the whole southern province in the future.

Sri Lankan professionals have become aware of the ethical challenges in palliative care[17] arising from cultural factors such as their own cultural identities, language and nonverbal communication, involvement of families and relatives, and addressing the patient's moral and spiritual background. As mindfulness meditation is culturally inherited in Sri Lanka, it is understood that utilization of meditation in improving patient outcomes may be useful. It is a form in which distracting thoughts and feelings are not ignored but instead acknowledged and observed nonjudgmentally as they arise, in order to detach from them and gain insight and awareness.

Nepal. Early developments in palliative care in Nepal are encouraging. Pain relief services are available at certain hospitals, and there is a hospice that is active and promises to educate health professionals. Professionals have been trained in India and collaborate with centers in the West.

Approximately 80% of Nepalis follow Hinduism, 11% follow Buddhism, 4% follow Islam, and 5% follow some other spiritual practice. Buddhist and Hindu practices are used in performing health rituals. There is a strong belief in reincarnation and that the actions of an individual's current life reveal whether that individual has achieved enlightenment. As one achieves enlightenment, the cycle of reincarnation ends. If an individual has not achieved enlightenment, that individual continues to be reincarnated to complete a proper form of life. Some people look to ayurvedic medicine, which uses dietary nutrition to relieve the body of imbalances, to care for illness; others turn to shamanic, biomedical, or other systems. Traditionally, the dead are cremated on river banks; a son is usually expected to perform the funeral rituals. Some Buddhists may practice "sky burials," which is when corpses are cut up and left at sacred sites for vultures.[18]

Bhutan. Bhutan has mainly Buddhists and Hindus, and death-related rituals are similar to those in India and Nepal. There is no scholarly information available on palliative care services in the tiny kingdom nation with the highest happiness index. Tibetan medicine and other herbal medicine systems are popular. One Bhutanese surgeon has trained in palliative care in the Calicut training program, but the exact number of palliative care services and professionals in Bhutan is not clearly known.

AREAS OF IMPROVEMENT FOR PALLIATIVE CARE IN THE INDIAN SUBCONTINENT

In all countries of the Indian subcontinent, all areas of palliative care—services, education, and research—need to be developed further, combining traditional systems and practices with modern methods.

The obstacles to palliative care and opioid usage can be surmounted by demonstration—by educating professionals, patients, and families about models of care that work, as shown in a study in Taiwan.[19] Training the caregivers in the patient's family in nursing skills leads to fewer hospitalizations and more time spent at home, reducing the need for travel to the hospital.

The main barriers to efficient home care that nurses face in their practice are 1) family beliefs in alternative medicine and 2) pressure to reduce morphine dosage inappropriately because the patient's family fears addiction. However, these barriers can be tackled efficiently (although the process is time consuming) through nurses educating families about palliative care. Maddocks[20] has discussed palliative care education in developing countries in detail.

Models of palliative care vary based on the availability of resources. WHO states that "home-based care is generally the best way of achieving good quality care and coverage in countries with strong family support and poor health infrastructure."[21] As an example, the Palliative Care program in Sarawak, Malaysia has been shown to be sustainable and not costly.[22]

Payne recently gave an approximation of the extent of palliative care services available in the countries in the Indian subcontinent. According to her, there are 284 palliative care services in India, seven in Bangladesh, six in Nepal, two in Pakistan, and one in Sri Lanka.[23] She has suggested that the key features for the development of palliative care in Asia should build on religious and cultural traditions (with due respect given to views on family decision making), information and communication preferences, building capacity, and expertise at all levels, while negotiating resources, integrating palliative care into oncology services, and providing access to affordable and available medication.[23] A model for integrating palliative care services within radiation therapy has also been proposed.[24]

PALLIATIVE CARE AND THE CULTURES OF THE INDIAN SUBCONTINENT

Hindus. Among Hindus, certain customs and rituals for a dying person include putting the person on the ground (and not the bed) so that the soul is released back into the ground and not retained; pouring holy water (from the Ganges or any other holy river) in the person's mouth and sprinkling it on the body to purify and rid the person of sins committed during that person's lifetime; and chanting hymns and lighting incense to ensure a peaceful death and passage to heaven. In clinical practice, one comes across patients seeking religious conversion during their last days of life, creating conflict within the family and community. Religious groups have successfully participated in community palliative care programs.[4]

Family and community interconnectedness, *karma*, and reincarnation are major beliefs in Hinduism. Health care decisions may be made by the most senior family member or the eldest son. *Karma* is a combination of cosmic and moral cause and effect that can cross lifetimes and includes life lessons learned for spiritual growth. The belief in reincarnation gives great comfort to the dying and their families because they know their loved one will be reborn into a new life and is not gone forever. Enduring physical suffering may lead to spiritual growth and a more fortunate rebirth.[25] The Hindu view on the end of life has been well described by Firth.[26]

End-of-life care for Sikhs is similar to that of Hindus, but there are no good descriptions of Sikh practices and beliefs about death in the medical literature. (See the essays on Sikhs in Chapters 10–14.) Although there are many Muslims in South Asia, end-of-life issues among Muslims are described in detail in chapter 6 and will not be repeated here.

Buddhists. Buddhism itself is not monolithic. There are substantial variations in ideas of what is good and what is not good between Buddhists of Sri Lanka, Vietnam, China, Japan, and Tibet. Much of what people believe to be "Buddhist" is quite culturally specific. There are also wide variations between different types of Buddhist practice. Some Buddhists enjoy long chanting ceremonies and elaborate rituals, and some prefer absolute simplicity and an emphasis on quietude.

Another key concept in Buddhism is impermanence. Because Buddhists believe in beginningless time and an uncountable series of lives, they also believe that everything is constantly changing—nothing is fixed. For some people, the changeability of life is a source of anxiety; but Buddhism believes that it is useful to become accustomed to change and that strength comes from being adaptable.[27]

People who are dying are about to let go of—or lose—everything that they knew and had in this life. Buddhists would prefer to think about this as "letting go" rather than losing. The things of this life were never things that could be kept eternally. A dying person is letting go of his or her name, nationality, friends, and possessions. Belief in *karma* means that, if the person is able to give away personal possessions to others who will use them in a good way (such as to good people or worthwhile charities), then the deceased will continue to benefit from the *karma* accrued from this action in a future life. Death is sad and often untimely, but from the Buddhist point of view, there is continuity, and there is a future. If a person has suffered a lot, he or she can be reassured that all this *karma* has finished—it has been experienced—it is over. Impermanence means that, although the person is losing his or her particular identity of this life, he or she will acquire another one in the next life. There is some comfort and security in that idea. It is not the case that the person is about to cease to be; merely they are changing the clothes of their identity.[27]

In conclusion, palliative care in oncology centers is gradually developing in the Indian subcontinent, with cultural and traditional aspects emerging as significant factors. Currently, there is a gross lack of adequate palliative care services; but the next decade should see modest growth. Policy makers seem to have been impressed by the role of palliative care. End-of-life care that is traditional and acceptable to the society is desirable. Educating all health professionals is of key importance. Once services are established and palliative care education starts rolling, local research could provide answers to local questions and problems.

REFERENCES

1. Chaturvedi SK, Chandra P. Palliative Care in India. *Support Care Cancer*. 1998;6: 81–84.
2. Wright M, Wood J, Lynch T, Clark D. Mapping levels of palliative care development: A global view. *J Pain Symptom Manage*. 2008;35(5):469–485.
3. Rajagopal MR, Venkateswaran C. Palliative care in India: successes and limitations. *J Pain Palliat Care Pharmacother*. 2003;17:121–128.
4. Chaturvedi SK. Ethical dilemmas in palliative care in a traditional developing society, with special reference to Indian setting. *J Med Ethics*. 2008;34:611–615.
5. Sureshkumar K, Rajagopal MR. Palliative care in Kerala. Problems at presentation in 440 patients with advanced cancer in a south Indian state. *Palliat Med*. 1996;10:293–298.
6. World Health Organization. *Symptom Relief in Terminal Illness*. Geneva: World Health Organization; 1998.
7. *International Narcotics Control Board. Availability of Opiates for Medical Needs*. New York: United Nations; 1996.
8. Devi BCR, Tang TS, Corbex M. What doctors know about cancer pain management: an exploratory study in Sarawak, Malaysia. *J Pain Palliat Care Pharmacother*. 2006;20:15–22.
9. Rajagopal MR, Joranson DE, Gilson AM. Medical use, misuse, and diversion of opioids in India. *Lancet*. 2001;358(9276):139–143.
10. Ghooi RB, Ghooi SR. Freedom from pain—a mirage or a possibility? Experience in attempts to change laws and practices in India. *J Pain Palliat Care Pharmacother*. 2003;17:1–9.
11. Shaikh AJ, Khokar NA, Raza S, et al . Knowledge, attitude and practices of non-oncologist physicians regarding cancer and palliative care: a multi-center study in Pakistan. *Asian Pacific J of Cancer Prev*. 2008;9:581–584.
12. Abbas SQ, Muhammad SR, Mubeen SM, et al . Awareness of palliative medicine among Pakistani doctors: a survey. *J Pak Med Association*. 2004;54:195–199.
13. Spruyt O. Community-based palliative care for Bangladeshi patients in east London. Accounts of bereaved carers. *Palliat Med*. 1999;13(2):119–29.
14. Somerville J. Palliative care: the experience of informal carers within the Bangladeshi community. *Int J Pall Nurs*. 2001;7,:240–247.
15. Jayaweera I. *Home based palliative care service*. Cancer Care Association, Sri Lanka. http://cancercaresl.com/hbpc/. Accessed October 20, 2012.
16. Kumar S, Mathews N. Neighbourhood network in palliative care. *Indian J Palliat Care*. 2005;11:6–9.
17. Dayasiri MBKC. Ethics of palliative cancer care in Sri Lanka. A cross-cultural perspective. *AMJ*. 2010;3(12):772–776.
18. Nepalese—Cultural approaches to pediatric palliative care in central Massachusetts—LibraryGuides at University of Massachusetts Medical School. http://libraryguides.umassmed.edu/content.php?pid=94770&sid=1158109. Accessed July 17, 2013.
19. Liu WJ, Hu WY, Chiu TY et al. Factors that influence physicians in providing palliative care in rural communities in Taiwan. *Support Care Cancer*. 2005;13:781–789.
20. Maddocks I. Palliative care education in the developing countries. *J Pain Palliat Care Pharmacother*. 2003;17:211–221.
21. World Health Organization. *Cancer Pain Relief with a Guide to Opioid Availability*. 2nd edition. Geneva: WHO; 1996.

22. Devi BCR, Tang TS, Corbex M. Setting up home-based palliative care in countries with limited resources: a model from Sarawak, Malaysia. *Ann Oncol.* 2008;*19*:2061–2066.
23. Payne S. Comparative practices on end-of-life and palliative care in Asia and globally. Paper presented at: Asian Oncology Summit; April 2012; Singapore.
24. Bansal M, Patel FD, Mohanti BK, et al . Setting up a palliative care clinic within a radiotherapy department: a model for developing countries. *Support Care Cancer.* 2003;*11*:343–347.
25. Thrane S. Hindu end of life: Death, dying, suffering, and *karma. J Hosp Palliat Nurs.* 2010;*12*(6):337.
26. Firth S. End-of-life: a Hindu view. *Lancet.* 2005;*366*:682–686.
27. Cousens D. Palliative Care and Buddhist Cultural sensitivity. Paper presented at: Providing Culturally Sensitive End-of-Life Care: Cultural Perspectives on Death and Dying; April 26, 2006; Austin Hospital, Australia.

CHAPTER 5

Historical Perspectives on End-of-life Care in Global Context

Latin America

EDUARDO BRUERA, MARVIN OMAR DELGADO-GUAY

INTRODUCTION

Worldwide adoption of effective hospice and palliative care measures has faced an array of challenges, many of which remain pertinent even today, especially in developing countries. Latin America and the Caribbean comprise a developing region, with 45 countries and a population of 576 million. Spanish is the most prevalent language, followed by Portuguese. Latin America has the highest income gap in the world.[1,2] Many national health systems focus mainly on disease prevention, prenatal assistance, and treatment of undernourishment. Unfortunately, most must deal with poor administrative systems, poverty, and inadequate infrastructures.[3] The average number of deaths in the region was 3.465 million (mortality, 6.6/1000 inhabitants), with the majority due to cancer, cardiovascular diseases, and infectious diseases.[4]

In Latin American countries, the need for palliative care is increasing. There is an increase in the prevalence of chronic diseases. The population is aging. Life-threatening diseases are diagnosed late, and facilities that provide curative treatments are lacking.[3,5]

Palliative care availability, accessibility, and affordability are inadequate. Unfortunately most countries in Latin America and the Caribbean do not meet the need for palliative care. Approximately 80% of these countries do not recognize it as a discipline, and it is not included in the public or private health systems. Only Chile, Costa Rica, and Cuba have national palliative care programs.[3,5] It was estimated that more than 90% of palliative care that is available is found only in large cities. Only 5%–10% of patients who need palliative care receive it. Unfortunately, however, more than 50% of patients cannot pay for these services or for palliative care medications.[3,5] Most health systems in Latin America are underfunded. Although they pay for futile interventions, they often do not pay, or underpay, for palliative care services. Even though there is adequate availability of different opioid pain medications, there is poor accessibility because of their high cost, a lack of health care personnel trained in how to prescribe and use them, and restrictive regulations.[3,5] Other barriers to the delivery of palliative care in Latin American countries have been identified (Table 5.1).

HISTORY AND CURRENT STATUS OF PALLIATIVE CARE

From 1981 to 1985, some health care professionals in Latin America began to become interested in the management and treatment of the severe pain and distressing symptoms that patients with advanced cancer often experience. This generated a great interest in a group of clinicians to obtain more training and to adapt models of care for these patients. These models of care were found in Canada, Italy, England, and the United States. With the support of WHO collaborating centers, an effort was initiated to develop and teach palliative care in Latin America. World leaders traveled to Latin America from different places around the region to teach the principles of palliative care and symptom management. Among those who traveled to Latin America to teach palliative care were E. Bruera, M. Baynes, K. Foley, N. Coyle, J. Stjernswärd, R. Twycross, and V. Ventafridda.

Table 5.1. ISSUES RELATED TO THE APPROPRIATE DELIVER OF PALLIATIVE CARE IN LATIN AMERICAN COUNTRIES

Major issues

Insufficient knowledge by physician, nurses, and other
    health professionals about palliative care
Poverty
Unfunded programs
Drug availability
Taboo around death/disclosure of diagnosis
Inadequate communication about diagnosis and prognosis
Lack of appropriate research infrastructure
Lack of support from hospital administrations
Low public awareness
Uncommitted government/Ministry of Health
Accreditation

History by country. Following the WHO guidelines, the first palliative care program in Argentina was created in Buenos Aires, Argentina in 1985 with the help of the Prager-Bild Foundation. The palliative care team, which included physicians, nurses, social workers, and a psychologist, received training through this foundation. Some of them visited hospices in England to adapt models of care for their patients. In September 1986, the National Academy of Medicine in Buenos Aires, Argentina organized the first International Conference of Hospice and Palliative Medicine. Twenty years later, around 80 teams were operating countrywide, and palliative care activity could be identified in each major and medium-sized city throughout the country. In the main, palliative care services are hospital based, with few home-care programs. The Pallium Latino America training initiative was launched in the early 1990s to support clinical practice, with courses offered at various centers across the country. Links have been established with the International Centre for Palliative Care in Oxford, and courses are accredited by the Universidad del Salvador School of Medicine (Buenos Aires). A major step forward was taken in 2000, when the Argentina Ministry of Health and Social Activities approved national standards for the organization and implementation of palliative care services; palliative medicine was recognized as a specialty that same year.

Costa Rica is a small country with an established health system committed to providing quality care at a reasonable price to every citizen. With a government-sponsored network of 29 hospitals and more than 250 clinics throughout the country, the Caja Costarricense de Seguro Social (CCSS) has primary responsibility for providing low-cost health services to its four million inhabitants. On October 1, 1990, Costa Rica created the first Latin American pediatric palliative care unit at the Children's National Hospital of Costa Rica, Central America. Since that time, this palliative care unit has been offering inpatient consultation services and house-call visits to patients with advanced and terminal illnesses. The Clinic for Pain and Palliative Care was established in the Calderón Guardia Hospital in the early 1990s and later became recognized as the National Center for Pain Control and Palliative Care (1999). A national pain control and palliative care policy was adopted in 2001.[6]

Argentina and Costa Rica are among 35 countries in the world in which hospice/palliative care services are achieving a measure of integration with mainstream providers and gaining wider policy recognition.[6] In Brazil there are more than 14 operational services. In 1992, the first Mexican palliative care unit was founded at the Hospital Civil de Guadalajara by Gustavo Montejo Rosas. Since then, several other institutions have developed pain and palliative care programs and hospices in different states throughout Mexico; however, home-based care is rarely provided, mainly because of financial constraints, such as lack of funding for transport.

In Colombia, early initiatives were led by psychologists, such as Isa de Jaramillo, who created the Omega Foundation (Bogotá, 1987), and Liliana

De Lima, who established a palliative care program in La Viga. When services expanded, hopes were pinned on "Law 100," which passed in the mid-1990s and aimed to integrate health services and give patients broader access to care. Palliative care clinical and educational programs have continued to flourish in different states of the country.

A number of "hospices" providing shelter and care for AIDS patients are operating in Guatemala. In 2005, in Guatemala City, Eva Rossina Duarte founded the first palliative care program in the country, as part of the care provided to patients with advanced cancer at the Instituto Nacional de Cancerología de Guatemala. This program has continued to grow and develop and is now an independent department at the same hospital. In the same city, Silvia Rivas founded the first pediatric palliative care program, which is dedicated to the care of pediatric patients with cancer and their caregivers at the Unidad Nacional de Oncología Pediatrica.

Developments in Nicaragua are at an early stage, but interest has been forthcoming from the country's Ministry of Health. A pain control unit has been established at the National Radiotherapy Center, and the professional trained in pain control works there on a voluntary basis.

Initiatives in Bolivia are also at an early stage, with activity centered on the palliative care unit in Santa Cruz de la Sierra, where the National Cancer Institute is located. In 2005, the Association Boliviana de Hospicio y Cuidados Paliativos organized an event to mark World Hospice and Palliative Care Day. Journalists and representatives from national and local health authorities were invited to hear presentations and receive information about the importance of palliative care for the patient and family.

Activists in Paraguay have issued a position statement favoring a public health approach to palliative care; initiatives are currently centered on the National Cancer Institute and the Hospital de Clinicas in Asuncion.

In the Caribbean area, palliative care services began in Cuba at the beginning of the 1990s. Three services are currently operational: two in Havana and one in Cienfuegos. In 2005, the British academic Dr. Richard Harding visited Cuba as a Travelling Fellow (from the International Association of Hospice and Palliative Care [IAHPC]), and while there, he helped to develop a palliative care education program. In Jamaica, the Consie Waters Cancer Care Hospice, which has eight beds, was founded in 1985 and initially maintained close contact with St Christopher's Hospice, London. Nearby Hope Institute is a hospital-based palliative care team led by a former medical consultant from England; both services are in Kingston, Jamaica. Foundations for palliative care services are also being laid in several other Caribbean islands.

Current status and areas for improvement. In 2001, a regional organization known as the Latin American Association for Palliative Care was launched by six palliative care professionals: Hugo Fornells and Roberto Wenk from Argentina, Liliana De Lima and Rene Rodriguez from Colombia, Eduardo

Méndez from Uruguay, and Lizbeth Quesada from Costa Rica. The following year, the Association's first meeting was held in conjunction with the 6th Latin American Palliative Care Congress in Guadalajara.

The Pain and Policy Studies Group/WHO Collaborating Center at the University of Wisconsin has been active in bringing together clinicians and policymakers from countries throughout the Latin American region. For example, a workshop held in Ecuador in December 2000 assembled cancer and palliative care clinicians, national drug regulators, and cancer-control officials from Bolivia, Chile, Colombia, Ecuador, Peru, and Venezuela to develop action plans aimed at ensuring the availability of opioid analgesics for palliative care. Activities like this continue to develop to improve all aspects of palliative care in Latin America.

In 2002, the Asociación Latino Americana de Cuidado Paliativo (ALCP) was created. The objectives of the ALCP are to support the development of palliative care in the region, to mobilize resources for the countries, to promote changes in legislation and regulations to improve access to the treatments and medicines, to support and coordinate the Latin American Congress of Palliative Care, and to develop a network of international cooperation for the region.

Several Latin American congresses in palliative care have taken place, promoting the educational efforts, academic impact, and research advances of the palliative care programs in the different countries of the region. However, research in palliative care in Latin American is still scarce.[7,8] Health care research in Latin American countries, in general, has been underfunded and underestimated as a priority, considered a luxury rather than a necessity.[9] In addition, there is a gap in scientific production in palliative care between low- and middle-income countries and high-income countries.[10]

Over the last 30 years or so, there has been a significant increase in the number of palliative care programs in Latin America, and a growing commitment to making practice evidence-based has been emerging. There is an impetus to move palliative care further upstream in the disease progression, thereby seeking integration with curative and rehabilitation therapies and shifting the focus beyond terminal care and the final stages of life. There is also a growing interest in extending the benefits of palliative care to those with diseases other than cancer, in order to make "palliative care for all" a reality. All of these programs continue to benefit from the strong personal motivation of leaders. Latin American countries, despite many barriers, continue to work to improve the care and quality of life of patients with advanced illnesses and their caregivers.

PALLIATIVE CARE AND LATIN AMERICAN CULTURE

Latin America today is a product of 500 years of mixing the people and cultures of the indigenous populations, European colonialists and immigrants, and Africans, who arrived via forced migration and enslavement.[11] In addition to this cultural diversity, Latin American culture is also influenced by national origin and social class.

It is important to consider the heterogeneity of the Latin American populations living in the United States, where there is considerable variation in health care access and utilization patterns by country of origin, English-language proficiency, insurance status, and length of time in the United States.[12] However, the predominant use of the Spanish language and shared cultural themes create definite similarities among Latinos in the United States.[13] Latinos are the largest ethnic minority group in the United States, currently accounting for 16% of the US population, a proportion that is projected to grow to 30% by the year 2050.[14] For many Latinos in the U.S., the experience of illness is influenced by their experience as immigrants. Regardless of country of origin or degree of acculturation in the United States, a number of culturally based beliefs and attitudes that permeate the Latino community in the United States may influence illness experience, decision making, and care at the end of life.[15] Because there are so few data on the social, economic, and religious aspects of care at the end of life in Latin American countries themselves, we present a review of studies regarding Latinos in the United States. From them, one can extrapolate reasonably to Latinos in Latin American countries.

There is mixed evidence about rates of advance care planning in the Latin American communities. In a recent multicenter study of patients with advanced cancer, only 29 of 62 of Latino patients (47%), compared to 249 of 312 of white patients (80%), had an advance care plan.[16] However, in a study of 239 elderly white and 224 elderly Latino patients in New York City, only 35% had completed a health care proxy, and rates did not differ by ethnicity.[17] Rates of hospice use among Latinos appear to be similar to whites. A third study of 40,930 elderly patients with advanced cancer found that Latinos had slightly lower rates of hospice use compared with whites (38% vs. 42%).[18]

It has been reported that, in Latin America, physicians often do not disclose bad news or poor prognosis with their patients and are expected to keep up patients' hope.[1,19,20] Interestingly a study of 91 patients with advanced cancer in Cuba found that only 41% knew that they had cancer. Those patients who knew their diagnosis reported less anxiety compared with patients who did not know.[20] However, Blackhall et al.[21] showed in a US survey that not informing the patient of a poor outcome was preferred by about a third of older Mexican Americans, compared with less than 15% of whites or African Americans. Moreover, evidence suggests that Latin American patients expect physicians to take a more directive role regarding decisions about life-sustaining treatment.[22,23]

Religion and spirituality. In a recent study of a diverse group of US patients with advanced cancer, religiousness was associated with wanting all measures to extend life, even after adjustment for race and ethnicity (odds ratio, 1.96; 95% CI, 1.08 to 3.57).[24] More research is needed to investigate different aspects of the communication of adverse outcomes and about spirituality and the decision-making process in Latin American patients.

One can safely say, however, that spirituality and religiosity are commonly enmeshed with Latino cultural values and daily lives. They serve as foundations of strength and coping with life's struggles, as well as playing an important role as alternative therapy for health and well-being.[25-27] In Latin America, spirituality and religiosity are important components of mind-body alternative therapies when used for the purpose of healing or to maintain health.[28-33] Latino theological literature describes spirituality as integral with Latino culture.[34-40]

Spirituality among Latinos is intricately woven within the historical events of Spanish/Christian colonization of the indigenous people of Mexico, the Caribbean, and Central and South America. Latinos of the Americas embody this shared history of colonization, which has an impact on cultural and spiritual perspectives and values.[34] Religious symbols, rituals, and meanings that exist within the structure of organized Hispanic Catholicism are mixed with the influences of indigenous cultural roots.[35]

There are some enduring cultural values among Latinos in which their faith experiences are embedded, such as *Personalismo*, which is an important Latino cultural value that is characterized by warmth, closeness, and empathy in one's relationship with others. In faith experiences, this translates to a direct and intimate relationship with one's conception of a universal being, which may include Christian concepts of God, Jesus, the Virgin Mary, the Virgin of Guadalupe, or various other saints.[41]

Another Latino core cultural value that influences spirituality is *Familismo*, which is characterized by an enduring commitment and loyalty to immediate and extended family members.[36] The extended family forms a collective support network with strong ties of solidarity, interdependence, and loyalty.[15] Faith experiences are often embedded in one's relationship with the family and members of the community, which may or may not include involvement with the church. The role of Latino women in the family and local community is a key component.[15,42,43] Clinicians should be prepared for large families to be present at the bedside and to be involved in care.

Another cultural script that can be present in many clinical situations is *Fatalismo* or fatalism. It is a belief in fate—that one's future is preordained or not under one's control. *Fatalismo* has been primarily studied as a belief or attitude that may deter Latinos from participating in cancer screening and other preventive services.[44,45]

Religion and spirituality (*la espiritualidad*) have a powerful influence on many Latinos. In the United States it has been reported that a high proportion of elderly Latinos are Catholic.[46] However, whereas according to a recent Pew study of 4016 US Latinos, 92% consider themselves religious, the religious diversity of Latinos is increasing overall: 68% are Roman Catholic and 15%, Evangelical or "born-again" Protestants (*Evangelistas*).[47] Latino Evangelicals in the United States pray more, attend religious services more frequently, and evangelize more frequently than Catholics, and they are more likely to believe the Bible to be literally true.[47] Nearly one in ten (8%) Latinos do not identify with any religion. Differences in religious identification among Latinos coincide with important differences in demographic characteristics. Most Latinos pray every day, most have a religious object in their homes, and most attend a religious service at least once a month. By significant majorities, Latinos who identify with a religion believe that miracles occur today just as they did in ancient times.

Amid this overall religiosity, important differences emerge among Latinos of different religious traditions and between Latinos and their non-Hispanic counterparts.[47] There has been an increasing trend toward evangelical Pentecostalism in the United States and particularly in Latin American countries.[48] For example, the religious landscape of Brazil is changing. Although Brazil has the world's largest Catholic population, the growing evangelical Christian movement has made inroads into the heretofore Catholic hegemony.[49]

Not all Latinos, however, relate to Christianity; some may be atheist or agnostic, or they may identify with non-Christian faith traditions.[47] Nevertheless, within the context of religious denominational diversity, Latinos tend to have an active, intimate relationship with their conception of God, and popular religiosity is a prevalent value.

It has also been reported in focus groups conducted in the United States that Latino surrogates indicated that suffering was to be borne as part of a test of faith.[15,50] This view can act both as a risk factor and as a protective factor for adjustment and coping. The view that pain and suffering are a test of faith can interfere, for example, with pain management and the ability of family members to prepare for the death of their loved one.[51] This concept has also been reported in the literature on attitudes of African Americans toward end-of-life care and may represent a common expression of perseverance and struggle in the face of discrimination and subjugation.[52-54]

In some Latino cultures, there is high degree of acknowledgement of death. In fact, death is even celebrated in some Latino cultures. The holiday celebrated on November 2 of every year in some Latin American countries illustrates this: *El Dia de los Muertos* (Day of the Dead). This ancestral holiday focuses on honoring and celebrating the dead and the coming together of family when there has been a death.[13]

Latin America has a strong history of a very tight interaction between spirituality, religion, and health care. Major religious institutions, mostly Roman Catholic, led the way in the establishment of the first hospitals and medical schools in Latin America. Chaplains as well as prayer rooms and chapels are available in the vast majority if not all health care institutions in the region. There is also a strong presence of shamanic and traditional-healer practices when patients become ill. There is also a strong tradition for family members to engage in spiritual and religious practices when a member of a family is ill. This permeation of spirituality and religion into all aspects of the serious illness is quite universal across the region, and it affects individuals across the socioeconomic spectrum.

Palliative care clinicians in Latin America and those who care for patients from Latin cultures need to be aware of the very strong spiritual and religious needs of the families and also of the varieties of ways in which these patients and families can access these types of support, either by providing them access to chaplains within the palliative care team or by facilitating and encouraging patient access to religious leaders or traditional healers. Maintaining communication and a friendly welcoming attitude towards these individuals will further personalize care for patients and families in the region, and it is usually associated with increased satisfaction with care on the part of the patient and family, and, generally, with a better bereavement after the patient's death.

A key goal of palliative care services is to alleviate patient suffering. In a multicultural and spiritual region such as Latin America, palliative care services continue to evolve and to grow, but always with cognizance of the patient's cultural and spiritual needs. The care and the quality of life of patients with advanced and terminal illness will continue to improve every single day. Educational and research activities are fundamental to assuring the development of palliative care activities in Latin America.

REFERENCES

1. United Nations. Department of economic and social affairs: Population division. World Mortality. New York: United Nations; 2011. http://www.un.org/esa/population/publications/wmchart2011/wmchart2011.pdf. Accessed August 30, 2012.
2. United Nations. World population prospects: The 2002 revision. New York: United Nations; 2002.
3. Bruera E. Palliative care in Latin America. *J Pain Symptom Manage*. 1993;8(6):365–368.
4. World Health Organization. Mortalities. WHO Global Infobase; 2004. https://apps.who.int/infobase/Mortality.aspx. Updated 2011. Accessed August 20, 2012.
5. Wenk R, Bertolino M. Palliative care development in South America: A focus on Argentina. *J Pain Symptom Manage*. 2007;33(5):645–650.
6. Wright M, Wood J, Lynch T, et al. Mapping levels of palliative care development: A global view. *J Pain Symptom Manage*. 2008;35(5):469–485.
7. Pastrana T, De Lima L, Eisenchlas J, et al. Palliative care research in Latin America and the Caribbean: From the beginning to the declaration of Venice and beyond. *J Palliat Med*. 2012;15(3):352–358.

8. Wenk R, De Lima L, Eisenchlas J. Palliative care research in Latin America: Results of a survey within the scope of the declaration of Venice. *J Palliat Med*. 2008;11(5):717–722.

9. Moloney A. Latin America faces hurdles in health research. *Lancet*. 2009;374(9695):1053–1054.

10. Pastrana T, Vallath N, Mastrojohn J, et al. Disparities in the contribution of low- and middle-income countries to palliative care research. *J Pain Symptom Manage*. 2010;39(1):54–68.

11. Gonzalez BE, Borrell LN, Choudhry S, et al. Latino populations: A unique opportunity for the study of race, genetics, and social environment in epidemiological research. *Am J Public Health*. 2005;95(12):2161.

12. Weinick RM, Jacobs EA, Stone LCet al. Hispanic health care disparities: Challenging the myth of a monolithic Hispanic population. *Med Care*. 2004;42(4):313–320.

13. Talamantes MA, Gómez C, Braun KL. Advance directives and end-of-life care: The Hispanic perspective. In: Braun KL, Pietsch JH, Blanchette PL, eds. *Cultural issues in end-of-life decision making*. Thousand Oaks, CA: Sage Publications; 2000:83–100.

14. US Census Bureau. Percent of the Projected Population by Race and Hispanic Origin for the United States, 2008 to 2050. Census Bureau Home Page; 2008. http://www.census.gov/population/www/projections/tablesandcharts/table_4.xls. Accessed August 28, 2012.

15. Smith AK, Sudore RL, Pérez-Stable EJ. Palliative care for Latino patients and their families. *JAMA*. 2009;301(10):1047–1057.

16. Smith AK, McCarthy EP, Paulk E, et al. Racial and ethnic differences in advance care planning among patients with cancer: Impact of terminal illness acknowledgment, religiousness, and treatment preferences. *JCO*. 2008;26(25):4131–4137.

17. Morrison RS, Meier DE. High rates of advance care planning in New York City's elderly population. *Arch Intern Med*. 2004;164(22):2421–2426.

18. Smith AK, Earle CC, McCarthy EP. Racial and ethnic differences in end-of-life care in fee-for-service Medicare beneficiaries with advanced cancer. *J Am Geriatr Soc*. 2009;57(1):153–158.

19. Holland JC, Geary N, Marchini A, et al. An international survey of physician attitudes and practice in regard to revealing the diagnosis of cancer. *Cancer Invest*. 1987;5(2):151–154.

20. Justo Roll I, Simms V, Harding R. Multidimensional problems among advanced cancer patients in Cuba: Awareness of diagnosis is associated with better patient status. *J Pain Symptom Manage*. 2009;37(3):325–330.

21. Blackhall LJ, Murphy ST, Frank G, et al. Ethnicity and attitudes toward patient autonomy. *JAMA*. 1995;274:820–825.

22. Blackhall LJ, Frank G, Murphy ST, et al. Ethnicity and attitudes towards life sustaining technology. *Soc Sci Med*. 1999;48(12):1779–1789.

23. Caralis PV, Davis B, Wright K, et al. The influence of ethnicity and race on attitudes toward advance directives, life-prolonging treatments, and euthanasia. *J Clin Ethics*. 1993;4(2):155–165.

24. Balboni TA, Vanderwerker LC, Block SD, et al. Religiousness and spiritual support among advanced cancer patients and associations with end-of-life treatment preferences and quality of life. *JCO*. 2007;25(5):555–560.

25. Campesino M, Schwartz GE. Spirituality among Latinas/os: implications of culture in conceptualization and measurement. *ANS*. 2006;*29*(1):69.

26. Levin JS, Markides KS, Ray LA. Religious attendance and psychological well-being in Mexican Americans: A panel analysis of three-generations data. *Gerontologist*. 1996;*36*(4):454–463.

27. Reyes-Ortiz CA, Rodriguez M, Markides KS. The role of spirituality healing with perceptions of the medical encounter among Latinos. *J Gen Intern Med*. 2009;*24*:542–547.

28. Hsiao AF, Wong MD, Goldstein MS, et al. Variation in complementary and alternative medicine (CAM) use across racial/ethnic groups and the development of ethnic-specific measures of CAM use. *J Altern Complement Med*. 2006;*12*(3):281–290.

29. Barnes PM, Powell-Griner E, McFann K, et al. Complementary and alternative medicine use among adults: United States, 2002. Advanced data from vital statistics; No. 343. Hyattsville, MD: National Center for Health Statistics; 2004;*2*(2):54–71.

30. Mikhail N, Wali S, Ziment I. Use of alternative medicine among Hispanics. *J Altern Complement Med*. 2004;*10*(5):851–859.

31. Kronenberg F, Cushman LF, Wade CM, et al. Race/ethnicity and women's use of complementary and alternative medicine in the United States: Results of a national survey. *Am J Public Health*. 2006;*96*(7):1236.

32. Ortiz BI, Shields KM, Clauson KA, et al. Complementary and alternative medicine use among Hispanics in the United States. *Ann Pharmacother*. 2007;*41*(6):994–1004.

33. Graham RE, Ahn AC, Davis RB, et al. Use of complementary and alternative medical therapies among racial and ethnic minority adults: Results from the 2002 National Health Interview Survey. *J Natl Med Assoc*. 2005;*97*(4):535.

34. Rodriguez J. *Our lady of Guadalupe: Faith and empowerment among Mexican American women*. Austin, TX: University of Texas Press; 1994.

35. Hinijosa J. Culture, spirituality and US Hispanics. In: Deck AF, ed. *Frontiers of Hispanic Theology in the United States*. Maryknoll, NY: Orbis Books; 1992:154–164.

36. Diaz-Stevens AM. Latinas and the church. In: Dolan JP, Deck AF, eds. *Hispanic Catholic Culture in the U.S.: Issues and Concerns*. Notre Dame, IN: University of Notre Dame Press; 1994:240–277.

37. Loya G. The Hispanic woman: pasonaria and pastora of the Hispanic community. In: Deck AF, ed. *Frontiers of Hispanic Theology in the United States*. Maryknoll, NY: Orbis Books; 1992:124–133.

38. Rodríguez J. Latina activists: toward an inclusive spirituality of being in the world. In: Aquino M, Machado, D, Rodriquez J, eds. *A reader in Latina feminist theology*. Austin, TX: University of Texas Press; 2002:114–130.

39. Solivan S. *Spirit, Pathos, and Liberation*. Sheffield, England: Sheffield Academic Press; 1998.

40. Pineda-Madrid N. Notes toward a Chicana feminist epistemology (and why it is important for Latina feminist theologies). In: Aquino M, Machado D, Rodriquez J. *A reader in Latina feminist theology*. Austin, TX: University of Texas Press; 2002:241–266.

41. Cervantes J. The integration of religion and spirituality in counseling and psychotherapy with Chicano/Latino families. Paper presented at: National Latino Psychological Association Conference; November 18, 2004; Scottsdale, AZ.

42. Peña M. Feminist Christian women in Latin America: Other voices, other visions. *J Feminist Stud Religion*. 1995;*11*(1):81–94.

43. Aquino MP. Latina feminist theology: Central features. In: Aquino M, Machado D, Rodriquez J. *A reader in Latina feminist theology*. Austin, TX: University of Texas Press; 2002:133–160.

44. Pérez-Stable EJ, Sabogal F, Otero-Sabogal R, Hiatt RA, McPhee SJ. Misconceptions about cancer among Latinos and Anglos. *JAMA*. 1992;*268*(22):3219–3223.

45. Otero-Sabogal R, Stewart S, Sabogal F, Brown BA, Perez-Stable EJ. Access and attitudinal factors related to breast and cervical cancer re-screening: Why are Latinas still underscreened? *Health Educ Behav*. 2003(*30*):337–359.

46. Stolley JM, Koenig H. Religion/spirituality and health among elderly African Americans and Hispanics. *J Psychosoc Nurs Ment Health Serv*. 1997;*35*(11):32–38.

47. Suro R, Escobar G, Livingston G, et al. *Changing faiths: Latinos and the transformation of American religion*. Washington, DC: Pew Research Center; 2007. http://www.pewhispanic.org/2007/04/25/changing-faiths-latinos-and-the-transformation-of-american-religion/. Accessed March 29, 2012.

48. Solivan S. Hispanic-Pentecostal spiritual healing practices. Paper presented at: Harvard Spirituality and Healing in Medicine Conference; March 1999; Chicago, Ill.

49. Estatistíca. 2010 Population Census: General characteristics of the population, religion and persons with disabilities. http://www.ibge.gov.br/english/estatistica/populacao/censo2010/caracteristicas_religiao_deficiencia/default_caracteristicas_religiao_deficiencia.shtm. Accessed July 17, 2013.

50. Braun UK, Beyth RJ, Ford ME, McCullough LB. Voices of African American, Caucasian, and Hispanic surrogates on the burdens of end-of-life decision making. *J Gen Intern Med*. 2008;*23*(3):267–274.

51. Del Gaudio F, Hichenberg S, Eisenberg M, et al. Latino values in the context of palliative care: Illustrative cases from the family focused grief therapy trial. *Am J Hosp Palliat Med*. 2012;1–8. DOI: 10.1177/1049909112448926.

52. Crawley LV, Payne R, Bolden J, et al. Palliative and end-of-life care in the African American community. *JAMA*. 2000;*284*(19):2518–2521.

53. Crawley LM. Palliative care in African American communities. *J Palliat Med*. 2002;*5*(5):775–779.

54. Crawley LM, Marshall PA, Lo B, et al, End-of-Life Care Consensus Panel. Strategies for culturally effective end-of-life care. *Ann Intern Med*. 2002;*136*:673–679.

CHAPTER 6

Historical Perspectives on End-of-life Care in Global Context

Middle East and North Africa

MOHAMMAD ZAFIR AL-SHAHRI

INTRODUCTION

The Arab League consists of 22 countries, 18 of which speak Arabic as the primary language. The discussion in this chapter is focused on these 18 Arab countries that are geopolitically part of the Middle East and North Africa. The population of these countries exceeds 333 million, of which more than 95% are Muslims and 68% live in countries with low or lower middle income according to the World Bank classification (Table 6.1).[1]

In the year 2008, cancer cases in these countries were estimated to have exceeded 237,000 and cancer deaths to be more than 172,000 (Table 6.2).[2]

This high death rate may be explained by the fact that, as in other developing countries, the majority of cancer patients present for treatment with advanced stages of disease. For these patients, then, cure is no longer an option, and palliative care is the most appropriate approach. When the needs of terminally ill patients with non-cancer diagnoses are taken into account, the necessity and urgency for good end-of-life care in the Arab World is even more evident.

HISTORY AND CURRENT STATUS OF PALLIATIVE CARE

Palliative care in the Arab World is probably most developed in Saudi Arabia. It was first introduced in the early 1990s at King Faisal Specialist Hospital

Table 6.1. POPULATION AND ECONOMY OF THE ARAB WORLD
(ESTIMATES FROM THE YEAR 2010)

Country	Population (in thousands)	Muslim population (%)	Income category (World Bank classification)
Algeria	35,468	99	Upper middle
Bahrain	1,262	81.2	High
Egypt	81,121	90	Lower middle
Iraq	31,672	97	Lower middle
Jordan	6,187	92	Upper middle
Kuwait	2,737	85	High
Lebanon	4,228	59.7	Upper middle
Libya	6,355	97	Upper middle
Mauritania	3,460	100	Low
Morocco	31,951	99	Lower middle
Oman	2,782	99	High
Qatar	1,759	77.5	High
Saudi Arabia	27,448	100	High
Sudan	34,206	100	Lower middle
Syria	20,411	90	Lower middle
Tunisia	10,481	98	Upper middle
United Arab Emirates	7,512	96	High
Yemen	24,053	100	Lower middle
Total	333,093	95.3	

and Research Center (KFSHRC) in the capital, Riyadh, as a home palliative care service. This later developed into a comprehensive palliative care program involving inpatient, outpatient, and home care components as well as a postgraduate training fellowship program for physicians pursuing subspecialization in palliative medicine.[3-5] Pioneers who received palliative care training at KFSHRC were able to initiate palliative care services in several other institutions in Saudi Arabia as well as in other countries such as Egypt, Qatar, United Arab Emirates, and Bahrain. Kuwait has recently inaugurated a multistory, dedicated palliative care center that is now partially operational, with a capacity of approximately 100 inpatient beds. Kuwaiti physicians are now being sponsored to join the palliative medicine fellowship program at KFSHRC for subspecialty training. In Jordan, there is localized provision of palliative care in a major cancer center in Amman. The establishment of a private palliative care clinic that provides clinical and professional training services is another interesting Jordanian experiment that is now a few years old. A recently initiated palliative care service is evolving in a cancer center in Khartoum, Sudan, led by a Sudanese physician who received palliative care training overseas.

Table 6.2. CANCER BURDEN IN THE ARAB WORLD (ESTIMATES FROM THE YEAR 2008)

Country	Cancer incidence	Mortality
Algeria	28,736	21,012
Bahrain	534	294
Egypt	68,805	50,807
Iraq	19,901	15,359
Jordan	4,912	3,445
Kuwait	1,960	880
Lebanon	7,092	4,859
Libya	5,045	3,837
Mauritania	1,978	1,542
Morocco	27,597	19,734
Oman	1,432	1,043
Qatar	618	364
Saudi Arabia	13,277	8,868
Sudan	21,860	16,690
Syria	9,468	6,232
Tunisia	11,938	8,437
United Arab Emirates	1,645	832
Yemen	10,249	7,873
Total	237,047	172,108

Both Morocco and Tunisia have localized palliative care services, but on a limited scale that is too far from meeting the needs of the populace.[6]

Other Arab World countries are either lacking any appreciable palliative care services or, at best, are in a primitive capacity-building stage at present.[7] In the last two decades, there has only been a very modest increase in the medical use of morphine in the Arab World, whereas worldwide consumption has grown considerably in the same period (Table 6.3).[8]

This further emphasizes the huge gap between the rapidly growing need and the alarmingly slow progress in palliative care services in the Arab World. Improving awareness among health care policy-makers and professionals as well as in the community at large may boost the development of palliative care in the region. However, establishing and expanding palliative care training programs for local health care professionals would probably be the best way forward.

PALLIATIVE CARE AND ARABIC CULTURE

Islam, the religion of the vast majority of Arabs, is both a belief scheme and a system of living in accordance with the teachings of the *Qur'an*. Islam is the

Table 6.3. CONSUMPTION OF MORPHINE
EQUIVALENT PER CAPITA IN THE ARAB WORLD

Country	Consumption of morphine equivalent (milligram per capita)	
	1980 (±1 year)	2009 (±1 year)
Algeria	0.02	0.48
Bahrain	0.44	6.48
Egypt	0.09	0.88
Iraq	0.25	0.18
Jordan	0.24	3.93
Kuwait	0.57	6.97
Lebanon	0.24	4.34
Libya	0.20	1.62
Mauritania	0.14	0.01
Morocco	0.04	0.76
Oman	0.14	2.30
Qatar	0.32	2.48
Saudi Arabia	0.41	4.75
Sudan	0.09	0.08
Syria	0.18	2.79
Tunisia	0.06	3.63

reference through which Muslims commonly see, interpret, and value things, including health, sickness, and death. However, the extent to which this discussion applies to individuals may vary to a lesser or greater degree due to the uniqueness of every human being, a fact that holds across races, faiths, cultures, languages, and geographical variations. Within Muslim communities, some variations exist between schools of thought, as well as between individuals within the same school of thought, who may vary in their interpretation and (or) the level of observance of religious teachings.

The religion of Islam. The word *Islam* in Arabic refers to the absolute submission to the will of Allah (who created the universe) by conforming interiorly and externally to His law. Islam is based on five pillars of religion (*Arkan ul Islam*) and six pillars of faith (*Arkan ul Iman*), as shown in Table 6.4.

Islam acknowledges no priesthood, and, therefore, Muslims invoke Allah directly for their needs. Every Muslim is entitled to read the *Qur'an* and the *Sunnah* (sayings and deeds of the prophet Muhammad, peace be upon him [pbuh]). The major principles and guidelines in the *Qur'an* and the *Sunnah* are commonly understood by people of variable education. However, learned scholars (*Ulama*) are often needed for interpreting the sacred scriptures and educating others about the Islamic viewpoint on complex matters. For practical reasons, a spiritual care provider for patients may not have to be a learned

Table 6.4. PILLARS OF ISLAM AND PILLARS OF FAITH

Pillars of Islam (Arkan ul Islam)	
Shahadah	Bearing witness that there is no one who deserves to be worshipped save Allah and that Prophet Muhammad is the messenger of Allah
Salah	Prayers five times a day
Zakah	Almsgiving
Sawm	Abstinence from food, drink, and sexual intercourse during daytime throughout the ninth lunar month (Ramadan)
Hajj	Pilgrimage to Makkah once in lifetime for those who are physically and financially able

Pillars of faith (Arkan ul Iman) To believe in:	
Allah	There is only one God and He alone has the right to be worshipped
Angels	Angels of Allah exist as honored beings
Books	The Noble Books Allah has revealed to His Prophets
Prophets	The Prophet Muhammad and all previous Prophets (including Adam, Noah, Abraham, Moses, and Jesus, who are Prophets of Allah)
Day of Judgment	The day when all people will be resurrected for Allah's judgment according to their beliefs and deeds
Alqadar	Divine Predestination

scholar but certainly needs to have received reasonable formal education in Islamic studies and jurisprudence.

The meaning of suffering. Muslims attribute the existence of disease and the suffering associated with it to Allah's will, as they believe in Divine Predestination (*alqadar*). This belief, however, does not mean to Muslims that man lacks freewill. Rather, Muslims believe that human beings can choose to do good or bad and that they bear responsibility for their own choices and its consequences. Furthermore, Islamic teachings promote prevention and treatment of disease. According to Islamic guidance, suffering should be perceived as a mode of atonement for person's sins, as the prophet Muhammad (pbuh) imparted, "No fatigue, no disease, nor sorrow, nor sadness, nor hurt, nor distress befalls a Muslim, even if it were the prick he receives from a thorn, but Allah expiates some of his sins for that."[9] This approach of interpretation may help patients and families to cope well with the psychological impact of serious and life-limiting illnesses. Nonetheless, some Muslim patients may perceive suffering as punishment inflicted on them by Allah as a result of their sins. This "negative" perception may potentiate the suffering experience a patient is already going through. The role of a competent spiritual care provider is pivotal in such cases, where he (or she) may help the patient to adopt the positive approach of perceiving suffering. Islamic teaching emphasizes that relieving suffering of a human being or an animal is greatly virtuous.[10]

Expression of suffering. Islam coaches Muslims to experience and express patience at difficult times. Nonetheless, Islam also allows for moderate expression of suffering in a way that does not reflect any degree of rejection of *alqadar*. This may lead some patients to report physical symptoms more readily than psychological and emotional suffering. Expressions that might reflect existential suffering such as "why me?!" are rarely heard of when caring for Muslim patients. Stoicism, on the other hand, may lead some patients to underreport severe symptoms, assuming that reporting such symptoms echoes impatience. A spiritual care provider may be of invaluable assistance in providing such patients and health care providers with the necessary support and guidance to get symptoms better reported and eventually better assessed and controlled.

Spiritual healing practices. The prophet Muhammad (pbuh) said, "Seek treatment, because Allah did not send down a sickness but has sent down a medication for it—known to those who know it and not known to others— except for death" (p. 71).[11] Treatment options as perceived by Muslim patients include mainstream medicine, spiritual cures, and traditional medical practices. The spiritual medical practices involve repeatedly reciting verses of the *Qur'an* and certain prophetic prayers. Black cumin (Nigella seeds) and honey are also believed to possess healing effects, as per Islamic sacred scriptures.[11] Drinking water obtained from *Zamzam* (the well in the Holy Mosque, Makkah) is a very commonly used spiritual healing modality as a result of prophetic recommendations.[10] The *Sunnah* forbids wearing amulets. However, the use of amulets for healing purposes is not infrequent among Muslims in some communities. Cauterizing, as a traditional medical method, is still practiced, although it was discouraged by the prophet Muhammad (pbuh).[11] The use of spiritual healing modalities is fairly common in the Arab World and probably even more so when a particular disease proves to be poorly responsive to mainstream medical treatment. Patients and families would probably feel more comfortable if the health care team were to avoid judgmental attitudes and show sensitivity to those spiritual healing modalities even at very advanced stages of life-threatening disease.

Potential spiritual concerns. At different stages of disease trajectory, patients may go through various aspects of deterioration in functional status that may hinder their ability to perform worship rites. For instance, having a colostomy or being unable to control sphincters may lead the patient to suffer from being unable to feel ritually clean. Other examples include an inability to stand up and face Makkah during prayers; an inability to perform fasting during Ramadan; and an inability to perform self-hygiene in a way that ensures modesty and dignity. A spiritual care provider should be able to support patients and families by reassuring them that all worship rites and religious duties are waivable and (or) modifiable one way or another to make them attainable for patients according to their abilities.

The illicit use of drugs known to have effects on sensorium, such as opioids, is firmly prohibited for Muslims. However, medical prescription of opioids is largely considered allowable based on the principle of necessity.[12] At times, the spiritual care provider may need to show religious evidence (such as a religious verdict) to convince patients of the permissibility of the medical use of opioids in relieving suffering. In the terminally ill, when it becomes hard to preserve a state of balance allowing for optimum symptom management (through opioid use, for instance) and a normal level of mentation, the benefits and risks should be made clear to the patient who may, or may not, choose to tolerate a little higher profile of symptoms for the sake of preserving the level of mentation.

The concept of death. Muslims believe that everyone shall die, with the timing, location, and cause of death being predestined by Allah. Muslims also believe in an afterlife, where people will go to heaven for eternal joy or to hell for either temporary or eternal suffering based on their righteous or improper deeds in their worldly life. Muslims do not believe in the reincarnation of the soul of the dead person into other persons or creatures. However, they do believe in a temporary form of intermediate life between worldly life and the day of resurrection. This special temporary life is known as the life of *Barzakh* (barrier). Life is sacred in Islamic teachings, and people do not own their lives; therefore, they have no right to intentionally end their lives. Hence, euthanasia and physician-assisted suicide are strictly prohibited.[13]

Death and funeral rites. When death approaches, a spiritual care provider, or an individual of wisdom, will typically remind the dying of the unlimited kindness of Allah and will inspire him (or her) to hope for Allah's blessings and compassion. The prophet Muhammad (pbuh) said, "None of you should die without having good expectations in Allah" (p. 15).[11] He once visited a dying young person and questioned him, "How do you feel?" The man replied, "By Allah, O Messenger of Allah, I have hope in Allah and I fear my sins." The prophet said: "These two qualities do not dwell together in a person's heart in this situation (of dying) but Allah will grant him what he hopes, and save him from what he fears" (pp. 15–16)[11]

The bonds and obligations in the Arabic family structure are major. In some instances, the patient's final requests are difficult for the family to accomplish. Therefore, the patient's relatives may fall under an extensive emotional burden. In these situations, the interdisciplinary team is advised to be reassuring of the patient's family, to prevent the potential of developing intense feelings of self-blame.

According to Islamic teaching, once death occurs, the body of the deceased should be handled with the highest possible degree of dignity; and those present around the dead body are encouraged to perform good prayers for the dead and for themselves, as the angels will say *"aameen"* (so be it) when they hear these prayers. The relatives of the deceased are encouraged to be patient and to gracefully accept Allah's decree. They are allowed to weep but not to wail.

Hastening the funeral rites is highly encouraged in Islam, and the health care team should bear this in mind while completing routine procedures.[14] Funeral rites for Muslim patients are simple and normally of low cost, ensuring that within a few hours the dead body could be washed, shrouded, carried to the mosque for funeral prayers, and finally transported to the graveyard for burial.[15] The condolences start as soon as the death is confirmed, without a definite time limit for giving condolences. However, many Muslims are used to giving condolences within the first three days after death. The communal obligations for participation in the funeral rites may have a significantly comforting effect on the grief of the bereaved family.

Palliative care in the Arab World is at different stages of development in various Arab countries. However, the current state of palliative care development is too far from matching the progressively growing needs. For substantial progress in palliative care programs to take place in the Arab World, improving palliative and end-of-life care awareness among health care policy-makers and professionals is a prerequisite. Arabs normally perceive meanings of life, disease, and death through religious teachings. In order to ensure culturally plausible palliative and end-of life care for Arab patients and their families, competent spiritual care providers are invaluable to the health care team.

REFERENCES

1. United Nations. Country profiles. World Statistics Pocketbook. New York: United Nations; 2011. http://unstats.un.org/unsd/pocketbook/country_profiles.pdf. Accessed August 14, 2012.
2. International Agency for Research on Cancer. Cancer fact sheet. GLOBOCAN 2008. Lyon, FR: International Agency for Research on Cancer; 2008. http://globocan.iarc.fr/factsheet.asp. Updated December 15, 2012. Accessed August 14, 2012.
3. Gray AJ, Ezzat A, Volker S. Developing palliative care services for terminally ill patients in Saudi Arabia. Ann Saudi Med. 1995;15(4):370–377.
4. Brown S, Black F. Palliative care in the kingdom of Saudi Arabia. Eur J Palliat Care. 2001;8(5):196–198.
5. Al-Shahri MZ. Cancer pain: Progress and ongoing issues in Saudi Arabia. Pain Res Manage. 2009;14(5):359.
6. Porchet F, Schaerer G LP, Leruth S. Intercultural experiences of training in the Maghreb. EJPC. 2005;12(1):35–37.
7. Wright M, Wood J, Lynch T, Clark D. Mapping levels of palliative care development: A global view. J Pain Symptom Manage. 2008;35(5):469–485.
8. Pain and Policy Study Group. Country profiles. Pain and Policy Study Group; 2012. http:// http://www.painpolicy.wisc.edu/countryprofiles. Accessed August 14, 2012.
9. Al-Bukhari, MI. Sahih Al-Bukhari (Summarized, Arabic-English). Khan M, trans. Riyadh, Saudi Arabia: Dar-us-Salam; 1994:934.

10. Al-Jauziyah I. *Healing with the medicine of the prophet (pbuh)*. Riyadh, Saudi Arabia: Dar-us-Salam; 1999.
11. Al-Jibaly M. *The inevitable journey part 1—Sickness: Regulations and exhortations*. Arlington, TX: Al-Kitaab & As-Sunnah Publishing; 1998.
12. Al-Shahri M, al-Khenaizan A. Palliative care for Muslim patients. *J Support Oncol*. 2005;3(6):432–436.
13. Abdalati H. *Islam in focus*. 6th ed. Riyadh, Saudi Arabia: Al-Jumah Press; 1993.
14. Philips AAB. *Funeral rites in Islam*. Dar Al Fatah: Sharjah, United Arab Emirates; 1996.
15. Al-Shahri Z, Fadul N, Elsayem A. Death, dying and burial rites in Islam. *European Journal of Palliative Care*. 2007;13(4):164–167.

CHAPTER 7

Historical Perspectives on End-of-life Care in Global Context

Asia Pacific

RAMASWAMY AKILESWARAN,
NORSHISHAM BIN MAIN, CYNTHIA GOH

INTRODUCTION

The Asia Pacific region represents those countries that are located in Asia and those close to the Western Pacific Ocean. The countries in this region include the Asian countries as well as Australia, New Zealand, Japan, Russia, the United States, and Canada. For the purpose of brevity and clarity, although the development of hospice and palliative care will include the member countries of the Asia Pacific Hospice Palliative Care Network, the discussion of spirituality and religion will be limited to the Southeast Asian region.

Southeast Asia is a large region located to the east of India and south of China. It consists of two parts—one located on the Asian mainland and the other, an island chain that extends into the South China Sea. Mainland Southeast Asia includes the countries of Cambodia, Laos, Myanmar, Thailand, and Vietnam. The Malay Peninsula projects from the mainland into the South China Sea. It includes the small state of Singapore and the country of Malaysia. Malaysia also occupies part of the island of Borneo, along with the tiny nation of Brunei and a section of Indonesia. The other islands constitute the nations of Indonesia and the Philippines.[1]

Religion is an integral part of life in Southeast Asia. Several religions are practiced in the various countries of the region. A particular religion predominates in some of the countries, with other religions also being practiced in these countries. This may be illustrated by Indonesia, which houses the largest Islamic population in the world, but also includes a proportion of people that practice Christianity, Buddhism, and Hinduism. Similarly, on the Malay Peninsula, Buddhism is the most popular faith on the mainland, but Islam dominates the southern half and the southern islands. Isolated pockets of Islam coexist with predominant Buddhist populations in Cambodia and northern Thailand. Muslims account for around 40% of the Southeast Asian population, or some 220 million people.[1]

Many of the religions seem to have been introduced into the region by traders and immigrants from other parts of the world. Hinduism was the state religion in many Southeast Asian states from the fifth to the fourteenth centuries. After the fourteenth century, Buddhism replaced Hinduism in most parts of the region except Bali, Indonesia.[2] Angkor Wat in Cambodia and Borobudur in Java, Indonesia are some examples of the religious centers of Hinduism in the past. It is believed that the influence of Hinduism declined in the region because of its elitist doctrine based on the caste system. Buddhism, Islam, and Christianity gained popularity as they were more egalitarian in nature and put salvation into the hands of the individual. Islam is believed to have come into the region through Muslim traders from the Middle East. Islam is the state religion of Malaysia and Brunei, and 90% of Indonesians are Muslims.

Animism or spirit worship has also existed alongside all the other religions in the region. Ancestor-spirit worship is an integral part of religious practice even today in many parts of the region. This is considered an important part of one's responsibility of paying respects to one's ancestors on a regular basis. Taoism, which originated in China, is practiced in the region as well, with the Taoists' firm belief in ancestor worship. Practices such as burning of paper money, paper and bamboo models of cars, air-conditioners, mobile phones, iPods, and iPads are noted in an effort to remember the spirits of ancestors and provide them with the required comforts in the nether world. One could also witness the cooking of rice, eggs, and so on for the deceased spirit when the body of the deceased is still at home. The "Hungry Ghost" festival is celebrated in the seventh lunar month of the Chinese calendar. It is believed that, on the first day of the seventh month, the spirits join the mortal earth and have to be fed and entertained so that they will be happy and return to their abode by the end of the month. It is common for the family of the deceased to cover the mirrors and deities at the homes of the deceased with red paper or newspaper. This is believed to prevent the soul of the deceased from being trapped in the mirror or bringing bad luck to those who view the coffin or body in the mirror. One may also see bits of red paper stuck at the entrance to the elevator leading to the deceased's home.

The Philippines and East Timor are two predominantly Christian countries in the region. Christians in both countries are largely Roman Catholics, as this religion was introduced by the Spanish and Portuguese traders and evangelists from these countries.

Confucianism, which is believed to have originated with the Chinese sage Confucius in the fourth and fifth centuries B.C. E., is still prevalent in Vietnam, Singapore, and the resident Chinese in the region.

It should be evident that many different religions are still being practiced in Southeast Asia even today. All these religions still have a significant effect on the beliefs and culture of the people in these countries, which in turn influence the acceptance of and reactions to hospice and palliative care in the region.

HISTORY AND CURRENT STATUS OF PALLIATIVE CARE

The first-known hospice and palliative care program in Asia was started quietly by Roman Catholic nuns in Seoul, Korea. Prior to this, hospice programs, also run by religious orders, were already in existence in Australia.

It was not until Dame Cicely Saunders started St Christopher's Hospice in London in 1967 that the hospice movement started in many countries in the Asia Pacific. Cicely Saunders visited Australia, and her lectures resulted in many individuals being inspired by the concept. One such individual was Dr. Rosalie Shaw, who went on to start the first hospital-based palliative care service in Australia at the Repatriation General Hospital in Perth, Western Australia in 1981. St Christopher's Hospice was a Christian foundation, and many in Cicely's Foundation Group, which was the think tank that undergirded the development of the concept of care at St Christopher's, were Christians. In fact, the name "hospice" in English can be traced back to the medieval hospices run by religious orders across Europe and constituted places of refuge, safety, and care for pilgrims journeying to religious shrines—in particular, to Rome or Jerusalem. In Asia also, many hospice services seem to have been pioneered by Christians, often Roman Catholic institutions or individuals, even in countries in which the predominant population is not Christian, as evidenced in Japan, Korea, Taiwan, Hong Kong, Singapore, Malaysia, and Indonesia.

Though the earliest development of hospices in Asia was in Korea, when the nuns of the Little Company of Mary started a hospice in Seoul, the Korean hospice movement did not take off until the 1980s, after Professor Kyung-Shik Lee started a hospice unit at the Catholic Hospital at Kangnam St Mary's Hospital in 1982. By 1995, there was a WHO Collaborating Centre for Hospice and Palliative Care at the College of Nursing of the Catholic University of Korea, which spearheaded nursing training palliative care. The arrival of the Asia Pacific Hospice Conference in Seoul in 2005 provided impetus for the government to fund studies and pilot projects for national palliative care service provision.[3]

The first hospice service in Japan was inspired by Cicely Saunders and St Christopher's Hospice. Psychiatrist Professor Tetsuo Kashiwagi established a hospital team in 1973 at the Presbyterian-run Yodogawa Christian Hospital and later an inpatient unit, which became the service model for palliative care in Japan for more than two decades. Hospital-inpatient hospice care achieved funding by the National Insurance in 1990. It was not until 1993 that the first free-standing inpatient hospice, the Peace House Hospice, came to be built. Hospice home care was the last to be developed and funded in Japan and is the area of growth currently.

In Taiwan, volunteer hospice home-care programs started in the mid-1980s under the leadership of Chantal Co-Shi Chao, a nurse educator affiliated with the Catholic Sanipax Socio-Medical Service and Education Foundation. The first inpatient hospice unit was opened in 1990 at the Presbyterian Mackay Memorial Hospital in Taipei, championed by radiation oncologist Dr. Ernest Lai. The Presbyterians started the Hospice Foundation of Taiwan, which funded Mackay Hospice and research and education programs in hospice care. The third charitable foundation which is also a major contributor to hospice care in Taiwan is the Buddhist Lotus Hospice Care Foundation, based in Hualien in the south of Taiwan.

In Hong Kong, the first hospice ward was started at the Roman Catholic Maryknoll Hospital in 1982. Other units started soon after, including the free-standing Bradbury Hospice, which opened in 1986, built with money from the Jockey Club and the Keswick Foundation. The palliative care unit was run by the Haven of Hope Hospital, a hospital started by Christian missionaries in 1955 to serve leprosy and later tuberculosis patients. In 1991, the Hospital Authority of Hong Kong took over the funding and running of hospice services, which led to a time of growth of palliative care services, mainly hospital-based units with hospice home care services linked to them.

In Singapore, the hospice movement commenced in 1985, when the Catholic Canossian sisters at St. Joseph's Home extended their mission from care of the elderly to care of the dying. This gave rise to a secular volunteer movement, which started hospice home-care services and formed the Hospice Care Association (HCA), now HCA Hospice Care. Other religious groups to start hospice services in the community include Assisi Hospice in 1989, run by the Roman Catholic Franciscan Missionaries of the Divine Motherhood; Agape Hospice Care, run by the Methodist church; Metta Hospice Care, run by the Buddhist Metta Welfare Services; and Bright Vision Hospital, run by the Singapore Buddhist Welfare Association. What these services have in common in multiethnic Singapore is that they serve patients of all races and religions, and all have strict policies not to proselytize. The staff running the services are usually multiracial and religiously diverse. For example, most of the hospice home-care nurses at the Buddhist Metta Hospice Care program are Muslim, and at Bright Vision Hospital, the first team consisted of a Sikh

Director of Nursing, a Malay Muslim ward sister, a Chinese Christian doctor, and a Chinese Buddhist pastoral care worker. Palliative care was integrated into the Singapore health care system when palliative care services were started in all government hospitals, as mostly consultative services with no designated inpatient beds.

In Malaysia, hospice services began simultaneously in 1991 at the Penang branch of the National Cancer Society, and at the Catholic Assunta Hospital in Kuala Lumpur, which started Hospis Malaysia. As in Singapore, the staff was multiethnic and from different religions, and served the whole community, regardless of race and religion. This reflects a very practical approach to care, because the needs of the patients and families are often similar, whether physical symptoms, emotional needs, or social and financial support needs. Culture and religion play a minor, though sometimes important part, when cultural attitudes or religious practices impinge on the physical care, or when social norms affect caregivers and place of care.

Current status. The present state of palliative care provision reflects to a large extent the economic development and general health care service provision of the different countries in Asia. In the most economically developed areas, such as Japan, Taiwan, Hong Kong, and Singapore, palliative care services are well developed and funded by national insurance or subsidized by the government. Cancer palliative care is particularly well developed and the chief growth areas are in non-cancer palliative care, such as end-organ failure and dementia. Palliative care is well integrated into the healthcare system. The discipline is recognized as a medical specialty, and education and training of the workforce is well developed. Research collaborations are occurring within and among these countries, facilitated by the Asia Pacific Hospice Palliative Care Network (APHN).

There are some palliative care services in the majority of states in Asia, although coverage may be patchy, especially outside major urban centers. In countries like Malaysia, Philippines, Indonesia, and Thailand, there is coordination to a varying degree of palliative care efforts by the government or national palliative care bodies.

Different challenges are faced by countries like India and China, with their huge populations. Although there are centers of excellence in some of the large cities, coverage of the poorer, less developed regions of the countries remain a challenge, again linked to economic development and general health care provision there. The public health approach, such as that developed in north Kerala in the form of Neighbourhood Networks for Palliative Care,[4] may be one solution to the challenge of coverage.

There are a significant number of states in Asia and the Pacific where palliative care provision is very limited or non-existent. These include Cambodia, Laos, Myanmar, Bangladesh, East Timor, Papua New Guinea, and many of the

Pacific island nations.[4,5] There are currently individuals and organizations, like the APHN, working to encourage palliative care development through educational efforts.

The APHN is the regional network for palliative care.[6] Established in 2001, its members comprise both individuals and organizations. It runs a directory of palliative care services in the region and acts as a link for individuals to access information, particularly on education and training in palliative care. Major programs run by the APHN include education initiatives aimed at countries with early development of palliative care services and a regional research network. It also runs the biennial Asia Pacific Hospice Conferences.

PALLIATIVE CARE AND ASIA PACIFIC CULTURES

Many examples of how religious beliefs and practices affect palliative care delivery in the community in many of these countries are seen on a regular basis by palliative care practitioners. Some of the more commonly encountered issues are highlighted below.

Muslim patients with colostomies or fistulae are unable to pray due to their inability to complete their ablutions. The case of the son (only child) of a Muslim widow insisting on taking the patient home despite her having a place at an inpatient unit in a community hospital exemplifies some of the issues this raises. The Muslim community generally believes that children should care for their parents at home, as this makes it easier to pray and have the *Qur'an* read to the patient. Yet the patient's nursing-care needs, including the rectovaginal fistula, could hardly be cared for by her son in this particular instance.

Chinese ancestor worship interfering with the person's wishes is exemplified by a case in which the eldest daughter-in-law, whose duty was to care for the ancestral shrine, was unable to convert to Christianity. This was because, after conversion, she would no longer be able to do her duty and would also be separated from her husband and his family in death.

Families may believe strongly that illness is due to spells cast by rivals or enemies and take the patient to other spiritual healers to rid him/her of the spells. Sometimes bizarre practices are used, including beatings, branding with incense, or imbibing potions. These are common among Malays, Chinese, Filipinos, and others.

Christian churches and Chinese and Hindu temples known for their healing services or as potential places for answering prayers are constantly frequented by devotees of different religions. An example is a Roman Catholic Church run by the Redemptorist brothers at Novena in Singapore. Waterloo Street Kuan Yin Temple and the Hindu Krishna temple next door see devotees visit one temple and then the other in a single trip.

Malays approach traditional healers or *bomohs* who may prescribe medications or practices. Malay Muslims are also known to go to holy men, who may offer prayers and sometimes holy water to sprinkle or drink.

Some of the solutions for spiritual distress are prayers and offerings at temples, and "merit giving" by others on behalf of the patient is seen among Buddhists and Taoists.

The redemptive qualities of physical suffering may act as a barrier to effective pain management. Some patients, such as those who are Roman Catholics, Buddhists, and Hindus, believe that, if they suffer in this life, they may suffer less in the next life.

There is also a belief that traditional Chinese medicines (TCM) cannot be taken alongside Western medicines. A common belief is that TCM and opioids must be taken at least two hours apart. Therefore it is impossible for patients to take oral morphine every four hours and lactulose three times daily if Chinese herbal infusions have to be taken twice daily and not within two hours of Western medicines.[7] Awareness of practices and adjustment of drug regimes to twice-daily, slow-release preparations may allow better pain relief.

It is important to have an understanding of patients' and families' priorities in the prescribing of medications—traditional "cures" give a hope of stopping the disease, whereas measures like pain killers merely reduce suffering; so the former always have priority over the latter.

Islam. Islam is one of the major religions in Southeast Asia. Muslims make up about 25% of the population in this region. Indonesia has the largest number of Muslims. The religious practices of the Muslims in this region follow that of the Sunnis, the largest branch of Islam. There are cultural influences on the practice of Islam; however the fundamental principles and practices remain the same. The basic fundamentals are known as the five pillars of Islam. All Muslims believe in the *Syahadah*, that there is only one God, Allah, and Creator of the universe and that the prophet Muhammad (peace be upon him) is His messenger. The *Qur'an* is the holy book for the Muslims throughout the world.

In Islam, the time spent in this world is part of a journey that is meant for devotion to God. This journey is continued after death as a spiritual journey. Human life is considered sacred, and acts that hasten or take a life are forbidden. Muslims also accept that death is inevitable and is a part of life. Death is predestined, although the date, time, place, manner, and cause of death are not known.

Muslims are thus encouraged to maintain health and to seek treatment in illness to fulfill their obligations. However, in the event of severe illness with poor recovery or a terminal illness, they will accept the inevitability of death. It is observed that most will strive to maximize their devotion and seek forgiveness for past sins in preparation for their next journey into the hereafter.

It is this devotion that brings forth the desire to return home from hospital so that the ill Muslim patients may be able to achieve this. This also gives the family and the extended relatives and friends the opportunity to spend more time with the patient. During this period, most will spend time reading holy verses from the holy *Qur'an*. It is for this reason that most patients will also want to remain alert and oriented even up to the point of demise so that they may die while reciting the *Shahadah*.

Some patients choose to decline any potentially sedating medications with the intent of maintaining their wakefulness. It is imperative that patients and their family are informed of any such medications when it is prescribed. Even if prescribed, some patients may not take them and may consequently be labeled as noncompliant. It is best to discuss this and frame it in the context of the goals of care, where a balance is sought between pain control and level of consciousness. When symptoms are severe and the doses of opioids required are sedating, health care professionals should explore these goals again. Suffering may be perceived as test of faith; however, when that suffering leads to deterioration in care due to caregiver burnout or distress, it may be necessary to seek the help of religious persons.

The concept of maintaining health and life leads some Muslim patients and their relatives to want to pursue treatment and other interventions up to the point of death. They perceive that withdrawing or stopping treatment is akin to giving up on life in itself. This can create conflicts with health care professionals. It is best that discussions pertaining to this involve a religious leader (*Imam*) or a religious teacher (*Ustaz*) so that they can help work through the issues with the patient, the family, and the health care team.

After the death of the patient, family members, neighbors, and friends are informed so that they may visit the deceased to pay their final respects. Muslims are encouraged to visit fellow Muslims who are ill or have died. During this period, Muslims spend time reading holy verses for the patient. Families in mourning are not advised to remain calm but are counseled instead to weep in moderation. However, excessive weeping, wailing, or hysterics are not encouraged and are perceived as contrary to the accepted belief that everyone will die and return to God.

The body is cleansed in a prescribed ritual prior to shrouding. This is done by those of the same sex as the deceased and those familiar with the cleansing ritual. A congregational prayer is then held for the deceased before the body is buried. Burial usually takes place on the same day. Health care professionals involved in the care of the patient should try to facilitate this by ensuring that the required procedures, such as procurement of the certificate of cause of death and so on, are completed as quickly as possible. The body is placed several feet underground and facing the direction of the holy city of Makkah.

Subsequently, prayers are offered for the deceased at three days, seven days, 44 days, and 100 days after the death. This is more of a cultural practice among the Malays of the Southeast Asia region. It provides a means of bereavement support for the family of the deceased.

In summary, the religious practices of Muslims in the region are similar to Muslims in the rest of the world. There are some variations accorded from the culture of the different races. Muslims prioritize religious practices over cultural practices. Those who provide palliative care for Muslims have to consider the sensitivities involved, just as for members of other religions.

Hinduism. Hinduism is believed to be the world's oldest religion, dating back over 8000 years, as mentioned in the ancient scriptures and writings. Jainism, Buddhism, and Sikhism are believed to have originated from Hinduism. It is still practiced by a sizeable minority in the Southeast Asian region. Its influence on the local culture is visible in the Hindu temples, new and old, dotting the entire region. The number of practicing Hindus varies in the region. For example, 4% of the resident population in Singapore is Hindu. Deepavali, one of the major Hindu festivals, is a public holiday in Singapore and Malaysia.

Two important Hindu concepts, *Karma* and reincarnation, play an important role in influencing the end-of-life decision making for Hindus. *Karma* can be simplistically stated as, "As you sow, so will you reap." Birth, death, rebirth and *Moksha* or salvation is part of what is called *Samsara* or worldly life. Palliative care is aligned with Hindu philosophy, as death is a part of life, and prolonging life through artificial means in a terminal illness is thought to interfere with *Karma*.[8] Interventions such as intubation, artificial feeding, or very aggressive care in the face of a terminal illness go against Hindu thinking. Contemplating or completing suicide also goes against Hindu philosophy by interfering with nature.

Traditionally, Hindus wish to pass away at home and family members of a dying patient try their best to fulfill this wish for the patient. When death is imminent, the close relatives of the patient are notified so that they can visit the patient before he or she passes away. The dying patient is usually placed with his head facing east, a lamp is lit near the head and the relatives pray, read the scriptures, and sing hymns. Close to the moment of death, even when the patient is unconscious, a family member chants a holy mantra in the patient's right ear. Sacred ash or sandalwood paste is applied to the patient's forehead. Vedic chanting is continued, and drops of water from the river Ganges or milk is trickled into the patient's mouth. All these rituals signify purity of thought for the patient while passing away. Being culturally sensitive to these death rituals even in an inpatient hospice setting can make a significant difference to how the family members remember the patient's passing away.

Immediately after death, the body is laid on the ground or in a cot with the head facing south. A lamp is lit near the head and incense is burned. A cloth is tied under the chin and over the top of the head. The thumbs and the big toes are tied together. Usually no embalming or removal of organs is allowed. Cleaning and bathing of the body is done in preparation for the cremation. Except for infants and children up to the age of three years, who are buried,

Hindus are cremated on the same day of death, if possible. Hence, it is important for all the formalities concerning the certification of death and so on are done as quickly as possible to facilitate early cremation. The collection and immersion of ashes is done on the day after cremation; the urn of ashes is not kept at home or in a columbarium, as is done among followers of other religions in the region. Memorial services for the dead are a very important ritual for the family members and are arranged on various days immediately after death and then annually. This helps the family members with their grief and bereavement as this event is communal, with friends and others involved in the ritual.

In a study of 560 nurses who cared for dying patients in Ethiopia, Kenya, India, and the United States, nurses from all four countries identified spiritual interventions such as praying with or praying for the patient and reading from holy texts as helpful or being important to patients and families. The similarities between cultures were more common than the differences. Nurses from all four cultures stressed compassion, respect, and individualizing care based on patients' needs as most important factors for dying patients.[9]

The belief system of Hindus can thus be used for end-of-life discussions with Hindu patients and caregivers and can be the basis for decision making in discontinuing treatments or medications for dying Hindu patients in the Southeast Asian region.

Buddhism. Buddhism is a very important religion in Southeast Asia, and a large number of its followers are from this region. This religion was founded in India in the sixth century B.C. by Siddhartha, a royal prince. After Siddhartha attained enlightenment, he was called Gautama Buddha. There are two main variants of Buddhism: Theravada and Mahayana. Myanmar, Thailand, Cambodia, Laos, Vietnam, and Singapore are some of the countries where Buddhism has a large number of followers.

Buddhists follow the four noble truths and the eight-fold path, as propounded by the Buddha. The *Sangha*, the order of Buddhist monks established by Buddha, is still followed today in the Buddhist society. Buddhists also read the *Dharma* or *Dhamma* and follow its precepts. Meditation is a very important part of the Buddhist way of life.

During the dying phase, the Buddhist patient is expected to be alert and not oversedated or made unresponsive. Thus, patients themselves or family members request that the patient not be given high doses of opioids or any other medications that would make them very drowsy or cloud their thinking. This is requested to enable patients to have clear minds so that they can concentrate on the chanting that is usually ongoing at that time. The Buddhist chanting is done by the caregivers or, in most instances, there is a recorded version that is played continuously near the patient. When a patient passes away, some Buddhists may prevent doctors or health care workers from touching or moving the body for eight hours following the death. This is done so as to prevent the soul from being disturbed. However, when doctors need to examine the patient for signing the certificate of cause of death, they can inform the patient's family members that they will do a quick examination without disturbing the body overtly; and this is usually acceptable to most family caregivers. During the patient's wake and funeral, Buddhist monks are invited to chant and pray for the patient's soul.

Giving alms to Buddhist monks and helping the needy is a way of life for Buddhists. So, patients themselves or caregivers are inclined to do this whenever possible, even during the final phase of a patient's life. Earning enough merits in this life is seen as a help or a way to merit a better afterlife.

Christianity and other religions. The Christians in the region, Roman Catholics and Protestants, follow practices similar to those followed by other Christians elsewhere in the world. The local culture may influence some of the beliefs and practices, but, in general, the principles and practices of Christianity in Southeast Asia is similar to that seen in any other part of the word.

Judaism, Zoroastrianism, Baha'ism, and so on are some of the other religions, which have a small number of followers in the region. There are also the "Free Thinkers" who do not adopt any particular religion or faith.

Conflicts due to religion. Due to changing lifestyles in the region, the younger generations have started embracing religions that are different from those followed by their parents or even their siblings. This can lead to conflict with the patients when they are from the older generation or with those of their siblings who practice a different faith.

For example, an elderly patient may have been a Buddhist or a Taoist. The patient's young son or daughter may have converted to Christianity and is now interested in converting the patient as well before he/she passes away. This can lead to numerous conflicts when the patient does not want to convert or when the siblings see that a certain religion is being imposed on their parent against their wishes. Sometimes, this incites tension within families when the patient is alive or conflict over which funeral rites have to be performed once the patient passes away. There have been instances where patients have said that they have consented to conversion just to make their children happy, even though they feel guilty about going against their own God. There have also been anecdotes where patients have been converted when they are not conscious, and this has led to conflicts among siblings over which religious rites have to be performed when the patient passes away. Health care professionals dealing with such situations have to be very sensitive to the circumstances and people involved when such a conflict arises. The conflict may be easier to deal with if the patient is conscious and can speak his or her mind on the matter. The challenges arise when the patient is not conscious or is cognitively impaired. Religion can then become a stumbling block rather than a harmonizing tool for patients and caregivers.

Spiritualty, religion, and faith are extremely useful in helping patients cope with death and dying in most instances and it is useful to know the basics of various religions or faith in the region in order to be able to deal with it in a more professional manner when the need arises. The use of a spiritual guide or a religious master at the right time can also help palliative care workers deal with a sensitive issue with which they may not be comfortable.

REFERENCES

1. Southeast Asia/Malaysia/Indonesia/Philippines/Oceania. In: Esposito, JL, ed. *The Islamic World: Past and Present.* Oxford Islamic Studies Online; 2004. http://www.oxfordislamicstudies.com/browse?_hi=4&_f:region=islam:regionOf Activity&region=Southeast%20Asia/Malaysia/Indonesia/Philippines/Oceania. Accessed February 7, 2012.
2. Kleinmeyer C. *Religions of Southeast Asia.* DeKalb, IL: Northern Illinois University; 2004.
3. Shaw R. The development of palliative medicine in Asia. In: Bruera E, Higginson IJ, Ripamonti C, et al., eds. *Textbook of palliative medicine.* London: Hodder Arnold; 2006:58–63.
4. Kumar S. Learning from low-income countries: What are the lessons? Palliative care can be delivered through neighbourhood networks. *BMJ.* 2004;329(7475):1184.
5. Lynch T, Connor S, Clark D. Mapping levels of palliative care development: A global update. *J Pain Symptom Manage.* 2012;17(10): 472–474.
6. Goh CR. The Asia Pacific hospice palliative care network: Supporting individuals and developing organizations. *J Pain Symptom Manage.* 2007;33(5):563–567.
7. Thrane S. Hindu end of life: Death, dying, suffering, and *karma. J Hosp Palliat Nurs.* 2010;12(6):337.
8. Coenen A, Doorenbos AZ, Wilson SA. Nursing interventions to promote dignified dying in four countries. *Oncol Nurs Forum.* 2007;34(6):1151–1156.

CHAPTER 8

Overview of Health-care Delivery Systems and Workforces in End-of-life Care in the Global North and South

CHARLES VON GUNTEN

A BRIEF HISTORY OF HEALTH CARE

From the beginning of recorded human history until the development of public health and antibiotics in the mid-twentieth century, people typically died quickly, often of infectious diseases or accidents. Evidence of cancer and atherosclerotic heart disease has been found in preserved bodies (embalmed or naturally preserved) in all parts of the world. There is the perception that these noncommunicable causes of disease are more common now than in earlier times. Although it is technically true, it is more accurate to say that more people now live long enough to die of these causes than ever before.

Professional health care is as old as human history. Preparation for the work has varied, but is best characterized as one of apprenticeship. Until the last 60 years, in addition to assuring that custodial needs were met, the majority of the specialized effort of the health care professional was expended on the subjects of diagnosis and prognosis to answer the questions "What is wrong with me?" and "What will happen to me?" It is only since the scientific method began to yield changes in health care after World War II that there has been the perception that the body, like a machine, can have its parts understood and "fixed." Ever more elaborate and sophisticated treatments have eclipsed the central role of prognosis and the care of the "whole" patient in the context of his or her family. Much has been made of the perception that death is "a choice" rather than inevitable. This approach to health care can be paraphrased from the medical literature in the 1970s as "if only patients could leave their damaged physical vessels at the hospital for repair, while taking their social, emotional, and spiritual selves home."

Contemporary health care and workforces are now molded to this model. The "best" hospitals look like laboratories, and the "best" health care workforce wear lab coats. The preparation and socialization of physicians, nurses, pharmacists, social workers, counselors, chaplains, and other health care workers is conducted over years within this social construct. It should not be a surprise that the care of the dying does not fit with this model. From my point of view, this contemporary pattern must be placed in its broad historical perspective. It can then be seen to be a recent aberration that needs correction, rather than as a wholesale restructuring of the health care system and its workforce.

A HISTORY OF THE CARE OF THE DYING

In Europe, from the fall of the Roman Empire around 350 C.E. to the Protestant Reformation and Renaissance, monasteries were the main repositories of expert knowledge. Each monastery was quite isolated and integrated knowledge from a variety of sources: Druid, Celtic, Christian, Greek, Roman, Jewish, and Muslim.

In response to the biblical parable of the Good Samaritan, in which a good person provides for the care and nurture of a sick man found by the side of the road, monasteries developed the practice of taking in the sick. The earliest description of this was one developed by a woman of Rome in the fourth century.

The words hospice, hospital, hotel, and hospitality all stem from the same Latin root word, *hospes*. There were no distinctions between these—people were housed, fed, and cared for until they recovered or died. There was no distinction between care of the body and the spirit—it was all one activity.

By the twelfth century, there is evidence of the development of hospitals, distinct from hospices, as places to care for the sick. In England, a monk who returned from the Crusades in the Middle East established St Bartholomew's Hospital in London in 1106 C.E. Later documents suggest that admission policies began to change so that only those with a chance to live should be admitted and the dying left to the hospices, because the hospital did not want a bad reputation.

The Age of Enlightenment led to extraordinary changes, among them the Protestant Reformation. The development and promulgation of methods of inquiry, including tools such as the microscope and the scientific method of experimentation, led to new explanations and descriptions of health and illness.

Dividing body from spirit. The history of health care until the time of the Renaissance and Reformation has to be understood in the context of an undivided body and spirit. There was one human being. The contrasting view that a person is composed of two parts, physical body and spirit (soul), has roots that can be found in ancient Greek approaches to medicine first articulated around 400–600 B.C.E. The Roman system of health care that subsequently developed in the years 100–400 C.E. continued this approach. Christian Europe adopted Greco-Roman medicine, and although the impetus for care was spiritual, it tended to the body as a reservoir for the soul. The French philosopher Descartes (who most people remember as saying, "I think, therefore I am") sharpened this dualistic view. He advocated that human beings were composed of body and spirit as separate entities.[1]

Descartes proposed that this conceptual division permitted secular medicine to focus on the body while leaving the spirit to religion. The scientific method was employed to dissect, experiment, and understand the functions of the body in health and disease. Trained health care workers could undertake this approach without contravening the authority of religion over the spirit.

One way to see this is a reassertion of the way the Greeks and the Romans approached human illness. Sadly, it had the unintended consequence of implying spiritual care was not part of health care, an assertion that was not part of Greek and Roman medicine. The care of the body was left to those who study and practice the natural sciences; the care of the spirit was left to those who study the divine and supernatural.

The Cartesian approach led directly to the development of new knowledge in the natural sciences and improvements in health and health care. The discovery of the physiology and pathology of the body, the action of bacteria and viruses, how the blood moved, the distinction of normal from malignant cells, improved sanitation, concerted efforts by public health, and the development of a wide range of antibiotics and other medical interventions have increased life expectancy from an average of 31 years in the 1300s, to 48 years in the 1800s, to an average of 80 years by 2012 (82 years for women compared with 78 years for men); and every year the statistics continue to improve.[2]

The shift in focus has been so complete that, in contrast to death being expected, death has become alien to health care. The divide that Descartes established opened up new possibilities for medical research, but had the unintended consequence of seeing the body as a complex machine—only requiring better engineering to be able to "fix" it. Anything related to personhood came to be considered "non-medical" and outside the realm of orthodox health care.

Contemporary health care workers, whether they are doctors, nurses, social workers, counselors, therapists, or others, are a product of this pattern. They have been socialized and professionalized to think of health care as separate from religion and spirituality; they care for the body, not the spirit. Chaplains alone are the health care professionals whose job it is to somehow bridge these two. However, in an environment that so divides them, their task and training generally make them feel like afterthoughts rather than essential elements of modern health care.

Many health care organizations now market themselves with the implicit message that death can always be overcome. Consequently, anyone working in health care cannot be faulted for feeling that they have failed if they do not save their patients from death. One way of viewing this historical development is to see it as a response to the absence of spiritual care as part of the health care professional's response to the ill person. Blame Descartes.

END-OF-LIFE CARE TODAY

From a global perspective, most people come to medical attention with advanced incurable disease. Of the 58 million people dying annually (45 million in developing countries, 13 million in developed countries), at least 60% (35 million) would benefit from modern approaches to good end-of-life care.[3] Assuming at least two family members involved in each patient's care, palliative care could improve the quality of life of more than 100 million people annually worldwide. As a public health strategy, it makes more sense to put limited financial resources into prevention and palliation rather than into expensive treatment that will not change the prognosis. Even in the developed world, when patients present earlier to the health care system, and there is a greater chance that their life can be prolonged, a comprehensive approach to their care that integrates palliative care throughout their illness experience will provide them with better quality of life.

If one only looks at death from cancer, two-thirds of the 10 million new patients with cancer each year (7 million) will die within a year of diagnosis.[4] Even in the developed world, about half of all people diagnosed with cancer will die of the disease. With accelerating worldwide implementation of public health approaches to communicable disease, there will be a vast increase in death from noncommunicable diseases; the need for end-of-life care will increase dramatically over the next 50 years. By 2025, there will be 1.2 billion people 60 years of age or older; by 2050 the number will increase to 2 billion. Since the major risk for cancer is age, the incidence of cancer will double to more than 24 million new cancers per year by 2050.[4] Age is similarly the most important risk factor for atherosclerosis, which causes heart attacks, heart failure, strokes, and dementia.

Unfortunately, even though the knowledge and experience to control pain and diminish suffering exists, the tragedy for most of the world's population is that palliative care is not available to them. In fact, it is tragic that the existing knowledge cannot be applied to the 45 million deaths that occur because of inadequate education, government health policy, and the unavailability of essential medications.[5]

Health care systems across the world can be seen to be in various stages of being able to afford and implement these public health strategies, and these basic approaches to prevention and treatment of communicable diseases. In much of the developing world, it is only in the last 10 years that any health care policy attention is being given to noncommunicable diseases, because the communicable diseases are the overwhelming cause of treatable illness.

In the developed world, more than 90% with access to basic medical care can expect to die after being diagnosed with a life-threatening illness. They will experience multiple, often concurrent, physical symptoms and psychological, social, spiritual, and practical issues. Most of these problems add to a patient's and family's sense of suffering and reduce their quality of life, particularly if they are present for a long time.[6]

In one study of patients with cancer, inpatients had an average of 13.5 symptoms, whereas outpatients had an average of 9.7 symptoms.[7] In patients with AIDS, symptom prevalence has been reported to be even higher.[8] Patients with congestive heart failure, emphysema, or dementia suffer from a range of symptoms that are similar. In all studies of symptom prevalence, pain, nausea/vomiting, constipation, and breathlessness are common. As patients lose weight and become weak and fatigued, loss of function becomes increasingly present. For many people, the loss of their independence is devastating and a source of considerable suffering.

Hospitals as places of care. Hospitals were a further development of the approach to the care of the sick in the medieval monasteries. The reason for their growth in size appears to be due to efficiency. It is much more efficient for a physician to go from room to room than to make a series of home visits. Similarly, it is much more efficient for the apprenticeship model of training to have all of the sick people in one place and have the trainees apprentice there. There is no indication that hospitals developed because of evidence that they provided better outcomes for the sick. The origin of hospitals as places of charity care is also easily perceived. Those with enough money would prefer to be at home and pay to have the doctor come to them, rather than go to a place where a large number of sick people were all housed together.

It is only in the last 60 years that the reputations of hospitals, with specialized facilities for the delivery of specialized treatments, have been attractive enough for the middle and upper classes to go there. This was another motivation for having the dying pushed out of hospitals—because it damages the business of health care.

Throughout the world, surveys show that people prefer to be ill and die at home *if* it is not too much burden on their family. Sadly, hospitals everywhere have become places for the sick to go and to stay until they get well, or die. Hospitals that have thousands of beds (and in some parts of the world, have up to five people per bed, including under the bed) are as much as a manifestation of the inability for families to provide care as of the promise of the hospitals to do something for the people who are there. In the most developed parts of the world, chronic care facilities have arisen for the provision of nursing care for those who cannot return home or who have no homes. In most of the developed world, only 10%–20% of people die at home; most die in an institution.[9] Interestingly, since research that shows that people can be well cared for and can die at home, a solution to the economic challenge of caring for an ever-increasing population of institutionalized dying is apparent.

As care for patients with life-threatening illnesses has shifted into institutions, a generalized lack of familiarity with the dying process and death has evolved among the public. Only a minority of people, including physicians, have ever watched someone die. Most nonprofessionals have never seen a dead body except, perhaps, at a funeral parlor. Fantasy about what death is really like is fueled by media dramatization, rarely reality. This has had the unfortunate effect of driving the behavior of bringing sick people to hospital, whether or not there is anything that can be done to change the condition of the person; the motive is fear.

The modern hospice movement. Cicely Saunders trained to be a nurse in England in the 1940s. She came from a Christian background in the Church of England. She hurt her back and had to stop working as a nurse. She became a social worker. In caring for patients with terminal cancer in hospital wards, she thought they could be much better managed if their "total pain," with its physical, psychological, social, and spiritual components, was addressed. She imagined a place where doctors, nurses, social workers, chaplains, and others provided care for the patient and family as a unit. In the 1950s, she visited existing hospices around London (Trinity Hospice, St Joseph's Hospice, St Luke's Hospice) and observed the giving of oral morphine with much better pain control than she saw in the hospital, where the practice was unknown. She did not find a model of care that she imagined would be best for the dying she observed.[10,11]

In an extraordinary demonstration of leadership, Cicely Saunders trained to become a physician, and then built her own institution in order to pilot her ideas of good end-of-life care. Most importantly, this was an academic hospice where patient care, education, and research could be conducted. She changed care for the dying around the world because physicians, nurses, social workers, chaplains, and others were invited to visit, train in the conduct of the care, then return home to do likewise.

The details of hospice care in the United Kingdom and its development in other parts of the world are described in other sections of this book. The principles and the model, however, are important to review if one is to understand the development of health care workforces in end-of-life care.

Training of health care staff for the dying. Saunders summarized her observations of the care of dying by characterizing their suffering as "total" pain, with physical, emotional, social and spiritual dimensions.[10] The care of the patient could only occur in the context of the patient's family. She then defined a "core" health care team to meet those needs as comprising a physician, a nurse, a social worker, and a chaplain. Other disciplines played important supporting roles to the main team: pharmacists, physical and occupational therapists, nutritionists, psychologists, counselors, music therapists, and others. In addition, subspecialties of physicians, such as psychiatrists or anesthesiologists and occasionally surgeons and radiation oncologists, needed to play a role.

Since health care training is still, fundamentally, an apprenticeship model, St Christopher's Hospice was an academic hospice where health care professionals who were already trained could study for periods of days to years to develop special skills. People who trained at St Christopher's went on to found, develop, and staff hospices and specialist teams serving people in hospitals, nursing homes, and their own homes around the world. If one is to understand how health care staff can be trained to serve in the health care workforces of the world to provide good end-of-life care, this model must be fully grasped.

Age-appropriate assessment of the patient and family as a unit and looking at the goals of care with the participation in interdisciplinary, interprofessional care that can address physical, psychological, social, and spiritual needs is how all care begins. The trained health care professional helps the patient and family manage advanced illness and the prospect of death, assured that comfort will be a priority, values and decisions will be respected, spiritual and psychosocial needs will be addressed, practical support will be available, and opportunities for emotional growth and closure will exist.

The structure of a training program in a particular country or setting will need to relate to the structure of health care in that country. In all cases, it helps to frame the discussion at the primary, secondary, and tertiary levels of health care. In primary end-of-life care, there is no need for specialists. All doctors, nurses, and others working in the health care system need to learn basic approaches to end-of-life care. As in the rest of health care, most illness proceeds in a usual way; usual approaches are enough. It is a mistake to think that highly specialized places for the care of the dying are needed. They are not.

Secondary levels are where specialist skills are available. St Christopher's Hospice and all inpatient hospice units are examples of secondary levels where patients whose needs exceed the abilities or capacities of that available in the primary care setting will need to go. It also refers to specialist teams that may see people at home, or in hospital, or in a nursing home, for help and advice to the primary team.

Tertiary levels are where the most difficult cases are seen, and where the education, training, and research that improve the quality of care are done. Although there is a role for individual reading in textbooks or other sources as well as for classroom-type experiences where groups of people are learning together, there is no substitute in health care for the apprenticeship experience. New trainees of any discipline need to participate in the care of patients, observe others providing the care, and then attempt to provide the care under observation, where guidance, correction, and improvement can be undertaken. Health care is a skill; it can only be learned in the doing. Health care is not just the knowing.

The training of specialist physicians, nurses, social workers, chaplains, and others requires the acquisition of knowledge and skill that exceeds that of others in society. Formal training and recognition of a specialist-level skill in end-of-life care will relate to the formal training of health care professionals in general. The development of practice standards for end-of-life care and well-defined competencies for the various disciplines involved supports the designation of palliative care as a specialty. The major clinical skills central to end-of-life care are the assessment and management of physical, psychological, and spiritual suffering faced by patients with life-limiting illnesses and their families. Communication and teamwork are critically important to achieving desired patient and family outcomes.

Although these knowledge domains and skills overlap with the knowledge, attitudes, and skills that characterize other disciplines that care for patients with advanced illnesses, the specialty practice of end-of-life care is distinguished from other specialties by 1) a higher level of clinical expertise in addressing the multidimensional needs of patients with life-threatening illnesses, including a practical skill set in symptom control interventions, 2) a high level of expertise in both clinical and nonclinical issues related to death and dying, 3) a commitment to working within an interdisciplinary team approach, and 4) the strong focus on the patient and family as the unit of care. Specialist-level skills complement the core competency that should be maintained by disciplines, particularly as it addresses the quality-of-life concerns of patients and families during the period of advanced illness and the needs that specifically arise in the period surrounding the patient's death.

The medical knowledge needed to relieve suffering and improve end-of-life care is greater now than in it has ever been in the history of medicine. Yet consistent application of this knowledge is not yet routine. Specialization, and specialist training, can be seen as responses to the growth in medical knowledge and the need to make that knowledge practically available to patients and their families. Such growth in this knowledge provides a way to understand why not just health care, but spiritual care should be given by physicians, as it was in the time of the ancient Greeks, Romans, Chinese, and Egyptians in the millennia before the Common Era.

A central challenge in the training of a worldwide workforce with the skills needed for good end-of-life care center is the development of an apprenticeship model. Health care practice is not learned from a book or a lecture. It is a skill that is learned by watching others do, then doing it under supervision. Too much time has been wasted in "duffle bag" medicine, where an expert from another country drops in for a lecture or two, then goes home. Nothing changes. Similarly, sending people "away" to another country for years to train teaches them to do medicine in the host country—it does not train them to return to their own country to practice in that setting and culture. Even in a developed country, there is often an expeditious attitude of "What's so hard about this? You're a doctor aren't you? You're a nurse who has seen dying people? Do end-of-life care." No one would make that case for the training of a surgeon or for a circulating nurse. The answer is formal training in a recognized specialty.

How does formal training lead to improved end-of-life care? Formal training centers where standards are set and demonstrated are critical to the dissemination of a skilled workforce in each country. It stands to reason that, if primary end-of-life care skills are to be broadly available, then all health care professionals will need to spend time working in a specialist setting where they can practice under supervision. This means that in every country, every health care professional will need to spend some clinical clerkship time with a specialist service.

Formal recognition of that training within each country will be an important element. Human beings are social, and look to others for signals that what they are doing is "right." Consequently, a consistent effort to recognize the specialty of palliative care began in England, and spread to the rest of the English-speaking world. Now, such recognition is also spreading to other countries around the world. A formally recognized field can attract the "best and the brightest" to commit their careers to further developing the field. This means that researchers will pursue efforts to extend and refine the knowledge base of the field, teachers will train the next generation of specialists, and administrators will devote resources to the clinical, research, and teaching needs of the specialty. Highly skilled specialists will be available to help with the most difficult patients and support their colleagues in improving care for all patients.

There is an important analogy to be made. Although all health care workers care for patients who have hearts, not all of them are cardiologists. For everyone looks to cardiologists for setting the standard, however, it is from cardiologists that they get their knowledge and skills for practice at the primary care level. Cardiology is an established specialty over the entire world. There are specialist doctors, nurses, social workers, counselors, pharmacists, and others. The same is true for the field of end-of-life care. We must have recognized specialists and role models that set the standards, and provide the education and research, to guide the rest.

Does establishing specialty training in end-of-life care have any possible negative consequences? Specialization can further fragment health care and drive up costs by adding yet another person with "specialist" skills. Additionally, some are concerned that the responsibility for end-of-life care will be "dumped" into the laps of the specialist services, further widening the divide between the living and the dying, the successful and the unsuccessful, the winners and the losers. Yet, what patients desire and need is continuity. In addition, there is a risk of alienating health care workers already doing good end-of-life care, but not identifying themselves or practicing as specialists or having had the "right" training. An additional concern is that widespread training in end-of-life care will lead to a dilution or co-option of some essential essence of what makes end-of-life care "special."

These concerns are neither unique to end-of-life care nor inevitable. Formal training in itself neither increases nor decreases the likelihood of these outcomes occurring. The root causes for these potential problems must be sought and prevented or redressed. They do not mitigate the driving rationale for improving end-of-life care as part of the broad goal of improving the health of the public.

Structure of training programs. Conceptualizing a training scheme for end-of-life care requires relating it to the structure of training for all people working in health care in a country. As a general rule, public education means the provision of "grade school" to all its citizens without differentiation into a specialized track. In some countries, entry into health care training occurs immediately after public school or "grade" school. In others, the differentiation toward training in a profession happens earlier in the grade school curriculum. Only a few countries require a baccalaureate degree before entry into health care training. In others, some elements of a baccalaureate education are included in the health care training curriculum. A better way of conceptualizing an end-of-life care training scheme is to answer the question, what knowledge and skills are expected?

All health care education is based on the observation that health care workers learn their art through practice. A program that teaches end-of-life care skills relies on a well-functioning clinical program that routinely delivers high quality end-of-life care to patients and their families. Since all learners progress in skill from novices to expert, the trainee must be able to exercise supervised decision-making capacity in the provision of end-of-life care as part of the training experience in his or her discipline.

End-of-life care from those trained is exercised in two roles: consultant and manager. Those roles are exercised in a variety of settings: hospitals, specialist units, specialty hospitals, long-term care (including nursing homes), day hospitals, ambulatory clinics, and home care. The clinical program in which end-of-life care training is based needs to have enough breadth and depth of clinical experiences so that the trainee can routinely demonstrate the required skills before graduating from the program.

Health care workers should be exposed to patients with a wide variety of disease conditions (e.g., cancer, congestive heart failure, chronic obstructive pulmonary disease, dementia, HIV/AIDS) and a wide variety of socioeconomic and cultural backgrounds. Trainees will want to have the opportunity to see patients in inpatient and community settings. Training programs will demonstrate that clinical care and clinical teaching in all settings is provided in a collaborative manner among physicians and other health care professionals. This collaborative practice model will use interdisciplinary team meetings for review and clinical decision making. A consultation model, longitudinal care, and exposure to bereavement support need to be part of the training experience.

THE ROLE OF RELIGIOUS BELIEF IN END-OF-LIFE CARE DELIVERY

In surveys of patients and their families, 75% think their spiritual care is *as important* as their physical care; 65% think their doctors, nurses, and other health professionals should participate in that spiritual care.[12] Taking the broadest view, these statistics should seem appropriate, given the history of the development of health care. However, taken from the narrow view of the last 60 years, these are startling and troubling for those who think the natural must be separated from the supernatural in modern medicine.

It is inescapable that any program training people for health care practice in end-of-life care needs to impart approaches that incorporate the religious and spiritual beliefs of the patients and families. This is not to say that the health care professionals need to be expert in religious beliefs and practices, or that they themselves need to have the same beliefs in order to provide care.

There is a pernicious pattern of human thinking that divides issues into black or white, in or out, and right or wrong kinds of categories. This kind of thinking will not help integrate body and spirit, natural and supernatural, into one health care approach to the end of life. In fact, it is rather clear that broad knowledge of any religion or spiritual tradition does not give clear guidance in the care of any particular patient and family.

Good end-of-life care requires teamwork and the inherent implication that there will be compromise, give and take, and modification in order to facilitate the best care of an individual patient and family. At the end of the day, the best quality of measure of end-of-life care is that the needs and expectations of the patient and family are met.

SUMMARY

The broad sweep of medical history of the care of the dying integrates body and spirit together as the subjects of care. Hospices, as places to care for the dying, developed in medieval Europe. After the 1500s, for a variety of reasons, that tradition was lost to contemporary health care as secular medicine performed research and treated the physical body, whereas the spirit was left to religion. Research has now proven that the more holistic model demonstrated by Cicely Saunders in the first academic hospice has broad applicability to the provision of health care and the training of the health care workforce. The challenge now is to ensure there are enough places with enough skilled experts to train all of those in health care who will care for the dying. Good end-of-life care can happen anywhere that knowledge and skill is brought together.

REFERENCES

1. Descartes R. Meditations on first philosophy. Translated and edited by John Cottingham. Cambridge: Cambridge University Press, 1996.
2. World Bank. Life expectancy at birth, total (years). The World Bank Data Web site. http://data.worldbank.org/indicator/SP.DYN.LE00.IN/countries/1W. Published 2013. Updated 2013. Accessed April 3, 2013.
3. World Health Organization. Chronic disease report. Chronic Disease Report Web site. http://www.who.int/chp/chronic_disease_report/full_report.pdf. Published 2013. Updated 2013. Accessed April 3, 2013.
4. World Health Organization. Global action against cancer. Global Action Against Cancer Now Web site. http://www.who.int/cancer/media/GlobalActionCancerEnglfull.pdf. Published 2005. Updated 2005. Accessed April 3, 2013.
5. United Nations. Millennium project. Millennium Project Web site. http://www.unmillenniumproject.org/. Published 2006. Updated 2006. Accessed April 3, 2013.
6. Center to Advance Palliative Care. America's care of serious illness: A state-by-state report card on access to palliative care in our nation's hospitals. http://reportcard-live.capc.stackop.com/pdf/state-by-state-report-card.pdf. Published 2008. Updated 2011. Accessed April 3, 2013.
7. Portenoy RK, Thaler HT, Kornblith AB, et al. Symptom prevalence, characteristics and distress in a cancer population. *Quality of Life Research*. 1994;3(3):183–189. http://www.jstor.org/stable/4035093.
8. Solano JP, Gomes B, Higginson IJ. A comparison of symptom prevalence in far advanced cancer, AIDS, heart disease, chronic obstructive pulmonary disease and renal disease. *J Pain Symptom Manage*. 2006;31(1):58–69. doi: 10.1016/j.jpainsymman.2005.06.007.
9. Gomes B, Calanzani N, Gysels M, et al. Heterogeneity and changes in preferences for dying at home: A systematic review. *BMC Palliat Care*. 2013;12(1):7. doi: 10.1186/1472-684X-12-7.
10. Saunders CM. *Beyond all pain: A companion for the suffering and bereaved*. London: Spck; 1983:88.
11. Saunders CM, Summers DH, Teller N. *Hospice: The living idea*. London: E. Arnold; 1981:198.
12. Roberts JA, Brown D, Elkins T, et al. Factors influencing views of patients with gynecologic cancer about end-of-life decisions. *Am J Obstet Gynecol*. 1997; 176(1 Pt 1):166–172.

CHAPTER 9

The Spiritual Care of Patients and Families at the End of Life

CHRISTINA PUCHALSKI

INTRODUCTION

Spirituality plays a significant role in the lives of patients and families across the life span but in particular when facing serious illness and dying. People and families dealing with serious illness, loss, disability, or pain encounter profound suffering. As Art Lucas, a board-certified chaplain and a leader who himself struggled with and died from pancreatic cancer, said to me as we were preparing for a joint presentation, "Once a person is given a diagnosis of a serious illness, or a family member faces the illness or the loss of a loved one, life is never the same." What Art was not aware of was that, two years before our meeting, my mother had died; one year before our meeting, my father was diagnosed with cancer; and just three days before our conversation, my beloved cat, Zoey, was diagnosed with an aggressive form of cancer. Indeed, life changes; and those changes can bring on fear, anxiety, and deep suffering. Often, as I was doing that morning, the suffering is borne in silence. And in the silence lay a myriad of deep spiritual questions: "Why? What will happen? Where is God for me now? Who am I in the midst of this illness or loss? How can I cope with the loss? What is my path now?"

Spiritual care is rooted in the recognition that the suffering of patients and loved ones needs to be recognized and supported. It includes asking patients about their pain, their suffering, and what is important to them. But the ultimate expression of spiritual care is compassion. As McNeill wrote: "Compassion asks us to go where it hurts, to enter into places of pain, to share in brokenness, fear, confusion, and anguish. Compassion challenges us to cry out with those in misery, to mourn with those who are lonely, to weep with those in tears. Compassion means full immersion into the condition of being human."[1(p4)] This full immersion means that clinicians need to have the training and resources to support our humanity not only as health care workers but as professionals whose vocation is the service and accompaniment of those we serve in the midst of their suffering. Spiritual care thus encompasses the doing: the asking about patients' and families' spiritual resources and the identifying of spiritual distress. However, it also involves the art of being present to the other in full compassion as fully human spiritual beings.

HISTORICAL ASPECTS

Historically, compassion and spiritual care were an integral part of the mission and practice of health care institutions and providers. Medical care was primarily supportive and palliative, with few options for curing disease. The healers utilized a holistic approach of physical, psychological, social, and spiritual care. The first hospitals in the United States were started by religious and service organizations, whose service and calling were manifest in a focus of care on the whole person. Health care systems gradually moved to a more disease-oriented model, somewhat neglecting the nonphysical aspects of patients' and families' suffering. The field of hospice and palliative care, however, recognized the essential role spirituality plays in end-of-life care, as well as in the care of seriously ill patients and their loved ones.

Since the inception of hospice care and the subsequent development of palliative care, spirituality has been recognized as an essential element of palliative care. Dame Cicely Saunders, the founder of the modern hospice movement, described the concept of "total pain" as encompassing spiritual distress as well as psychosocial and physical distress.[2] Her model was eventually described as the biopsychosocial-spiritual model, which is the framework for the profession of palliative care.[3] The model emphasizes the totality of patients' and families' experiences in the context of illness or dying. Integrating all dimensions of patients' and families' experiences with illness is key to whole-person care.

Spirituality, particularly in palliative care is supported by ethical as well as empirical literature.[3-6] Studies have demonstrated that spiritual care affects health care outcomes including quality of life, coping, and end-of-life decision making.[7,8] Surveys demonstrate that patients want their spiritual issues formally addressed in the clinical setting[9,10] and want their spiritual needs attended to by health care professionals.[11-13]

In 2004, the National Consensus Project for Quality Palliative Care (NCP) developed guidelines and domains in palliative care.[14] Spiritual care, defined as attending to spiritual, religious, and existential issues, is one of the eight distinct domains within the NCP Guidelines. In spite of these guidelines, the implementation of this domain of care was challenged by the lack of clear definition, roles, and assessment and treatment models. Although there were courses in medical and nursing schools, there was, until recently, minimal professional education in spiritual care. So, inspired by our many colleagues who wanted to provide better spiritual care, Dr. Betty Ferrell and I co-led the National Consensus Conference to develop recommendations for implementing the spiritual care domain of the NCP Guidelines for Palliative Care. The project was a collaboration of the George Washington Institute for Spirituality and Health (Puchalski) and the City of Hope National Medical Center (Ferrell). Forty interdisciplinary leaders in palliative care and spiritual care were invited to develop specific and practical recommendations for the implementation of interdisciplinary spiritual care in palliative care, which was defined as starting from the initial diagnosis of a serious or chronic illness. Specific recommendations as well as models for spiritual care implementation and interdisciplinary spiritual care education were developed. The resultant recommendations were then reviewed nationally, approved through a consensus process, and published for widespread dissemination as a consensus document titled "Improving the Quality of Spiritual Care as a Dimension of Palliative Care"[15] as well as a book entitled *Making Health Care Whole: Integrating Spirituality into Patient Care.*[16]

IMPLEMENTING SPIRITUALITY IN CLINICAL SETTINGS

The key to implementing spirituality in clinical settings is to have a practical model for implementation that allows all clinicians to recognize and integrate patients' spiritual issues into the treatment or care plan. The National Consensus Conference developed a model that is based on a generalist-specialist model in which board-certified chaplains are recognized as the spiritual care experts. This model is also premised on the professional obligation of all clinicians to attend to all dimensions of a patient's and his/her loved one's suffering—the psychosocial and spiritual as well as the physical. Finally, this model is relational. We defined the concept of a transformational healing relationship. This means that healing occurs within the context of the relationship between the clinician and the patient. The transformation is bidirectional; that is, both the patient and clinician are affected and even changed in the context of that relationship. It is the clinician's obligation to provide a compassionate and open environment of trust in which the patient can share his or her inmost concerns, including the experience of their suffering as well as their sources of strength, hope, and meaning. The clinician's "tool" is compassionate presence. This type of presence conveys to patients that the clinicians are fully there for them, that their clinicians will listen with respect and without judgment or filtering, and that the clinician will honor whatever is shared. In this sense, many clinicians see this type of encounter as sacred.

To implement this model fully, there are three important aspects that will be discussed:

1. Clinical aspects of identifying spiritual distress and patient resources of strength
2. Integration of patient's spiritual beliefs into a treatment or care plan
3. Practice of compassionate presence.

CLINICAL ASPECTS OF SPIRITUAL CARE

The National Consensus participants debated extensively over the notion of a spiritual diagnosis. Spirituality is a difficult concept to define, much less diagnose. However, we felt it was crucial to frame spirituality within a diagnostic category for several reasons. Spiritual distress is a significant source of suffering for patients. It must be addressed just as any other source of pain and distress. To address spiritual distress, it has to be integrated into a medical model, or the patient will continue to suffer with the source of that suffering ignored. Recognizing that the full dimension of patients' suffering cannot be fully understand, the following model helps in defining how part of spirituality may be reduced into a clinical model framework, which we title a "Whole Person Care Model" (Figure 9.1).

This model describes how spirituality is central to the whole person and impacts all the other dimensions. The center of the circle, one's deepest inner core, cannot be fully understood or diagnosed. But a diagnosis is possible at the outer rim, where spirituality intersects with the other domains of one's personhood. Clinicians make spiritual diagnoses, ideally in an interdisciplinary team setting with the input of board-certified or eligible chaplains.

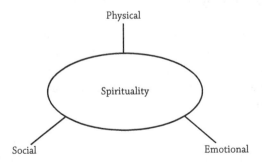

Figure 9.1: The "Whole Person Care Model."

The consensus conference attendees also reached full consensus on a definition of spirituality:

> Spirituality is the aspect of humanity that refers to the way individuals seek and express meaning and purpose and the way they experience their connectedness to the moment, to self, to others, to nature, and to the significant or sacred.[15(p 887)]

The definition is based on two core concepts: meaning and connection. At the end of life that meaning is what has been defined as "ultimate meaning"—that which gives us meaning even when our life as we know it is ending. Connection is who or what provides that sense of connection for the person. It might be someone the patient loves, or it could be God or another understanding of the sacred, or it might be an experience in nature, the arts, philosophy, or a significant experience that helps define that for the patient.

Based on this definition the clinician can inquire about meaning and connection in a patient's life. He or she can identify resources of spiritual strength, which might be values, beliefs, practices, or communities. Clinicians who develop treatment or care plans also could identify and diagnose spiritual distress, which would, in general terms, be a lack of meaning and/or connection as per the definition.

There are tools used to identify spiritual distress or spiritual resources of strength. All patients receive a spiritual screening, history, and assessment by the appropriate health care professional. The goal of the screening is to identify if there is a need for an immediate referral to a chaplain. The goal of the spiritual history is to learn more about the person's spiritual or inmost story, to identify spiritual resources and strengths, and to diagnose spiritual distress. Spiritual assessments are done by chaplains in a narrative reflective process. The assessment is used to further delineate the spiritual issues, confirm or change the diagnosis made initially by the clinician, and help determine an appropriate plan of care with regard to the patient's and family's care plan.

Spiritual screenings are admissions questions to screen for spiritual distress; screening is usually limited to one or two questions:

- Is spirituality or religion important for you? Are your spiritual or religious beliefs helping you right now? A yes/no combination to these questions triggers a referral to a board-certified chaplain.[17]
- Do you have any spiritual beliefs, practices or values that you want integrated into your care?

Spiritual histories are more detailed and to be done by clinicians who determine treatment or care plans. The spiritual history can be done by a tool, such as the FICA,[18] HOPE,[9] or SPIRIT.[19]

The general algorithm for the process of identifying spiritual distress is first to ask if the patient has any source of distress and then, through a logical clinical discernment process, decide the source of the distress: physical, emotional, social, spiritual, or some combination of these. This is depicted in Figure 9.2.

Once a diagnosis or possible diagnosis is made, the clinician needs to refer to the appropriate person that would need to be involved in the care of the patient. For emotional or psychological distress, one would consider a mental health professional; for physical distress, a physician or nurse; for social distress, a social worker; and for spiritual distress, a chaplain or other spiritual care professional, such as a spiritual director or pastoral counselor.

Spiritual distress can present in many different ways, from existential distress to religious-specific distress. Table 9.1 lists potential spiritual diagnoses.

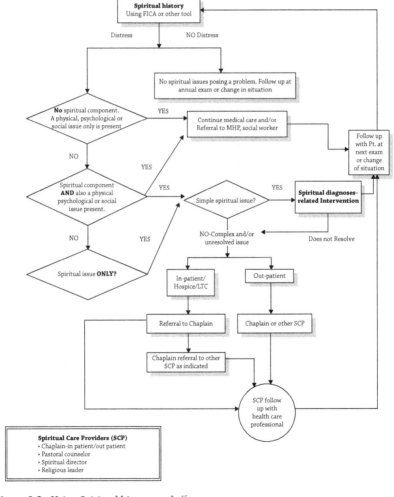

Figure 9.2: Using Spiritual history tools.[15]

Table 9.1. SPIRITUAL DIAGNOSES

Diagnoses (primary)	Key feature from history	Example statements
Existential	lack of meaning/questions meaning about one's own existence/concern about afterlife/ questions the meaning of suffering/seeks spiritual assistance	"My life is meaningless""I feel useless"
Abandonment by God or others	lack of love, loneliness/not being remembered/no sense of relatedness	"God has abandoned me""No one comes by anymore"
Anger at God or others	displaces anger toward religious representatives/inability to forgive	"Why would God take my child... its not fair"
Concerns about relationship with deity	closeness to God, deepening relationship	"I want to have a deeper relationship with God"
Conflicted or challenged belief systems	verbalizes inner conflicts or questions about beliefs or faith/conflicts between religious beliefs and recommended treatments/ questions moral or ethical implications of therapeutic regimen/expresses concern with life, death and/or belief system	"I am not sure if God is with me anymore"
Despair/ hopelessness	hopelessness about future health, life/ despair as absolute hopelessness, no hope for value in life	"Life is being cut short" "There is nothing left for me to live for"
Grief/loss	grief is the feeling and process associated with a loss of person, health, etc	"I miss my loved one so much" "I wish I could run again"
Guilt/shame	guilt is the feeling that the person has done something wrong or evil; shame is a feeling that the person is bad or evil	"I do not deserve to die pain-free"
Reconciliation	need for forgiveness and/or reconciliation of self or others	"I need to be forgiven for what I did" "I would like my wife to forgive me"
Isolation	from religious community or other	"Since moving to the assisted living I am not able to go to my church anymore"
Religious specific	ritual needs/unable to practice in usual religious practices	"I just can't pray anymore"
Religious/spiritual struggle	loss of faith and/or meaning/religious or spiritual beliefs and/or community not helping with coping	"What if all that I believe is not true"

This list is based on work from the National Comprehensive Cancer Network (NCCN),[20] as well as the literature in spirituality and health. It should be recognized that this is a preliminary attempt to create taxonomy of spiritual distress. More research is needed in this field.

TREATMENT PLAN

There are two possible pathways to treat or attend to a patient's spiritual distress or suffering once a diagnosis is made—the simple and the complex, as described in Figure 9.2. For simple spiritual issues, a clinician might be able simply to be present to the patient and listen to the patient's story. Often the patient might come to some understanding simply in the context of being fully heard by a compassionate listener. Other types of interventions might include dignity-based therapy, meaning-oriented therapy, art therapy, journaling, yoga, mindfulness, or the patient's own self-identified resources, such as meditation, prayer, or self-care. For more complex spiritual issues, such as the need for forgiveness or reconciliation with self or others, severe existential distress, or lack of connection or love of others or God, referral to chaplains or other spiritual care professionals is indicated.

Once the clinician obtains the information from the history, he or she can integrate it into the treatment plan. This includes making a diagnosis of spiritual distress or pain, or identification of spiritual issues or spiritual goals if appropriate, and determining and implementing the appropriate spiritual interventions.

A more holistic assessment and treatment plan addresses all dimensions of the patient, not just the physical. So the biopsychosocial-spiritual assessment and plan is the model recommended (Figure 9.3). This model emphasizes the need for all clinicians to address all dimension of the patient and document those in the chart. Treatments are then targeted to the dimensions that have active issues; resources of strength are also notes. There is an ongoing follow up and modification of the plan as needed with the different members of the health care team.

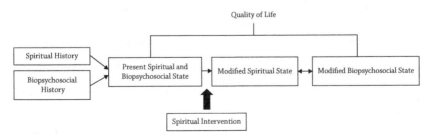

Figure 9.3: The biopsychosocial-spiritual treatment plan.[3]

COMPASSIONATE PRESENCE

In the final analysis, the spiritual care model is a relational model in which the patient and clinicians work together in a process of discovery, collaborative dialogue, treatment, and ongoing evaluation and follow up. Thus, an integral part of this model is ongoing professional development of the clinician with regard to his or her ability to provide compassionate, patient-centered care. This would include attention to the spiritual needs of the health care professional as related to the call to serve others in an altruistic, compassion-based model of professional practice. Clinicians should also attend to their own biopsychosocial-spiritual issues, with the goal of having balance in their lives and healthy approaches to stress management and to the issues that arise in caring for seriously ill patients. Being aware of one's spirituality and sense of vocation is the first step to providing compassionate care.

Compassion is an attitude, a way of approaching the needs of others, and of helping others in their suffering. But more importantly, compassion is a spiritual practice, a way of being, a way of service to others, and an act of love. Health care professionals and organizations want to provide compassionate care, but the research presented indicates the need for greater personal awareness, knowledge, and skill building of compassion and spirituality to be able to possess and maintain the ability to provide compassionate care. One might even consider compassionate care as a spiritual discipline. Compassion can be thought of as spirituality in action.

Innovative models for integrating spirituality and compassion into health care must be developed to help health care professionals and institutions build their capacity for spiritually grounded compassionate care. The model must take into account several dimensions of spirituality, including the health care professional's sense of transcendence, meaning and purpose, call to service, connectedness to others, and transformation. In addition, the model must address compassion as a spiritual discipline that includes being fully present to others, viewing compassion as a moral imperative with universality for all suffering individuals, open to the divine and holy in others, and with full knowledge and experience of the profound nature of suffering. Based on these conceptual frameworks for spirituality and compassion, the elements of the model are illustrated in Figure 9.4.

This model includes the behaviors, knowledge, and skills of spirituality in health care that promote compassion as a spiritual discipline. These include awareness of one's own spirituality or inner life, an ongoing personal formation that includes the caregiver's own spirituality, and the commitment to medicine as vocation, where one's call to serve is rooted in altruistic or agape love of those one serves. It is only then that the clinician can practice compassion with patients and families.

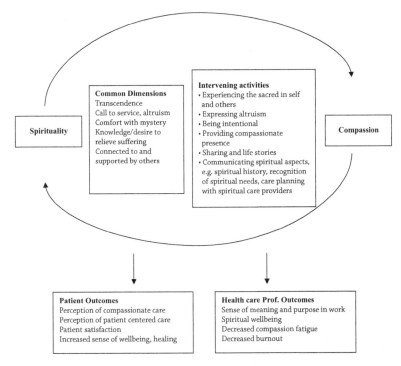

Figure 9.4: Model of spirituality and compassionate health care.

The model involves the development and refinement of skills that will enable the health care professional to engage in compassionate care for individuals who are suffering, and to support themselves and others in compassionate care. The skills include cognitive intent to be present, emotional and spiritual awareness, and, finally, a practice that enables one to be present and in the moment. These skills may include one or several spiritual disciplines or practices, such as meditation, prayer, mindfulness training, religious rituals, and other practices intended to help an individual to be open to the presence of the divine and sacred in their own lives and the lives of others. These skills will also help the health care professional develop intelligent wisdom and the ability to empty oneself of distractions, personal and professional, to more effectively focus concerns on others.

CONCLUSION

Spirituality is an integral part of all our patients, their families and our lives. As Art Lucas noted, illness and loss trigger deep issues related to the finality of life as we know it. These issues, if ignored, can cause deep suffering in people's lives. Often it is in the context of health care systems that patients, families, and clinicians become aware of these spiritual issues. Suffering, if supported, may be transformed in a person's life where healing might be possible; healing as a restoration of coherence or inner peace.

My mother's and Zoey's deaths, my father's diagnosis of cancer, albeit with successful treatment, all have impacted my own life in deep and profound ways. Life was and is never the same. But the loss and suffering have opened the door to so many new and different gifts. Art's presence, as well as those of my loved ones, enabled a transformation, a healing. We all can offer that to our patients and their families through our presence to and our love for them. This, then, is the very simple and very profound basis of spiritual care—love. Love to our patients, families, each other, and to ourselves.

REFERENCES

1. McNeill DP, Morrison DA, Nouwen HJM, Filártiga J, ebrary I. *Compassion, a reflection on the christian life*. New York: Doubleday. 1982:141.
2. Saunders CM. *The management of terminal malignant disease*. Vol 1. 2nd ed. London: Edward Arnold; 1984:252.
3. Sulmasy DP. A biopsychosocial-spiritual model for the care of patients at the end of life. *Gerontologist*. 2002;42 Spec No 3:24–33.
4. Sulmasy DP. Is medicine a spiritual practice? *Acad Med*. 1999;74(9):1002–1005.
5. Astrow, A. B., Wexler, A., Texeira, K., et al. Is failure to meet spiritual needs associated with cancer patients' perceptions of quality of care and their satisfaction with care? *J Clin Oncol*. 2007;25:5753.
6. Ferrell B, Coyle N. *The nature of suffering and the goals of nursing*. Oxford; New York: Oxford University Press; 2008:127.
7. Puchalski CM, Lunsford B, Harris MH, et al. Interdisciplinary spiritual care for seriously ill and dying patients: A collaborative model. *Cancer J*. 2006;12(5):398–416.
8. Cohen SR, Mount BM, Tomas JJ et al. Existential well-being is an important determinant of quality of life. Evidence from the McGill quality of life questionnaire. *Cancer*. 1996;77(3):576–586. doi: 2-0.
9. Koenig HG, McCullough ME, Larson DB. *Handbook of religion and health*. New York: Oxford University Press; 2001:712.
10. Yi MS, Mrus JM, Wade TJ, et al. Religion, spirituality, and depressive symptoms in patients with HIV/AIDS. *J Gen Intern Med*. 2006;21 Suppl 5:S21–7. doi: 10.11 11/j.1525-1497.2006.00643.x.
11. Tsevat J, Sherman SN, McElwee JA, et al. The will to live among HIV-infected patients. *Ann Intern Med*. 1999;131(3):194–198.
12. Kimmel PL, Emont SL, Newmann JM, et al. ESRD patient quality of life: Symptoms, spiritual beliefs, psychosocial factors, and ethnicity. *Am J Kidney Dis*. 2003;42(4):713–721.
13. Clark KL, Loscalzo M, Trask PC, et al. Psychological distress in patients with pancreatic cancer—an understudied group. *Psychooncology*. 2010;19(12): 1313–1320. http://ovidsp.ovid.com/ovidweb.cgi?T=JS&CSC=Y&NEWS=N&PAGE=fulltext&D=medl&AN=20119937. doi: http://dx.doi.org/10.1002/pon.1697.

14. Dahlin, C. *The National Consensus Project for Quality Palliative Care Clinical Practice Guidelines for Quality Palliative Care.* 3rd ed. 2013. http://www.nationalconsensusproject.org/Guidelines_Download2.aspx.

15. Puchalski C, Ferrell B, Virani R, et al. Improving the quality of spiritual care as a dimension of palliative care: The report of the consensus conference. *J Palliat Med.* 2009;*12*(10):885–904. doi: 10.1089/jpm.2009.0142; 10.1089/jpm.2009.0142.

16. Puchalski CM, Ferrell BR. *Making health care whole: Integrating spirituality into patient care.* Conshohocken, PA.: Templeton Press; 2010.

17. Fitchett G, Murphy PE, Kim J, et al. Religious struggle: Prevalence, correlates and mental health risks in diabetic, congestive heart failure, and oncology patients. *Int J Psychiatry Med.* 2004;*34*(2):179–196.

18. Borneman T, Ferrell B, Puchalski CM. Evaluation of the FICA tool for spiritual assessment. *J Pain Symptom Manage.* 2010;*40*(2):163–173. doi: 10.1016/j.jpainsymman.2009.12.019; 10.1016/j.jpainsymman.2009.12.019.

19. Maugans TA. The SPIRITual history. *Arch Fam Med.* 1996;*5*(1):11–16.

20. National Comprehensive Cancer Network. NCCN Guidelines. http://www.nccn.org/professionals/physician_gls/f_guidelines.asp.

III

Spiritual Beliefs and Practices for a Good Death

Introduction: *On a Good Death*

MARK LAZENBY, RUTH McCORKLE, DANIEL P. SULMASY

One of us first trained in theology and philosophy of religion and wrote on the big questions of life and death (ML). It became clear that theology and philosophy were the handmaidens of those who worked with people in their everyday lives as they struggled to make sense of the questions of life and death—especially death. This led to training as an oncology nurse practitioner and to a career of asking the philosophical and clinical questions of life and death—especially death. How could a philosopher-nurse not ask the question of what is a good death? That question, of course, has been asked by philosophers—and nurses—from time immemorial. One nurse's reflections on a good death, however, stood out from among the rest. It was this essay that proved the rightness of being a philosopher-nurse. This essay, by another one of us (RM), is titled, simply, "A Good Death."[1] This one-page essay, in a few paragraphs, explores a good death from the question of what is a good birth. The questions of life and death become one. In this unit of the book, the questions of life and death, as with McCorkle's short essay, become one. What are the opportunities in our lives to plan and prepare for a good death? How do we provide a good death to our dying loved ones? How do we care for the families who remain? How do we care for families during all the phases of death?

The phases of death—this is what that one-page essay is really about—the phases of death.[1] As with a good birth, which has three phases (prenatal, labor and delivery, and postnatal), a good death has three phases. In the predeath phase, a good death involves participating in planning one's final days. At the time of death, it involves the dying having control over the circumstances and the living respecting those choices—even when they would chose differently. After death, it involves caring for those who remain—caring for them in the way that makes sense according to their beliefs and practices.

That is how this unit of the book is organized—by the phases of death. In this unit we explore the first phase, predeath, through three case studies: one about emergencies that lead to death; another about when disease moves from life-threatening to life-limiting; and finally, one about prolonged dying. In the fourth case in this unit, we explore the second phase, death itself; and in the fifth case, the third phase—after death.

These case studies are as universal as the phases of death themselves. They involve young children and young professionals, with lives full of promise and responsibility. They involve older people—men and women—and the demands of a modern society on them and on their families. They involve the rich and the poor, the privileged and the struggling. They involve how we die and how we live after those we love have died. They involve different places and cultures around the world. The difference between a good death in the global north and the global south is, in our view, a difference of circumstance, not substance.

After each case study, some of the world's leading palliative care and hospice clinicians and some of the world's leading bioethicists describe how, in that phase of death and in the circumstances of the case, we can help the dying and the families of the dying make safe passage. Safe passage, according to these clinicians and ethicists, invariably comes back to creating the environment in which people are assured that it is safe to believe and to engage in spiritual rituals and practices—safe, that is, to have the circumstances that, for them, in their particular cultures, bring about a good death.

After the clinicians and ethicists, thinkers from among the world's most prevalent spiritual traditions describe the spiritual beliefs and practices in which faithful people would engage and elucidate for us what safe passage means within their traditions. Irene Taafaki explores safe passage from the indigenous spiritual perspective. Taafaki and her group conducted anthropological research among people in the Marshall Islands using the case studies in the book, and from this research, wrote these essays on the indigenous spiritual view of the phases of death. James Amanze, from Botswana, describes the spiritual beliefs and traditions of Africans through the African Independent and Pentecostal Churches. Soraj Hongladarom, of Thailand, and Ruiping Fan, of Hong Kong, explore Buddhist and Confucian beliefs and practices at the end of life, respectively. John Graham, of the United States, describes the end-of-life spiritual beliefs and practices of Evangelical Christians, as Jan Holton, Carol Taylor, and Uma Mysorekar, also of the United States, do for mainline Protestant Christians, Roman Catholics, and Hindus, respectively. Herbert Brockman, a rabbi in the United States, tells us about Jewish spiritual traditions and beliefs around death. Najmeh Jafari, of Iran, and Tariq Ramadan, originally from Egypt but now living in England, limn the traditions of Shi'a and Sunni Muslims. Surjeet Kaur Chahal, of India, describes the Sikhs' spiritual traditions. And Jan Nielsen, a Unitarian Universalist minister in the United States, tells us of the beliefs and practices of people who are spiritual but who may not identify with one religious tradition, the so-called "spiritual but none." As exemplified in the Unitarian Universalism, Nielsen tells us in her first essay (Chapter 10) that the "spiritual but none" "draw wisdom not only from the world's religions, but also from the findings of science as well as the writings of poets and philosophers, both ancient and contemporary." Essay after essay, across all the situations and phases of death, the overwhelming message of these thinkers is: our spiritual beliefs and practices define us, and if we pay attention to them and make room for them in our homes, our hospitals, our hospices, our places of worship, and our daily lives, we create the environment necessary for safe passage—for a good death.

This book began with a poem contributed by Elizabeth Alexander. A poet who wrote and read a poem for the inauguration of the United States' first African-American president[2] and a poet who herself has faced the suddenness of death, Alexander's poem, "Autumn Passage," presents, in beautiful metaphor, the picture of safe passage from this life into "something else." Whatever "something else" means to you in your spiritual tradition, read this poem with the hope and promise that safe passage brings. Read it aloud to your patients. Read it aloud to your loved ones. Read it to yourself—as you face and contemplate safe passage from this life.

The book ends with a coda, meant mostly for clinicians, but patients and families may draw strength and counsel from it too. It ends with a poem by T. S. Elliot, one from his *Quartets*. This poem sets our gaze on what is to come. That is where the book ends—with the beginning of the next life.

REFERENCES

1. McCorkle R. A good death. *Cancer Nursing*. 1981;4(4):267.
2. Alexander E. *Praise song for the day: A poem for Barack Obama's presidential inauguration, January 20, 2009.* Saint Paul, Minn.: Graywolf Press; 2009.

CHAPTER 10

When Emergencies Happen

Case

MARK LAZENBY, RUTH McCORKLE, DANIEL P. SULMASY

Huang-Fu came out of the womb alert and bright. There was no doubt to his father, Dao, and his mother, Lien, that he was smart. Toddling when he was nine months old, talking when he was a year and a half, and playing the violin at four, he was born with a bright future. That was, after all, why they named him Huang-Fu; it means rich future.

Dao and Lien gave Huang-Fu everything a smart boy could need: violin lessons, soccer lessons, and every imaginable piece of technology that would fit into the living room of their tiny urban apartment.

Both Dao and Lien had grown up in rural villages, but they too were bright. And their brilliance had taken them to the city, where they met in engineering school.

Every day they work hard, and when they get home from work and school, they teach Huang-Fu to work hard on his studies. They want the best for him. And they want him to know that, if he works hard too, his future will be even brighter.

With his brightness, though, comes a lightning-quick speed, and a kind of impetuousness. Lien has told him more than once to be careful when he crossed the street to catch the bus to go home from his kindergarten. But this day, this one horrible day, she turns her head to say hello to a friend when, without her noticing, Huang-Fu sees the bus coming and dashes across the road.

Now Huang-Fu, only six years old, lies in the intensive care unit in the hospital of the very university where Dao and Lien met. Both of his legs are broken, but all his internal organs are unharmed. His heart beats normally. His liver and kidneys function well. And his lungs are fine. It's just that he's in a coma, and without the ventilator, he wouldn't know when to breathe.

When the car hit him, it threw him some ways down the road, and he landed on his head. The bleeding in his brain probably started as soon as he hit the ground.

The doctors tell Dao and Lien that nothing more can be done to save Huang-Fu's life. His future, they say, rests only in giving his organs to other children who need them. But Lien is certain—certain—that Huang-Fu hears her. She has not left his side once during these 24 hours he has been hospitalized.

Dao, not being much of a religious man, now finds that he must walk to the temple just outside the hospital's walls. There, he lights a candle and prays for wisdom in these dark circumstances. Back in the intensive care unit, he puts his arm around Lien's quivering shoulders and holds the limp hand of his only child, his only son. "I didn't see him cross the road," Lien finally speaks to Dao. "I only remember hearing the ambulance coming. I never knew that car hit him." Dao grips her tighter, holds her stronger. "He can't die," she sobs. "He cannot die. He is all we have."

The Clinical Issues

IRA BYOCK

As a doctor and as a father, I read the story of Huang-Fu's vibrant young life and devastating accident with a deep ache in my chest. Although the description of his condition is sparse, some facts can be surmised. Trauma surgeons, neurosurgeons, and critical care specialists are exceedingly reluctant to stop striving to save the lives of patients. That is doubly true when the patient is a child. A physician has said to Dao and Lien that there is no hope of their son surviving; that means the injury to Huang-Fu's brain is literally lethal.

Criteria developed through years of deliberative processes, involving authorities in medicine, ethics, law, and theology, allow patients to be declared dead when there is no electrical activity in the brain, including the brain stem, and no brain function, by repeated examinations and objective physiologic tests, such as EEGs and brain scans. Such individuals have no consciousness, are unable to breathe without mechanical ventilation, and are being maintained on intensive life support. Recovery in such situations is not merely rare; it is impossible.

Given that this determination has been made—and while honoring the person of Huang-Fu, acknowledging the tragedy of his injury, and treating his broken body with reverence—it is ethically and legally accurate to consider that he has died. Huang-Fu is incapable of suffering. But his parents are.

The clinical opportunities in this situation are reduced to two categories: First, clinicians must respond to the grief of Dao and Lien, supporting and guiding them through the searing pain of their loss. Secondly, if—and only if—it is acceptable to Dao and Lien, clinicians can explore the opportunity to donate Huang-Fu's vital organs to save the lives of other children.

These goals may seem to be in tension with one another. At the present time, Dao and Lien are unable to let go of their son. How could they feel otherwise? They are clinging to hope for his recovery and cannot imagine losing him or their lives without him. Yet, if their hope only resides in Huang-Fu's survival, it is false hope.

Although the couple deserves some time—at very least a day or two—for the stunning shock of their son's death to be absorbed, there is clinical wisdom in providing this very bad news clearly. When death is certain, as it is in this situation, saying gently, "Your son has died" is a compassionate act. The statement will evoke intense grief, but it is their grief to own. Equivocation on the part of clinicians, though well meaning, can complicate a family's pain. When matters of life and death force doctors to cut deeply, sharp blades, deftly wielded, are merciful.

We are told that Dao is not very religious, but his walk to the temple implies some felt connection to a cultural tradition. In my practice, I commonly draw on skillful spiritual counselors to help illuminate a path through this very dark, foreboding terrain. Perhaps a cleric, members of a congregation or cultural group, or the hospital's chaplains can extend support to the couple during this terrible time. Perhaps there are rituals in their tradition that can provide some comfort. Lien feels a crushing sense of guilt. Perhaps their faith tradition or community can help Lien forgive herself and realize that she did nothing wrong. Sometimes the weight of grief is made lighter when it is borne in community.

We cannot know whether or not Dao and Lien will be able to accept the bitter opportunity to donate their son's organs. Although the practice of organ transplantation after brain death is not universally endorsed by all religious denominations, the guidelines for organ donation have earned broad agreement. Affirmation of life is a common theme of religions.

As unimaginably hard as it can be to accept the death of a child, for many people the knowledge that their loss can benefit others may provide some solace. Huang-Fu's vital organs can save the lives of children who are waiting for a heart, liver, and lungs. Additionally, his kidneys, skin, corneas, and marrow can contribute immensely to the health of others. Knowing that part of their son will live on—both literally and figuratively—may help Dao and Lien find some meaning in this truly tragic event.

The Ethical Issues

ARTHUR CAPLAN

The tragic accident that left Huang-Fu in a coma in a hospital intensive care unit is almost too emotionally trying to discuss. Having one's only child involved in a terrible accident that is likely to prove fatal places emotional demands on parents and on doctors that are at the edge of human endurance.

A few medical facts need to be established in trying to navigate through this tragedy. Huang-Fu is very young. At age six, he has a capacity for more resiliency in the face of trauma than older adults would. His age and the fact that he has only been in the hospital for 24 hours point toward a tiny bit of uncertainty about his prognosis. Given the gravity of his head injury and the massive bleeding that is occurring, it is unlikely that he will survive for long. His parents ought not to be given false hope. But the reality is that more time ought to be given to see whether there is any chance for his recovery.

The doctors must explain that the prognosis is very grim but that they are willing to wait a few days to see if Huang-Fu shows any signs of stabilizing. At best this means he will survive but probably not regain consciousness—ever. At worst, he will continue to decline and die. The doctors must make sure the nurses understand that the next few days will prove crucial to caring for Huang-Fu. Hospital administrators, worrying about the cost of his care, must know that a short period of watchful waiting is about to begin which will most likely end in the death of Huang-Fu.

During this time, spiritual and psychological counseling ought to be offered to Dao and Lien. There is a grave risk that their marriage might founder amidst the guilt and recrimination that will follow hard on the heels of this accident. Lien may even be thinking about harming herself out of guilt at not preventing this tragedy. If they will accept it, early counseling is very important to help them at this most difficult time.

If Huang-Fu does stabilize he will surely be very impaired. His parents need to understand that and not have false hopes about his recovery.

If he does not and his bleeding continues, then a decision will have to be made about ending his life support. The doctors should explain as early as they can that they will make a recommendation to this effect if it proves necessary after a few more days of watchful waiting.

The parents must understand that if things do not go well, Huang-Fu cannot recover and his dying will not be artificially prolonged. They will then have to decide if they wish to be present when the machines are turned off. They will also have to decide if they wish to discuss the possibility of organ and tissue donation.

If Huang-Fu does continue to bleed in his brain, my hope is that his parents will have the strength to consider organ and tissue donation. The medical group should be preparing to have a knowledgeable and sensitive person approach them. They will surely not want to see their beloved son "suffer," so this issue must be addressed head on, as must the attitudes of their religion about making the gift of life to others, even when it means removing tissues from their son's body. If the parents can find comfort in having Huang-Fu help another child or children, then donation could prove therapeutic for them.

If the parents do not wish to have this discussion at all, they should not be forced to do so. If, after the discussion, they do not wish to have their son utilized as an organ or tissue donor, then those wishes must be respected.

Whatever the choice is about donation, the hospital should make arrangements to contact Dao and Lien a week after their son's death and then again a month later. The parents will need support and assistance in finding the psychological, emotional, and spiritual help they will almost surely need to cope with the loss of their beloved only son.

The African Independent and Pentecostal Churches Response

JAMES AMANZE

In African Independent Churches, the story of the car accident met by Huang-Fu would be received with great shock. When a car accident happens, such as the one described in the story, many African Independent Church members look for the ultimate cause that made the car hit Hung-Fu. Like in many African societies, the ultimate cause of the accident would be a witch, angry family spirits, or other evil spirits. It is strongly believed that these can cause an accident to happen.

Once an accident has occurred, the person is taken to hospital for treatment by medical doctors. However, apart from taking the patient to a modern hospital, African Independent Churches also resort to spiritual healing. This is done by consulting a prophet-healer, who normally uses the Bible to identify the ultimate cause of the accident. The Bible is opened randomly, and whatever is read in it is interpreted as the cause of the accident. Once the ultimate cause of the accident has been identified, the prophet-healer prescribes medicines or rituals that should be performed in order to heal the person who has been involved in the car accident. The rituals may take the form of prayers, sacrifices of animals, or use of holy water mixed with ashes or some other concoctions, as well as holy oil. Prayers for the sick person can be held at home or in church, depending on the advice of the prophet-healer. Even in cases where a person is declared brain dead, members of African Independent Churches would still pray for the healing of such a person, because they strongly believe that God can bring to life even those who are dead.

When accidents take place, people ask many theological questions, such as "Why has God done this to our child? Why has this accident happened to us and not to other people? Have we done something wrong to the ancestors or to God? What can we do to appease God and the ancestors?" Prophet-healers claim to have answers to some of these questions. They provide such answers by consulting the Bible under the inspiration of the Holy Spirit. As regards the donation of the organs of the child for further medical use, the majority of people would reject the request. Many African Independent Church members believe that, in order to be an ancestor at the resurrection, a person needs to have his or her body intact and not dismembered.

Pentecostals believe that car accidents are an attack by the devil. In a situation like that of Huang-Fu, if parents are on the spot, they would rebuke the devil not to take the life of the child. They would not blame the child, the parents, or the driver of the car but would blame the devil. The immediate instinct of the parents would be to resist the death of the child through prayer, though the doctors would say that the brain of the child is dead. They would see the accident as an attack by a foreign body which works against God, the source of life.

Pentecostal churches normally teach that occurrences such as car accidents are caused by the devil and only prayer through Jesus and the Holy Spirit can reduce or stop life-threatening injuries. When a person is involved in an accident, the immediate action is to take the person to hospital for medical attention. However, apart from medical care in the hospital, Pentecostal Churches emphasize the power and significance of prayer in order to bring about deliverance. Families of those who are involved in car accidents are encouraged to have faith in God, because he has the ultimate power to heal those who are injured, even at the point of death. People are taught that God is always a victor over the powers of evil.

When car accidents occur, Pentecostals ask a lot of theological questions, such as "Why did God allow this accident to happen? Is this accident a result of God's displeasure? Are we being tested by God to find out whether we maintain our faith in him?" In most cases, such questions remain unanswered; but pastors try as much as possible to comfort the family and help them to come to terms with their tragedy. One of the things the churches do is to invite members of the community to come together for prayer. Prayers for healing, during which the faithful sing and pray with the family, are held at home. All Pentecostals in the African context have a strong belief in miracles, including the possibility of having a clinically dead brain miraculously healed. This is one of the reasons why Pentecostals are not willing to have the organs of their loved ones donated for further medical use. They believe that, even at death, a person can be brought back to life by the saving power of God. The idea of donating the organs to the hospital for further medical use, would, therefore, be rejected by the majority of Pentecostals in Africa under the influence of African Traditional Religions, which would generally not entertain the idea.

In situations like that of Huang-Fu, people are given some counseling in the form of teaching. Pentecostal churches emphasize the sovereignty of God. They teach that God is in control regardless of whether a person with brain injuries lives or dies. Faith is the central message. People are told that they must have faith in God, because he is able to restore life even to people whose brain may be beyond healing. This is because God has power to raise the dead from the grave.

The Buddhist Response

SORAJ HONGLADAROM

The case of Huang-Fu is a sad one, where a bright young boy is struck down by a terrible accident. It is a situation no one wants to happen. But such things indeed do happen. Now he is in a coma, having suffered extensive and severe brain damage. His story shows that he appears to be brain dead, as he cannot breathe on his own without a ventilator. The doctor told Huang-Fu's parents that nothing more can be done to bring him back and the only option is to withdraw the life-support system and donate his internal organs for those who are in need of them.

Huang-Fu's story raises a very difficult dilemma. Withdrawing life support certainly means that Huang-Fu will stop breathing and will die. Many Buddhists in Asia still believe that it is the heart that lies at the center of being alive; as long as the heart is beating the person is believed to be alive. But there is nothing in the Buddhist teaching that says that the heart is at the center of life. It is true that when Buddhist texts mention death they usually refer to the conditions traditionally associated with it, such as having cold body, swelling, being eaten by worms and so on. But due to modern medical technology, it is now possible for someone to be "dead" in a certain sense without having a cold body. However, it is only because the ventilator is working that the person is kept "alive" that way. When the brain is totally dead, the part of the brain that controls breathing dies too. Without it, the body will stop breathing naturally. Only when the ventilator breathes for the body so that the heart and lung system is kept working does the person, in this case Huang-Fu, appear alive. As there seems to be nothing in the Buddhist texts that specifically say that death occurs when the heart stops beating, the belief that the heart is center of life seems to come from the pre-Buddhist era. Still, it has a quite powerful hold on much of the population.

According to the canonical texts, however, death occurs when the soul leaves the body. Since there is no way to check this scientifically, it could be argued that when the whole brain ceases to function, the soul has already departed the body, because the function of the soul is no longer possible on this body—no possibility of any return to consciousness. Nonetheless, there have been reports that some patients who have been declared brain dead did come back to consciousness; in such a case, the Buddhist would say that their souls have not actually departed the body and there should be a more reliable way of telling whether the patient is actually brain dead or not.

Suppose that Huang-Fu's brain is irrevocably damaged; it would be wise for his parents to consider donating his son's organs to those who could benefit from them. If they do not allow this, the organs will be wasted; furthermore, the parents will incur tremendous merit by deciding to donate their son's organs, because doing so will help other suffering patients to live. Compassion—the feeling that one needs to do something to help alleviate others' suffering—is a supreme Buddhist virtue; and Huang-Fu's parents have a very good opportunity to help others that way, since there is actually no hope of seeing Huang-Fu coming back any longer. Here the Buddhist approach to organ donation is that it is a supreme act of generosity to donate one's bodily organs to someone who is in need for them. There is a well-known story about a bodhisattva—someone who aspires to become a Buddha in order to be able to help sentient beings—seeing a very weak tigress who is unable to hunt and feed her cubs. Overwhelmed by compassion toward the tiger, the bodhisattva laid himself down so that the tigress could eat him in order to become strong again. Other Buddhists do not need to go that far, but the story points to the idea that to give one's possession to those in need of it is a very powerful act of compassion and a great source of merit which will bring one much closer to the Ultimate Goal.

The Confucian Response

RUIPING FAN

The Confucian religion is a family-based and family-oriented religion. The integrity, continuity, and prosperity of the family constitute a central concern of the Confucian faith and provide powerful motivations for family members to live a Confucian, virtuous way of life by taking care of each other. The main features of Confucian familism were laid out in the five cardinal Confucian classics, namely *The Book of Poetry*, *The Book of History*, *The Book of*

Rituals, *The Book of Changes*, and *Spring and Autumn Annals*. They were compiled by Confucius (551–479 B.C.E.) and his disciples, reflecting the Sinic civilization that had already existed for at least two thousand years before Confucius. In this civilization, humans follow the Mandate of Heaven, a quasi-personal God, to live their lives. The Mandate of Heaven is not shown in a system of explicit principles or rules that are derived from divine laws such as the Ten Commandments offered in the Judeo-Christian Bible, but is implicit in the fundamental signs, images, and structures of the universe manifested in the eight trigrams, 64 hexagrams, and 384 lines of *The Book of Changes*.[1] These signs, images, and structures were revealed by Heaven and recognized by the sages to mirror the essential constituents and dynamics of the universe so as to direct human actions. Specifically, the 37th hexagram, *jia ren* (family members), indicates the basic Confucian symbolism of the family: a stove (fire) used to cook food for a family to share and the virtue (wind) that is emanated from this way of life. In short, Confucian familism is grounded in the recognition of the resonance between the reality of the family and the deep reality of the universe, which carries significant implications for health care and life and death decision making.

The Confucian familist way of life becomes possible through the guidance of Confucian rituals (*li*). *Li* comprise a series of familial and social behavior patterns, ceremonies, and conventions that inform appropriate human relations and interactions, such as birth, capping (a coming-of-age ceremony), wedding, burying, sacrificing, greeting, and bowing. The Confucian rituals have been established by the sages to follow the Mandate of Heaven and incarnate the grounding symbols of the family. Performing the rituals is the normal way of learning and exercising Confucian virtue (*de*), so as to love other humans properly. Indeed, the fundamental Confucian virtue of *ren* calls for universal but non-egalitarian love: although one is required to love every human being through appropriate ritual performance, one has metaphysically grounded and ritually guided moral obligations to look after one's family members more than others. Normally, Confucian grandparents, parents, and children make shared decisions regarding important family issues (such as a family member's health care) and live as an autonomous unit apart from the rest of society.

This case is a family tragedy taking place in East Asia, where Confucianism has asserted immense cultural influence along with Buddhism and Daoism. As a religion, Confucianism is not quite exclusive in practice. "The temple" mentioned in the case that "Dao must walk to" would most probably be a typical East Asian temple in which Confucian, Buddhist, Daoist, and even other local spiritual statues are all established for people to pursue their blessings. A Confucian physician would sympathize with the terrible pain that Dao and Lien are suffering by losing their beloved only son, Huang-Fu. She would also appreciate shared decision making among family members in the Confucian familist way of life. Crucially, in this case, the hospital and physician must recognize that there are Confucian family-based, ritual-like medical practices that they should observe in order to handle the case well. In addition to talking to Dao and Lien, for instance, they should also attempt to communicate with Dao and Lien's parents for pursuing an adequate decision about Huang-Fu's organ donation. Such a ritual-like practice is supported by at least two reasons based on Confucian familism. First, Dao and Lien's parents also have a right to join the decision making for their grandson, because the size of the Confucian family usually includes three generations, if not more. Second, since Dao and Lien stand in unbearable grief, their parents are in a better position to understand Huang-Fu's literally lethal brain injury and appreciate that Huang-Fu can save other children by donating his organs. They can find more effective ways than the physician to explain the situation to Dao and Lien. Nevertheless, if the family decides not to offer such donation, the decision must be respected, because Confucianism holds that Huang-Fu is the child of this family, which has the legitimate authority to decide one way or another.

The Evangelical Christian Response

JOHN GRAHAM

First, it is important to know that Evangelical Christianity bases its understanding of the nature of God and humanity upon Scripture (the Bible). Scripture provides an unfolding revelation of the nature of God made most perfect in the Gospels, which tell of the life, death, and resurrection of Jesus, the Son of God. The four Gospels—Matthew, Mark, Luke, and John—are "Good News." But, can there be any good news for a couple upon the impending death of their most precious and only child—the child of promise?

Christianity says the couple can know from Scripture that their son is precious to God. Huang-Fu was created in the image of God (Genesis 1:27) and is loved by God with a love that is greater than their own love for their son (1 John 4:10). The question which comes to mind is, "If God loves Huang-Fu, how could God let him die? Surely, God could raise this boy to life. So, why doesn't God do that?"

This is a good question. It is called the Theodicy question, which tries to justify the ways of God to humankind. Evangelical Christians will say that, ever since Adam and Eve sinned in the Garden of Eden, all of creation is fallen and we are all subject to sin and death. Others will say God established the laws of nature at creation, and, if you step in front of a moving vehicle, you will be injured, perhaps fatally. The easiest solution may be to say that this is part of a great mystery that will be understood when we see God face to face in heaven. "Then we will know, even as we are known" (1 Corinthians 13:12 New King James Version).

This case brings up the question of whether Evangelical Christianity would allow the withdrawal of life-prolonging treatment. The answer is yes, withdrawal of life-prolonging treatment is permitted when there is little or no hope of recovery. Excessive and heroic efforts to prolong life can even be seen as a lack of trust in God and the Christian hope of eternal life.

As a pastor, when there is no reasonable hope of recovery, I would counsel a family to release their loved one, withdraw life-prolonging treatment, and place him or her in the hands of a loving God. I would also encourage everyone to have a signed Advanced Directive and Do Not Resuscitate documents, which can help a family know the will of their loved one in advance.

Choosing to withhold life support when there is little hope of recovery and releasing one's organs for transplantation upon death is a great gift of love. So, organ transplantation is almost universally approved among Evangelicals and is seen as a sign of Christ's love. As a pastor, I would counsel a family to release a deceased loved one's tissues and organs for transplantation. And, as I have done, I would counsel everyone to register as an organ donor. I do not want to be buried with organs that could have saved another person's life.

Mentioning life after death introduces an important understanding of Evangelical Christianity. Life is not limited to the time we have on this planet, be it short or long. Human life is eternal. Evangelical Christianity traditionally says that all who accept God's salvation through Jesus Christ's death on the cross will be saved and will spend eternity with God and the heavenly hosts (John 3:16).

Also, the Christian understands that after death we will be given a new body, a body free of blemishes, one fit for eternity. Paul writes in 1 Corinthians 15:40–44 (NKJV)

> There are heavenly bodies and there are earthly bodies; but the splendor of the heavenly bodies is one kind and the splendor of the earthly bodies is another...So will it be with the resurrection of the dead. The body that is sown is perishable, it is raised imperishable; it is sown in dishonor, it is raised in glory; it is sown in weakness, it is raised in power; it is sown a natural body, it is raised a spiritual body.

If this couple's son dies, knowing he will raised to eternal life with an incorruptible and glorified body may give them comfort in the hour of their grief and may help them release their son to God's tender care, knowing that one day they will be reunited with Huang-Fu in heaven.

The Christian belief that Jesus Christ lived, suffered, and died as one of us, also means we can go to God who understands our suffering. Hebrews 4:15 (NJKV) says, "For we do not have a high priest who is unable to sympathize with our sufferings, but we have one who has been tempted in every way, just as we are, yet was without sin. Let us then approach the throne of grace with confidence, so that we may receive mercy and find grace to help us in our time of need."

No one can fully appreciate the agony the boy's mother, Lien, is experiencing. She feels responsible for not watching out for her son as he dashed across the street. In these kinds of situations, a Christian knows he or she may go to Christ and leave our burden with Him, knowing Christ has invited us to bring all our cares to the One who cares for us (Peter 5:6–7). This is God's invitation to all who suffer and are burdened. We can bring our burdens to God and find rest for our weary souls (Matthew 11:28-30).

The Hindu Response

UMA MYSOREKAR

Hinduism or Hindu Dharma, also known as Sanatana Dharma or Universal religion, affects every aspect of life for Hindus. Hindus worship God in a form or a formless manner, according to one's own knowledge, desire, need, and spiritual elevation. Hindus believe that God will come to them in every form one desires and prays according to one's needs and wishes.

One of the principles of Hinduism is the law of *Karma*; and *Karma* means not only action, but also the result of an action. It denotes an action that brings back results in this life or future lives. The doctrine of *Karma* is therefore based upon the theory of cause and effect. Every human action inevitably leads to results, good or bad, depending on the moral quality of the deed. There is no such thing as an action without results.

The accident that left Huang-Fu in a coma in a hospital is the worst tragedy any parent has to deal with. The entire family, particularly the grandparents if alive, will become involved in the case and the decision making. They will be a great support to the parents. In Hindu tradition, the family network is strong, especially if there are older members. Their advice and guidance are extremely valuable.

The first thing that would be done is to offer prayers to the family deity or go to a temple and do special services for the recovery of the child. They would also seek the help of astrologers to interpret the horoscope of the child. Many Hindus believe in horoscopes or birth charts, and knowledgeable astrologers can often direct the families to perform some *poojas* or services, like *Havans* such as *Mrityunjaya Homam*, *Dhanvantari Homam*, *Ganapati Homam*, *Navagraha Homam*, and so on, for the recovery of the child.

Parents, even if they are not religious, are asked to go to a temple and offer prayers. Even while in the hospital, parents and grandparents or other family members will be praying for recovery of the child. Even though the physician may have told the parents of the inevitable, there is always hope against hope. "Maybe a miracle will happen. God is merciful and He will not do this to us."

This is the faith the majority of Hindus have. Others also believe that destiny cannot be changed and whatever will be, will be.

Prayer is the basic tenet of Hinduism and is a path by which God can be reached. Man thinks of God with devotion, and prayers are a call from the heart of the devotee during which he asks for God's help and guidance and at the same time sings His praises. Prayers, therefore, stand for asking, requesting, and appealing. The purpose of prayer is, first, to cultivate godly attributes in oneself; second, to rid oneself of evil thoughts and desires by meditating on God; and, third, to express gratitude to God. Prayers therefore strengthen one's resolve, decrease fear, lead to peace of mind, and set one on the path of righteousness. All of this will eventually lead to introspection and self-realization. To help in this process, one utilizes images of deities, symbols, mantras, japas, meditation, and eventually contemplation of the absolute.

In addition, prayer is the road to fulfillment. Through prayer, one seeks grace from God and receives comfort in times of distress. It also works wonders, and its power of healing is beyond comprehension of a human mind. All prayers are equally effective. Some prayers, such as chanting of "Vishnu Sahasranama" (the 1008 holy names of Lord Vishnu) are considered to be the easiest and the best means by which mankind can attain lasting happiness, peace of mind, relief from all bondage and sorrow, and, ultimately, salvation. Similarly, recitation of *Hanuman Chalisa*, consisting of 40 stanzas praising Lord *Hanuman*, renowned for his strength and courage, will help overcome all obstacles.

Hindu teachings, with their ancient foundations, make no direct reference to contemporary organ transplants. Hence, moral concerns are more or less a matter for the individuals concerned. Those involved in the organ-request process should be aware that the religion does not seem to explicitly deter the patient from donating. Health care professionals requesting donations from the Hindu community need not be reluctant to ask, although it is possible that some may have personal reservations.

Even though withdrawal of life-prolonging treatments in extremely grave situations, when death seems almost certain, is acceptable among Hindus, it is not so easy when the victim (such as Huang-Fu) is a child. The family will expect everything be done no matter what it takes. Religious people hold on to strong faith that God will save their child.

The Indigenous Response

IRENE TAAFAKI

For Marshallese people (Ri-Majōl), life is not defined by the condition of the brain or the heart but as the drawing of breath, the last of which is the sacred *aū*. As long as a patient is seen to be breathing, whether on their own or through a ventilator, they are alive. While the patient breathes, there is a consciousness, and it is believed they can hear no matter what their physical condition might be. In this state the patient remains connected: aware that family and friends are present, which gives them strength to survive. They will remain strong to wait for the arrival of a special loved one who will utter the last words of comfort, encouragement, or permission to rest. Then natural death will occur with the final expiration or *aū*.

It will only be after time has passed, and when the family is absolutely convinced that there is no hope of recovery, that it will be collectively agreed that the patient's life-prolonging treatments be withdrawn. The world view of Ri-Majōl is shaped by the deep conviction in a spiritual force or power —*Anij*— that exists beyond the human plane, and also belief in supplication to that power: the first response of Ri-Majōl to the tragic situation of Huang-Fu and any decisions of his parents to begin or withdraw life-prolonging treatments is that there is always the possibility of healing and the hope of a miracle.

In the case of an accident and the subsequent hospitalization (or home or clinic care on the outer islands within the Marshall Islands), neither the patient nor their immediate family would be left alone to manage the tragedy. Immediately the community would be aware of the accident, and large numbers of relatives and friends would gather to provide support. This would likely include the Marshallese chaplain, those who will offer help, and other silent supporters representing the solidarity of the community. Although only one or two members of the family may stay at the bedside, the larger group will remain close by—convinced that this collective presence will strengthen the spirit of the patient and their immediate family. Among the Marshallese diaspora in Hawaii, Guam, and the United States, this practice continues, and people will travel many miles to be with the patient and their next of kin.

Life support will never be withdrawn from a patient until all options and efforts to restore health are exhausted—the first being the application of those traditional medicines known to bring the patient out of a coma. Herbal and nonherbal treatments will be proposed and tried in anticipation that eventually one will be effective. Local medicine will also be prepared and given to relieve the anguish of close relatives of the patient. Particular faith is given to the efficacy of those treatments given to healers through dreams, as these are seen to be inspired or revealed by spirits, and therefore stronger.

Practical wisdom and decision making is also informed by a repertoire of recollections and anecdotes of the experiences of others—*bwebwenato*. There are stories of those who have awoken from a coma that will be shared to bolster the conviction to wait and avoid premature withdrawal of life support:

MC "I have a brother who was in an accident and he was admitted. They said he was brain dead. He had a crack on his head. Dead up here (head) but still breathing. My father is a preacher and believers all of them—my brother, older one. They had to make a decision. They just leave him like that. My older brother say (*sic*)...there is a saying...don't ever put a period where God put a comma. So after a few months, he recovered."

MR (to me): see? (to MC) Is he alright?

MC: He's in military. *E bar pad jōkan* (He is also there [far away]).

Organ donation is a very new concept to Ri-Majōl, and as yet little understood: there is no facility for transplants in the Marshall Islands, but there is no cultural objection to either giving or receiving organs, except among Marshallese who have embraced Christian faiths opposed to such medical practices. However, the notion of extending the existence of the deceased through organ donation would neither provide the family with a rationale for donating the organs of the newly deceased, nor would it provide any source of comfort to the grieving. The strong conviction of Ri-Majōl in the continuation of the life of the soul (*jetōb*) throughout eternity is the real "future" for the deceased.

The Jewish Response

HERBERT BROCKMAN

I read the case of Huang-Fu with a deep sense of pain and anguish. As a parent, it is unimaginable to have to suffer such an inexplicable tragedy. And then to ask a parent to decide when it is truly over, to admit that hope is lost, is even more unthinkable.

At the same time, as a person of faith and as a rabbi, I am awestruck by the responsibility of walking with families through their grief. As my very first mentor warned when I was about to begin my rabbinic duties, "the job of the rabbi is to disturb the comfortable and to comfort the disturbed." It is this confluence of the prophetic and the pastoral roles that calls us, not only to grieve ourselves—as we must, to care for ourselves—but to help others, to lead others, through a process that may encourage them from grief to some sense of healing.

At such times I am reminded of the image of the shepherd, a common religious reference, who leads his flock from the rear. In any approach to the family of Huang-Fu, this image is appropriate.

How are we to understand such a tragedy? Judaism does not find redemption in suffering and death. The notion that somehow the God of Israel is served by tragedy would be grotesque. Whereas in other faith traditions, some might argue that it is all a divine mystery, Judaism assumes that God's goodness and justice is a priori. It is left to humans to wrestle with the conflict. Confronted with the idea that the righteous may suffer, the rabbis recalled that, when Noah was informed of the coming deluge, he merely asked about the size of the Ark he was to build in order to save his family. For this, he earned the title, "a righteous man *in his generation*." It was a qualified approbation. On the other hand, when Abraham learned of God's intention to destroy Sodom and Gomorrah, he challenged God, arguing that "(to) sweep away the righteous (innocent) along with the wicked" would bring calumny on God's own name. "Can the judge of all the earth do unjustly?" It was this challenge that earned him the honor of becoming first patriarch of the Jewish people and set the value of "just-ness" as the highest moral category.

No belief exists in my tradition that would justify the tragedy of Huang-Fu. What we are left with are the practical and immediate issues regarding end-of-life questions—namely, in this case, the decision to withdraw life-support treatment, allowing natural death to occur, the question of when death can be declared, and the issue of organ transplantation. Jewish tradition has much to say about making these decisions.

What we know from this case is that Huang-Fu is in a coma and that the physicians believe it is irreversible. Lien, Huang-Fu's mother, feels that her son hears her and she refuses to "give up." Jewish tradition distinguishes between interventions that directly bring on death and those that interfere with the dying process, including the removal of external sources that prevent death. The first is proscribed, whereas the latter may be encouraged. There are to be found in rabbinic literature a number of instances when it was considered praiseworthy to cease life-prolonging actions and allow death to occur. The obligation to keep someone alive is balanced: "One may not hasten death, but may remove that which hinders death" (Shabbat 32:5, 151b).[2]

In the case presented here, Lien is not prepared for this to happen. The decision will take some time. There has to be a balance between supporting Lien and moving toward the reality of the situation. Prolonging suffering is never optimal. In Jewish tradition, the mourning process can only begin following the funeral. This is one of the principles behind the practice of having the funeral as soon as possible—to allow for the grieving to begin. "There is a time to be born, and there is a time to die" (Ecclesiates 3:2 Rabbi's Manual).

Judaism is similarly clear on what constitutes death. What distinguishes us as human beings is that we are sentient beings. Therefore, in general, a "flat brain wave," unresponsive to any treatment or other medical process, is regarded as death, although some Orthodox Rabbinic authorities maintain that the cessation of the vital functions of heart and lungs constitute death.

The question of organ donation is essentially moot. The body, though treated with the utmost respect, dignity, and modesty, is ultimately the container for the soul. "The body returns to the dust from which it came"

(Genesis 3:19 Rabbi's Manual). As such, the ability to harvest organs for the sake of others falls under the category of *pekuah nefesh* ("saving a soul"). It is encouraged over any other obligation. Put succinctly, the religious obligation is "to cure the sick, to bury the dead, and to comfort the mourner" (Gittin 60a).[2]

The case, in the end, is not about Huang-Fu as much as it is about Dao and, especially, about Lien. Being supportive, yet encouraging them to move forward, is important work. The God of Israel is seen not only as a creator and preserver of life, but as a "comforter in death." The tradition teaches that the "Shechina" ("divine presence") is at the bedside of the sick (Yoreh Deah 335:4).[3] It is the obligation of the caregivers and community to help the family experience that Presence in the midst of their grief through their presence. Prayer is used to call upon the Divine to be with and to walk with this family into the future and the painful process of healing.

The Mainline Protestant Christian Response

JAN HOLTON

It is an immense tragedy when a child suffers such a senseless accident and loses his life. Even before Huang-Fu's birth, Dao and Lien see his future as filled with everything bright and hopeful. They are good and loving parents who worked hard to give him every opportunity for a successful future. But in one moment's time, it all came to a horrible end.

The sudden and catastrophic aspects of this accident make the spiritual and pastoral concerns quite complex. Life-changing moments such as these can cause the absolute collapse of one's emotional and spiritual worlds, throwing into question the role of a God who would allow the suffering and death of an innocent child. A spiritual caregiver should be prepared for questions such as: "Where is God? Why would God let this happen?" Or, simply, "Why?" All are entirely predictable and acceptable spiritual questions in the midst of this crisis. Nevertheless, in this raw stage of the crisis, caregivers should resist the urge to find sure answers and instead recognize these questions as cries of lament emerging from deep pain and loss.

In order to help the family face the psychospiritual implication of the accident, a spiritual caregiver should begin by seeking clarity about the child's condition. To most laypersons the language of *coma*, even if clinically appropriate, does not equate to brain death. For a family to begin the process of decision making about organ donation, the spiritual caregiver must help the family clarify with medical professionals whether or not Haung-Fa is clinically dead. Only then can the family begin the long and difficult process of accepting the reality of their son's death, grieving his loss, and, perhaps, offering his organs as a final gift.

Organ donation marks a paradoxical time that joins two or more families by tragic circumstance. What is a tragic, devastating time of loss and grief for one family can be a time of great healing and joy for others. Some parents of a mainline Protestant tradition who find themselves in situations similar to Lien and Dao's may turn to their church for guidance. Mainline Protestant traditions encourage organ donation and see it as a gift that models the love given through the death of Jesus Christ. Despite widespread institutional acceptance, however, there is often substantial personal spiritual resistance to the idea. This may reflect the influence of a complex, lingering, centuries-old concern for burial of a whole (intact) body. This, in turn, is likely rooted in the Doctrine of the Resurrection originating in the early church. Many creeds still actively recited in weekly worship in mainline denominations across the United States and elsewhere state a belief in the resurrection of the *body* as a basic tenet of the Christian faith. Most mainline denominations, however, also informally translate the notion of resurrection as being *spiritual* in nature rather than physical. Even so, the underlying influence on disposition of the entire body at death remains. For Christians who practice their faith in mainline denominations, some of this sentiment may unconsciously influence decisions regarding organ donation. A spiritual caregiver, along with a team of medical and social work professionals, is essential to helping parents like Lien and Dao through this difficult decision-making process.

Once brain death has been established, prayer and rituals for the dying may help Dao and Lian begin the process of transition necessary for saying goodbye to their son Huang-Fu. Blessings, prayers, and liturgies of Protestant anointing may serve to help the family name the loss they are facing as well as commend their loved one into the hands of a loving God for eternal healing and rest.

The death of an unbaptized child can engender in parents what feels like an especially difficult spiritual concern for the state of the child's soul. In the mainline Protestant traditions the salvific relationship with a loving God is not a theological question for young children, who are unbaptized at the time of death. Nonetheless, some parents may request baptism, one of two sacraments in the Protestant church, just prior to or even after death. In such cases clergy should regard such a request as a pastoral care concern based on the fear and grief of parents, and thus not an issue to be debated on doctrinal grounds. Those denominational traditions that practice infant baptism and those who baptize at a later age at profession of faith differ little in this regard.

The Shi'a Muslim Response

NAJMEH JAFARI

As a mother of a six-year-old child, this tragic event filled my heart with sorrow. In my working life as a physician, I have been faced with this situation many times, and I have witnessed the denial, grief, and tears of parents. The sudden and unexpected death of Dao and Lien's only beloved son, Huang-Fu, exposed them to significant pain and distress. They now face a difficult decision: Should they turn off life support for their brain-dead child?

It seems that the most important step in this situation is for Dao and Lien to accept their son's death. The injury to Huang-Fu's head was lethal, and there is no hope for him to wake up. If they were faithful Shi'a Muslims, they would believe that, though death is an inevitable part of human existence, life is sacred; all life originates from God and returns to God. As the *Qur'an* (21:35) teaches, "Every soul shall have a taste of death: and we test you by evil and by good by way of trial, to Us must you return."

Whether to accept legal brain death, which is the irreversible end of all brain activity, as death or not is a challenging issue in Islam. Most Shi'a scholars accept legal brain death as the condition in which "complete cessation of all functions of the brain occurs," but some of them are of the opinion that "human life does not end by brain death with a beating heart."[4] To determine brain death, it is required that "expert physicians ascertain that the cessation is irreversible, and the brain is in the state of degeneration."[5] Although Shi'a scholars are familiar with the concept of brain death, most of them would prefer to wait for nature to proceed its way rather than withdraw ventilation and circulatory support; however, some of them believe that "delaying the inevitable death of a patient through life-sustaining treatment is neither in the patient's nor the public's best interests because of limited financial resources. Withdrawal of life-sustaining treatments in such instances is seen as allowing death to take its natural course."[4]

After brain death, however, there is a ground for suggesting the possibility of donating organs in order to save lives of the recipients whose lives cannot be saved otherwise. Some scholars believe that the beating heart in the brain-dead patient does not mean the end of life, and organ transplantation is impermissible. However, prominent Shi'a scholars, such as Ayatollah Khomeini, accept organ transplantation from the brain dead. "It is authorized to use organs such as heart, liver, etc. of a definite brain dead with permission of organ owner for transplantation if someone else's life is dependent on it."[6] Saving a life is of paramount value in Islam, as the following verse from the

Qur'an (5:32) illustrates: "if any one saved a life, it would be as if he saved the life of the whole people." Regarding this religious belief and considering the thousands dying each year while wait-listed for organ transplantation, the decision making will be easier for Dao and Lien.

Transplantation of an organ from the brain dead to a living human being needs informed consent by the dead (before death) or his heirs; "presumed consent" is not acceptable in Shi'a Islam. In this case, the informed consent from the father of Huang-Fu is necessary, and he should not be forced to give it.

Usually organ transplantation is assisted by charity organizations. Therefore maintaining relationships with local Islamic-community leaders and educating them on the issue of organ donation is an effective approach to facilitating organ donation in a sensitive and effective manner.

For the family, the death of a loved one is a very difficult time. This needs to be taken into account when providing information about organ and tissue donation and discussing consent and related issues. It can be done through spiritual counseling by an expert spiritual healer. Shi'a Islamic doctrine is full of spiritual advice for Muslims in this situation. It holds that human existence continues after the death of the human body and that death is a transition for the soul from the material world to a spiritual world of purgatory. There is a direct relation between conduct on earth and the life beyond. It should be mentioned to Huang-Fu's parents that he was innocent in his life, and therefore, in the other world, his spirit will be freed and he will be purified from the pains and sorrow of the natural and material world; he will have his "rich future" in heaven with the Lord. The Holy Qur'an (32:11) states: "The Angel of Death, put in charge of you, will (duly) take your souls: then shall ye be brought back to your Lord."

For faithful Muslim parents, the belief that this accident is a test from God may bring them peace and divine blessing. The Qur'an (2:155–157) puts it this way:

> Be sure we shall test you with something of fear and hunger, some loss in goods or lives or the fruits (of your toil), but give glad tidings to those who patiently persevere, Who say, when afflicted with calamity: "To God We belong, and to Him is our return." They are those on whom (Descend) blessings from God, and Mercy, and they are the ones that receive guidance

The unexpected death of their beloved Huang-Fu surely has caused Dao and Lien grief. As faithful Muslims, however, they are encouraged to be patient and to bear this tribulation with fortitude; for in so doing, they can rest upon God's blessings and mercy.

The Sunni Muslim Response

TARIQ RAMADAN

Dao and Lien, parents of Huang-Fu, a six-year old child who has been involved in a tragic road-traffic accident, are being informed by the medical doctors, 24 hours after he has been hospitalized, that nothing more can be done to save his life. Although his internal organs are unharmed, Huang-Fu is in an irreversible coma and breathing only by way of a ventilator. Having explained these facts, the doctors are now asking the parents about the possibility of donating Huang-Fu's organs to other children who need them. The doctors advise that this is the only future now for Huang-Fu. According to the Islamic tradition, there are certain points that doctors and a Muslim family should be aware of in a medical emergency such as this.

First and foremost, it is essential for the Muslim family to listen to the conclusions drawn from medical evidence by the doctors. Communication—honest, open, and informed dialogue—between doctors and the family is absolutely critical throughout the entire process. This is on three levels: informing the family of the status of the patient, a discussion of options for organ donation, and finally a discussion about removal of the life-support device.

While informing the family, doctors must be aware that they may be dealing with a particular culture, so their task is not only about imparting knowledge but also about being sensitive in the way they communicate the information. From a Muslim perspective, the best way in Islam is for the doctors to acknowledge the right of the parents to know what is happening without undue delay and to inform them in a gentle but clear, direct way so that there is no room for misinterpretation. The doctors in this case study are doing exactly this, explaining the situation clearly to the parents—that there is no hope, that Huang-Fu is in a coma, that his breathing is being done by a ventilator and that without this he wouldn't know when to breathe. In Muslim-majority countries, sometimes perhaps because of the culture of that particular country, doctors delay in informing the family as they try to find a way to convey the message. But from an Islamic perspective, whatever the cultural context, it is critical to inform the parents as soon as the medical conclusions have been drawn by the doctors. As difficult as the news is to comprehend, Dao and Lien must accept that the final word on the status of their son is that of the doctors. From an Islamic viewpoint, this is the first critical step.

Next, as the family absorbs the news and begins to experience the absolute shock of the situation, the doctors should carefully explain that religious and psychological counseling is available—the parents should be given the opportunity to talk to the different experts who can help them from a religious, cultural, and psychological viewpoint. Specifically, a Muslim family should be offered the opportunity to have an Islamic religious expert (for example, an

Imam) or a psychologist speak with them. It is very important for the doctors to keep talking to the family throughout the entire process and to inquire as to whether they have specific beliefs. Within the Islamic tradition, building knowledge is important but it is also important to understand the aspirations and expectations of the Muslim family. This is relevant both within the first 24 hours and in the days following.

Dao and Lien then have to decide whether to allow the doctors to give Hung-Fu's organs to other children. Organ donation is permitted in Islam— the only restriction being not reproductive organs. Doctors should therefore outline all the possibilities in a way that will enable the Muslim parents to understand how their son's body could help the lives of others. Again, this conversation should be between the doctors and the family and, if necessary, the Imam should reassure the family that this is permissible within the teachings of Islam. Sometimes it may be that the patient has at some previous time consented to be an organ donor. This decision should be upheld by the family. It is very often the case, however, as in an emergency situation of a young child, that prior consent is not available. So, although the doctors (and Imams, if present) should make clear that from an Islamic perspective organ donation is possible, the final decision must ultimately be that of the parents. They can agree or not agree to organ donation for their child, knowing that it is possible in Islam but that it is their own personal choice. The parental decision must be accepted by the doctors and the Imam. The parents should be supported and not be made to feel guilty whatever their decision, since in Islam such freedom of choice for the parents at the end of their child's life is very important.

Finally, there must also be a discussion between the doctors and the parents about when to stop the life-support device. According to Islamic teachings, this decision has to be made by the doctors, once they have confirmed that there is no point in continuing with the device. But the doctors must discuss this fully and sensitively with the family, being aware of the psychological environment. The Muslim family should be fully informed throughout the process, so that they know exactly what is happening, but they should accept the fact that the final decision is for the doctors. Mainstream Islamic attitudes suggest that a dying person may receive whatever contemporary medical treatment and technology is available to try to survive and eventually be cured or healed, but also counsel that a person not act against what nature intended by using devices to keep someone artificially alive when, without those devices, he or she would otherwise die (futile medical care). In Islam, the family must accept the doctors' recommendation of when to begin to withdraw the life-prolonging treatment and grant permission to allow their child to be taken off the life-support device (for example, the ventilator). At this point it is important to acknowledge that, although a Muslim family is welcome to speak with an Islamic religious expert, the discussion about removing life support is really very much between the doctors and the family alone.

So, in summary, the first step for a Muslim family is to absorb the assessment of the situation, based on the advice from medical doctors. Communication with the family is critical and should be undertaken as soon as possible in an appropriate way, with doctors offering the family access to relevant Islamic religious experts and psychologists. Doctors should then leave room for the family to absorb the information, react, and be able to receive support from these counselors. Organ donation is permissible in Islam, and if consent has not been provided by the dead person before the time of death, the decision should be made by the family. The choice is theirs alone. Doctors make the final decision about stopping life-support devices. Their decision should be based upon medical knowledge and expertise, but always including continual dialogue with the family. Doctors should make it clear to the family that they respect their suffering, but knowing the facts as they are, they should explain the speed at which the next steps should be undertaken. Timing is critical if organ donation is to be successful and action has to be taken promptly once the patient has died.

The Roman Catholic Response

CAROL TAYLOR

Dr. Byock makes clear that Huang-Fu's medical team have determined that Huang-Fu is dead and recovery is impossible. His mother understandably refuses to accept that he is dead. If Dao and Lien were Roman Catholics, they would have grown up listening to narratives of miraculous cures in the New Testament Scriptures, such as the raising of Lazarus from the dead (John 11:1–4). We can well imagine Dao and Lien caressing their son's ventilated and warm body, praying as Lazarus' sisters Martha and Mary prayed, "Lord, if you had been here, my brother [son] would not have died. [But] even now I know that whatever you ask of God, God will give you."

The doctors and nurses caring for Huang-Fu and needing to remove the no-longer-effective life-sustaining treatments are challenged not only by the parents' understandable refusal to accept brain death criteria but also their deeply held conviction that a miraculous cure is possible if only their faith is strong enough. Belief in a personal God who knows and loves us is a double-edged sword. It comforts as we contemplate being called "home" to eternal union with God, and on the other hand gives us hope that the one we love will be spared for the moment. Life is sacred for Catholics but does not have absolute value, since the full perfection of human life is not in the here and now.

What Catholics call "the spiritual works of mercy" include comforting the afflicted and praying for the living and the dead. Catholic health care's healing ministry would prioritize supporting Huang-Fu's parents, who are exquisitely vulnerable in their suffering—especially Lien, who feels responsible for her son. Professional caregivers, priests, and lay ministers would utilize healing presence to stand in solidarity with the suffering parents. In this fashion, they would incarnate Jesus, who was often reported to be perturbed and troubled in the face of human suffering and to weep (John 11:33–36). Suffering is known to "make" or "break" humans. The Paschal mystery, Jesus' suffering, death, and resurrection, may be a source of hope for Huang-Fu's parents. Similarly, they may be comforted by the belief that God did not spare his "only begotten Son" and by the example of his Sorrowful Mother, Mary. The Catholic Rosary (prayer beads) highlights mysteries in salvation history and includes both sorrowful and glorious mysteries commemorating Jesus' suffering, death, and resurrection. The Ethical and Religious Directives for Catholic Health Care Services state:

> For the Christian, our encounter with suffering and death can take on a positive and distinctive meaning through the redemptive power of Jesus' suffering and death. As St. Paul says, we are "always carrying about in the body the dying of Jesus, so that the life of Jesus may also be manifested in our body" (2 Cor 4:10). This truth does not lessen the pain and fear, but gives confidence and grace for bearing suffering rather than being overwhelmed by it. Catholic health care ministry bears witness to the truth that, for those who are in Christ, suffering and death are the birth pangs of the new creation. "God himself will always be with them [as their God]. He will wipe every tear from their eyes, and there shall be no more death or mourning, wailing or pain, [for] the old order has passed away" (Rev 21:3–4).[7]

Dao and Lien would have been asked if they wanted the Sacrament of the Anointing of the Sick for Huang-Fu prior to the diagnosis of brain death. The sacrament is administered by a priest who lays his hands on the head of the sick person and anoints with the blessed Oil of the Sick the forehead and hands, praying, "Through this holy anointing may the Lord in his love and mercy help you with the grace of the Holy Spirit. May the Lord who frees you from sin save you and raise you up."[8] This sacrament is highly valued as a means to a good death.

Catholics support organ donation. Three directives specifically address this topic:

> 63. Catholic health care institutions should encourage and provide the means whereby those who wish to do so may arrange for the donation of their organs and bodily tissue, for ethically legitimate purposes, so that they may be used for donation and research after death.

64. Such organs should not be removed until it has been medically determined that the patient has died. In order to prevent any conflict of interest, the physician who determines death should not be a member of the transplant team.

65. The use of tissue or organs from an infant may be permitted after death has been determined and with the informed consent of the parents or guardians.

Great care would need to be exercised throughout the entire process of withdrawing previously life-sustaining treatments and organ procurement to ensure that Huang-Fu and his parents are treated in a competent, compassionate, and respectful manner consonant with their inherent human dignity, theirs by virtue of being human and created in the image and likeness of God (Genesis 1:27).

The Sikh Response

SURJEET KAUR CHAHAL

The tragic case of Huang-Fu in coma is emotionally very upsetting, and it is very difficult for the parents Dao and Lien to even imagine losing their son. They are emotionally attached to their son, and there is no rational solution that would really appeal to them. In this trying situation, sociocultural and spiritual responses may help the parents to cope with this horrifying experience.

First and foremost, if we see this case from the perspective of Sikh religion, the parents and doctors need to wait and watch the situation. All efforts should be made to stabilize Huang-Fu. One of the most important factors that would play a role here is that God's ways are wondrous and miraculous and that it may be possible for Huang-Fu's condition to improve.

This would imply that Dao and Lien have faith in God's miraculous powers. However, there is also a possibility that Huang-Fu's condition deteriorates. In this situation, after a review by the doctors, it would not be inappropriate to turn off the machines. Seen from the Sikh perspective, a great emphasis is laid on service to humanity. The highest form of service to humanity is sacrifice for the benefit of others. In the case of Huang-Fu, if his conclusion does not stabilize after about a month's watchful waiting, it would be accepted, according to the tenets of Sikh philosophy, that instead of artificially prolonging Huang-Fu's life, his organs should be donated. This would also help Huang-Fu's parents to cope up with his loss in a better way. Since this human body is just one form that the soul takes, by donating Huang-Fu's organs, his soul would rather accumulate positive *karmas* by donating his organs for others. This would perhaps relieve Hung-Fu's parents of any feelings of guilt.

Huang-Fu's parents need spiritual counseling after his death, which is usually provided by members of the spiritual congregation, friends, and family, as per the Sikh tradition.

Thus to sum up:

1. Weight of guilt can be reduced by accepting the Will of God.
2. This human life is one of the forms in which one takes birth. It is all under God's Will—how He will keep and sustain this body.
3. Service to humanity—this Sikh value would help the parents accept donating Huang-Fu's organs. Also, by donating his organs, Huang-Fu will live on through the bodies of others. His soul, of course, does not die. It is only five elements of his body that revert back to the five elements (the root chakra to earth; the sacral chakra to water; the navel chakra to fire; the heart chakra to air; the throat chakra to ether).
4. Uncertainty of prognosis leads to acceptance of miracles—that is—wait to see if there is a chance of recovery.

The Unitarian Universalist Response

JAN K. NIELSEN

Unitarian Universalism is a faith without a creed or official set of beliefs and practices. Unitarian Universalists draw wisdom not only from the world's religions, but also from the findings of science as well as the writings of poets and philosophers, both ancient and contemporary. Some Unitarian Universalists believe in God or some form of higher power, while others may consider themselves agnostic or atheist. Some Unitarian Universalists engage in spiritual practices like prayer or meditation while others may not. Some Unitarian Universalists may believe that our essence continues in some other form or realm after we die while others believe that after our bodies die, our lives come to an end. Unitarian Universalists focus less on the question of an afterlife and more on living a meaningful life in the here and now. Unitarian Universalists include people whose religious roots may lie in traditions such as Buddhism, Christianity, Hinduism, Islam, or Judaism as well as an increasing number of people who previously identified with no faith tradition at all. Because Unitarian Universalism allows for a broad diversity of beliefs and practices, some who might describe themselves as "spiritual but not religious" are finding their spiritual homes in Unitarian Universalist congregations.

When called to counsel either a Unitarian Universalist or someone who identifies "spiritual but not religious," it is important to make no assumptions about the person's spiritual beliefs and practices. After first listening with compassion to Dao and Lien, the wise counselor then might ask some straightforward questions, such as:

- "How do your spiritual beliefs speak to what has happened?"
- "Were you raised in a faith tradition as a child?"
- "Do you find the word 'God' meaningful?"
- "Do you use other words to name the sacred or transcendent?"
- "Do you pray or meditate?"
- "What do you believe happens when we die?"

When providing spiritual care for people whose beliefs and practices may be unclear or unfamiliar, first invite them to share their spiritual perspectives and then decide what to say and do.

Dao and Lien are facing a tragedy no parent should have to endure. Their precious and only child, Huang-Fu, cannot survive without a ventilator. His brain is bleeding but his internal organs are unharmed and could be used to help other children sustain their lives. When life brings tragedy and presents hard questions, people who have left the religious traditions of their childhoods or the traditions practiced by parents or grandparents may find themselves drawn to the rituals and practices of the faith traditions of their roots. Even though Dao does not think of himself as a religious man, he now finds he must walk to a temple where he lights a candle and prays for wisdom. Especially when death is near, people who have not considered themselves religious may yearn to hear familiar sacred words or music or long to do something with their hands like hold prayer beads or light candles. Dao's prayer for wisdom is one a Unitarian Universalist might find most meaningful. A Unitarian Universalist facing a tragedy like this might pray, not for a certain result, but instead for wisdom or courage or peace.

A spiritual caregiver might offer to pray with Dao and Lien as they struggle to accept what has happened and decide whether they should agree to allow Huang-Fu's organs to be given to other children who need them. After sharing a time of prayer or meditation with Dao and Lien, it could be important for the spiritual caregiver to say, with clarity and compassion, that what happened was no one's fault. These heartbroken parents should also be reminded that no God would will anything like this to happen. We do not know why bad things happen, but when they do, we humans are called to make wise and caring choices. Because most Unitarian Universalists do not believe the intact body is necessary for whatever might lie beyond this life, cremation of the body after death is widely accepted among Unitarian Universalists and organ donation considered a wise choice. While gently encouraging Dao and Lien to find ways to honor their son's bright spirit, a spiritual caregiver might suggest that by allowing their son's healthy organs to be given to other children who need them, they can make this life better for others and at the same time allow Huang-Fu's life to give life to others.

REFERENCES

1. Legge, J, Trans. *The Chinese classics*.Vol 1–5. Safety Harbor, FL: Simon Publications; 1970.
2. Epstein, I. Ed. *Babylonian Talmud*. London: Soncino Press; 1932.
3. Ramah, Shulchan aruch, Yoreh Deah 335:4; cf Telushkin, *A Code of Jewish Ethics*. Vol 2. New York: Bell Tower;2009
4. Al-Mousawi M, Hamed T, Al-Matouk H. Views of Muslim scholars on organ donation and brain death. *Transplant Proc.* 1997;29:3217.
5. Parliament of Iran. Deceased or Brain Dead Patients OT Act; 2000:H/24804-T/9929.
6. Khomeini SR. Rulings regarding brain death. In: Rohani M NF, ed. *Ahkam-e pezeshki*. Tehran, Iran: Teymurzadeh Cultural Publication Foundation; 1997:174.
7. National Conference of Catholic Bishops. *Ethical and religious directives for Catholic health care services*. 5th ed. Washington, D.C.: US Catholic Conference; 2009.
8. UCSSB. *Catechisms of the Catholic Church*. 2nd ed. Liberia Editrice Vaticana: Vatican City; 1997. http://www.usccb.org/beliefs-and-teachings/what-we-believe/catechism/catechism-of-the-catholic-church/epub/index.cfm.

CHAPTER 11

When Disease Progresses

Case

MARK LAZENBY, RUTH McCORKLE, DANIEL P. SULMASY

Growing up in a traditional Muslim family, Eman knew the importance of her name: it means "Faith" in English. Faith is everything to her parents—her traditional parents. Her father wears a robe and a head covering, a *kufiya*. And he prays five times a day. Every Friday, he makes the journey downtown to the main mosque for noontime prayers. He does not smoke; he tells his five sons and Eman, his only daughter, that good Muslims do not pollute their bodies with tobacco. Eman's mother, who always wears a head scarf, a *hijab*, outside the home, is devoted to her family. While she does her housework, she prefers to have a cassette of a famous Imam reciting the *Qur'an* playing in the background than to have the TV on.

Gifted and disciplined in primary school, Eman won a scholarship to a private secondary school. After graduating from secondary school with honors, she was admitted to her country's most competitive medical school in a city a few hours' drive north of her hometown. It was her childhood dream to become a physician, the most prized of professions among her peers growing up. Almost daily in secondary school, she'd write her name on scrap pieces of paper as "Dr. Eman," just to get the thrill of how it looked. Ten years ago, she proudly graduated with a Bachelor of Medicine and Surgery. Dr. Eman—a reality. Her parents, not owning a car, made the journey by bus to attend her commencement ceremony. Accepted into a challenging internship program in the same city where she went to medical school, she went on to do a two-year residency in obstetrics. During her residency, she married a young surgeon, Ahmad. After she finished residency and started practicing full-time as a obstetrician, she and Ahmad had two children—Amina and Khalid—now three and two years old. Although she continues to wear the *hijab* to honor her parents, she does not believe that good Muslim women should remain in the house.

A few months ago, Eman went to see a friend and colleague, a gynecologist who works in the same hospital: she had developed a pus-producing sore in her right armpit. According to her friend, the sore looked like an obstructed hair follicle. The follicle, and the sweat gland underneath it, both looked infected, she said. She prescribed an antibiotic. Eman felt that the antibiotic cleared up the infection, but her armpit continued to feel uncomfortable. Then she noticed an enlarged node. She took another course of antibiotics, which she bought herself from the pharmacy. After all, Dr. Eman could prescribe her own medication now. But the node did not recede after taking the medication. In fact, a rash developed where the sore had been. Eman feared that the rash looked a lot like *peau d'orange*, an indication of a terrible but common enough form of breast cancer Arab women seem to be prone to. She remembered her mother talking about a beloved aunt who died as a young woman from what was thought to have been breast cancer, but of course, this aunt never sought treatment. Eman dismissed this fear as the fear every young health professional has. Doctors often think they have every illness they see in the clinic. Still, she could not quiet her anxiety. So she spoke with a professor from her old medical school with whom she kept in touch. The professor took one look at Eman's rash and quickly ordered a mammogram. The radiologist noticed something suspicious. Eman went for a biopsy. It confirmed her fear. She had inflammatory breast cancer.

Eman told Ahmad, and together they agreed that they would try to keep life as normal as possible for Amina and Khalid. And she was adamant: she was going to keep working as long as she could. So while continuing in her practice delivering babies, she received chemotherapy as an outpatient. After two cycles, however, she felt pain between her shoulder blades. An MRI found that the cancer had migrated to one of the bones in her back. And the MRI also found the cancer had moved to her liver.

Eman has told her parents that she is ill, but she has not told them that the cancer is incurable. With her father and mother and her husband at her bedside, she now is a patient in the very hospital where she has delivered babies as an attending obstetrician for the last seven years. Hairless and riddled with pain, she shakes from fever. The chemotherapy has driven her white blood cell count so low she cannot fight off infections. But still, she wants more treatment. She is, after all, only 35 years old, and has two little children to care for—two little children to raise. She confided in her oncologist that, despite the odds, she has faith she will beat this cancer.

The Clinical Issues

BETTY FERRELL

The story of Eman is a story of a woman struggling for survival while facing terminal disease. Her life and illness experience are greatly influenced by rich and sacred cultural and spiritual beliefs. Eman is a human, a woman, a spouse, a mother, a wife, daughter, and a physician. She is far more than an inflammatory breast cancer.

The clinical and medical decision issues for Eman will be based on more than the survival statistics for her pathology and the response rates of her treatment options. The last sentence of this case, "she has faith she will beat this cancer," is a reminder of the human experience of life-threatening illness. Eman hopes for survival. Her hope is likely deeply grounded in each of the relationships of her life; perhaps especially important being her role as mother to two young children.

Eman's health care providers may see the process of decision making as a matter of statistical odds. From this biological lens, medical decisions may be based singularly on the odds of tumor response and may ignore the patient's need to maintain hope. Eman may sacrifice personal comfort, symptom burden, and treatment toxicity if aggressive treatment offers even minimal survival benefit. What is the price or the value of a week or a month of additional time for a mother to spend with her children? That question can be answered by only one member of health care team—the patient.

The nodal point in the case of Eman is recognition of the unique story of her life and relationships, from her perspective, and how these factors will influence the ultimate decisions about her disease and the quality of her remaining life. Treatment options that offer the possibility of extended life despite harm may far outweigh a known outcome of death.

The treatment choices of cancer are too often seen as competing and polarized options. Cancer is either treated aggressively with chemotherapeutic agents, surgery, and other tumor-directed modalities while ignoring the *human* surrounding the tumor, or treatment of the tumor is abandoned and care becomes directed only toward patient comfort. For patients such as Eman, the decision to seek intense disease-focused therapy is deeply rooted in the need to survive and to fulfill her commitment to those she loves.

Beyond Eman's personal relationships with her parents, spouse, and children is the relationship with her health care providers. The dynamics of patient and health-care providers are made extremely complex when the patient is also a colleague. Eman the patient is also Eman the physician. Her treatment decisions will be informed not only by what she is advised as a patient but by what she knows, values, and has experienced as a physician providing care. As an obstetrician, she has lived a professional life valuing new life, healthy birth, and the sacred nature of birth and the bonding of mother and child. These profound life experiences do not disappear as she becomes "the patient"; rather, they illuminate every aspect of decision making she must now face to sustain her own life.

Health-care providers advise patients on treatment choices based on their awareness of the eventual outcome as we believe it to be. We advise Eman based on our knowledge of 6-month, 1-year, or 5-year survival. But Eman is living her one life today. She is living breast cancer prospectively, but our advice is retrospective, based on the lives of others. Her decision today to enter a clinical trial, seek alternative therapy, or to postpone what we consider to be urgent if it will interfere with her ability to attend a daughter's dance recital must be honored. We must also avoid suggesting to patients that their treatment decisions are unchangeable. If she commits to treatment and finds it to be unendurable, she should feel support in altering her decision.

The Ethical Issues

MARGARET MOHRMANN

Eman is immune deficient, febrile, and in significant pain. Her metastatic cancer is incurable, as she and her husband know. She wishes to continue curative treatment in the belief that she will "beat the odds." The poignant truth is that the word "incurable" still leaves room for that belief; the conviction that she will "beat the odds" determines her choices and sets the ethical valence of this story.

She is from a culturally traditional and religiously observant Muslim family and wears the *hijab*, but we do not know the place or depth of religious belief in her adult life, beyond an indication that it may matter to her to be a "good Muslim woman." We do not know the larger culture within which this tale is unfolding (her medical degree indicates that it is not the US), nor anything about the beliefs, policies, and practices of the hospital staff.

Despite these morally important lacunae, certain ethical requirements can be noted. First among them is welcoming, attentive respect for who Eman is and what she cares for, a respect based less upon on autonomy than a steady recognition of whose life is at stake, who is rightly the center of consideration. The primary role of other actors is to assist Eman in living this final period of her life—including its necessary decisions—in ways that reflect her commitments and enable her to honor whom and what she most values.

This task requires clarity about her condition and the probable effects of attempts at remission, as well as her priorities. The story suggests that her children are her primary concern; she will need help to discern how best to enact her care for them under these conditions. Decisions about curative versus palliative treatments are more truly about what her remaining time will be like. Eman's fidelity to her family and to herself requires that she decide within the reality of her medical condition; it is the moral task of those around her to assist and support her, gently and compassionately, within that reality.

That Eman is a woman should matter little to this analysis, but because our perceptions are inescapably gendered, we must be careful particularly to avoid making gendered assumptions about what she "must" want. We do not know what being "a good Muslim woman"—or a mother, wife, daughter—means to her or entails for her decisions. She may choose to continue curative treatment because she is fiercely committed to doing everything she can, however futile, to stay alive for her children. Or she may want to seek palliative treatment only, but feel constrained to put up the fight she thinks is expected of her. She may need support for the former stance (plus assurance of assiduous palliation of side effects) *or* permission for the latter. The only way to know which approach is fitting is to listen to her.

This situation calls for virtuous perception and action much more than for analysis of conflicts between patient autonomy and physician or family paternalism. Responsibility, honesty, compassion, patience to endure, and humility in the face of the undeniable tragedy, incorrigible unknowns, and forced choices before her are virtues asked of all as Eman, her family, and her doctors and nurses together seek the best possible way of going on.

The African Independent and Pentecostal Churches Response

JAMES AMANZE

Eman's story is typical of many situations in Africa and people deal with such serious physical ailments every day. What happens among African Independent Churches is representative of what happens in African society generally. Initial signs of a disease are always fought with simple treatments bought at pharmacies or ordinary shops. However, if the person does not get healed after some time, suspicion begins to arise concerning the cause of the disease. The ultimate cause is normally not considered to be bacteria or germs, but a person such as witch or sorcerer. Sometimes the cause of the disease is attributed to evil spirits or angry ancestral spirits in the family. When western medicine fails, members of the African Independent Churches would approach a prophet-healer in their church or in any other church who is regarded as having the power of healing. The prophet-healer would initially use the Bible under the inspiration and guidance of the Holy Spirit to diagnose the disease and prescribe the necessary treatment. The treatment would consist of administering holy water mixed with ashes, commonly known as *sewacho* in Botswana, to bathe or drink, use of holy oil to apply to the body, prayer, laying on of hands and offering of animal sacrifices. Sometimes African traditional medicine is used.

When the situation becomes very critical and the use of the Bible and Christian prayers prove ineffective, the patient and the family turn completely to the use of traditional medicine. At this point they believe that the God of their ancestors from whom human beings spring to life will intervene and heal the sick person. This is done by invoking the healing power of God through the ancestors, who are always watchful, beneficial, and have the interests of their descendants at heart. However, they can sometimes be malicious, in which case their forgiveness is sought. In this context, faith plays a major role, and family members never give up the fight to the very end. The help of diviners is always enlisted to find out the ultimate cause of the disease. The belief is that once the ultimate cause has been identified and neutralized, the problem will come to an end. The person will be healed henceforth. Elements of faith and hope persist until the person dies. If the person does not get healed, the belief is that the ultimate source of the disease was not identified or it was too potent to be dealt with. When everything fails, members of the family leave things in the hands of God, whom they consider to be the source of life.

In Pentecostal Churches, when someone is suffering from a serious disease such as cancer, people believe that such a person can be healed by God, though they know that extreme stages of cancer are incurable. Many Pentecostals across Africa strongly believe in miracles such as those recorded in the Old and New Testaments. Pentecostal Churches teach that if people pray hard the disease will disappear, because there is nothing impossible with God. Since many Pentecostal Church members believe that diseases such as cancer are caused by the devil and evil spirits, they also believe that it is possible for a person to be healed and cured by faith in God. Pentecostals believe in both spiritual healing and physical curing. This is how they think about all diseases, including cancer. They believe that since diseases are caused by the evil one, the triune God can overpower the devil and destroy the disease.

Pentecostals teach that the devil is always at work attacking those who believe in Jesus. As such, Christians must be prepared all times to fight back against the devil through prayer in order to secure their lives. At times, churches teach that in order to heal a person with cancer such a person needs to be exorcised. Again, the churches teach that a person who is afflicted with cancer should maintain his/her faith in God, though the pain maybe unbearable. This is because the reward of the kingdom of heaven is obtained through pain, tribulations, and trials. Biblical references from the book of Job and the suffering of Jesus in the Gospels are read and interpreted so that the message suits the prevailing situation.

When a person is suffering from cancer, a lot of theological questions are asked such as "Why does God allow this to happen to our family member? Does God see us, does he hear us?" In order to fight the disease, members of the Pentecostal Church pray, lay hands on the sick, fast, and read the Scripture as a way of asking God to intervene and to strengthen the sick and the family. They may help to buy medicine if they are given the prescription from a doctor. If the medicine is purchased, they always pray before it is given to the patient.

Pentecostals believe that there is nothing impossible with God. He can even raise the dead from the grave. Great emphasis is placed on faith in order to fight the disease through the power of God. Many Pentecostal churches have healing schools which teach people about healing. People are taught to claim their healing from God. Healing is considered as a covenant promise made by God to the believer. It is one of the benefits of the believer in Christ. Healing is one of the benefits one gets for being a Pentecostal, but it must be claimed when one is sick. If claimed with faith, it is always given.

The Buddhist Response

SORAJ HONGLADAROM

The case of Eman is a sad situation in which a promising young clinician suffers from an incurable cancer. She has a loving husband and two lovely children, but her battle with the cancer is keeping her further and further away from her beloved career. Nonetheless, she is determined to carry on for as long as possible. She has not told her parents about her real condition, and presumably her own children have not been told that their mother is suffering from the incurable disease either.

It is really sad to see this kind of situation, but in real life this kind of thing happens all the time. Since Eman is a practicing Muslim, perhaps she realizes that the minds of human beings cannot fathom the infinite nature of God. Perhaps God has another design for her and the fact that she, a bright young doctor with a promising career with everything that a girl could hope for, is suffering from the disease is one of his unfathomable plans. She might also think that her decision to continue to fight the cancer and to continue as if life were still normal is also part of God's plan. She will continue to fight, but whether she ultimately succeeds or not (which is quite unlikely considering her present condition) is up to God.

Eman's attitude would not have been too different had she been a Buddhist instead. Instead of thinking about God, she would have been thinking of the law of *karma*, which states in general terms that everything that happens does so according to causes and conditions. Her present condition is a result of previous causes, which are so numerous that it is impossible to lay them out in any detail. She would have realized that the fact that the cancer happens to her instead of another person is a result of a long chain of causes and effects that stretch far beyond her own present lifetime. However, this is definitely not a chain of fatalism—she still has her own free will to decide, and in this case she has decided to continue to fight the cancer, trusting in the power of modern science that someday a cure might be developed which could save her. If she were a good Buddhist, she might have recalled one of the teachings of her Master that death is inevitable and the fact that a misery is happening to her right now could be a blessing because it means that her past negative *karma*s are bearing fruit right now. From now on she will be cleared of these negative *karma*s, and her path toward realization of the Ultimate Goal of Nirvana, or being released from the chain of samsara, will be much smoother.

Eman's decision to continue to fight the cancer would not contradict her Buddhist belief (had she been a Buddhist) because she has full trust in modern medicine. She knows what kind of consequences she will have to face as a result of her decision here and accepts them. Moreover, even though she realizes that the chance that such a miracle cure will be available on the market in a short period of time is quite minimal, she decides to fight on nonetheless. Buddhism would say that this is perfectly all right for her, because it shows her commitment to her career and, more importantly, her genuine desire to make herself useful to others in her role as an obstetrician. Since she has a pure motivation, she incurs a lot of positive *karma*s that will be very helpful to her later on.

Her decision to continue the fight might not be agreeable to other Buddhists, however; they might choose instead to enter into palliative care and start to prepare themselves for the ultimate end, and, of course, for their next lives. Since either decision does not violate the Buddhist precepts (neither of them causes negative *karma*s), Buddhism in general does not forbid either curative or palliative choice in this type of situation. As for the question whether the fact that Eman is a woman has anything to do with this issue, Buddhism would say that it has very little because gender is not relevant to the character of the karmic results of her action.

The Confucian Response

RUIPING FAN

This is another very sad case! Eman is a mother of two small children, and is also a brilliant young physician. But she is now found with an incurable metastatic breast cancer. Facing this case, a Confucian physician would inevitably recall the remarks made by Confucius on the incomprehensibility of the ultimate meaning of disease and death. Indeed, Confucius sees the final cause of life and death in the hand of the transcendent, or Heaven. He believes that "life and death have their determined appointment" (*Analects* 12:5). The meaning of such an appointment goes beyond the grasp of the finite knowledge of the human beings. When a virtuous student was found with a fatal disease, Confucius went to see him and sighed in sorrow: "It is the appointment of Heaven! That such a man should have such a sickness!" (*Analects* 6:8). Confucians "do not complain [of their suffering] against Heaven" (*Analects* 14:37). All they ought to do is attempt to help the sick in proper ways in specific cases like this one for Eman.

In this case, Eman wants more chemotherapy, even though it has made her hairless, riddled with pain, and shaking from fever, while her cancer has nonetheless already migrated to her backbone and liver. As a physician herself, she is definitely aware of what this state of affairs implies in the medical sense. But "she has faith she will beat this cancer." This can be understood as a wish to create a kind of miracle to cure the disease. More accurately, however, she is willing to endure more pain and symptom from the chemotherapy in order to gain more time to be with her relatives, specially her two small children. Does her decision to undertake more aggressive treatment invoke the issue of medical futility?

Confucians would not put aside her wish by reference to the consideration of medical futility. The reason is not that physicians should pursue a miracle—such a hope, even if religiously reasonable, is medically unreasonable. Nevertheless, a hope of extending her life through more chemotherapy is undoubtedly medically reasonable. From the story, we know that one of her central concerns is to care for her family members, especially her two small children. Confucianism sees such concerns most valuable and respectable. For Confucians, it is a shared familist way of life that is fundamentally important for authentic human existence. Accordingly, as long as it is medically indicated that more aggressive treatment will contribute to her survival, whether for one more month or one more year, the treatment cannot be considered medically futile. Eman and her family may reasonably judge whether the time gained is worth the pain suffered, but it is not an issue of futility.

This does not mean, however, that Confucianism would take this case primarily as a matter of personal autonomy, that is, as a matter that simply depends on Eman's self-determination, one way or another. Instead,

Confucians hold that proper medical decisions should be directed by moral autonomy, following the moral will.[1] The moral will is not the free expression of any arbitrary decision, but is the determination to will what is grounded in the way of Heaven (*tien dao*), such as the virtues of benevolence (*ren*) and righteousness (*yi*). Accordingly, the Confucian tradition does not grant any dominant personal autonomy regarding life-or-death decision making. Instead, the individual must be joined by the family members to make shared decisions in order to pursue the moral will, with each side—the patient and the family—carrying a veto power in the normal situation. This family-based approach to medical decision making can be supported by at least two Confucian reasons. First, since a patient is understood to be metaphysically and ethically inseparable from his or her family members, family members naturally possess a right to join the medical decision making. Second, a severely ill patient is easily overcome by extreme passions to require too much, too little, or too radical medical treatment than what should appropriately be undertaken. Family members' joining in medical decision making can help patients accomplish adequate determinations, realizing the proper, virtuous mutual care and interdependence of family members in conformity with the way of Heaven.

In this case, Eman's husband and her parents are clearly available close family members who also have a right to join the decision making. They should respect Eman's wish, but this does not mean that they should always follow her view. Suppose that after administering one more course of chemotherapy, Eman's condition worsens so that continuous aggressive treatment would imply only more suffering but no greater chances of survival. In such a case, her husband and parents should try to change her view and turn to palliative treatment. Physicians should appreciate and honor the right of the family to join the decision making and protect the medical interests of Eman.

The Evangelical Christian Response

JOHN GRAHAM

Eman was raised in a devout Muslim home, symbolized by the *hijab* which she wears to honor her parents. She is a 35-year-old physician and obstetrician-gynecologist, married with two children. Her life was all before her when she learned it might be cut short because she had a rapidly progressing, inflammatory form of breast cancer. Chemotherapy was tried but the cancer is unrelenting. She is in the hospital, in great pain, balding, and infected because chemotherapy has depressed her immune system. Yet, she has not lost hope, she has faith she will "beat this cancer."

Although Eman is Muslim, in every way she fits the picture of people of all faiths who struggle with an illness that threatens to cut life short. I have known many Evangelical Christians who have had the same experience and, like Eman, they too have expressed faith that they will "beat this cancer." And, on occasion, I have seen Evangelical Christians who did not want others to know the severity of the illness.

In the story as given, we are not told the reason Eman can say she has "faith" she will beat this cancer. What is the source of her faith? Is it in medicine, or in herself, or the love she has for her children (a love that won't let go), or is it her faith in Allah? We are not told. However, the fact she "wants more treatment" because she has two little children to care for, may indicate her faith is in medicine—that the right chemotherapy combination will arrest the spread of her cancer. Evangelical Christians may also not have identified the source of the faith they have that they will beat "this cancer."

If I were Eman's pastor, I would want to talk with her about where she has placed her faith. Biblically speaking, a believer's faith is to be focused ultimately on God; to have the assurance that God is present and—if it is God's will—that God will intervene (miraculously, if necessary) to bring forth healing, even if medical science has nothing to offer. Evangelical Christians who have studied the Bible intently are aware that Jesus and his disciples healed all manner of disease (Luke 6:19; 10:8–9). Some Evangelicals say the age of miracles ended with the canonization of the Bible. Yet, most Evangelicals pray for others to be healed; and when they are sick, they ask others to pray for them. For many, the expectation is always present that, even at the last minute, God will heal them, to His honor and glory.

It may be important to help Eman to see that, although God uses medical science as one instrument to heal people, the ultimate healing instrument God has is eternal life.

The other thing I see in Eman's story is that she did not feel comfortable to tell her parents that she had an incurable cancer. She simply told them that she was "ill." Surely they will know, but one has to wonder why she could not share this with her parents. Perhaps she wanted to shield them from pain but, by not telling them the truth, she may have shielded herself from the intimacy that only her mother could give. The same is true for her own children. In the story as presented, I don't see where Eman and her husband have shared with their children the seriousness of her illness. As their pastor, I would encourage her to consider doing that.

Evangelical Christianity would not demand Eman continue curative-oriented treatment if there is no indication of it being effective and if the side effects and continued hospitalization make it difficult for her to be with her family the last remaining days of her life. Yet, that is a decision only she can make. As her pastor, I would encourage her to put the remaining days of her life in the hands of God and to seek God's Will. I would hope she could put her trust in God rather than in medicine, which is no longer effective and, in fact, has depleted her immune response. This doesn't mean she must go home. She may need to remain in the hospital to receive pain-alleviating medications, but her loved ones may be more accessible were she moved to a palliate care unit or to a hospice.

This brings up the issue as to when to begin end-of-life care. Eman is in the hospital and a multidisciplinary consultation with her oncologists and a Palliative Care Team (including clergy, an imam) is the most effective way to improve end-of-life care. As her pastor, I would encourage her to seek consultation of this kind to help her and her husband make the best decisions in the days ahead. Most importantly, her children should be included, so that they can receive the counseling they will need now and upon losing their mother. All of her loved ones need to know when it is time to say goodbye. A multidisciplinary consultation, including clergy, can help make these kinds of decisions.

Evangelical Christianity speaks of a "good death," meaning, at the end of life, to submit one's life into the hands of God, to be at peace knowing one's sins are forgiven, and to look expectantly to eternity with God and Jesus Christ, who promises to receive her into glory. According to a 2000 Debate of the Age Health and Care Study Group, reported in the British Journal of Medicine,[2] a "good death" will include:

- knowing when death is coming, and understanding what can be expected
- being able to retain control of what happens
- being afforded dignity and privacy
- having control over pain relief and other symptom control
- having choice and control over where death occurs (at home with family and friends, or elsewhere)
- having access to information and expertise of whatever kind is necessary
- having access to any spiritual or emotional support required
- having access to hospice care in any location, not only in hospital
- having control over who is present and who shares the end
- being able to issue advance directives which ensure wishes are respected
- having time to say goodbye as well as having control over other aspects of timing
- being able to leave when it is time to go, and not to have life prolonged pointlessly

These twelve principles can be incorporated into health care services for end-of-life care organizations and institutions. And, none of the above conflict with the principles of Evangelical Christianity. The list includes "having access to spiritual and emotional support," which acknowledges the need for pastoral counseling as the end of life approaches. Most importantly, a "good death" is to die in the warm embrace of one's loved ones, with the firm assurance that one's eternal destiny is with a loving God.

The Hindu Response

UMA MYSOREKAR

Hinduism is one of the oldest and largest religions, with over a billion followers all over the world. Hinduism also known as universal religion, and Sanatana Dharma teaches that all living beings are manifestations of Supreme Brahman or Ultimate Reality and that Atman or the individual soul is divine and eternal. Hinduism influences all aspects of its adherents' lives every single day.

Hindus believe that, as all streams and rivers lead to the same ocean, all genuine religious (spiritual) paths lead to the same goal. Worship of every form of "GOD" and celestial forces leads to the same God. Each one is allowed to pray to and worship a formed or a formless deity according to one's own knowledge, desire, need, and spiritual elevation. Hindus believe that God will come to them in every form desired, and they pray according to their needs and wishes.

One of the principles of Hinduism is the Law of *Karma*. *Karma* means not only action, but also the result of an action. The consequence of an action is really not a separate thing. It is a part of the action, and cannot be divided from it. Breathing, thinking, talking, seeing, hearing, eating, and so on, are different kinds of *karmas*.

Eman's story is indeed tragic. She is a woman, a wife, a mother, and a physician facing the challenges of survival in the face of an inevitable terminal illness.

Hinduism views suffering as an integral part of human life. It is firmly believed that suffering, aging, sickness, and death are afflictions of human life from which mankind finds no escape except by way of liberation. In Eman's case, her suffering is intensified due to her strong attachment to her daughter. Attachment is the cause of bondage and sorrow. She wanted to be an ideal mother giving the best for her daughter, although she knew especially as a physician that the odds were against her. She was hoping against hope. The Hindu scriptures teach that suffering is a result of past *karma*, and therefore one has to endure it with detachment and acceptance, keeping faith in God and performing actions as an obligatory duty and sacrificial offering to God. Intensifying one's faith in God and becoming more spiritual gives a person such as Eman the inner strength to face with courage the pains from the disease and the pain of bondage with her daughter. The outcome of spiritual living is to transcend both pleasure and pain.

Having accepted suffering, sickness, and so on as part of human life, Hinduism essentially teaches the way to live with suffering. The resolution to suffering only comes with the experience of God. It is only when we become identified with the spirit that suffering ends. This is the way Hindu philosophy helps one to cope with suffering. Hindu philosophy also encourages worshiping with devotion through many practices such as *poojas*, yoga, and the study of sacred scriptures such as the *Upanishads*, the *Vedas*, the *Bhagavad Gita*, and so on.

Prayer for health is a highly prevalent practice among Hindus. People who use prayers for health concerns report high levels of perceived helpfulness. Prayers can intuitively take one closer to the solutions one needs to resolve the problems. Hinduism encourages one to live with a positive attitude that will give inherent strength to deal with the suffering. Special *poojas* services are performed in temples for the sick, and many times family members take part in these services. Joint family systems are fairly common among Hindus, and this is a great source of strength for a sick person like Eman, as she will feel confident that her dear daughter will be well looked after even after she is gone.

Many Hindus may want to use alternate therapy such as meditation, Ayurveda, and homeopathy. These may be encouraged along with the conventional therapy.

Spiritual healing (faith healing) refers to the process of caring for diseases of the body or mind with the help of faith. It is a fairly well known fact that, in the healing process, the attitude of mind plays an important role. A spiritual attitude helps to create a healthy mind and reduce anxieties and worries. Spiritual practices such as prayers, meditation, and so on are found beneficial because they improve the inner strength needed to fight the disease. Family plays a great role in giving a patient like Eman the moral strength she needs. Hindu families are resolved to help to use this strength to reaffirm their belief that life does not really end with death. This, therefore, continuously helps to uplift her spiritually to face death with dignity and to be fearless; and it also constantly reassures her that her dear children will be well taken care of.

The Indigenous Response

IRENE TAAFAKI

Marshallese (Ri-Majōl) will do all possible to continue curative-oriented treatment and go to extraordinary lengths to explore all options for a recovery. They relate closely to a patient who has faith that she will beat progressive cancer, which is a disease unfortunately quite familiar to Marshallese people after the eleven years of nuclear testing post-World War II. Options, arranged by the family on behalf of the patient, will include the use of traditional medicines, relocating the patient to find the best treatment environment for healing to take place, and spiritual healing through supplication and prayer.

Ri-Majōl retain great confidence in their traditional medicines, and herbal remedies are often a first resort when serious illness is suspected or diagnosed.

Once allopathic treatments commence, traditional remedies will also be taken alongside western treatments such as chemotherapy. Considerable effort is made to send Marshallese herbs and herbal preparations long distances to treat patients in hospitals overseas. Stories about the efficacy of traditional medicine in offsetting the negative side effects of chemotherapy support their use, and one of the key purposes of the Cancer Survivors Support Group is to disseminate information on such treatments. Ri-Majōl are well aware of the skeptical attitude towards such traditional treatments among Western-trained doctors using mainstream treatments, and will more often than not keep this self-medication secret.

> B:You were taking the local medicine.
> Mac: Iaar jab kwalok [I didn't tell].
> Mi: We don't tell them.

Ri-Majōl also hold strong belief in the "right place" for healing to occur. If a patient is not responding to treatment in one location, then another will be chosen. In the past this might involve movement from one house to another, from the side of the lagoon to the center of the island, as directed by the traditional healer. Nowadays, as finances allow, the family will facilitate this movement from hospital to hospital, or even further—arranging for treatment in Majuro, Manila, Hawaii, or the US mainland in the hope of a cure.

In former times, healing prayers and chants were uttered over the patient by spiritual healers known as *ri-allōk* prior to or during the administration of traditional medicine. Patient safety was further ensured by having a traditional healer remain with the sick. By not leaving the patient alone, family members could ensure that the patient's spirit would not be taken away. Now, as a strongly religious and predominantly Christian community, prayer is said before the administration of medicine. Priests and pastors as well as family members will engage in morning and evening prayer, whether at home or in hospital—a practice known as *nokin*. Constant accompaniment (*Kōrwane*) with the patient remains essential. In some cases a combination of traditional and Christian practice will be quite acceptable. Other forms of traditional healing by those understood to possess "the gift" will include therapies to remove pain, and though largely palliative, are believed to work and contribute to the healing process.

When a cancer patient understands that the disease has metastasized, recognizes that there is no hope and the inevitability of death, then acceptance occurs. This sometimes requires the patients themselves to convince their families to recognize the futility of further treatment. It would be highly unlikely for this to be in reverse. A family would never ask the patient to acknowledge the futility of any further treatment and the inevitability of their death. Not only would this be regarded hastening death *bwijerro* (see Chapter 12) but the family always maintains faith in a miracle.

At the point of acceptance, the family will continue to ensure every possible attention to the palliative care of the patient. This extends to informing physically distant close and extended family members so that they can make arrangements to say their farewells, and the need to support the immediate family of the terminally ill. For those living outside the Marshall Islands, arrangements will include practical considerations such as the availability of accommodation outside of the medical facility.

As a matrilineal society, the Marshall Islands values women, sustains their rights, and recognizes their equal partnership with men. There would be no distinction in the extent a family would go to in order to find an effective treatment for any member, whether male or female, infant or elderly.

The Jewish Response

HERBERT BROCKMAN

Eman's response to her tragic illness seems both culturally and religiously informed. And although the medical profession must focus on the methodologies of treatment options and the statistics of survival or cure, it is clear that much more is involved—especially for Eman in her role as physician, daughter, wife, and mother. The decisions about treatment or non-treatment will be hers and hers alone. Those who care for her and about her will gently "accompany" her on her journey.

First, Eman regards her work "delivering babies" as essential. Her insistence on continuing this life-giving and life-affirming effort by receiving chemotherapy despite suffering the accompanying debilitating effects, suggests how important this is to her. Even when it became clear that the disease had spread, she continued to seek ways "to beat this cancer," to hope, "since she has two little children to care for...."

Whereas to some this may seem naïve and wistful, Eman can continue to find ways "to care for" her children. I often wonder whether a patient's acceptance of the "reality" of his or her circumstances is at least as much for the family and caregivers as it is for the patient herself. An anonymous poet wrote:

My strength gives less and less
Be good to me, be good to me
Be my narrow bridge across a sad abyss,
Across the sadness of my days....

How can one help to be that "narrow bridge?" Perhaps the answer lies in helping the patient see her role beyond death, through the process of preparing her family, especially her children, to see that sadness and hope need not be contradictions. Sharing both can be vital. Even when finally there is acceptance, dying need not be a passive acceptance; it can be active and influential.

I shall never forget one of the first patients I visited at the Baltimore Cancer Research Center. As I entered her room, taking note of the frail person in the bed, bald from her therapy, I introduced myself. Her husband, who had been standing nearby, immediately left the room. The patient turned to me and asked, "Rabbi, when you die, what do you do with your shoes?" For a moment I was taken aback. I had had no training in a hospital setting. Only the truth loomed before me. "Well, I don't know," I managed to get out. "But actually there is a tradition in Judaism that shoes especially were to be given away only to strangers, to those in need. Even in death, perhaps especially, it is important to find ways for the living to benefit."

She looked at me for a moment. "Thank you rabbi—thank you for talking to me about dying. No one else will. When I asked my husband, about dying, he just said, 'Stop that! You're going to make it!' He then went and called the nurse. She came in and asked, 'Can I help you dear?' When I told her I was dying she immediately left the room and within a moment a doctor entered. He introduced himself as Dr So-and-So, a psychiatrist. I told him, 'Thank you doctor, but I'm not crazy, I'm dying.' Thank you, rabbi, for being willing to talk to me about dying"

For the next month I visited the woman several times a week. I told her about the difference between passive dying and active dying, that she could still find ways to be active and influential.

Judaism teaches that there are two realms that exist: the earthly and the heavenly. It is we, human beings, who are entrusted with "completing" the original creation here on earth while the heavenly is God's realm. The two are connected by mystery.

Islam, too, envisions the idea of two realms. Eman's "ground of being," whether an active part of her personal faith or not, can be a present reality. In Judaism, we are taught, "Though you may not complete the task, neither are you free to desist from it."[3] Exploring ways with Eman "to complete the task," to leave a legacy to her family, especially for her children, can be life-affirming.

How to do this? In Jewish tradition, along with preparing a "last-will-and-testament," and the more recent "living will," we find an older tradition that became known in the Middle Ages as an "Ethical Will." Whereas the first describes how one's tangible assets are to be distributed upon death, and the second records the individual's end-of-life decisions, the ethical will is meant to pass on one's values, blessings, life lessons, hopes, and dreams.

Helping patients prepare such testaments empowers them. It assures that their life-giving influence will continue. In this case, Eman's maternal voice will continue to influence her children long after her passing. Perhaps, in this unexpected way, Eman will "beat this cancer." And in this knowledge will be both sadness and the hope for which we all search.

The Mainline Protestant Christian Response

JAN HOLTON

At the heart of this narrative is the tension between the power of belief, or faith, and medical science. Like those from traditions around the world, Eman's life is surrounded from beginning to end with religious faith. As a doctor, Eman has built her profession on the power of medicine to alleviate suffering and bring good to the world. In spite of this, as a person of faith, when facing a terminal diagnosis, she does not yield to science alone but holds to a belief that *faith* is not only the greatest good but also her greatest weapon.

Like Eman's experience, most mainline Protestant denominations believe that science and medicine are not contrary to religious faith but are, in and of themselves, gifts from God. Advances in medical science have improved the likelihood of surviving catastrophic injury as well as progressive diseases. We benefit from science in terms of overall longevity and quality of life. Medicine can, however, also prolong life without attention to quality, thus extending life-saving efforts or curative treatment beyond what is appropriate or even desired. It takes great wisdom and diligent efforts of discernment to distinguish between benefit and excess. Care, therefore, can and should be taken that end-of-life decisions are made in consultation with patients, physicians, families, and religious professionals.

Spiritual care providers should consider why Eman holds onto the hope of restored health in spite of medical evidence to the contrary *and* her resistance to telling loved ones of the terminal diagnosis. How might these be connected? For many, the belief in the power of God to restore one's health is connected to a positive outcome—getting well. To question one is to question faith in the other. To make matters more difficult, the decision to accept death risks being perceived as a betrayal of love itself—a giving up on life with those whom one loves.

In mainline Protestantism, however, there is more one faithful response to progressive and terminal disease. Indeed, accepting death, making the decision to end curative treatment, and acknowledging God's faithful presence in, through, and after death can all be expressions of the faithful life. Christians believe that, even when faced with the fragility of human life, we can still claim victory over death through the sacrifice made in the death and resurrection of Jesus Christ. Even at the end of life, God is active and present. God never abandons God's beloved people.

The human reality of grief, however, remains. It is an overwhelming task for any mother to comprehend the idea that she will not live to see her children grow up. It is an understandable response to wish to protect one's children from the terrible reality of a parent's death. Being a parent herself may even increase Eman's desire to protect her own parents from the truth of her diagnosis. Nonetheless, should she choose to openly accept her death and invite her loved ones into this sacred time, they gain the opportunity to witness the power of love and hope to persevere in the face of loss. Ultimately, though, it will remain Eman's choice.

Prayer is a long-held tradition among many religions, including mainline Protestants. Whereas some denominations rely on traditional written liturgies, others prefer extemporaneous prayers drawn from the immediate context. In a situation such as Eman's, either form of prayer can be an effective means for the act of *naming,* that is, giving voice to the struggles of illness, the witness and love of family and community, and resistance to or the acceptance of approaching death. Tradition declares that through prayer we are connected to generations of Christian believers who have gone before. Prayer allows one to name both fear and possibility while lifting all to the heart and mystery of God's power in healing. Although it may be our inclination to focus the desire for healing on the physical body, tradition and sacred Christian texts remind us that God's healing comes in many forms, the ultimate of which is revealed to us when we are received into God's presence after death. Prayer and other rituals help frame the human experience, especially suffering and death, with hope and possibility by giving voice to the realities of the present situation, articulating feelings of the one who is ill and his or her loved ones, and framing all within the presence and love of a faithful God.

The Shi'a Muslim Response

NAJMEH JAFARI

Eman's story is a familiar tragedy for me and reminds me of the moments I was working as a spiritual healer of Muslim women with breast cancer. Like Eman, most of my patients believe that they will fight cancer and that God will help them in this hard situation. This belief originates from their religious perspectives. As a "Muslim woman," Eman believes that death does not happen except by God's permission; "Nor can a soul die except by Allah's leave, the term being fixed as by writing" (Qur'an 3:145). So, if God wants her to survive, surely she will live more.

She has been a productive woman at work and home. She is the mother of two young children. Hence, she has enough reasons to survive. She hopes to survive because she believes that God has created a treatment for every illness, as said the Prophet Mohammad: "Seek treatment, for every illness God created a treatment."[4] Therefore, it is a mutual responsibility of the patient and physician to do everything possible to prevent premature death.

Muslims believe that the real healer is God. In the *Qur'an* (26:80), the Prophet Abraham is quoted as saying: "And when I am ill, it is He Who cures me." Indeed, one of the names of God is "the Healer" (al-Shafi). Eman may seek help from God and search for her cure in spiritual moments. She will pray because she believes that God will be with her, as God said in the *Qur'an* (2:153): "O ye who believe! seek help with patient perseverance and prayer; for Allah is with those who patiently persevere."

Eman wants to continue her treatment and every moment of life is precious for her. She wants to live to deliver more babies as an obstetrician, to care for her children as a mother, and to be a good wife for her spouse. But when the disease progress, Eman and her family may find the curative treatment is futile, and in this step she has to accept God's will and start her journey to Allah. "To God We belong, and to Him is our return" (Qur'an 2:156). She knows that death is a part of the overall divine plan and a transition to another, higher form of life: "We have decreed Death to be your common lot, and We are not to be frustrated, from changing your Forms and creating you (again) in (forms) that ye know not" (Qur'an 56:60–61). Muslims are encouraged to be ready for the moment of death.

Eman's suffering at the end of life can be seen as the divine will for her purification and spiritual maturity. The Prophet Mohammad said: "Hours of sickness sweep away hours of sins."[5] This interpretation helps Eman and her family to cope with this life-threatening illness. However, this does not mean that the pain should not be alleviated. Every effort should be made to meet her physical, psychological, and spiritual needs. She needs medication to alleviate pain and opportunities for communication with family members, as well as spiritual healing. Spiritual care in this situation helps Eman to maintain her balance, calmness, and general wellbeing. This may provide a chance for her to remember God, seek God's help with patience and prayer, and ask for forgiveness. She may need to pray in mosque, read or have read aloud to her the *Qur'an* or other religious literature in hospital, or have a visit from an Imam. Health care providers should consider these spiritual needs and maximize their efforts to support her in carrying out her religious rituals. Furthermore, her spouse, mother, and father are in need of religious support, and health care providers can encourage them to pray for their beloved one. Group prayers for Eman, by family members and friends (if it is possible in the hospital setting) may help them to resolve their own fear and distress.

The Sunni Muslim Response

TARIQ RAMADAN

Eman, a 35-year-old professional woman, wife, and mother of two very young children has been diagnosed with an incurable form of cancer that, after two cycles of chemotherapy treatment, has now moved to the bones in her back and her liver. Eman wants to continue with curative-orientated treatment despite both her obvious physical suffering and pain and the advice from her physician that such treatment is now futile because the medical facts verify that the disease has reached an irreversible stage.

In such a sensitive situation, it is important to be aware of the existing knowledge of the patient, her religious background, and her cultural environment. Yet, from an Islamic perspective, although it is very important to consider all these factors collectively, the crucial starting point is to obtain the correct medical facts. So here it is critical for the hospital physicians to honestly inform Eman about her exact situation and to explain all the options available for her future care. Every patient has the right to be informed—correctly, promptly, and with clarity. In this case study this is even more poignant because the patient is a physician—she can understand more complex medical details about the nature of the current and future stages of her terminal disease and should therefore be informed to an equivalent level in order to have as valuable a picture as possible to enable her to evaluate her situation and consider her options for future treatment and care.

Beyond gaining knowledge of the facts and the patient being informed of their specific situation is the need to respect the patient's autonomy. This autonomy is founded on two factors. The first is to respect Eman's religious background and get a sense of her surrounding culture. For example, the fact that Eman has discussed her medical situation to varying degrees of detail with different members of her family (husband, parents, children) and her oncologist is important. Also, through her religious background, growing up in a traditional Muslim family, Eman maintains hope through her faith in God that she will beat this cancer. However, keeping hope in the name of one's religious principles needs to be balanced with the second factor—having a clear understanding of the medical facts from the doctors. Islam teaches it is necessary for believers to face science and acknowledge the facts, so to keep hope in God to go beyond nature is not always the right translation of the Islamic understanding of God's will. It is instead about the need to face reality and, in so doing, to try to find the best way of spending the remaining time that one has with the people one loves and at the same time to prepare one's family for the inevitable—the fact that one's life with them is soon to come to an end. Muslims believe that human life is not one's only life and that there may be something beyond this life which is the secret of God's will. So at some point Eman may be able to accept her circumstances and seek further comfort from her faith, relying upon God's will and hoping that there is a meaning in having the cancer beyond the limitation of her human rationality. For Eman, with confirmation from her doctors that her treatment is not working, it may be time not only to keep hope beyond the facts, but moreover to be ready to accept the facts and find a way to deal with her situation as best she can and try to spread patience and understanding for her family.

Eman should be encouraged to consider all the options on the basis of the plain facts. There are two options for Eman. First, beyond the facts, she can continue to hope that it is possible to reverse the irreversible and decide to continue with curative treatment. Indeed, within mainstream Islamic tradition, it is acceptable for Muslims to find whatever way possible, and receive whatever means, to be cured of a disease. This is how Eman appears to have been dealing with her situation until now. It is also acceptable within Islam for the patient to change his or her mind about treatment at any stage. For example if Eman were to decide that the treatment that she is receiving is making her feel too poorly and is too much to cope with, she can stop that treatment.

With Eman suffering so much now, and because the treatment is not working, it is becoming more and more difficult for her and her family to bear. This is when Eman's husband (and even perhaps her parents) could become involved and talk with Eman. This could enable them all to acknowledge that they are each struggling with a situation which is not going to improve; that the facts confirm the disease is irreversible and that Eman is suffering unnecessarily. Within Islam, a second option of palliative treatment is acceptable here. Such treatment is designed to relieve symptoms and make the patient as comfortable as possible, while at the same time acknowledging the irreversibility of the disease—keeping hope but at the same time dealing with the situation and opting for end-of-life care to ease the suffering of the patient. Seeing Eman suffering less and being slightly more comfortable could help the family to come to terms with the situation. This is also part of a deep faith, where "faith" is not to hope in something beyond nature but to accept the natural reality and the way that Eman's situation is now evolving towards her own death. So, if cure is really not possible, then in Islam it is acceptable for the patient to receive all available contemporary medical means to manage and lower the level of suffering, depending on the guidance of the attending physicians.

Mainstream Islamic teachings also accept and respect a patient's decision if he or she does not want to seek a cure or accept medical treatment for remedy or pain-relief and just wants to accept this disease as a test from God, a message that life is to end and to use these thoughts in a spiritual way, in a journey to become closer to God. However there can be no attitude of fatalism, and the majority of Islam religious experts (scholars) encourage patients to accept medical treatment to manage their suffering as the disease progresses, especially in end-of-life care.

In summary, the first critical factor is for the patient to acquire all the facts and to be informed about them and know exactly from a medical viewpoint what the next stages are. Next, it is important to respect the autonomy of the patient and, while taking into consideration any religious principles and cultural environment of the patient, to give hope but to make it clear that this hope cannot go against the facts. In facing the facts, the patient has the two options—curative or palliative treatment. This is where the family and patient should take an agreed decision and try to think not only about the way in which the patient must deal with her own fate but also about the way she can help her family to deal with the reality. Any state of denial here in the name of faith, although understandable, could be counterproductive. In Islam, faith is not to deny the facts but instead to address them and try to give them meaning. In this instance, palliative care might be a better option for Eman from an Islamic viewpoint, but all this should only be proposed and not imposed on her, always respecting that the next steps of care should ultimately be the patient's personal decision, in discussion with his or her family. During difficult times such as these, acceptance by everyone involved of the inevitable can only truly be achieved through respecting autonomy, by communication, and through understanding of the deep teachings and lessons that we draw upon from our individual faiths and cultures.

The Roman Catholic Response

CAROL TAYLOR

Had Eman been raised in a traditional Catholic family, she would thank God every day for the blessings of a loving family (parents, spouse, and children), an excellent education, and meaningful work as an obstetrician. Disciplined, hard working, and virtuous, she would know that all these are gifts from a loving God. As she learns that her inflammatory breast cancer is metastasizing and the probability of cure is remote, she may begin to question God's love and mercy or wonder why God's tender hand of blessing is no longer gently resting on her. How could a loving God allow her to die when she has two young children to love and raise?

Although Eman's professional caregivers must work diligently to continue to treat her cancer and infections, they face the greater challenge of ministering to her suffering. As she learns that her hope for a cure is no longer realistic, Eman is likely to despair and raise anguished questions about meaning and worth. If Eman derives her value from being a mother to Amina and Kahlid, now three and two years old, a wife, a dutiful daughter, and a competent and compassionant physician—and all this is threatened by the cancer that has weakened her—her suffering will be intense. Cassell defines suffering as the distress humans experience when their integrity and self is threatened.[6]

For a Roman Catholic, learning that life is finite raises questions about what ultimately gives meaning and purpose to our existence. In the encyclical *Spe Salvi* Benedict XVI writes:

> We need the greater and lesser hopes that keep us going day by day. But these are not enough without the great hope, which must surpass everything else. This great hope can only be God, who encompasses the whole of reality and who can bestow upon us what we by ourselves cannot attain.... [Our] great, true hope which holds firm in spite of all disappointments can only be God—God who has loved us and who continues to love us "to the end," until all "is accomplished (cf. John 13:1 and 19:30)."[7]

The Catholic health care ministry witnesses to the belief that God has created each person for eternal life.

Pastor Ted Creen describes hope as the ingredient in life that enables an individual both to consider a future and to actively bring that future into being.[8] Hope has the capacity to embrace the reality of the individual's suffering without escaping from it (false hope) or being suffocated by it (despair, helplessness, hopelessness). Professional caregivers can help Eman to envision a future beyond the here and now and to use the time and energy she has to meet the universal spiritual needs of meaning and purpose, love and relatedness, and forgiveness.

The critical clinical question for Eman is whether and when to transition from cancer treatment to purely palliative goals. The Ethical and Religious Directives for Catholic Health Care Services address the stewardship we have over human life. "We are not owners of our lives and do not have absolute power over human life. We have a duty to preserve our life and to use it for the glory of God, but the duty to preserve life is not absolute, for we may reject life-prolonging procedures that are insufficiently beneficial or excessively burdensome."[9] Continuing chemotherapy is morally optional for Eman but professional caregivers have an obligation to talk with Eman about whether or not cancer treatment offers a reasonable hope of benefit that balances the burdens she is experiencing. In their deliberations, caregivers are guided by their commitment to respect the inherent dignity of human life in all its dimensions. Directives 56 and 57 offer precise language:[9]

> 56. A person has a moral obligation to use ordinary or proportionate means of preserving his or her life. Proportionate means are those that in the judgment

of the patient offer a reasonable hope of benefit and do not entail an excessive burden or impose excessive expense on the family or the community.

57. A person may forgo extraordinary or disproportionate means of preserving life. Disproportionate means are those that in the patient's judgment do not offer a reasonable hope of benefit or entail an excessive burden, or impose excessive expense on the family or the community.

Eman herself and her family and professional caregivers and ministers can pray for a cure, for research advances that dictate new treatment options, or for God's will. If Eman's cancer continues to advance, prayers for a happy death can be prayed.

The Sikh Response

SURJEET KAUR CHAHAL

Eman's case is a typical case of faith in God's miraculous powers. Despite the odds, Eman has faith that she will be able to fight the disease and will be cured. She is aware that normally it is difficult for a patient in her situation to get cured. However, a patient like Eman would be quite justified in having faith in the belief that God will cure her. According to Sikhism, if God has created this body, he can always cure the patient.

As far as the decision of Eman to continue curative treatment is concerned, it is very much acceptable as per the Sikh tenets. Her decision is motivated by her desire to look after her children, to care for them. It is based on her desire to do her best; whatever she can for her children. What matters in Sikhism is not the outcome but the motive of the action. Whether she can do much or not, she has a desire, an intention to look after her children. In spite of all the pain and suffering caused by chemotherapy she still wants to continue with curative care, for she puts duty before self.

In a medical sense, treatment may be futile, but the hope that it may cure or the hope that God's wondrous ways may cure her is a very important consideration. In such a situation, the concerned patient usually prays to God to cure him/her. Besides personal prayer, more importantly in Sikhism, a congregational prayer is almost always performed, wherein the entire congregation in the *Gurdwara* (the Sikh place of worship) prays for the patient to get cured. Additionally, groups or friends go the patient's house/bedside in the hospital and pray for his/her recovery. All this has a great curative effect on the patient and also more importantly it helps the patient emotionally.

After repeated chemotherapies, if Eman realizes that she can no more be of much use to her children and, rather, her children are being neglected because the family members have now to attend to her, end-of-life care treatment should begin. However, there are no strict guidelines. It all depends on the case and the decision of the patient, which must be respected.

However, there are certain other attitudes too. The concerned patients may pray and not ask for cure but for strength to accept God's Will. A patient may accept the Will of God and pray that whatever he does is acceptable as sweet and pray for strength to accept God's Will. The Gurus regarded suffering as a result of a person's *karma*. Sikhism believes in the theory of *Karma*. According to the theory of *Karma*, in this life we are reaping the fruits of *karmas* or deeds which we have done in this birth or in earlier births, because Sikhism believes in the theory of rebirth and reincarnation.

Devout Sikhs believe that they must have the moral courage to bear the suffering without sinking into pain and grief. A person should pray for the grace of God to enable him or his family members to put up with pain in the spirit of acceptance and surrender.

The Unitarian Universalist Response

JAN K. NIELSEN

If a mother's worst fear is that she will live to bury a child, her second worst fear is that something will happen to her before she has seen her children through a safe passage to adulthood. Eman achieved her dream of becoming a physician and, though she continued her practice delivering babies through two cycles of chemotherapy, the cancer has now spread in her body. Eman wants to do everything she can to survive for her young and beloved children, Amina and Khalid. Despite her knowledge that her cancer is incurable, Eman is determined to continue treatment; she has faith that she will beat the cancer.

A spiritual caregiver might begin by allowing Eman to tell, and perhaps retell several times, her story. All she may share—her profound grief, her fears, her deep love for her children, her questions and beliefs about life and faith—should be held by the compassionate presence of someone willing to listen without judgment. The caregiver should neither attempt to impose any agenda to persuade Eman to end treatment nor to offer advice about her desire to continue treatment. Eman's life has been turned upside down; cancer has robbed her both of her dream of raising her children and of a sense of control over her life. Right now, one of the few ways Eman can exercise control is through her determination to continue treatment, and her children give her two very good reasons to want to survive. No one should try to coerce away from Eman that last bit of control, and hope.

After listening deeply to Eman and taking time to get to know her spiritual perspectives, a spiritual caregiver might ask Eman if she would like to share in a time of meditation or prayer. A spoken prayer for Eman might ask that she find within herself the wisdom and courage to make wise and loving decisions and the strength to do what is right. A caregiver might then talk with Eman about what it means to have faith. From a Unitarian Universalist perspective, faith can mean giving one's heart, perhaps to a person or to one's most cherished values and hopes. Eman is giving her heart to her dream of living to see her children grow up. A caregiver might invite Eman to give her heart also to the understanding that, even if her body is unable to beat the cancer and she dies, her love for her children will continue to embrace them for the rest of their lives for, as the poets of the ages teach, love is stronger than death.

While Eman is still able to make decisions about her care, her spiritual caregiver might invite her to think about her spiritual legacy—what she would like to pass on to her children. Someone might offer to record Eman speaking to her children, or she might write or dictate letters to her children, sharing her thoughts about life, her most cherished values, and her hopes for their lives, as well as her deep and abiding love for each of them. This spiritual legacy, whether in the form of a video recording or a handwritten letter, could be the gift that allows Eman to let go of her body and make safe passage from this life with faith that both her legacy and her love will be with her children always.

REFERENCES

1. Chan J. Moral autonomy, civil liberties, and Confucianism. *Philosophy East and West*. 2002;*52*(3):281–310.
2. Smith R. A good death. *BMJ*. 2000;*320*(7228):129–130.
3. Goldin H. *Ethics of the Fathers*. New York: Hebrew Publishing Company; 1962.
4. Majlesi MB. *Bihar al-Anwar*. Vol. 59. Beirut: Al-Vafa Institute; 1982:66.
5. Majlesi MB. *Bihar al-Anwar*. Vol. 67. Beirut: Al-Vafa Institute; 1982:262.
6. Cassell E. *The Nature of Suffering and the Goals of Medicine*. New York: Oxford University Press; 1991.
7. Benedict XVI. *Spe Salvi*. 2007. http://www.vatican.va/holy_father/benedict_xvi/encyclicals/documents/hf_ben-xvi_enc_20071130_spe-salvi_en.html. Accessed on July 17, 2013.
8. Creen T. *Moving Mountains or at Least Managing Them*. Belleville, ON: Essence Publishing; 2002.
9. National Conference of Catholic Bishops. *Ethical and religious directives for catholic health care services*. 5th ed. Washington, D.C.: U.S. Catholic Conference; 2009;*25*.

CHAPTER 12

When Dying May be a Long Process

Case

MARK LAZENBY, RUTH McCORKLE, DANIEL P. SULMASY

Martha had always been smart. Growing up in her tiny Texas town, she excelled at her studies. And when all the young men were off fighting wars, she went to university and earned a degree in chemistry. After college, she went to graduate school on a full scholarship at a prestigious university in Boston. She thrived on the vibrant intellectual life. She met Robert, a recent business school graduate. They married. And while Martha was finishing up her doctorate, she gave birth to their first child, Eleanor. Martha balanced Eleanor, all of ten months old, on her hip when she bent down to be hooded by her doctoral mentor. She was the first in her family to go to college. She was the first PhD her adoring parents had ever known.

Soon, two more children followed, Paul and Rachel. And Robert and Martha made the great migration to New York City, for Paul to take a job on Wall Street. The hustle of New York City energized her, and she happily fell into raising her children. In her spare time, she taught a college course here and there. After she got her children into high school, she took a full-time faculty position in the chemistry department at a prestigious college in the city. It was convenient, only a few blocks away from the apartment she and Robert had made their family home. As the years went on she made a few discoveries and wrote some important papers. But most of all, she was proud of her students. One of them had been short-listed for a Nobel Prize.

Over the years, her children graduated from high school and college, and had children of their own. Robert had had two open heart surgeries for clogged arteries. And then one day, he had a massive heart attack and died in the emergency room. At the time of her widowhood, Martha was 70, a grandmother eight times over, and still teaching.

She taught until she was 72. Always a devout Episcopalian who had taken her children with her to church as often as she could, she now threw herself into the work of her local parish. At church, she made sandwiches for the homeless one night a week, sewed clothes for children of lesser means, and served on the altar guild year after year.

Life had taken her three children all over the world. Paul, who had married a Nepalese woman he met in college, was living and working as a dentist in Katmandu. Rachel had moved to Geneva, where she and her partner had jobs in a NGO. And Eleanor, now divorced, lived on the other side of the country. A lawyer, Eleanor was busy with her practice and raising her two boys, one in college and the other a senior in high school.

Three years ago, a few women from the church phoned Eleanor. They had noticed that Martha was not bathing as often. Sometimes, they said, Martha would ask them to help her walk home; she had grown afraid of getting lost. Eleanor flew to New York right away. She took her mother to see a geriatrician for a full evaluation. Martha, the brilliant chemist and gifted teacher, now had Alzheimer's disease.

Martha protested that she could still live alone. But out of fear and concern, Eleanor hired help. First only a home-health aide was needed to stay during the day. But then Martha started wandering around the halls of the apartment building in her pajamas at night. More than once at bedtime the doorman had to take her back to her apartment. He tried to convince her as best he could that she lived in Number 9B. But Martha protested, "Don't be silly. I live in Texas. My daddy hitched the horse right over there. I know he did, but I just can't find it," she exclaimed with bewilderment. Eleanor then got round-the-clock care.

Eleanor could not cope anymore. The constant flying back-and-forth had taken its toll. And the expense of the care was too great. She asked Paul and Rachel if they could help, but neither had money to spare. She knew this. The expense of round-the-clock care, coupled with college tuition, nearly broke her. And she was emotionally wasted and physically washed up.

Martha's Alzheimer's disease was progressing. She had to be admitted to the hospital twice—once for a urinary tract infection and once for pneumonia. The pneumonia, the doctors told Eleanor, was due to her mother's uncoordinated swallowing, a consequence of her progressing disease. When Eleanor visited, Martha now needed to be reminded who she was. Martha then developed pneumonia again and was admitted to the hospital a third time.

Now 82 years old, emaciated, and demented, Martha is in the geriatrics ward on constant intravenous hydration. The geriatrician and geriatric nutritionist tell Eleanor, who has been sitting by her mother's bedside for the past 48 hours, that they must start intravenous nutrition in order to get her mother strong enough so that a feeding tube can be surgically placed into her stomach. "It is really unsafe to let her eat anymore. The food will just go down the wrong pipe and she'll develop pneumonia again," he says. Eleanor was saddened that she and her mother had never discussed this before; they never discussed what her mother would want if she were in these awful circumstances. But after speaking with her brother and sister, Eleanor tells the doctor that she cannot stand to see her brilliant mother in this condition. "All my siblings and I want is for Mother to be at peace," she tells the doctor. "Is a feeding tube really necessary? Isn't there any way you can give her something to make her slip away into sleep, I mean permanent sleep?" she asks.

The Clinical Issues

ASHLEY E. SHREVES, R. SEAN MORRISON

Mary's story illustrates the sad trajectory of Alzheimer's disease and related dementias, which are characterized by progressive and relentless declines in cognitive and physical function. One of the particular challenges of caring for persons with dementia is that they cannot direct their own medical care. Clinicians and families, thrust into the position of surrogate decision makers, are often poorly prepared to select from an ever-growing list of medical therapies and options.

Ideally, in the early stages of her disease, Mary would have engaged in discussions with her clinicians about the kind of care she wanted. Such a discussion would have focused on Mary's goals in the setting of her present state of health and her predictable future state of cognitive and functional decline. In this discussion clinicians might ask such questions as:

- "Tell me, what would be a 'fate worse than death for you'?"
- "What for you makes life worth living?"
- "If your disease progresses to the point that you can't feed yourself or have difficulty swallowing, would you want a feeding tube placed?"
- "Is there a state in which you could envision not wanting life-prolonging treatments, such as antibiotics or intravenous medication, and would instead want all efforts focused on comfort?"

Answers to these questions should be carefully documented and codified in legally recognized advance directives, such as a living will. Additionally, and perhaps most importantly, a surrogate decision maker should be identified and legally documented. Ideally, Mary would have designated her daughter her surrogate decision maker and, while she was still of sound mind, had a conversation about what kind of care she wanted. Healthy, community-dwelling older adults are fairly uniform in their treatment preferences when fully informed about advanced dementia, and this can be a useful surrogate to guide families confronting treatment options in the latter stages of the disease. About 90% want comfort-focused care *only*.[1,2] It is reassuring that Mary's daughter's request that her mother simply "be at peace" is thus, statistically, the most likely goal that her mother would have had for herself. Recognizing that alleviating symptoms is an appropriate and desirable goal for someone living with advanced dementia, Mary's daughter should assess all potential treatments for their ability to achieve that goal—the goal of comfort.

In the final stages of dementia, patients often lose interest in food or lose the ability to swallow.[3] Although these are medically anticipated complications, they often raise concerns about "starvation" and the suffering associated with that state. Whereas many families and clinicians are concerned that lack of nutritional intake in the setting of dementia and other serious illness is associated with "hunger pangs" and discomfort, it has been clearly demonstrated that patients near the end-of-life do not experience hunger and that feelings of thirst can be easily alleviated with good oral care.[4,5]

In addition, as swallowing dysfunction worsens, patients are at risk for swallowing food into the lungs and getting pneumonia.[6] Families are often asked to decide whether a feeding tube should be inserted into the stomach. And physicians often promote feeding tubes, saying that they reduce swallowing food into the lungs. However, they do not.[7] Tube feeding can even result in additional suffering from complications from the tube itself. And people being fed through a tube no longer experience the pleasure of tasting food—and doing so with other people at mealtimes. The question for Mary's daughter is, will tube feeding will alleviate her mother's suffering? Mary's daughter can be reassured that careful spoon feeding will both enhance Mary's quality of life and will be consistent with the treatment goal of providing comfort.

Mary's daughter's question regarding "something [to be given] to make her [mother] slip away" signifies an interest in exploring possibilities for active termination of her mother's life. In fact, it is not uncommon for patients to consider death a preferable alternative to Alzheimer's dementia.[8] Whatever one's views on euthanasia, Mary's suffering can be addressed. Palliative care is medical care that focuses on improving the quality of life for seriously ill persons and their families. Palliative care is provided by a team of interdisciplinary professionals—physicians, nurses, social workers, and chaplains, for example. The team provides an added layer of support to patients, families, and clinicians. The palliative care team focuses on reducing distressing physical, emotional, and spiritual symptoms. They also help patients and families establish realistic goals of care and match treatment to those goals. They even coordinate transitions across health care settings.[9] Thus, even in a situation such as Mary's, strategies and therapies exist to promote dignity and comfort.

The Ethical Issues

DANIEL CALLAHAN

One of the most important consequences of longer lives throughout the world is the increasing prevalence of chronic disease. Although cancer, heart disease, diabetes, and stroke pose a number of difficult medical, economic, and ethical problems, those posed by dementia (particularly Alzheimer's disease) are particularly complex. It is a lethal disease that attacks the brain and thus the personhood of its victim. It is slow-acting, with the dying process stretching out for some years in many cases. It places a particular burden, economic and psychological, on families and loved ones.

Four types of ethical issues arise in providing medical and family care.

Advance directives. What ethical obligations do we owe to dementia patients who have left no information about how they would want to be treated, or not treated, in that condition? Should such decisions be left to physicians alone, to patient families alone, or to a negotiation between patients and families? Does the difference between Alzheimer's and the other disease of aging mean that the choice of final decision makers should be different?

Initiation of artificial nutrition or hydration. If the prognosis for life extension is good for artificial nutrition or hydration, should it be initiated, using the same standards that might be used to determine treatment for someone with cancer or heart disease? But if the prognosis is extremely poor, is that course of medical and ethical benefit? Or is there something different about artificial nutrition and hydration, closer to forms of ordinary nutrition and comfort care, that means it ought to be provided whatever the circumstances? And what about associated infections, such as urinary infections treatable with antibiotics, or kidney failure (ordinarily requiring dialysis)?

Persistent vegetative state. A condition brought to mind by considerations of Alzheimer's disease is the persistent vegetative state, with either no, or extremely low, probability of ever coming out of that condition—thus definitively putting that person beyond any meaningful inner life (so far as can be determined) or interaction with family members. Should such patients be maintained on artificial nutrition and hydration? Should associated infections or other threats to life be treated? Should such patients be treated as if they are the same as dead, or, if not, to what extent?

Assisted suicide or euthanasia. Assisted suicide is not possible in this case, since Mary herself cannot take an overdose of medicine prescribed to end her life. Only euthanasia, the direct taking of a patient's life by a physician, is possible. If it is illegal in a country, would it be ethical for a physician to do it and take his or her chances with the law? What if one knows there is a practice, not openly acknowledged but common, to simply increase the dosage of opioids to a lethal, not easily detectible, level? Would it be right for a family member to ask for it? If illegal, should the law be changed to allow euthanasia, not only to enhance patient and family freedom of choice, but also to avoid the quiet, illegal practice? These and other ethical questions continue to arise in caring for patients at the end of life, especially those suffering from chronic diseases such as Alzheimer's disease.

The African Independent and Pentecostal Churches Response

JAMES AMANZE

Martha's situation in this story is fairly common in Africa across the religious divide. The African people consider life as the greatest gift that God has given to humankind. To be alive is a gift and not a privilege. In African Independent Churches, apart from being guided by Christian ethics, members are also guided by African Traditional Ethics, which maintain that no one except God has the right to terminate human life, regardless of the clinical condition in which a person is found. Thus, there is no situation in the African context in which people would contemplate to carry out mercy killing or enable a person to terminate his or her life. It is unthinkable.

In Africa generally, old age is appreciated as a symbol of wisdom, and to have very old people in the family is considered a blessing from God. It is considered a sacred duty to look after them even when they are in hospital and in a very serious condition, as Martha in the story. This is why in most African societies there are no old peoples' homes. This is because family members feel honored to look after the elderly, especially when they are completely helpless like Martha. African Independent Churches would consult a prophet-healer or a diviner to determine what caused Martha to have Alzheimer's disease. Treatment would be administered to her in accordance with the prophet-healer's or diviner's diagnosis. Prayers would be said for the healing of Martha in church or at home. When healing in the Church fails, some African Independent Churches revert to African traditional medicine as a matter of last resort.

African Independent Churches teach their members to take care of the sick and the elderly like Martha and to love them until they die naturally. Euthanasia is not accepted. Relatives of the sick person would leave everything in the doctors' hands to decide whether to stop medication or not. In most cases, if the doctors discover that the patient cannot be cured in hospital, they advise family members to take the sick person home. This advice is given especially if the cost of keeping the patient in hospital is escalating. Family members take that as a sign that the patient will not recover and that the doctors want the patient to die peacefully at home. Relatives normally act on the advice of the doctors. Even when this advice is given, members of the Independent Churches would continue to pray for the recovery of the sick person. It is strongly believed that God has the power to heal regardless of the sick person's condition, even at the point of death. Some churches may advise family members to offer sacrifices to God through the ancestors in order to invoke his healing power. Prayers continue until the person either dies or recovers from his/her illness. Family members would accept the death of a very old person as having gone to rest to become an ancestor. In the spirit world, ancestors act as God's intermediaries between God and the living.

In Pentecostal Churches, though a person may be old and very sick like Martha, church and family members would continue to pray for his/her full recovery. Pentecostals believe that it is morally wrong to wish someone to die. Although they know that people should die when they are old and sick, Pentecostals never say "let the person die because his/her time is over." They believe that their duty as Christians is to pray for people to have long life and not to terminate life, no matter how old and sickly one is.

Many Pentecostal Churches have a strong belief in miracles of healing. They teach their members that when someone is sick they should pray for a miracle to take place. Because of this strong belief in miracles, family members would find it very difficult to ask the doctors to terminate the sick person's life. They believe that God can bring the dead to life. Euthanasia is considered as unbiblical and unethical. What they normally do is to pray to God so that God can give the doctors wisdom to find the right medicine to treat the old sick person.

A number of theological questions are asked when people are found in a situation like that of Martha's. They ask, "Why does God allow us to suffer as a family?" Pentecostal Churches always pray for the sick in church. They ask God to do away with the sickness; they read scripture, fast, lay hands on the sick person, and pray for the family of the sick person for strength and courage. Generally speaking, when people see that the situation is not getting any better, they leave it in God's hands. Pentecostal members of the family would not consider the possibility of giving up nursing their relative, regardless of looking useless. They would not even consider the possibility of asking the doctors to switch off the supporting machines. Pentecostals believe that even if the supporting machines were to be disconnected, it would not matter very much. As a matter of fact, that would be a sign of faith that even without the supporting machines God has the power to restore the dying to life, regardless of their physical condition.

The Buddhist Response

SORAJ HONGLADAROM

Advances in today's medical technology have created a number of dilemmas that are very difficult to contemplate and to solve. In the old days, Martha's case would not have to be tackled because people rarely lived until the age when dementia could unleash its destructive power. Nowadays cases like Martha's have become all the more common, and this is the case not only in the industrial West.

In traditional Asian families, more than two generations live together under the same roof. There is a strong tradition of taking care of one's own parents, a showing of gratitude in return for the time when one's parents spent a great deal of effort raising one to adulthood. In the traditional setting, however, the situation in which the elderly parents suffer from progressing Alzheimer's disease does not often arise at all.

Eleanor's decision must be a traumatic, heart wrenching one. On the one hand, she cannot stand seeing her mother continue in this condition; dementia has set in and Martha is deteriorating before her very eyes. On the other hand, she needs to overcome the sense of guilt that accompanied her telling the doctor to do something so that Martha passes away in peace. Buddhism has a strong objection against killing, because killing and harming a sentient being goes directly opposite to compassion, which lies at the heart of Buddhism.

An advance directive or a living will would be very important in a situation such as this one. But in the case of Eleanor and her mother, in which there is no living will, the decision rests with Eleanor and her siblings. Martha is no longer able to make a decision on her own. Furthermore, supposing that Martha could make a decision on her own, it would run contrary to Buddhist principle were she to request her doctor to perform euthanasia on herself. Nonetheless, if her condition were such that her refusal to eat represents a natural progression of her disease, then, so long as Eleanor and her brother and sister agree, it would be all right if nothing were done to force feed her. In her advanced age and condition, refusing to eat can be natural, a stage in the dying process in which she is preparing herself for the next life. It would be an intervention against the natural course of things to put tubes into her stomach or to give her intravenous injections. She is not suffering from any disease that needs to be fought against. She is running along with nature. Buddhism fully recognizes this. Letting Martha die peacefully in this way is not the same as killing her. The Buddhist attitude is that when the end is coming, especially in Martha's case in which the situation is irreversible, one should go along with it and should not fight against it at all costs. Martha's children, especially Eleanor, should realize that arising and passing away is a condition that applies to everything in the world, with no exception. If possible, Eleanor should arrange for her mother to stay in a palliative care unit. It is futile to fight against dementia or Alzheimer's; it is much better for everybody to let Martha prepare for the next life in peace, with no painful intervention, no strong drugs with serious side effects. This is the time in Martha's life when, were she were a Buddhist, she should be meditating and pondering on the nature of things so as to get closer to the ultimate goal of Nirvana.

However, when it comes to assisted suicide or active euthanasia, Buddhism on the whole would advise against it. The reason is that this comes very close to harming one's own body, an act that runs against the principle of compassion. There is admittedly a fine line between not feeding Martha through the tube and, say, injecting her with poison. But the difference lies in the force that is directed against the body in the latter case, which does not seem to be there in the former. Of course if someone who is healthy and normal is denied food and is actively being starved, that would certainly count as harm; but that certainly is not Martha's situation.

The Confucian Response

RUIPING FAN

Confucianism has long recognized that elderly persons need special care. Such care involves not only physical but also mental and spiritual dimensions. In particular, Confucian familism emphasizes that adult children have a primary moral obligation to care for their aged parents. Such moral obligation is called filial piety (xiao) in the Confucian language. It is taken to be a foundational virtue in the Confucian family-oriented virtue ethics. As Confucius teaches, in order to follow the correct way (dao) to pursue the complete virtue of humanity (ren), "the gentleman (junzi) must devote his efforts to the roots, for once the roots are established, the way will generate therefrom. Filial piety and brotherly love (ti) are the roots of humanity" (Analects 1.2). For Confucians, no matter what else one does, one must first take care of one's parents in order to be a virtuous person. Indeed, Confucius stated that one's filial obligation could not be excused in the name of conducting studies or joining in politics. Instead, filial obligation is more fundamental than other obligations (Analects 1.6, 2.21).

Confucian filial obligation does not require every adult child to live under the same roof with their elderly parents to take care of them. In contemporary society, an ideal Confucian situation is that at least one adult child lives nearby elderly parent(s) to offer necessary assistance.[10] But Confucianism emphasizes that all adult children are obliged to support their parents in one way or another. In this case, Martha has three adult children, Paul, Rachel, and Eleanor. It is by no means only Eleanor who has moral obligation to take care of her mother as she is willing; Paul and Rachel are similarly morally obliged. They should have come to join Eleanor to give a helping hand. But they did not even come to visit their mother after they heard that she was diagnosed with Alzheimer's disease. From the Confucian understanding, living far away from their mother in Katmandu or Geneva cannot be taken as a legitimate reason for them not to undertake their most important moral obligation. A Confucian community would take inaction as extremely unfilial (buxiao) and extremely morally defective.

For Confucians, there are proper rituals to guide everyone in treating one's parents: the serving rituals when they are alive, the burying rituals when they die, and the sacrificial rituals after they are dead (Analects 2.5). The goal of the serving rituals is to have one's aged parents live happily. Confucius offers concrete instructions in this regard. In particular, in offering physical care and nourishment to one's aged parents, Confucius emphasizes that one must hold the attitude of reverence (jing) towards one's parents (Analects 2.7). In fact, as he points out, a much more difficult task than merely offering physical assistance to one's elderly parents is always offering such assistance with reverence and a happy expression on one's face (Analects 2.8). It is only in such a reverent way, Confucius states, that we can distinguish the child exercising the virtue of filial piety from an animal such as a dog or horse in following animal instincts toward its parents.

In the case of Martha, the most important thing is not to figure out what her advance directive would have been if it had been established in advance. Neither is it to decide whether artificial nutrition or hydration should be initiated. What the children should focus on is—through consultation with the professional team—to decide what methods and measures they should use in order to bring about the best possible life for Martha, their mother. Actually the answer is clear. As the experts addressing this case's clinical issues point out, "careful spoon feeding will both enhance Martha's quality of life and will be consistent with the treatment goal of providing comfort." Why shouldn't the children decide to do this? Even if they have no time to do it by themselves, they should all contribute money to hire someone to do it.

At this point, asking to end Martha's life through active euthanasia is not only illegal, but is also immoral. For Confucians, among a series of natural virtues and obligations, filial piety is always the central one. This is not only because filial piety is engaged in taking care of human life, since, according to the Confucian faith, human life is the most honorable of all life under Heaven. It is also because in revering one's parents through filial piety, one is, for Confucians, making them "the peer of Heaven and Earth";[11] that is, Confucianism holds that by reverently assisting their parents, the children are helping them reach the transcendent so as to accomplish eternity. Accordingly, serving the parents is the primary way of serving the transcendent and contributing to the great trinity of Heaven, Earth, and Man in the Confucian universe (XVI).[11] And that is why Confucians see that "filial piety is the supreme virtue of the fundamental Dao held by the sage kings to regulate the world" (I).[11] Confucians can certainly recognize the terrible difficulty that the children in this case confront, but they cannot accept their excuse of wanting their "mother to be at peace." Confucian filial piety requires them reverently to take care of, but not to kill, their mother.

The Evangelical Christian Response

JOHN GRAHAM

Martha's case highlights the issues raised when death is prolonged. Drs. Shreves and Morrison have outlined the medical aspects and Dr. Callahan has given a long list of ethical issues. There is the question of whether or not to initiate artificial hydration or nutrition, and what to do about patients in the persistent vegetative state. And, what if the family asks about assisted suicide or euthanasia? The American public is well aware of Dr. Jack Kevorkian, who participated in over 100 assisted suicides. Many also know that in 1994, the state of Oregon passed the Death with Dignity Act, which allows a physician to give assistance in dying by the prescription of lethal drugs.

Concerning assisted suicide, many Evangelical Christians would have felt as then-Attorney General John Ashcroft, who made an "Interpretive Rule" that physician-assisted suicide is in violation of the federally mandated Controlled Substance Act. Ashcroft said he would prosecute any physician in Oregon who prescribed lethal drugs to a patient. Eventually, the Oregon District Court ruled against Ashcroft, and the ruling was upheld in the 9th Circuit Court of Appeals.

Why did Ashcroft, an Evangelical, take this stance? Evangelical Christians believe that all life is a gift from God and quote Genesis, "God created man in his own image, in the image of God he created him; male and female he created them" (Genesis 1:27 NKJV), Evangelicals believe that to hasten a person's death is to "play God," which is the sin of murder. God alone can decide when a person dies. For many, assisted-suicide is a tiny step away from the horrors of the Holocaust. If it is Martha today, who will be next?

Although this is the traditional stance of Evangelicals, modern medicine has brought this view into question, because medicine can keep people alive who would have died a natural death long ago. In other words, does not medicine "play God" by extending the number of "appointed" days? Yet, most

Evangelicals value the life God has given and routinely ask every medical means be used to extend their life. Most want intravenous fluids and nutrition administered as long as they are alert and communicative. They want to be able to visit with family, friends, and loved ones as long as possible.

But what if a loved one has lost his or her unique personhood because of a disease such as Alzheimer's? Things may appear differently when family and friends can no longer communicate with their loved one. Does not being created in the image of God include the ability to have a meaningful relationship with God and those you love? Alzheimer's and other illnesses make that impossible. And, why prolong the inevitable? Why extend life when it means prolonging pain and suffering for one's loved one and a mounting financial burden for the family?

If I were the pastor of Martha's family, I would support their desire to not prolong the life of their 82-year-old mother who is now demented and near death. I would agree with their desire to let their mother die a natural death and not allow physicians to start intravenous nutrition or insert a feeding tube into her stomach. Instead, I would recommend they ask her physician to consider transfer to a palliative care unit in the hospital or to a hospice facility. Both of these services are designed to give dying patients dignity during the last few months of their lives. I believe this is what the family truly wants.

I would also encourage the family, when together, to remind each other of the stories about their mother before she became ill. And, when they are ready, I would encourage them to plan her funeral service to be a celebration of the life God gave and blessed. And, because Martha was a devout Episcopalian, I would help them plan an Episcopal service from the Book of Common Prayer that would celebrate the resurrection of Jesus Christ and affirm that their mother will also be resurrected and spend eternity with God and the people of God in heaven.

The questions raised about whether or not to initiate nutrition demonstrate the need for an advance directive to specify the will of the patient, made while he or she is alert and communicative. Martha and her daughter, Eleanor, spent many years together; yet Martha did not have an advance directive. Once the diagnosis of Alzheimer's was made and while Martha was still alert and cognitive, as her pastor, I would have encouraged Martha to create a legally-valid advance directive outlining the extent of care she wished to receive at the end of life. This document would have been great help to the family when emotionally charged issues such as whether or not to start intravenous nutrition are raised. It would alleviate unnecessary guilt on the part of Eleanor and her siblings, who do not want to prolong the life of their mother and extend her suffering when there was no reasonable hope of recovery. It is time to place their mother in the hands of a loving God with the firm assurance of God's gift of eternal life.

The Hindu Response

UMA MYSOREKAR

Hindu beliefs are intrinsically linked to health. Hindus believe that physical, emotional, mental, and spiritual health are all inseparably linked and therefore must be balanced to have good health. Magnetic influences, planetary influences, spiritual influences, as well as personal actions, beliefs, thoughts, diet, and exercise are all seen as having various effects on physical and mental health.

Treatments that do not address all these biological, physiological, and spiritual elements may not be considered effective by Hindus. Many Hindus attach stigma to mental illness and cognitive dysfunction. All illnesses, including mental illness, may be seen as a result of *karma* from this life or a previous one.

It is tragic that Martha, who raised a wonderful family and was also very successful in her career, ended up with a disease with mental disability. Hindus believe that the real problem is the bondage of mind to matter. Man's attachment is to his body and thereafter to those who are near and dear to him—his relationship in the physical world. All these bondages coupled with a lifestyle associated with materialism and so on produce a great deal of stress for human beings. Hinduism stresses yoga and meditation for a healthier and harmonious life. Another aspect of this holistic view regards meditation and mental health. While one sits in meditation, a gentle voice from an unseen depth guides one into a noiseless land—the shrine of silence, which is the sacred seat of the *Atman*. As one sits in mediation regularly, at the same time, in the same place, the mind gets nourished and relaxed, freeing one from mental illness.

A joint family system which is extremely prevalent among Hindus helps considerably to make some important ethical decisions for all those who are at the stage of dementia in which Martha finds herself. Terms such as living will (especially in the case of women), health proxy, and "do not resuscitate," and so on have not been popular at all among Hindus, and perhaps not even known. Generally, the oldest child or the oldest member of the family makes most of these decisions, including whether to continue treatment or not. Even if the clinician asks questions regarding matters concerning the end of life, such as tube feeding, palliative treatment, or interventions to prolong life, the Hindu patient will most probably not answer but instead will refer to a husband, oldest child, or any senior member of the family. Nowadays, however, with education, and information made available through news media, TV, magazines, Hindus are becoming more and more aware of their rights and duties.

For Hindus, culture and faith are inextricable. Although many modern decisions taken by Hindus seem more influenced by their popular nature than by the ideas of their faith, this distinction may not be as clear as it seems.

Hindus believe in the reincarnation of the soul (or *Atman*) through many lives, not necessarily all human. The ultimate aim of life is to achieve *moksha* or liberation from the cycle of death and rebirth. A soul's next life is decided by *karma*, as the consequence of its own good or bad actions in previous lives. It is believed that a soul cannot achieve *moksha* without good *karma*.

By actively helping to end a life, even one filled with suffering, a person is disturbing the timing of the cycle of death and rebirth. This is improper and it is believed that those involved in euthanasia will take on the remaining *karma* of the patient. The same argument suggests that keeping a person artificially alive on a life-support machine would also be not a right thing to do. The use of a life-support machine as a part of temporary attempt at healing, however, would be acceptable. A decision has to be made to discontinue life support either by parents or the spouse or other close relatives. In their absence, such a decision can even be made by a person or a body of persons as close friends. It can also be made by doctors attending the patient. A decision is taken to withdraw life support, even if religiously acceptable to Hindus, may, in certain legal settings, require approval by court. Passive euthanasia involving the withdrawal of treatment or food that would probably prolong the life is acceptable to Hindus. However, active euthanasia by administration of lethal compounds is not acceptable. The ideal death is a conscious death, and this means that palliative treatments will be a problem if they reduce mental alertness.

The Indigenous Response

IRENE TAAFAKI

Ri-Majōl focus their attention on the "now" and the life that exists. The strong and generally accepted confidence in the existence of an afterlife does not mean that Marshallese welcome or allow discussion about their death. On the contrary, to do so is received with fierce exclamation of *bwijerro*, which translates as "is this a death wish for me?" No matter how close to death a person might be, it is *bwijerro* to either refer to or make arrangements for one's own or a family member's demise, whether this is identifying the grave site, ordering the coffin, or preparing a grave or tomb.

Providing advance directives such as a living will would also be *bwijerro*. Dictating or signing such a document is unheard of amongst Marshallese, and those who learn of it reject it as a Western or *ri-pālle* practice. A recent exception to this taboo is the directive given prior to death regarding an individual's preference not to subject their bodies to chemical embalming. Nevertheless, despite such injunctions, it is generally recognized that families regularly choose to ignore the directive after the death in order to accommodate the cultural necessity for all family members to come from afar to be present before and after the funeral.

> M: When she (mother) said she doesn't want to be embalmed... I say, well, we need to talk about the grave then she says, oh you people, you really want me to go! (*bwijerro*)
> I: If your disease progresses... you would never ask...
> All: No
> M: That is ri-pālle style. (Laughter)

The aged of both genders are respected in Marshallese culture. Once women reach menopause, they are regarded as possessing greater wisdom, and their words and wishes are regarded seriously. Those with age-related dementia are not exceptions and remain an integral part of family life. Care is taken to ensure they are not left alone, and families practice *kau*—gathering around the sick or infirm. Usually, one member of the family will be assigned as the primary caregiver and will accommodate whatever the patient needs. This care is usually provided by a mature age younger daughter or granddaughter, since managing the bathing and bathroom functions of a male patient is taboo for the oldest daughter, and likewise cannot be provided by the son to his mother. Despite the infirmities of age, family members often vie to have the patient as part of their household, and the patient will be moved from house to house to meet the relative's wish to have them in their respective homes. An aged patient's idiosyncratic, unpredictable behavior and loss of memory is accepted, generally with good humor. They are made as comfortable as possible, massaged, kept upright with soft pillows, taken out on excursions (*jambo*) and, when unable to feed themselves, are hand-fed palatable soft foods such as *makmōk* (native arrowroot).

No matter how far the disease has progressed, the degree of dementia, or the length of the illness, life is regarded as precious and sacred. Sincere sympathy was expressed for Martha's progressive Alzheimer's disease, which rendered her as one "who could not remember her home"; and there was compassion for the lonely situation of the daughter seen coping without any other family support. This is unthinkable, given the close ties of traditional Marshallese society.

Death is dependent on the will of Anij (God) or, both in the past and present, believed to be the influence or action of a less powerful yet malevolent unseen spirit. However challenging a patient's tragic circumstance might be, ending their life unnaturally is not an option. The direct intervention of other people at the bedside is unacceptable, and, to the extent possible, the last breath (*aū*) should be a natural event. The notion of assisted suicide is incomprehensible and unacceptable to Ri-Majōl.

Similarly, although artificial hydration or nutrition will be agreed upon in order to maintain life, this will only be to the extent that it is acceptable to the patient, or while faith in recovery persists. If a patient were seriously demented, or were to suffer from an even more severe (but not progressive) condition such as persistent vegetative state, prolonging the agony of life by artificial means would not be regarded as sensible. Once there is absolute certainty by the family that there is no hope of recovery, the removal of artificial life support would be accepted. In such circumstances Ri-Majōl would request that patients be allowed the last opportunity to breathe on their own and die on their own, and will likely be heard to ask "do not hold on to them when they are ready to go."

The Jewish Response

HERBERT BROCKMAN

As I read Martha's sad and all too common story, I could not help but think of my own family's experience with my mother's growing dementia, which continued for over a decade. Concerning his mother, a colleague of mine, Rabbi Harold Schulweis, once described the position of children caring for dying parents by noting that they can say, "This is the woman who heard my first heartbeat, and her last heartbeat will be in my hand." What an awesome responsibility. To see the woman who not only gave one life, but nurtured and sustained one, once strong and protective, now weak and increasingly vulnerable can be emotionally devastating.

In the case preceding this one, I discussed the practice of writing an ethical will, along with the medical directive, or living will. In Martha's case, such a process, in addition to resulting in a legacy she would leave for future generations, could have the additional benefit of helping the family better prepare for the end-of-life decision making. In the case of long-term illness, this can be especially important. Often such discussions between family members and their loved one can relieve relatives of the onerous responsibilities of making such decisions on their own without knowing the wishes of the patient. They can also lead to a deeper understanding among family members, and to the healing of broken family relationships. At the same time, having these conversations can give the elderly and infirm at least some sense of control over their own lives.

In Martha's case, the family faced the inevitable question of the extent to which they should go to preserve her life, or to assist in her death. As her disease progressed, the normal life-functions began to fail. Not only her memory but nutrition and hydration become problematic, along with her body's ability to fend off infections, often leading to pneumonia. As organ failure begins, families begin to question the extent to which one can or should institute the artificial means by which to keep the patient alive. And, as the physical challenges mount, the emotional responses are inevitably exacerbated. How is one to balance the sense of respect and awe for life—for the miracles of creation and existence—on the one hand, and the inevitable desire to bring comfort and "peace" to a loved one on the other? In such cases, Judaism's balance between "not hastening a death" and "may remove that which hinders death" is instructive. At the point where "independent life" has ceased, the rabbinic tradition becomes applicable. For instance, in determining that point of the cessation of "independent life," most reform and conservative rabbinical authorities accept the notion of brain death according to the following criteria:

1. Lack of response to external stimuli
2. Absence of movement and breathing
3. Absence of elicited reflexes
4. A flat EEG

At this point it is no longer necessary or wise to continue external circulatory or respiratory efforts. Pain medication, however, is always permitted.

Acknowledging that death is a part of the cycle of life and accepting it as such is viewed as the necessary step to healing. Upon hearing of a death, the traditional response was to be "BARUCH DAYAN HA-EMET" ("Praised is the True Judge"). The mourner's prayer is also a doxology, praising God. Why the apparent contradiction? Why, just when one is grieving, is one called upon to praise? The answer lies in the recognition that the true value of a life is underscored by its transiency. Life is prized and to be preserved whenever possible; but in the end, when life ebbs, as it inevitably must, its true value is most clear. Indeed, "the human spirit is the light of God, (a light) penetrating one's most intimate being" (Proverbs 20:27; author's interpretation); but "that light of life is a finite flame. It burns, it glows, and then it fades and it is no more."[12]

As Rabbi Schulweis acknowledged: "When the messenger of death cannot be denied, I am prepared to accept the message. I am prepared to accept it not as a defeat but as a summation, not as a punishment but as a conclusion."[13]

The Mainline Protestant Christian Response

JAN HOLTON

Martha's intellectual vigor, pioneering spirit, and familial dedication make the diagnosis and debilitating reality of Alzheimer's disease especially tragic for both her and those who love her. Quickly, Alzheimer's attacked the very center of who Martha was. Fear of becoming lost replaced the confident, forward-thinking woman who raised her children to become independent successes in their own right. Instead of making a new future with purpose and meaning, the disease left her trapped in the past.

Strategies for spiritual care should be primarily focused on Martha's end-of-life comfort and care but also consider her caregiver daughter, Eleanor. Though Martha never discussed her wishes concerning medical care with her children, the advice to begin tube feeding has triggered in Eleanor a question as to what kind of care her mother would have wanted under these conditions. The children agree that they want their mother to be at peace. Martha's advanced Alzheimer's, however, perpetually creates conditions that require significant life-sustaining medical intervention and render her susceptible to continued suffering.

Most mainline Christian denominations engage a theology that recognizes medical science as a good gift from God and lauds its contribution to advancing not only the length but also quality of human life. It is one of the means by which God offers humans the abundant life described in Christian scripture in the Gospel of John (10:10 New Revised Standard Version): "I came so that they might have life and have it abundantly." But, like all good gifts, humans run the risk of clinging so tightly to the gift that it becomes both the means and the end. The church also recognizes that humans are finite creatures—life will come to an end. With the rise of medical technology, the mainline churches have responded by confirming the rights of individuals, family, or designated proxies to withhold treatment when there is no chance for recovery to a meaningful existence. The church encourages families to discuss personal choices regarding end-of-life care. In these cases, it affirms choices that refuse heroic measures to sustain life in order to allow a natural death. The church further affirms efforts to ensure, as much as is possible, a death with dignity that may include administering medications to alleviate or minimize suffering—even if such medications pose a risk of secondary harm.

There is a difference, however, between refusal of curative treatment and assisted suicide, or euthanasia, that is, the administering of medication with the intention to facilitate death. The latter of these is, at least on the surface, what Eleanor seems to suggest when she says, "give her something to make her slip away into sleep." The mainline Protestant churches hold that life is a gift from God. Direct measures to actively and intentionally facilitate death under any circumstances through the administering of medication, as opposed to allowing natural processes to take place, is not condoned. Effective spiritual care will help family members understand the difference between the desire for palliative care at the end of life—perhaps the intention behind Eleanor's statement—and the act of facilitating death such as is suggested by the unfortunate wording of the question.

In the mainline Protestant tradition, prayer is always an appropriate pastoral response to suffering. When prayer is joined with the power of human touch, for example a Protestant "laying on of hands," the one who is ill is connected to family and friends in a gesture of love while simultaneously inviting God's healing presence and peace through prayer. If this moment of ritual occurs close to death it may serve as a means by which Eleanor and other family members can begin the process of "letting go" of the physical presence of their mother by commending her into the hands of God. Such a "laying on of hands" may be a simple as holding hands or a more formal gesture of touching the head and/or shoulders. Permission to conduct this ritual should always be sought and special care taken when ministering to those with dementia so that it does not exacerbate fear and confusion.

The Shi'a Muslim Response

NAJMEH JAFARI

I lost my grandfather due to Alzheimer's disease a couple of days before writing this essay. Like Martha, he was a great man in his working and family life, and his long dying process was a very difficult time for our family. Hence, I can understand Eleanor's pain and her difficult situation in decision making.

Eleanor loves her mother, and it is very understandable for Eleanor to want "permanent sleep" for her. Eleanor is worried about her mother's will in this situation. She has blamed herself many times for not asking this question when Martha was in a good cognitive state.

If we consider Martha and Eleanor as Shi'a Muslims, there is no place for such feeling of blame. According to the Islamic view, human life is sacred and belongs to God: "Nor take life—which Allah has made sacred" (Qur'an 17:33); and death is the exclusive action of God: "Nor can a soul die except by Allah's leave, the term being fixed as by writing" (Qur'an 3:145). Hence, a person does not own his/her body, and there is no right for Martha to wish to die in this disabling situation. Martha's life is a divine trust and cannot be terminated by any form of active or passive human intervention, and her death is fixed by an unalterable divine decree (Qur'an 3:185; 29:57; 39:42). So an advance directive regarding this situation is useless in the Shi'a Muslim view.

If Eleanor asked about something to terminate her mother's suffering, Islamic doctrine has a clear answer: assisted suicide and euthanasia are forbidden. Euthanasia means "good or easy death" and signifies any active action to terminate the life of the patient who is suffering from an incurable disease. Muslim scholars regard euthanasia as an act of murder and a great sin in Islam. "[I]f anyone slew a person—unless it be for murder or for spreading mischief in the land—it would be as if he slew the whole people..." (Qur'an 5:32). Hence, the health care team should not have an active part in terminating Martha's life, even if it is at her guardian's request. The physician is obligated to provide the best care for Martha and alleviate her pain. If a feeding tube or intravenous hydration helps her to survive, they should be used, unless their use, or any such an act, shortens life. What if Martha were in a permanently vegetative state? This situation prolongs the dying process and has a high social, psychological, and economic impact on her family. In Islam there is no permission for doctors to terminate life in this situation either, and they are ordained to provide the basic human rights of hydration, nutrition, nursing and pain relief.

Eleanor and her siblings want "peace" for their mother and they are worried about her suffering by providing life-support care. In the Islamic view, suffering and pain are trials from God and are a means for self-purification of sins. "[A]nd bear with patient constancy whatever betide thee; for this is firmness (of purpose) in (the conduct of) affairs" (Qur'an 31:17). The Prophet Mohammad said that "Hours of sickness sweep away hours of sins."[14] In this religious view, Eleanor may consider this situation part of God's will to purify her mother of any sin; for her suffering Martha will be rewarded in heaven. However, health care providers are obligated to do their best to eliminate Martha's pain and suffering.

It should be emphasized that an important aspect in the care in Alzheimer's disease is providing support for the caregivers. Eleanor's shoulders will suffer the pain of the heavy load of caregiving. She needs psychological, economic, and spiritual support. Social support and psychospiritual counseling may be effective to keep her strong enough to tolerate her own profound suffering.

The Sunni Muslim Response
TARIQ RAMADAN

The story of Martha is quite painful. Once a gifted intellectual, she balanced her roles as supportive wife and mother of three children with an academic career in chemistry, teaching well into her seventies. Even in retirement, she played an active role in her faith community. Yet, now an 82-year-old widow, emaciated and demented, she is unable to recognize her own daughter and requires 24-hour nursing care. Martha's deterioration happened so gradually that she was unaware herself of the developing severity of her dementia, and so she did not at any point discuss with her family how she might want to be cared for in her later years. These past few years have been difficult for her family, in particular for her daughter Eleanor. Eleanor has struggled alone to organize and finance care for her mother, while at the same time holding down her own career and funding her two children through higher education.

Medical doctors are trying their best to reduce Martha's suffering. There is medical treatment available to her by way of the provision of intravenous nutrition in order to build up her strength enough to enable a feeding tube to be surgically placed into her stomach. The doctors have explained to Eleanor that this procedure will alleviate the need for Martha to take food through her mouth and thus risk catching pneumonia again, since she is unable to swallow properly anymore. It is quite clear that the progress of Martha's Alzheimer's is not yet in its final stages and she is not at imminent risk of dying. More rather the situation is one of a patient needing increased medical intervention to provide her with greater comfort while she continues to "live," potentially for quite some time yet. Eleanor wonders whether her once strong and independent mother might have wanted it this way or, without any quality of life, having reached such a helpless state. Would she have preferred just to be allowed to slip away or even be given something to speed up the dying process?

There are four key issues here. The first is the necessity for families to broach the sensitive subject of care choices in later life and engage in frank discussion with each other. If this is not realistic, then patients in the early stages of their disease need to be offered consultations with a clinician and the discussions formally documented. As was suggested in the case study, the creation of a living will can be used as guidance for the next steps towards the later stages of the disease. Such an approach would relieve the burden of decision making from the family. These issues need to be addressed while family members are well and not left until it is too late, as was the situation for Martha and her daughter Eleanor.

Secondly Martha has to make the decision as to whether or not to allow the initiation of artificial nutrition and hydration. Doctors have advised Eleanor both that her mother's physical health will improve and that her caregiving will become easier with such intervention. However, Eleanor is in a dilemma, not knowing whether her mother would want to be "kept alive" in this way or would be more comfortable and feel more natural receiving food through her mouth, even though it would inevitably take longer and thus cost more financially as well as increase Martha's risk of catching pneumonia again. In Islam, the use of technology is welcomed to ease the suffering and the risks for the patient.

Thirdly we are dealing here with a request for a kind of assisted suicide or euthanasia. This is a case of active euthanasia, meaning that it is a direct request coming from a family member asking medicine to help her mother to die; from an Islamic perspective, this is not permissible. However if there were, in a specific situation, an opinion from medical doctors that this was the final stage of the patient's life, then it is acceptable in Islam to seek ways to minimize the level and intensity of suffering, provided that the medical advice confirms that the patient's health condition cannot be reversed in any way and that the end of life is indeed imminent—for example, if the patient were to become permanently vegetative. The administration of morphine would be acceptable in this instance. The morphine would ease any physical pain that the patient was experiencing and furthermore speed up the dying process. As the dosage of morphine was increased, this medication would ultimately end the life of the patient. This is known as indirect passive euthanasia. In the Islamic tradition, passive euthanasia at this final stage of life is entirely acceptable because suffering in itself is not an objective; and thus it is permissible to provide pain relief medication to a patient to have a more comfortable life for the final few days, even though it will shorten her life. But acting against life or assisting a suicide when we are not dealing with the final stages of that life is, from an Islamic viewpoint, not permissible in ethical terms.

This case study highlights a broad critical issue that is not only a concern within families but also for society as a whole. With an increasingly aging population, how can we find acceptable, ethical ways to care for our elderly relatives who can sometimes be very demanding and, often in the long term, create unbearably challenging situations for the families involved? It is because it is so difficult for Eleanor, the daughter, that she might push toward making a decision which will end her mother's life prematurely. This is a social question, one that we have to address as a society—not by asking only the family or the other caregivers (professional and voluntary) to bear the entire burden of dealing with those who need care, but to encourage society overall to care about its human beings and its citizens. Within the Islamic tradition, this is an important concern: we need to find a way to care about the elderly, the sick, and the poor—people who are perhaps unable to contribute financially to the economy—in a way that respects their dignity to the very end of their lives. Beyond the discussion of this particular case study, we need to question the way our societies deal with this ethical issue. We need to challenge society to set some limits in the way that we act against the life of some patients and to confront society when the life of a person is perceived as useless in terms of financial gain and economic contribution. This raises a deep social and philosophical question that we should tackle.

The Roman Catholic Response

CAROL TAYLOR

We have yet to solve the challenge of caring adequately for individuals with chronic illnesses like Alzheimer's disease, especially in the United States, where there is no guarantee that basic health care services will be available to families when needed. Before addressing the challenges confronting Martha and her children, it is critical to note that among the seven basic principles of Catholic Social Teaching[15] are the life and dignity of the human person, the option for the poor and vulnerable, and solidarity. These principles call on all people of faith and reason to create a society where the needs of all, especially the most vulnerable, are met.

> To desire the common good and strive towards it is a requirement of justice and charity.... The more we strive to secure a common good corresponding to the real needs of our neighbors, the more effectively we love them. Every Christian is called to practice this charity, in a manner corresponding to his vocation and according to the degree of influence he wields in the [state]. This is the institutional path—we might also call it the political path—of charity, no less excellent and effective than the kind of charity which encounters the neighbor directly...[16]

Ideally, Martha would have exercised her legal and ethical right to select the person she most trusts to make her health care decisions when she is no longer able to do this and to make her preferences for end-of-life care known. When the family has more than one child it is helpful for parents to discuss their intentions and values with the entire family to prevent conflict later. Many Catholic dioceses and organizations make available to Catholics advance directive templates that are faithful to Catholic moral principles and teachings. Catholics are urged to make certain that their advance directives forbid any actions that the Catholic faith considers to be immoral, such as euthanasia or physician-assisted suicide. Similarly, Catholic hospitals, nursing homes and hospices will not follow advance directives that conflict with Church teaching.

> 60. Euthanasia is an action or omission that of itself or by intention causes death in order to alleviate suffering. Catholic health care institutions may never condone or participate in euthanasia in any way. Dying patients who request euthanasia should receive loving care, psychological and spiritual support, and appropriate remedies for pain and other symptoms so that they can live with dignity until the time of natural death.[17]

Thus when Eleanor asks her mother's doctors, "Isn't there any way you can give her something to make her slip away into sleep, I mean permanent sleep?" the answer from Catholic health care would be "We are sorry, but no." A chaplain or spiritual caregiver would be enlisted to help minister to Eleanor.

Catholics may also use an advance directive to request that they receive the sacraments of Penance, Annointing of the Sick, and Eucharist ("food for the journey") when they are at the end of life. They may also specify which prayers or Scripture passages they would like read at their bedsides.

Eleanor is also asked to authorize starting intravenous nutrition for her mother in order to get her strong enough for a feeding tube to be surgically planed into her stomach. Eleanor never had a conversation with her mother about what she would want in a situation like this. Eleanor is, however, troubled by seeing her brilliant mother in this condition, 82, emaciated, and demented. As Drs. Shreves and Morrison make clear, while it is not unusual for clinicians to suggest medical nutrition and hydration for patients with advanced Alzheimer's disease, it is no longer medically recommended. Tube feedings have been proven not to reduce swallowing into the lungs and can create additional burdens such as skin breakdown and the need for wrist restraints. Many Catholic nursing homes have initiated programs to train volunteers how to hand-feed patients with swallowing difficulties. Many Catholic families, including the parents of Terry Schiavo, believe that medical nutrition must always be offered. When the Ethical and Religious Directives for Catholic Health Care Services were revised in 2009, a more nuanced teaching emerged.[17]

> 58. In principle, there is an obligation to provide patients with food and water, including medically assisted nutrition and hydration for those who cannot take food orally. This obligation extends to patients in chronic and presumably irreversible conditions (e.g., the "persistent vegetative state") who can reasonably be expected to live indefinitely if given such care. Medically assisted nutrition and hydration become morally optional when they cannot reasonably be expected to prolong life or when they would be "excessively burdensome for the patient or [would] cause significant physical discomfort, for example resulting from complications in the use of the means employed." For instance, as a patient draws close to inevitable death from an underlying progressive and fatal condition, certain measures to provide nutrition and hydration may become excessively burdensome and therefore not obligatory in light of their very limited ability to prolong life or provide comfort.

Many Catholic clinicians and ethicists believe that patients in the advanced stages of Alzheimer's disease meet the criteria that make medical nutrition morally optional.

The Sikh Response

SURJEET KAUR CHAHAL

Martha is suffering from Alzheimer's disease. She is 82 years old and is on constant intravenous hydration. A feeding tube has to be surgically placed into her stomach. Eleanor, her daughter, is saddened that she does not have advance directives from her mother regarding the course of action to be adopted. Eleanor is contemplating whether there is any way to put her mother to permanent sleep.

The issues that need to be addressed in this case are whether intravenous nutrition should be started so that the feeding tube could be surgically placed. Firstly, it is necessary to make efforts to sustain Martha's life. Therefore initiating intravenous nutrition is necessary. Hydration should not be withheld even during the procedure, as withholding it may shorten life, although we are aware that the patient is already in the final stage of a terminal condition. In other cases, if temporary withholding of hydration benefits the patient, only in such cases it should be withheld, even though it may be discomforting. Similarly if we do not place the feeding tube and do not feed Martha this would amount to starving Martha to death, which would be looked upon as performing an act of omission. As a Sikh, we have the duty to help others, even if it is at the cost of causing inconvenience to us or to the other person. If the prognosis for life extension is good, certainly artificial nutrition or hydration should be started, as it is our duty to preserve this body as long as possible. However, if tube feeding may result in complications, especially in the later stages, it should not be inserted. If careful spoon feeding can be done, that may be the preferred alternative rather than placing the tube, which may be considered as an extraordinary means for sustaining life, which is not mandatory. The decision may be taken by the daughter Eleanor in the absence of advance directives. Therefore euthanasia or denying hydration or antibiotics during infections would not be permissible. The principle is to provide ordinary care and comfort.

However, if the benefits of treatment are limited and if a patient's death is imminent, the focus should be on treating symptoms and not on seeking to extend life at all cost. The aim should be to alleviate suffering and not to shorten life.

If a patient suffers from a persistent vegetative state with a low probability of coming out of that state, such a patient would not be leading a meaningful inner life. But the question arises, who are we as individuals to decide whether the patient's life is meaningful or not, and whether the patient should be kept alive or not. As far as the Sikh tenets are concerned, it is our duty to keep Martha alive so long as we can, even if she were in a persistent vegetative state. However, in this state, we may not adopt extraordinary means of sustaining life. We may allow natural death. Food should not be withheld with the intention of hastening death. Clinically assisted nutrition, only if it is ineffective or burdensome, need not be given.

As far as life-prolonging treatments are concerned, there are no fixed directives according to Sikhism. Every case is to be examined on its own merits. Very often, patients do give advance directives that extraordinary means may not be adopted to keep them alive. This advance directive is to be accepted, especially in cases of persistent vegetative state. After careful observation for some duration, artificial hydration and nutrition may be stopped, but active euthanasia is not permissible. No means that hasten death are to be adopted. One may not opt for life-prolonging treatments which are extraordinary. However, simple life-prolonging treatments such as antibiotics or intravenous medication are not to be stopped, even if they cause discomfort.

A patient should be looked after as long as possible. The patient has a right to get tender love and care. Just as parents have a duty towards children, similarly, children as well as the community have a duty towards such terminally ill patients.

The Unitarian Universalist Response

JAN K. NIELSEN

Martha's Alzheimer's has progressed, robbing her children of the vibrant, brilliant, and loving mother they knew and cherished. Now, when Martha is 82, Martha's doctors want to insert a feeding tube into her stomach; her difficulties with swallowing make it unsafe for her to eat on her own. Eleanor, her adult daughter, and the child most involved in Martha's care, questions the need for the feeding tube. All she and her siblings want, she says, is for Martha to be at peace. She then asks the doctors if they cannot just give Martha something to make her slip away into a permanent sleep.

So much of what her family knew as "Martha" is already gone—most all of her memory, her personality, her ability to interact with other people. It seems that Martha's essence, her consciousness, is gone; and yet, her body remains, although even Martha's body is now unable to survive without artificial means. Alzheimer's disease has left Martha in the ambiguous territory between life and death, and her loved ones are left to navigate the ethical, legal, moral, and spiritual issues—all with no direction from her, since her illness has taken away her ability to make decisions for herself. Martha left no written instructions nor did she discuss with her loved ones what she would want in these difficult circumstances.

Among Unitarian Universalists, preparing for the end of life is considered a wise and caring thing to do. Most Unitarian Universalists agree that declaring one's wishes for end-of-life care in writing, in advance of an illness that takes away one's ability to live with consciousness and dignity, is the right ethical, legal, moral, and spiritual choice.

All too often, however, it is common for people of all spiritual traditions, or of none, to put these things off. They wait to prepare and sign an advance directive declaring their wishes. Or they put off the hard and honest conversations with loved ones and wait to prepare and sign a document appointing someone to make decisions on their behalf. As in Martha's tragic situation, after the need for the documents becomes clear, it is too late. Waiting places the burden of making the difficult decisions on loved ones and also sometimes can leave the medical care providers with no choice but to continue expensive and invasive care for someone who has no possibility of a meaningful recovery.

When caring for a family left to make difficult end-of-life decisions without direction from their loved one, a spiritual caregiver might first invite the sharing of stories and memories about the person whose illness prevents them from telling their own life story. This can allow a burdened loved one like Eleanor to reconnect with the essence of the person they have lost. By remembering Martha's strength and independent spirit, Eleanor and her siblings might come to a deep and intuitive knowing that their mother would not want to exist in her current state. The spiritual caregiver might then facilitate a conversation among Martha's family about their choices.

In this case, Eleanor has requested that Martha be given something to help her slip into a permanent sleep. Although some Unitarian Universalists might be sympathetic to Eleanor's request, others would be reluctant to make or honor such a request because it could be seen as the taking of a life. Many Unitarian Universalist families, when faced with a situation like Martha's, decide instead that only hydration and comfort measures be administered. Rather than keep a loved one alive at all costs, death—an inevitable part of life—is allowed to come.

As they await Martha's passing, family and friends might gather at her bedside to share memories and to say good-bye. A spiritual caregiver might read aloud the words of sacred texts and poetry and lead the gathering in song or prayer, as the living gather round and bless Martha's safe passage.

REFERENCES

1. Volandes AE, Paasche-Orlow MK, Barry MJ, et al. Video decision support tool for advance care planning in dementia: randomized controlled trial. *BMJ.* 2009;*338*:b2159.
2. Deep KS, Hunter A, Murphy K, Volandes A. "It helps me see with my heart": how video informs patients' rationale for decisions about future care in advanced dementia. *Patient Educ Couns.* 2010;*81*:229–34.

3. Mitchell SL. A 93-year-old man with advanced dementia and eating problems. *JAMA.* 2007;*298*:2527–2536.

4. McCann RM, Hall WJ, Groth-Juncker A. Comfort care for terminally ill patients: the appropriate use of nutrition and hydration. *JAMA.* 1994;*272*:1263–1266.

5. Pasman HRW, Onwuteaka-Philipsen BD, Kriegsman DMW, et al. Discomfort in nursing home patients with severe dementia in whom artificial nutrition and hydration is forgone. *Arch Intern Med.* 2005;*165*:1729–1735.

6. Mitchell SL, Teno JM, Kiely DK, et al. The clinical course of advanced dementia. *N Engl J Med.* 2009;*361*:1529–38.

7. Sampson EL, Candy B, Jones L. Enteral tube feeding for older people with advanced dementia. *Cochrane Database Syst Rev.* 2009;2:CD007209.

8. Williams N, Dunford C, Knowles A, et al. Public attitudes to life-sustaining treatments and euthanasia in dementia. *Int J Geriatr Psychiatry.* 2007;*22*:1229–1234.

9. Morrison RS and Meier DE. Palliative Care. *N Engl J Med* 2004;*350*:2582–90.

10. Fan R. Which care? Whose responsibility? And why family? A Confucian account of long-term care for the elderly. *J Med Philos.* 2007;32(5):495–517.

11. Legge J. *The Hsiao King or Classic of Filial Piety.* Whitefish, MT: Kessinger Publishing; 2010.

12. Stern C. *Gates of prayer: The New Union Prayerbook.* New York: Central Conference of American Rabbis; 1975.

13. Schulweis HM. *Dying we live. Yom Kippur, 1995.* Accessed on July 17, 2013, from http://www.vbs.org/page.cfm?p=586

14. Majlesi MB. *Bihar al-Anwar.* Vol. 67. Beirut: Al-Vafa Institute; 264.

15. USCCB. *Sharing Catholic Social Teaching: Challenges and Directions.* Washington DC: United States Conference of Catholic Bishops.; 1998. http://www.usccb.org/beliefs-and-teachings/what-we-believe/catholic-social-teaching.

16. Pope Benedict X. Caritas in Veritate. *Encyclical Letter on Integral Human Development in Charity and Truth, Vatican.* 2009:29. The encyclical can be found in http://www.vatican.va/holy_father/benedict_xvi/encyclicals/documents/hf_ben-xvi_enc_20090629_caritas-in-veritate_en.html. Accessed July 17, 2013.

17. National Conference of Catholic Bishops. *Ethical and Religious Directives for Catholic Health Care Services.* 5th ed. Washington, D.C.: US Catholic Conference; 2009.

CHAPTER 13
At the Time of Death

Case

MARK LAZENBY, RUTH McCORKLE, DANIEL P. SULMASY

Mosupi was born on the day that a black man became president of his African country. That is why his mother named him Mosupi—it means witness. This little boy's birth was a witness to freedom. But his birth also bore witness to the HIV/AIDS virus that had swept across this land. When he was only three years old, his mother died from the virus. After his mother's death, Mosupi's grandmother raised him as her own, with all her love and with the hope and promise of the new times.

He was a slow child. Slow to grow. Slow to talk. And slow to play with friends. When he was five, he got a cold that wouldn't go away. His grandmother took him to the traditional healer. The healer was convenient; he lived in their village. After all, it was an hour's bus ride on a dusty, bumpy, gravel road to get to the doctor. The traditional healer prescribed beetroot and garlic. Mosupi ate plenty, even though he hated the taste. But by the time he was eight, he was constantly sick. So his grandmother finally took him into the city. The doctor told her Mosupi had HIV. She must take him at once to the pediatric infectious disease clinic, he said. At the clinic he got antiretroviral medications, which had only recently become available.

Mosupi perked up on those medications. He went through puberty, and gave his grandmother all the usual headaches. He made it through primary school and middle school. Then he stopped going. "I am just not smart enough, Granny." She understood. He was always slow. Not in school and no jobs to be had, Mosupi started hanging around older boys. As his grandmother suspected, he started smoking. She smelled it on him now and again. And Mosupi developed a relationship with a young woman, Naomi. They had a baby together, a little girl they named Mpho, which means gift. To them, she was a gift. Through all this, Granny woke Mosupi up early on Sunday mornings and took him with her to The Bible Church. Often, Granny, Mosupi, Naomi, and Mpho would all go together. These were happy Sunday mornings.

Along the way, Mosupi stopped going to the clinic to get his medications. It took a whole day to get them. He had to wake up at four in the morning to catch the bus for the ride into the city. After that, he had to wait hours at the infectious disease clinic to be seen. Then there was the bus ride home. Besides all this hassle, he hated how the medicines made him feel.

Over what seemed a period of a few short months, blotches started showing up on his skin. And he got painful white patches in his mouth. He grew gaunt. He hadn't eaten in days and had horrible diarrhea. His grandmother used all the money she had to hire a private driver to take them both to the hospital in the city. When they got there, the queue at the Accident and Emergency Department looked as if they'd be waiting for days. Flush, in pain, and too weak to stand, Mosupi sat next Granny. Together, they waited. That is the African way—to wait and wait, patiently.

Granny used Mosupi's mobile phone to call Mpho's mother to ask her to come. "And bring Mpho with you. Seeing her will cheer him up a bit," Granny said.

A nurse called Mosupi's name. With Granny's help, he stumbled to the triage area. He was so weak and so feverish that the nurse put him on a stretcher to lie down to rest. With no examining rooms available, the nurse pushed the stretcher up alongside the wall in back of another stretcher on which a man with a laceration from a bar fight had lain all night long.

There, on that stretcher in that hallway in the Accident and Emergency Department, alone and feverish and in pain, Mosupi at the age of 18 once again bore witness to the modern Africa into which he had been born. He died.

When the nurse noticed Mosupi was no longer breathing, she pulled the sheet over him, got a doctor to declare him dead. She went to the waiting room and called out for Mosupi's relatives. Mpho's mother and Mpho, who was just days away from her first birthday, had just arrived, to Granny's delight. The three of them followed the nurse back, Mpho in her mother's arms. Upon the sight of Mosupi's lifeless body, Granny and Mpho's mother wailed and wailed. Mpho buried her face in her mother's bosom, shielding her eyes from the scene that lay before her.

The Clinical Issues

DAVID KISSANE

Mosupi is dead. Named to celebrate the political ascendancy of his African people, Mosupi had been orphaned as a three-year-old boy as HIV/AIDS ravaged the country. Mosupi was first diagnosed with HIV at age eight and became non-adherent to his antiretroviral medication after dropping out of high school. Now the same family members that had gathered regularly together at the Bible Church each Sunday morning, his beloved Granny and his girlfriend, Naomi, carrying his one-year-old daughter, Mpho, are ushered into the hallway of the Accident and Emergency Department, where the 18-year old Mosupi has died alone on a stretcher against the wall. The women wail publically about his death. Mosupi is dead!

The doctor, who certified him dead, saw his dehydrated, cachetic body, covered with skin blotches typical of Kaposi's Sarcoma and immediately recognizable as another AIDS victim. Too late! Nothing to do here, it seems.

The nurse, who carries the emotional burden of the Accident and Emergency Department, witnesses their grief. No private room for the bereaved! No chaplain to anoint the deceased! The stark reality of poverty surrounds these three women, left again to take the nation forward without their men.

Where is the dignity of the dying here? Where is compassion for the bereaved? Bereft of the usual accompaniments of modern medicine, we see the harsh and raw reality in which a young man has died alone, ignorant of his terminal plight, and without adequate care that might have prevented his loss.

How might we have rewritten this tragic story? Let us assume that his death was indeed inevitable at that time in his country. A dying person presents close to his final breath. We want to triage this as a high priority for a private space which can be made sacred, and in which his family can continue to accompany him. Medicine needs to acknowledge the imminence of death and call a minister to help. A precious time of watchful accompaniment has arrived. Sociology points to the importance of ritual; spirituality responds to the need to find meaning in death and absence. Medically, we treat every symptom and sign that might relieve suffering, as simple as fluid for parched lips, a bed to rest on, a sheet to cover the body, a cool, wet towel to sooth the fevered brow. Psychologically, the model of family-centered care comes to the fore, to support not only the dying Mosupi but also his granny and his girlfriend, providing gentle touch, soft words, respectful silence, and guidance to embrace ritual and invoke their normal religious traditions that we hope will serve as a familiar and comforting pathway.

Family-centered care at the end of life brings together those closest to and immediately affected by the loss, and tries to create a compassionate and supportive frame in which relatives can be held in their grief. The medical environment yields to shift the tenor of care from technology and action to patient accompaniment and quiet respect. The family often needs guidance about the unfolding process, what to expect, and how they might help. The clinician seeks to appraise their resources, supports, religious tradition, and cultural norms. Attentively, the clinician should enquire about their needs.

Once death has occurred, its reality is proclaimed, with comment about the likely mode of dying given to offer explanation to help integrate understanding and eventually acceptance.

Medical schools the world over teach the following sequence of strategies in response to an unexpected death:

1. Call the relatives to come urgently, but safely, to the hospital. If only one relative seems available, search for other sources of support that can be rallied.

2. Usher them into a suitably private room.

3. Give a warning about the seriousness, a brief comment about your provisional diagnosis, and deliver the factual information thus: "I have some bad news...Mosupi seems to have been seriously ill with AIDS. We did all we could. I'm sorry to have to tell you that he has just died."

4. Patiently allow time for emotional expression, tissues for tears, touch for comfort, silence for the reality of the predicament to be integrated and confirmed. Name their grief, empathically normalizing and validating their reaction thus: "It is terribly sad...I sense that you are shocked. Many people find that it feels surreal...so unreal...grief is deeply painful, so very distressing!"

5. After a suitable time, invite the family to ask questions and, in the process, check their understanding about what has happened. "How much had you appreciated that Mosupi was so sick? What treatment had happened? How openly had you talked about this as a family?" Consider all of their needs. "Mpho is too young to remember what has happened, but she will sense your distress and need comfort. Will you stay with Granny and support each other?"

6. Consider their religious, cultural, ethnic and practical needs. Whom should be told? Would they like help? Do they have they a funeral director that will need to be told? Are there special needs in laying out the body? "Tell me if you practice a religion? Can I ask our chaplain (or minister) to come?"

7. Consider whether an autopsy is required by law or desirable medically if permission is given.

8. Educate briefly about health care needs with infectious or inheritable diseases, the related risks, the hope associated with active treatment and development of a care plan with optimal continuity. For example, "Can we arrange for Mpho and her mother to be tested for HIV, to give as much help as we can?"

9. Once the relatives appear to have integrated understanding and considered the practical steps that need attention, invite the family to accompany you to see the body of the deceased. Prepare them for what to expect and

accompany them to a private setting, where you can leave them with the deceased. "We recommend that you come and see Mosupi's body...appreciate that he is at peace. Will it help to say some prayers together by him? We will let you have some private time together with him."

10. Check back on them after a suitable time, reviewing again their understanding, answering any questions, considering fully their needs. Talk about the future care of the body, its transfer and what will occur. Offer a future meeting to discuss again what has happened, what pathology may have shown, what an autopsy might have found. "We find that a family meeting over the next month is very helpful for families...down the track...once the funeral is over. We like to review any pathology tests, answer your questions, and make sure that you understand all that has happened."

11. Discuss their transport home again, considering safety and support.

12. Ensure they are accompanied from the hospital, and respectfully bid goodbye.

The care plan outlined here shifts its attention from the deceased to those who continue living. Death is a normal part of life. The clinician attempts to educate the deceased's relatives about what it means medically and why it has occurred. The broad goal is to provide psychosocial and spiritual support to the family. When a physician has been a patient's usual care provider, they would indicate their willingness to complete a death certificate. In an Accident and Emergency Department, the physician would offer to reach out to the usual care provider, informing them of the outcome and ascertaining their willingness to help. When the jurisdiction mandates autopsy by law whenever death is unexplained, the family are educated about the requirement to report the patient's death to the coroner, who may choose to request an autopsy. If this is not mandated, the clinical service might still seek it to understand better what has occurred via a postmortem examination of the body, and thus to hope to improve care provision for the future. Extra certification about the mode of dying is generally needed when a funeral director is planning cremation of the body, and in most jurisdictions, an independent medical inspection of the deceased's body is mandated by law.

Mosupi's story of death from a fully treatable disease points to the medical neglect of underserved communities, with resultant challenges for our societies and care systems to identify optimal ways to follow-up with the sick and encourage both preventive and active care. Advocacy, education, access to care, and the cost of care are major public health concerns of the medical community. We seek the gradual shift of care paradigms from urgent crisis to preventive care, such that today, even bereavement care would begin for families during palliative care rather than waiting for death to arrive.

The Ethical Issues

ANNE DAVIS

Mosupi is a tragic example of the realities in Africa, where so many young people are infected with and have died from HIV/AIDS.

The two types of ethical issues here are the same for all patients: immediate and long term. But patients with HIV/AIDS are a special case because of the nature of the diagnosis and how it is perceived and experienced by patients, families, and communities.

Immediate Ethical Issues and Responses

Immediate responses use the ethical principle, *respect*: for:

- Mosupi's body in the context of scarce resources, including health care personnel, hospital space and privacy, and transportation;
- the family's immediate reaction in response to Mosupi's death; and
- the family's belief system about life, death, and obligations possibly influenced by tribal membership and traditional beliefs, the impact of Christianity or Islam, and burial rites.

Respectful treatment of a dead human body is a universally recognized ethical norm. To respect means that a person has and shows a high positive regard for the worth of someone or something...How are Mosupi and his family respected?

The role of stigma surrounding HIV/AIDS in the ethical care that Mosupi and his family receive or do not receive need to be taken into account. The beliefs of native healers, nurses, doctors, neighbors, and political and religious leaders about life and death can lead to disrespectful reactions, including the notion, widespread in some areas, that people who die from AIDS experience a bad death and do not deserve a good burial. "Bad" here is a judgmental word about Mosupi's behavior. Mosupi contracted HIV from his infected mother; however, the ethical principle, respect, remains, regardless of the diagnosis leading to his death.

Long Term Ethical Issues

Mosupi's death is the result of larger sociopolitical factors. This observation pushes us to examine ethical questions that go far beyond hospitals and Mosupi's illness. Such questions would include:

- How can people in Africa have access to ongoing health care and medications?
- What is possible in education and employment for Africa's youth?

- What role and responsibility do community leaders and politicians have to obtain scientific knowledge about diseases and help educate people using this knowledge?
- To help prevent HIV/AIDS should the government and community leaders promote the use of condoms and educate people in their use?
- With regards to HIV/AIDS, what is the ethical role and responsibility of various social institutions—government, religion, community, family—in education, prevention, and treatment?
- Do former colonial powers and other economically developed countries have any obligation in prevention and treatment of HIV/AIDS African patients?
- What would need to be accomplished in Mosupi's country to prevent his baby, Mpho, from contracting HIV/AIDS?

A Final Word

One of the most difficult but central questions in ethics is: How do individuals and groups maintain moral standards while at the same time respecting people who do not share some or all of those values?

The African Independent and Pentecostal Churches Response

JAMES AMANZE

In the era of the HIV/AIDS pandemic, many families in Africa have gone through the experiences of Mosupi's family, regardless of their religious affiliation. In Africa, human sexuality is considered sacred, and childbearing is a religious duty. In traditional Africa, the fact that Mosupi was already infected with HIV before his birth would not carry a moral stigma. He would still be considered as a gift from God through the ancestors to humanity. The moralization of HIV and AIDS is primarily a Christian problem. The genesis of the pandemic in a number of African countries was associated with myth, witchcraft, the work of evil spirits, anger of the ancestors for breaking societal taboos, and the like.

In African Independent Churches, Mosupi's illness would be taken as any other disease. Church people would pray for him during services for healing in the church or at home. Prophet-healers in many African Independent Churches claim that they have power to heal all kinds of diseases, including HIV/AIDS, through the power of the Holy Spirit. Some prophet-healers invoke the healing power of the ancestors to heal HIV/AIDS. A person in Mosupi's situation would be prayed for with the laying on of hands and the use of holy water, in some cases mixed with special ashes made from bones of sacrificed animals and cow dung. He or she would be given other forms of treatment, including African traditional medicine, depending on the diagnosis by the prophet-healer. Sometimes a ritual in the form of an animal sacrifice as a burnt offering to the ancestors can be performed under the supervision of the prophet-healer in the presence of relatives and church members.

In the event of death, relatives and the community at large would gather to lay the deceased to rest. The loss of Mosupi's family would always be considered as a loss of the entire community, because death, like birth, is a community affair. At death, the community grieves together. There is no such a thing as "private grieving" in Africa. Neither Mosupi nor his late mother would be vilified for having died of HIV and AIDS. However, such occasions are used these days to warn people to change their sexual behavior in order to avoid dying of HIV/AIDS related illnesses. By and large, the dead are considered to have returned to the ancestors and ultimately to God, where they came from. Mosupi's death would not be considered as punishment for sins committed by himself or his parents.

In Pentecostal Churches, the situation would be radically different. The death of Mosupi would carry a lot of stigma. This is because dying of AIDS is considered to be a result of sexual immorality either of the parents or of the deceased. The common saying among Pentecostals is "the wages of sin is death; you reap what you sow." Thus, death through HIV/AIDS has, for a long time, been considered a punishment from God. Because of the stigma involved in this case, Pentecostals would find it very difficult to tell other people that their child died of HIV/AIDS. When death occurs, a lot of theological questions are asked such as "If God is good, why does he allow us to die? Why does God not do away with HIV/AIDS?" When a person is sick with AIDS, church members pray, sing, fast, and lay hands on the sick. The church also may pull its financial resources together in order to buy recommended food for those with HIV/AIDS. They may also buy toiletries and so on.

When a person dies of AIDS, the church comes to comfort the family. Church members assure the bereaved that the deceased is in God's hands and that they must have faith in God, who is the source of life. Pentecostal Churches encourage the sick to repent of their sins before they die because they believe in a forgiving God. Pentecostals are happy if a person dies after repentance because God is not happy with the death of a sinner. This means that, if a person who contracted HIV/AIDS confesses before death, his or her sins are forgiven and can be saved. Pentecostals are not happy when an AIDS patient dies before repentance, because such a person dies in sin. By and large, doctors advise people to enable the sick person to confess his or her sins before death, so that his/her sins should be forgiven before meeting his/her Master Creator, who has the power over life and death.

In recent years, however, things have changed drastically, in that many Pentecostals do not believe any more that if a person dies of HIV/AIDS it is a punishment from God for sin. At present, people are more compassionate than ever before, in which case HIV/AIDS is considered as any other disease. However, Pentecostal Churches teach and preach against immoral behavior. The death of young people is considered a warning to others that those who live reckless lives will suffer the same consequences. In the event of death, prayers to comfort the bereaved are said regularly. No other traditional rituals for the dead are performed, unlike the case in African culture. Pentecostal Churches follow strictly Christian traditions.

The Buddhist Response

SORAJ HONGLADAROM

Mosupi is dead. Now, I see this case more as a case in political philosophy than in medical ethics. The political issue involved here is of course the poverty and indignity suffered by Mosupi and his people in Africa. According to Thomas Pogge, the rich nations in the West are doing next to nothing to help the poorer nations in Africa.[1] This is a clear case of global injustice. How could those in the richer nations of the West and Asia allow this situation to happen? With only a few dollars per person to spare, the people in the West, and in the richer countries in Asia could help solve the problems of hunger, poverty, malnutrition, and lack of adequate health care that beset these long-suffering souls in Africa. This glaring inequality among groups of nations in the world is the most gruesome example of injustice in the world today.

The indignity in the way Mosupi's body is treated is indicative of the political problems and injustices faced by African nations today. It is quite certain that, in Mosupi's own country, the rich elites are enjoying very good health care in a way that cannot be imagined by Mosupi's people. Perhaps they can fly to Europe on a regular basis just to see a doctor, or have a team of doctors in a rich private hospital in the capital city standing ready for them 24 hours a day. Whereas Mosupi has to spend one whole day just to ride a bus across his village to see his doctor and back, having to wait in an extremely long line before he can see his doctor for only a few minutes, the rich in his own country can just ride their chauffeured cars to the hospital at the time of their own convenience. The inequality can be found both internationally (between groups of nations) and domestically, as Mosupi experienced the gap between his own situation and that of his elite countrymen.

Buddhism typically does not address political issues directly. The strategy of the Buddha was that he was willing to go along with the political policies of the country in which he was living so that he could avoid conflicts with the political power. If the policy was unjust, he would try to teach the ruler to refrain from the unjust practice; but if this is not possible, then he would simply leave. Recently there has emerged a new form of Buddhist practice, however, called "socially engaged Buddhism,"[2] which aims at turning the Buddhist insights and teachings towards solving the social, economic, and political problems that are facing the world today. The Buddhist perspective on human equality and dignity can in fact be used to criticize these unjust practices that are causing suffering in the world. All human beings are capable of achieving the Final Goal of Nirvana; as such, all deserve respect and are equal in this regard because, deep down, every human being is a potential Buddha. This principle can indeed be used to found the idea of universal human rights. It is conceivable that if Mosupi's country did embrace these fundamental human rights principles as well as the rights to adequate health care as proposed by the World Health Organization,[3] the situation at least could have been ameliorated. Respecting human rights also certainly extends to respecting the deceased bodies too. They have to be treated with the dignity and respect that they deserve.

The Confucian Response

RUIPING FAN

Mosupi is a very unfortunate man in an African country. He was orphaned at three, raised by his grandma, and has now died of HIV/AIDS at 18. He has left three poor women, his grandma, his girlfriend, and his nearly one-year-old daughter behind him. We are not sure of the religious affiliation, if any, of the hospital in which Mosupi's body now lies. But the story does mention that Mosupi went to a Bible Church along with his grandma and girlfriend and had happy Sunday mornings. From a Confucian perspective, the hospital and the church should help Mosupi's wailing grandma and girlfriend handle his body properly and hold a funeral service for this tragically afflicted man.

As a family-based and family-oriented religion, Confucianism sees one's body as a gift from one's ancestors. It is not from one particular ancestor, but from all the ancestors of the family. Traditionally, Confucians take the actual scope of the family to include all members of nine generations (jiuzu): four generations ahead of oneself (one's parents, grandparents, great-grandparents, and great-great-grandparents) and four generations behind oneself (one's children, grandchildren, great-grandchildren, and great-great-grandchildren). However, the people belonging to two nearest generations (namely parents and children) hold the most intimate relations; that is, although it is understood that one's body is a gift is from all the ancestors, including remote ancestors, it is also emphasized that the body is most crucially from one's recent ancestors, especially one's parents. That is why in the beginning of the *Hsiao King* (the Classic of Filial Piety), it is clearly stated that "our bodies—to every hair and bit of skin—are received by us from our parents, and we must not presume to injure or wound them: this is the beginning of filial piety."[4] At death, one's body must be treated seriously and properly in order to show respect not only to oneself but also to one's ancestors.

From the Confucian understanding, the human soul (*hunpo*) is composed of the finest element (*qi*) of the universe. It is not created and inserted into one's body directly by God (*shangdi*); rather, it is transferred into one's life from one's ancestors, so that one's soul and one's ancestors' souls are essentially similar. One is therefore responsible both upwards to one's ancestors and downwards to one's descendants by being both a gift receiver and a giver in the Confucian way of life (*Analects* 2:4).[5] For Confucians, although God or Heaven (*tian*) creates and maintains the order of the universe, it is the Mandate of Heaven that ensures every child should be formed and born into a family through the union of a man (from one particular family) and a woman (from another particular family). In addition, Confucians believe that the human soul has two parts: *hun* and *po*. After death *hun* lives in the heavens near God, while *po* stays in the grave with the body.[6] *Hun* regularly returns to join the *po* by visiting the grave and to accept sacrifices from the descendants by visiting their homes. Ancestors give blessings to their descendants, and the descendants must be reverently filial to their ancestors, including attempting to avoid harming their own body so as not to make their ancestors worry about their health. Accordingly, Confucianism does not require that the body should never be cremated. Cremation is acceptable, since the *po* is certainly retained in the ashes. Confucianism does hold that insofar as possible, the cinerary casket ideally should be buried in a grave. Hopefully, Mpho, this poor man's daughter, will be cared for and cultivated to grow up and be able to provide certain memorial ceremonies for her dead father.

The Evangelical Christian Response

JOHN GRAHAM

Mosupi's case highlights the many problems facing the medically underserved throughout the world and in the United States: first, they have limited access to modern medicine and often turn first to tribal or household remedies instead; second, there is a lack of employment opportunities available to youth with limited education, often resulting in their getting involved with the wrong crowd and remaining financial burdens to their families; third, the glaring insensitivity of hospital personnel (perhaps augmented by the fact Mosupi has HIV); and, fourth, there are religious and societal issues—too often society and people of faith turn the other way and have not done what they could have done to alleviate this kind of suffering.

As an Evangelical Christian, what would I say to Mosupi's family were I their pastor? First, I would want to be present and listen as they share their heart-breaking story. Listen, as they share all their "what ifs" and concerns. "If only we had brought Mosupi to the hospital sooner, he would still be alive." "If only the government had done something. Why doesn't the government bring the drugs to our village so we don't have to make the long, expensive trip to town?" "Why didn't the nurse tell us Mosupi was about to die so we could say goodbye?" And, most importantly, "Why did God let this happen? We went to church every Sunday. We love God. Where was God when Mosupi died alone on that stretcher?"

At this moment, I believe I would want to comfort the family by telling them that I believe God was with Mosupi at the time of his death; for Scripture says "God will not leave us nor forsake us" (1 Kings 8:57; Isaiah 41:17 NKJV). With all integrity I would say, "Mosupi did not die alone. God was with him." I would also tell them that I believe that the angels of God were present at his side and that, at God's appointed time, they will escort Mosupi into heavenly places (Mark 13:27; Revelation 7:9-10).

After this, I would turn my attention to the living—to the grandmother and to Mpho's mother. I would tell them that I am here now and the people of our home church will be by their sides when they return home. I would ask if they need transportation back home (knowing that they do) and ask what they wish to do with Mosupi's body. I would contact pastors in the local Christian community, asking them to render aid in helping this family in their hour of great need. Perhaps they could provide transportation back home for the family and for Mosupi's body. I would contact our home church, informing parishioners there of Mosupi's death and of the family's plight. I would ask them to make preparations for the family's arrival and begin preparations for a memorial service to celebrate Mosupi's life in Christ.

Mosupi's funeral service would be a celebration of God's resurrection power made manifest in God's son, Jesus Christ, who was raised from the dead and ascended into heaven. The resurrection is the basis of every Christian's hope of eternal life. At his baptism, Mosupi was united with Jesus Christ in his life, in his death on the Cross, and in his Resurrection from the dead. Jesus was raised from the dead, and Mosupi shall be raised as well. The funeral service, in the midst of a loving community, will do much to help the family in their grief. But, their grief will not end there. The presence, prayers, and support of a loving community will be vitally important in the months ahead.

There are several issues yet to be considered. There appears to have been a lack of awareness on the part of Mosupi as to the danger of HIV. If he stopped his medications, one has to wonder if he used condoms when he had sexual relations with his partner. If not, there is the question of whether or not she and their baby, Mpho, have acquired HIV. They need to be tested. A pastor in this setting can have a great impact on people in his congregation, bringing knowledge of the disease to their attention.

Another thing to consider is how Mosupi and his family were treated at the hospital. They were separated from their loved one and he was left to die on a stretcher alone. And, following his death, there was little attention given to the family. Perhaps the diagnosis of HIV made a difference in the care they received. Yet, treating people with respect and dignity is crucial, especially when caring for someone who is near the end of life. Tragically, this was forgotten by Mosupi's caregivers and must have added to his family's pain. Health care professionals need to be sensitive to this, and the church can help bring this to the attention of leaders in health care institutions.

A final issue deals with the collective responsibility of society and organized religion to address the issue of the medically underserved in our communities and in the world at large. Global poverty is a societal problem which invites our collective attention. Sensitivity to the Mosupis of this world can do much to awaken an apathetic church and community. Together, we can address these issues and challenge our political leaders to respond appropriately.

The Hindu Response

UMA MYSOREKAR

Mosupi, as a little boy contracted HIV/AIDS from his own mother, but, unfortunately, due to poverty, did not receive proper treatment. Hindu religious teachings on healthy living and ethical consideration culminate in a spiritual objective if the information ascertained in the system is followed. From the Hindu religious point of view, no special perspective can be given on HIV/AIDS prevention and control.

Religion and medicine are intertwined in Hinduism. A Hindu form of health care called Ayurveda was practiced for thousands of years and addresses many physical, emotional, and mental illnesses and their treatments. Although such suffering is considered part of one's *karma*, it is acceptable to get relief and treatments. In fact, according to Hinduism, since the body encloses the God-likeness in the soul, it is important to maintain good health and to seek medical care.

Traditionally, Hindus prefer to die at home, although nowadays increasing numbers are kept in hospitals, especially when recovery is clearly not possible. When death is imminent, family, relatives from near and far, and close friends are notified. They all gather, and some family members will be chanting mantras such as *Vishnu Sahasranamas*, praying, and reading scriptures. The Hindu Temple in the area is contacted to depute a spiritual person (priest) to wherever the dying person is. Arranging a meeting with a priest or a spiritual person or allowing the patient and family to pray and sing devotional songs, and chant mantras or *slokas* are services recommended for a patient at the end of life. At the moment of death family members chant a mantra such as "*Om Namah Sivaya*" or "*Om Namo Narayana*" softly into the ear of the dying person. Holy ash or sandalwood paste is applied on the forehead. Holy water from Ganges or other holy river is trickled into the mouth. Hindus usually do not embalm the bodies. Postmortem examination is usually not acceptable, unless legally required.

The funeral is called *Antyeshti* or the last sacrament. Although a majority of Hindus believe in *karma* and rebirth, most of them consider death an inauspicious and sad occasion. Upon the death of a person, wailing and crying are common among close relations. When the death is unexpected and sudden, bereavement and grief are significantly greater. The general belief is that, at the time of death, a soul leaves the physical body though a small aperture in the skull and travels to other worlds and will return to earth based on its *karma*.

As death is considered inauspicious, the bereaved family usually stays away from normal social contact and engagements until the impurity caused by the death is washed away though rituals and purification ceremonies. Hindus usually cremate dead bodies with the exception that burial is performed in the case of saints, spiritual masters, and children. The place of cremation and the time of cremation are important. Cremating a body in a place of pilgrimage or on the banks of a sacred river is considered auspicious as it is believed to ensure a safe passage of the soul to the higher world. Cremation grounds are usually found outside the towns and villages in secluded places. In many urban areas and here in the United States they are replaced by electric crematoriums.

The body of a deceased person is usually cremated on the same day. Occasionally it is kept in the house (or funeral home) until important relatives living in distant places arrive to pay their last respects. Once the time of cremation is decided, the body is washed clean, sandalwood paste and turmeric are applied, and the body is decorated as the family desires. It is then wrapped in a white cotton cloth and taken to the cremation site or the crematorium. Just before cremation, the priest chants mantras and *slokas* from the *Bhagavad Gita* and *Upanishads*, and so on. This is to reassure the family present that the eternal soul has commenced its final journey, leaving the body behind.

About one or two days later, after the body is cremated, the sons of the deceased collect the ashes from the crematorium (or the cremation ground) in one or more urns. Ashes are dispersed in the ocean, or, if possible, into sacred waters of the Ganges, the Yamuna, or another sacred river. Hindus strongly believe that the contact of the ashes with the sacred water ensures liberation for the departed soul.

For a few days after the cremation, the family of the deceased is considered highly impure because of their coming into contact with the bio-magnetic energy accumulated around the dead body. They remain secluded, avoiding social contacts and visits to friends and families. The family members of the deceased remain occupied in various rites for 13 days.

The Indigenous Response

IRENE TAAFAKI

When a member of a Marshallese family dies, there will be no need for the hospital to call relatives to inform them; they will already be there. Every Marshallese belongs to a clan identified by the maternal blood line (*bwij*) and has an immediate kin comprising close knit relationships with uncles, aunts, and cousins. It is an organization with recognized leaders, spokesmen, and workers. If the medical staff allow, one or more members of the family will be close beside the deceased at the point of death—uttering words of reassurance, fanning, massaging, and offering sips of water. When the end of life occurs, they will witness the last breath. There follows space for grieving, with comfort provided through the strong support from relatives, friends, and the pastor or priest that serves the community wherever they reside.

When death occurs, the family leadership knows what to do. Instructions are immediately given to communicate with more distantly located family members to make arrangements to come to the place where the body lies. In the Marshall Islands, the public radio is used for this purpose. An early decision will be to identify those who will wash and prepare the body. If the deceased is of chiefly rank, then a special retainer will be called. For all others, the body is attended to by members of the family. However, the oldest child, whether male or female, cannot bathe his or her parents—that is taboo. Other older relatives will watch the process and contribute the requirements for it. The preparation of the body includes cleansing and anointing the body with fragrant coconut oil, dripping as much as 12 oz of pure oil slowly into the navel, and embalming using the leaves of the *kiden* (Beach Heliotrope), which is mixed with salt, pounded, and placed into all orifices, including the ear and nose but not the mouth. This embalming retains the freshness of the body for three to four days. Nowadays, chemical embalming is used to preserve the body, and this must be done by a certified mortician.

In death, as in life, the deceased is accompanied, and the dead body afforded the greatest respect. Ri-Majōl belief is that, since a person sprang from the clan's land, they must return to it for burial in a grave that faces to the east. When death occurs in the urban communities of Majuro and Ebeye, time is needed for relatives living overseas to arrange to travel home for the cultural rituals of the passing. If a Marshallese dies overseas, huge expense is incurred for the body to make the long journey back to be buried on the clan's land. Permission from the chief is obtained and usually he or his steward (*alab*) will be present at the burial to confirm this permission. This burial land (*uliej*) has its own taboos. For example, one may not harvest food from it. Because of the necessity to return to the land, there is reluctance among Ri-Majōl to cremate, though the recent challenges and cost of transporting coffins long distances have prompted a few families to defy custom, resort to cremation, and bring home ashes.

Marshallese believe that in life we are attached to a fine tentacle (*aoḷōk*), pulled through waters by (the god) Mejḷap. When people sicken, they lose hold of the thread, die, and are gathered into a vessel *waan kabool ḷal* (literally "to go around the world").

T: *Januōde im wanmanlok, enana mejatoto, enana lojet, enana aolep kain. Bwebwenato in Mejlep...ej boke aolep, ri-palle, ri-Majol...eppepe aolep armej. Elukkuun kwedkwedi neen armej bwe rewutlok jen ilele...wa ej eko-take* [January and onward, the air/weather is bad, the sea is bad. All people are floating (on the water attached to the longest tentacle of the Portuguese man-of-war [*aoḷōk*]).... They fall off the tentacle. The boat picks up people]

M: We're being strung right now...when it's high tide, we float...when it's low tide, we are dragging along the reef (everyone talking at once)...

I: What's his name?

All: Mejlep

T: *M., kwon ba...bwebwenato in mol...alon january elap naninmej.* [M., you say [commanding] this is a true story, in the month of January there is a lot of sickness]

M: You might say it is a true story, lots of sickness and death

C: *Bar juon etanak* [one more dream]. If you dream you are on the boat, you will die.

In the early morning following the third or sixth night after burial, the soul (*jetōb*) of the deceased will leave its physical body and make its way to the spirit world. Family members maintain a vigil to watch for this departure—and there are signs that confirm the passage. Throughout this time, the sadness of the loss is mitigated by *bwebwenato*—stories about the deceased and other topics to comfort the bereaved and lighten their grief. There is a spot or portal on the ocean side in Delap, Majuro through which all spirits of Marshallese pass and enter the canoes which then make their way to Nadikdik, an island near Mili Atoll. This is where, tradition has it, the souls of good and bad are separated, each to receive their justice.

Only after this journey of the soul has been taken, can the living leave the body alone.

The Jewish Response

HERBERT BROCKMAN

This is a human tragedy! Mosupi's death is not his or his family's alone. It underscores in the most vivid and personal terms the indecent and unjust ways we human beings treat one another. We have the means to prolong the lives of HIV/AIDS patients indefinitely but we seem to lack the political or moral will to do so. Lacking an economic incentive, we easily turn a blind eye. We have become inured to the suffering especially of people living in Third World countries. Little by little, it seems, our moral outrage and the capacity for human compassion diminishes. And what is lost is not just another human being, a Mosupi, but our own "stirring of the soul," our sense of life's mystery in a personal sense as well as in a collective human sense.

Even within families, I see this diminishment. The death of a loved one is a time for setting aside the "normalities" of existence for a chance to grieve, to pay tribute to the life of a loved one, and to life itself. Mourning is a time to focus our attention not on the "everydayness" but rather on the "extraordinariness" of life. Although the modern trend has been to give up many of the rituals that helped in the grieving process over the centuries, recently some Jews have begun seeking a renewal of them. Traditions were missing in the tragedy of Mosupi.

In Judaism, we begin with the recognition that life is sacred. A human being is made up of a soul that has been implanted at birth within a physical body. Upon death, the soul expires, or leaves the body, and finds its way to heaven. The custom arose that, upon death, the window of the room was opened to allow the soul egress.

The family would then tear an article of clothing, or, more commonly, a black ribbon as a sign that the "heart is rent." This symbol will remind and enable the community upon seeing the "tear" to perform the *mitzvah*, the obligation, of comforting the mourner.

The family may remain with the deceased until the removal of the body. In Jewish tradition, the body is "accompanied" until the funeral. In the more traditional communities, a burial society (*chevrah kadisha*) performs this ritual and will wash and anoint the body, dress the deceased in a shroud (since all are equal in death and distinctions are not to be made for rich or poor, scholar or dullard). As soon as possible, the burial will take place. Other than these preparations, the body is to be "disturbed" as little as possible. Even autopsy, unless the results could benefit another living person, is generally prohibited.

Respect for the body is to be shown at all times. Modesty is to be observed, with men preparing a male for burial and women preparing a female.

The body is then to be placed in a plain pine coffin or wrapped in natural material in order for the body to more easily return to its natural state. "The dust returns to the earth as it was" (Ecclesiates 12:7 Jewish Publication Society).

The promptness of the funeral is to allow the family to enter into the period of mourning. Their "grief work" begins with the actual funeral as they shovel the earth over the coffin. It is said that this is the final act of loving kindness one can do for a loved one—to help to bury them.

Although some in the Jewish community have practiced forms of cremation, it is believed that the process of decay should occur naturally. This custom of choosing burial over cremation has been reinforced by the deaths of so many Jews in the Nazi crematoria. A minority still practice cremation, however.

Among Ashkenazi (Eastern European) Jews, the practice of not bringing flowers to a funeral persists. Although this is custom and not "law," the reasoning does fit with tradition; namely, that the expense of the flowers would be better used as a contribution to charity in the loved one's name. This permits a person's memory to persist beyond the grave.

At this point the family then enters the period of mourning, which begins with the emotionally intense first seven days following burial and concludes on the anniversary of the loved one's death. Throughout, the community accompanies the family.

The Mainline Protestant Christian Response

JAN HOLTON

Many, like Mosupi and his family, struggle against the effects of poverty and illness such as HIV/AIDS. Each longs for the alleviation of suffering, and when the time of death approaches, each deserves a dignified death. Care for the poor among us is a basic principle of the Christian faith exemplified in the actions and teachings of Jesus Christ. It is an issue of justice and a fundamental response to human suffering. Mainline Protestant churches maintain the position that every person should have appropriate access to health care, especially palliative care, in the service of providing the opportunity for death with dignity. There is, however, disparity between levels of health care in the West and those found in many developing countries.

Mainline Protestant social and theological beliefs affirm support and care of the dying as responsibilities of the faithful. It is the task of spiritual caregivers, whenever possible, to provide comfort, direction, and spiritual support as death approaches. Most health care professionals in the West agree and are keenly attentive and sensitive to the needs of the dying and their loved ones. When this professional sensitivity is not present, it is the responsibility of spiritual caregivers to advocate on behalf of the dying and their families.

The presence of the community of loved ones at the time of death offers an active witness of love, facilitates a shifting of life narrative, and participates in spiritual accompaniment. Each of these acts has the opportunity to offer great comfort to the dying, and, in the process, change the shape of ensuing grief for loved ones.

The circle of family and friends that encompasses the dying provides what no medical professional can—love. Rather than leave one isolated and alone to face death, the comfort of loved ones gives strength to the dying. Sitting vigil through the long hours approaching death can provide witness to the labor of the dying body. This time of waiting is one in which families can share stories of joy, sadness, and laughter. As storied people, shifting these narratives to encompass the reality of approaching death can make room for the change that is to happen when the loved one is no longer in the family's presence. The mainline Protestant tradition recognizes that, even in the midst of loss, the stories of our lives connect us to the larger narrative of the Christian story. The Holy Gospels tell the stories of how many of Jesus's followers bore witness to his life and, in love, surrounded him as he approached death. Most importantly, a new story unfolds in the promise of resurrection.

Prayer and anointing are common rituals that enhance spiritual support at the bedside of those approaching death. In the mainline Protestant understanding, these are acts that call upon God's faithful presence for the one dying and affirm the fervent belief that, though illness or injury has foreclosed on one's earthly days, an eternal future in the presence of a loving God awaits. To facilitate a sense of agency in a time otherwise marked by feelings of helplessness, spiritual caregivers may encourage the active participation of loved ones in these rituals. For example, the simple act of touching a loved one during prayer or offering personal words of thanksgiving for the life of the dying are powerful contributions to the spiritual comfort and care of the dying and grieving alike.

Grief is a constellation of sometimes overwhelming emotions that can begin long before a loved one's last breath. Spiritual caregivers should be prepared for a variety of physical and spiritual responses. Tending to the body after death is a long held practice for Christians, as it is for many traditions. If death has occurred in a hospital, the physical practicalities often include removing medical devices and washing the body in preparation for a final viewing before its departure to a funeral home. Families may request to participate in preparing the body. They should be allowed to do so. In the mainline Protestant tradition, it is customary for spiritual caregivers to accompany families, in presence and prayer, through this last intimate farewell with their dying loved one before mourning moves into the public realm.

The Shi'a Muslim Response

NAJMEH JAFARI

Mosupi was diagnosed with HIV/AIDS when he was just eight, and ten years later, his body is lying unceremoniously on a stretcher alongside the wall in the hospital. Mosupi was born with the HIV virus replicating in his body. He experienced the fateful toll HIV infection takes in his country when his mother died when he was just three years old. Now, Mpho has had a similar experience in seeing her father die. While Mosupi's grandmother was looking for his loved one to "cheer him up a bit," Mosupi was nearing his last breath.

In Islam, the first and the foremost basic human right is the right to live; it is to respect human life. Mosupi deserves the best care, such as a private room to give him comfort, medicines to alleviate his suffering, and the presence of relatives for last words. In the final moments, Mosupi may have a sense of confusion, shock, nervousness, and fear. Were he a Muslim, he might have worries relating to the obligatory Actions of Islam (i.e., missed prayer or fasting), or about his daughter or possessions. When death approaches, close family and friends will try to support and comfort a dying person. Muslims are encouraged to visit dying loved ones and pray for their welfare in the next world. Also this provides a time when they seek each other's forgiveness. Granny and Naomi should have this chance to be present at his bedside to help him turn his thoughts to God and encourage him very gently to repent. Remembering God's mercy and asking for forgiveness may alleviate Mosupi's suffering and bring him peace. Close family and friends may help him to repeat the shahadatain of Islam, the testimony of belief in Allah and His Messenger. It is the declaration of faith: "I bear witness that there is no god but Allah and Muhammed is the Messenger of Allah."

Surroundings should be calm in these final moments, and those around Mosupi should pray for him or recite *Qur'an*. When his soul leaves the body and the Angel of Death takes it, those in the room should close Mosupi's eyes and cover his body temporarily with a clean sheet and lay him facing the *Qibla* (that is, in the direction of Makkah). Muslims believe that angels descend at the moment of death upon the dying believer and tell him neither to fear nor to grieve.

> In the case of those who say, "Our Lord is Allah," and, further, stand straight and steadfast, the angels descend on them (from time to time): "Fear ye not!" (they suggest), "Nor grieve! but receive the Glad Tidings of the Garden (of Bliss), that which ye were promised! We are your protectors in this life and in the Hereafter: therein shall ye have all that your souls shall desire; therein shall ye have all that ye ask for a hospitable gift from one Oft-Forgiving, Most Merciful" (Qur'an 41:32)

Granny and Naomi should have some private time together with him to express their grief. It is permissible to cry up to three days after the death, but not permissible to yell or weep. Muslims are encouraged to say "To Allah we belong, and to Him is our return" (Qur'an 2:156), and this will provide blessings and mercy from their Lord. They should be asked about their need for an Imam, a Muslim chaplain, to be present with them and to help them notify relatives.

In accordance with Islamic tradition, family or community members wash the body of the dead and bury him as soon as possible. Mosupi's body should be washed respectfully, in an Islamic manner, and then be wrapped in sheets of clean, white cloth, called the *kafan*. Cremation is not permissible in Islam. After washing and shrouding the dead body, the deceased is then transported for the funeral prayers and will then be taken to the cemetery for burial. Muslims rest in a grave on their right side facing the *Qibla*. After the burial, the family members collectively pray for the forgiveness of the dead.

Mosupi is dead and his soul is with his God. "Say: 'The Angel of Death, put in charge of you, will (duly) take your souls: then shall ye be brought back to your Lord'" (Qur'an 32:11). Granny, who had raised Mosupi, and Naomi, his girlfriend, need emotional and spiritual support. Muslims are encouraged to spend most of the first few days with the family of a deceased person and to prepare food for them, and remind them of Allah and Allah's mercy. Also, it is recommended for Muslims to visit the graveyard to pray for the peace of Mosupi's soul and to remember that after death is the afterlife.

The Sunni Muslim Response

TARIQ RAMADAN

The tragic story of Mosupi, a young man who died in such appalling, avoidable circumstances from a now-treatable disease, highlights some key ethical issues at two different levels. The first is the way that we deal with sick people in resource-limited societies. There is a need to increase access to proper medical care for people living in remote areas which will enable early and correct diagnosis of illnesses. There is a need to ensure that everyone is offered the correct medicine and the best possible treatment available, no matter who they are. Hospital admission procedures need improvement. We need to treat patients and their families more inclusively and with greater sensitivity when the patient reaches the final stages of life; and, finally, we need to improve support for the bereaved after death.

These are all critical issues. Yet to address them, it is essential to move upstream in the discussion and to consider the wider picture—that of our medical systems and the situation of medicine overall in Africa and other poor regions of the world. The entire medical system appears to be based on financial gain for transnational pharmaceutical corporations that continue to sell medicines at a price that is unattainable for many. Generic medicines could quite easily, and with relatively little loss of profit, be made available to everyone in any country. Medical systems are impacted by the economic system, with a few people making money from the many poor. These issues relate specifically to some critical teachings in Islam, which holds that all human beings are equal before God and have the right to be treated with equal dignity, no matter who they are or what their circumstances. Muslims are reminded of the responsibility to look after those who are less fortunate than themselves, in whatever respect.

In Islam, interpretation and understanding is key and can generate deep thinking and complex discussion between Islamic religious experts (scholars) and practitioners at grassroots level as they try to find ways to put the guidance that they recognize as coming from God into practice and address the challenges of our changing contemporary world. Here we need to consider what exactly we mean by "medicine" in a particular context; what do we mean by "health," and how should these be addressed in a comprehensive way? This is a discussion about human dignity in any social situation or level of poverty. Solutions can only be found if we look beyond the very narrow relationship between hospital and patients and instead address the whole system.

The story of Mosupi cuts to the very heart of these concerns. Early diagnosis and more readily accessible medication could have saved Mosupi's life. He was brought to the city hospital, and neither he nor his Granny were aware that he had reached the final stages of the HIV infection. Mosupi waited a very long time to be seen in the Accident and Emergency Department, even for an entry consultation with a nurse. Eventually he was given a bed to rest on and died alone in a corridor. His family was brought to his bedside after his death, without prior warning or explanation. They had to deal with their shock and immediate grief in that same corridor without privacy.

It is critical to find a way to provide the very minimum of conditions for everyone—a private area in the hospital, for a doctor to talk to the family and explain the expectation of imminent death, or, at the very least, prepare them with a discussion before seeing the dead body. The family should be given the opportunity to sit with the patient for the final few hours, or after death to absorb the situation and to have a private space and time for a dignified reaction. The family should be offered psychological, cultural, or religious support depending upon their beliefs. According to Islam, health care involves much more than treating the patient for a medical condition; to be a healer requires one to consider his whole being (emotional, physical, psychological, and spiritual). Simple improvements in communication which involve the family and their support systems can make a difference. Following through on the process beyond the death of the patient to aftercare for the bereaved and respecting what the family would like to do with the body according to their beliefs—all are important. Such basic thoughtfulness will allow the family to acknowledge and accept the loss of their loved one, to respect his body throughout the process, and to be able to grieve. These are all critical considerations for Muslims.

In terms of rituals, it is important and respectful for the family to be able to have some private time to say some necessary prayers and words to their dead relative. If necessary, in cases in which the cause of death is less certain, an autopsy is also permissible. The family also needs to wash the body and have the burial within 24 hours of death. A short prayer will be done before burial. Cremation is prohibited in Islam.

Humankind should struggle against poverty and put an end to stories like Mosupi's. If we want ethics in health care, we should have ethics in society. We have to start with the very essential ethical position that every human being, every life, has the same value as that of another human being, rich or poor, black or white, African or Western. To deal with health care ethically in our world today means to advocate for economic justice and fair trade by transnational corporations. Health care is business today. Indeed, business requires one to seek profit, but profit is sometimes given priority over human dignity, and this is in direct contradiction to the teachings of Islam.

The Roman Catholic Response

CAROL TAYLOR

I weep as I read the tragedy of Mosupi's death and his family's grieving. How can we reconcile this with the Catholic commitment to be a community of respect, love, and support to the dying and their families. Who journeyed in solidarity with Mosupi and his family as AIDS exacted its harsh toll of weakness, helplessness, and dependency? How long must Mosupi and his African people wait for a just world responsive to the needs of all? When will our commitment to the life and dignity of the human person, the option for the poor and vulnerable, and solidarity, each a basic principle of Catholic Social Teaching,[7] exact meaningful reform in our global community?

The Catholic Church is growing faster in Africa than in any other place in the world. It daily confronts the toll HIV/AIDS has taken on the continent. Pope Benedict XVI made two visits to Africa. The first was controversial because he told reporters during an in-flight news conference that condoms made the problem of HIV/AIDS worse. On his second visit, November 19, 2011,[8] he released an 87-page guide for the faithful in Africa, *Africa's Commitment*, which did not reference condoms but repeated earlier suggestions that abstinence until marriage and fidelity in marriage were the best ways to prevent the disease that has decimated Africa.[9] In this document Benedict suggests that there is potential for Africa to become a "spiritual lung for humanity." Among the traits he praised in Africans is their love of family on a continent where it's rare to find an "only child," and their deeply felt faith, whether it is in the context of Christianity or not.

Maureen Cavanaugh's KPBS-TV interview with Uganda-born Notre Dame University theologian, Fr. Emmanuel Katongole, is illustrative of the Catholic Church's recent efforts to address AIDS in Uganda.[10] Uganda utilizes the ABC Approach: A, abstain, B, be faithful, and C, condoms.

> I think it's a whole package, and I think I would like even to extend the package beyond the fighting of AIDS as a sexual disease to looking at AIDS as a social reality and a social disease that is connected with all the issues of impoverishment, of poverty, of lack of education, of the way, for example, men and women relate, and the lack of opportunities.

Viatiucm: the last sacrament of the Christian. We return to Mosupi and his grieving family. For those who are about to depart from this life, the Church offers the person the sacraments of Penance, Anointing of the Sick, and the Eucharist as *Viaticum* (food for the journey) given at the end of life. These are "the sacraments that prepare for our heavenly homeland."[11] The priest who has been called to minister to the dying lays his hands on the head of the sick person and anoints the forehead and hands with the blessed Oil of the Sick and prays, "Through this holy anointing may the Lord in his love and mercy help you with the grace of the Holy Spirit. May the Lord who frees you from sin save you and raise you up."[11]

Christian meaning of death. The Catechism of the Catholic Church explains that the Christian meaning of death is revealed in the light of the *Paschal mystery* of the death and resurrection of Christ in whom resides our only hope. The Christian who dies in Christ Jesus is "away from the body and at home with the Lord." For the Christian, the day of death inaugurates, *at the end of his sacramental life,* the fulfillment of his new birth begun at Baptism, the definitive "conformity" to "the image of the Son" conferred by the anointing of the Holy Spirit, and participation in the feast of the Kingdom which was anticipated in the Eucharist—even if final purifications are still necessary for him in order to be clothed with the garment of the heavenly wedding feast.[11]

Vigil, Funeral Litergy, Rite of Committal, and burial bereavement. Every Catholic, unless specifically excluded by the norms of law, has the natural right to receive the ministry of the Church at the time of death. In coordination with the pastor, the family of the deceased and the funeral director chosen by the family arrange the place and set the time for the Vigil, the Funeral Liturgy, and the Rite of Committal. The Vigil is often the first time family, friends, and members of the parish community gather in remembrance of the deceased for prayer, remembrance, and support. The Vigil may be celebrated in the home of the deceased, in a funeral home, in a suitable place associated with the church building, or in the church building. The Funeral Liturgy is a prayer for the mercy of God on the deceased and for solace for the living. In the celebration of the Eucharist, the Church commends the deceased to the mercy of God and most perfectly expresses the communion of the Church with those who have died. The Rite of Committal, a gathering of the faithful for prayer, is celebrated at the place of burial or interment of the body, but it is not permitted in the church building. The Church encourages the burial of Catholics in Catholic cemeteries. The Corporal Works of Mercy are a ministry of consolation which belong to the entire parish community. This includes prayer for the dead and may include the offering of a meal following the funeral. Bereavement ministry necessarily extends itself beyond the conclusion of the funeral rites to include the days and weeks after burial when those who mourn remain in particular need of the ministry of the Church.[12]

The sacred dignity of the human body. It is because of the entirety of God's action in human life, from its beginning at the moment of conception to its end in natural death, that the Church assigns great reverence to the body of one who has died. Given the sacred dignity of the body, the Church recommends that the custom of burying the bodies of the dead be observed to await the Resurrection. Cremation is now permitted, but it not very commonly practiced.[12]

The Sikh Response

SURJEET KAUR CHAHAL

Mosupi is a tragic example of poor patients in developing countries who are suffering from serious illness but are unaware of their plight. They cannot afford the treatment, are ill informed about their illness and usually prefer going to a traditional healer because it is convenient and cheaper. However, when traditional healing does not do the trick and their conditions worsen, poor patients who are Sikhs would report to a hospital or dispensary attached to one of the *Gurdwaras* (Sikh places of worship) in the city or village. If there is no such dispensary in the village/city the patients directly go to the *Gurdwara* and seek help there. Once their plight is made known, members of the community come forward to help such patients medically as well as financially.

If death is immiment, usually at least two or three members of the Sikh community reach the bedside of the patient to pray for the patient and to console and emotionally support the family. This is a practice even if the patient is poor, for such service to a dying patient is considered very holy and spiritually elevating.

At the time of death, the body is usually cremated as per Sikh rites. However, there are no unalterable, fixed, and stringent rules on the practices of cremation. The body may be even placed in a flowing river if cremation is not possible. Usually members of the Sikh community, when informed about the death of a patient, take over the responsibility of performing the last rites and rituals. All expenditure is also initially borne by them, so that the bereaved members of the patient's family are not burdened with the rites and rituals. The most important ritual is the performance of prayers along with the patient's relatives so that they get moral, emotional, and spiritual support. The prayers are read or sung by friends or professional priests. Subsequently, the body is cremated.

Another group focuses attention on the bereaved members. The family members are supported emotionally, financially, and, if the need arises, the rehabilitation of the family is also taken care of. Mosupi's death is inevitable. It is important, however, for the members of the community to support the family at the time of such a crisis. As per Sikh customs, the neighboring families and the members of the religious congregation, especially women, go to the house of the deceased, offer prayers for deceased, and console the family members. To combat the emotional loss, for ten days and thereafter once a month at least for a year, members of the community gather at the deceased's house to offer prayers for the deceased. It is only after the final rites are performed (that is, after ten days) that those who can afford to do so repay the expenditures incurred. Otherwise, expenditures are borne by the members of the community, who take it to be a holy service rendered to the dead. Rehabilitation of the family of the deceased is taken care of by close relatives.

If there are no such relatives, the community financially supports the family. This is considered a holy duty.

In the case of Mosupi, there is a possibility that other members, especially Naomi and Mpho, may have contracted the HIV/AIDS virus. Medical care should be directed towards the other members who may have contracted the disease. They are financially helped and guided to undergo various investigations pertaining to the treatment.

The Unitarian Universalist Response

JAN K. NIELSEN

Mosupi's story is tragic. He was born into poverty carrying a disease from which his mother had died when he was only three years old, a disease that would take Mosupi's life. Though he lived only to age 18, he brought joy to his grandmother and fathered the gift of a baby girl named Mpho. Just days before her first birthday, Mpho would witness her father's lifeless body and hear both her mother and Granny wail in grief over the death of a husband and grandson.

At the heart of Unitarian Universalism is its first principle: "the inherent worth and dignity of every person," which has theological roots in the Universalist understanding that all people, without exception, are children of God. No Unitarian Universalist would deem Mosupi as less than worthy because he had HIV. A Unitarian Universalist response to Mosupi's story would begin with compassion for the pain this family continues to endure and a commitment to honor their humanity.

A Unitarian Universalist called to provide spiritual care to this family might begin by finding a way to make sacred the space around Mosupi's lifeless body. If it is not possible to move his body to a private area, Granny or Naomi could place a colorful cloth over Mosupi's heart. The spiritual caregiver could make sure that Mpho feels safe and is not frightened by the first wails of grief from Naomi and Granny, either by gently stroking the child's back or holding her if her mother and grandmother cannot. Once Mpho's needs have been tended, the spiritual caregiver might invite Granny and Naomi, perhaps while holding Mpho, to stand on either side of Mosupi's body and to bear witness to his spirit by sharing memories and telling stories about his life. Perhaps some of the people either in the Accident and Emergency Department or in the waiting area could be invited to join in chanting or singing. The spiritual caregiver could bless Mosupi's body and lead a time of prayer, as a way to honor and make safe Mosupi's passage.

Most Unitarian Universalists would hear also in Mosupi's story a call to action and advocacy for increased access to quality medical care for HIV victims everywhere. Another core principle of Unitarian Universalism is an understanding that all life is connected. What hurts one, hurts us all. Within Unitarian Universalism, there is a long tradition of justice work, rooted in the understanding that life is a gift. Unitarian Universalists may not claim to know for certain what lies beyond this life, but most all agree that we all share the responsibility for doing what we can to make the gift of this life in the here and now the best it can be for all people.

REFERENCES

1. Pogge T. World poverty and human rights. *Ethics & International Affairs.* 2006;*19*(1):1–7.
2. King SB. *Socially Engaged Buddhism.* Honolulu, HI: University of Hawaii Press; 2009.
3. United Nations. Office of the High Commissioner for Human Rights. Human rights, health, and poverty reduction strategies. http://whqlibdoc.who.int/hq/2008/WHO_HR_PUB_08.05_eng.pdf. Updated 2008. Accessed August 1, 2012.
4. Legge J. Chapter 1. In: Legge J, ed. *The Hsiao King or Classic of Filial Piety.* Whitefish, MT: Kessinger Publishing; 2010.
5. Cf. Legge J. *The Chinese Classics.* Hong Kong: Hong Kong University Press; 1970.
6. Li Chi. *Book of Rites.* Vol. I. James Legge, trans. New York: University Books, Inc; 1967.
7. United States Conference of Catholic Bishops. *Sharing Catholic Social Teaching: Challenges and Directions.* Washington DC: United States Conference of Catholic Bishops; 1998. http://www.usccb.org/beliefs-and-teachings/what-we-believe/catholic-social-teaching/sharing- catholic-social-teaching-challenges-and-directions.cfm. Accessed on July 17, 2013.
8. Associated Press. "Pope's new document outlines role of Catholic Church in Africa." *Fox News*, November 19, 2011. http://www.foxnews.com/world/2011/11/19/popes-new-document-outlines-church-role-in-africa/#ixzz2BA3xmL21.
9. Benedict XVI. Post-synodal apostolic exhortation Africae Munus. http://www.vatican.va/holy_father/benedict_xvi/apost_exhortations/documents/hf_ben-xvi_exh_20111119_africae-munus_en.html. Published November 19, 2011.
10. Carone A, Cavanaugh M. KPBS interview with Father Katongole. http://www.kpbs.org/news/2010/mar/25/catholic-church-africa/. Published March 25, 2010.
11. United States Conference of Catholic Bishops. *Catechisms of the Catholic Church.* 2nd ed. Liberia Editrice Vaticana: Vatican City; 1997. http://www.usccb.org/beliefs-and-teachings/what-we-believe/catechism/catechism-of-the-catholic-church/epub/index.cfm.
12. Raleigh V, Diocese. General norms for the celebration of Roman Catholic funerals in the Diocese of Raleigh. http://www.dioceseofraleigh.org/docs/liturgy/norms_funerals.pdf. Updated 2008.

CHAPTER 14

After Death

Case

MARK LAZENBY, RUTH McCORKLE, DANIEL P. SULMASY

L uz had been the dutiful wife and mother all her life. She had married Gustavo when she was only 17. And by the time she was 18, she had given birth to their first child—a daughter, Maria. Over the years, Luz had borne seven more children. She had buried one of them, a baby who had died of a fever. And she had gone on to spend her entire life raising them.

Luz reveled in her wifely and motherly duties. She loved her family, loved them more than she loved her own life. Raising her children, cooking for them, and providing them a clean home warmed her heart. She even cleaned the mechanic shop Gustavo owned and her sons worked in. She was proud of how Gustavo's garage was not greasy. It was a garage a woman would feel comfortable bringing her car to and waiting in the little sitting area while Gustavo fixed it.

When he saw Luz mopping the floor of his garage's waiting room, Gustavo beamed. A man such as himself could do no better than Luz. Her ample size and curvy figure pleased him. He never had thought of another woman. Luz was his light—his only light.

A few years ago, Luz noticed that her ankles started to swell. And it was a little harder to breathe when she walked to the nearby open air market for the day's food. She went to the doctor and found out that her blood pressure was too high. And she had too much sugar in her blood. But the duties of wife and mother, and now grandmother, were more important to her than trying to lose the weight her doctor told her to. Besides, she just couldn't stop eating tortillas, as her doctor told her to. She just couldn't give them up. Her earliest and happiest memories included eating tortillas. And she had made them every day for her family. Gustavo loved them; she knew. She watched him roll them up and sop the beans with them. When he did this, her joy was complete.

She took the blood pressure pills her doctor had given her. But she didn't get her blood pressure checked as often as she should. Eventually, she ran out of the pills. She didn't have the time or energy to go to the doctor's office to get a prescription for more. Eventually, the swelling in her legs got worse, and her breathing had become almost impossible. She had taken to bed for a few days, complaining of headache, when finally, Maria demanded they take her to the hospital. But it was too late. Luz died of congestive heart failure on the wards a few days later.

The day after her death, her daughters cooked in Luz's kitchen for hours. And then that night, Luz's body was brought to the house and laid out in the living room in the coffin Gustavo had bought for her. Family and friends from all over the city came and sat by the coffin. They ate beans and rice, and of course, tortillas. They drank beer. And they chewed cocoa leaves until the sun came up. The funeral mass took place at noon in the cathedral. Afterward, Luz's sons carried her coffin to the cemetery on the hill next to the cathedral and lowered her into the ground themselves. Gustavo, stoic until then, doubled over in sobs as they shoveled the dirt into the grave.

After the burial, Maria held her father up as the entire family walked down the hill to the river that flowed on the outskirts of the city. They carried with them all of Luz's clothes. Luz's daughters and young granddaughters washed the clothes in the flowing waters of the river, while Gustavo and his sons and grandsons built a bonfire on the bank. The entire family took turns placing the clean, damp clothes on the fire. They raised their tear-streaked eyes into the sky and watched the steam and smoke from the burning clothes billow and carry Luz's soul into the heavens. She was free. Luz was in heaven. *Esposa, mamita, abuela*—wife, mother, grandmother, she was now with God.

Over the next few days, Maria and her sisters took turns cooking for Gustavo, and washing his clothes. But as the days wore on, he stopped going into the garage. His sons had to pick up the slack. And then, one month to the day after Luz's death, he stopped getting out of bed. As far as he saw it, there was no reason to go on living. He did everything for Luz. He had made his business so he could provide her a home. He made love to her to create a family for her. He ate her tortillas because he knew how it made her feel when she watched him eat them. Luz was his life. And now without her, there was no reason to go on living.

The Clinical Issues

MARY VACHON

Gustavo and Luz had truly lived a life of service, in the deepest meaning of the word—service to one another and to their family. The nodal point in

Gustavo's bereavement experience is the recognition of how much his service to Luz provided the primary source of meaning in his life. His children are now providing service to him. That is not how it should be.

Luz was described as "his light—his only light." We see the importance of food, service, and the funeral rituals from the family's cultural and religious background, but we do not understand the meaning-making potential of Gustavo's religious and spiritual beliefs at this time in his grief process.

We know that, as a young married couple, Luz and Gustavo faced the death of their child. We do not know how they coped with this loss, or whether their religious/spiritual beliefs helped; but they did have each other, and we know that "he made love to her to create a family for her." One child died, but seven children lived. Without being simplistic, there could be other children, but there was only one Luz. Can he now be helped through relationship with family and friends—or perhaps a priest, family physician or therapist—to see another Light or lights in his life?

The early grief literature speaks especially of men dying of "the broken heart" syndrome within a short time after their wives' deaths. One month after Luz's death, Gustavo refused to get out of bed, feeling there was no reason to go on living. In the Catholic tradition, some celebrate the "Month's Mind Mass," which is described as reflecting that "the pain of loss is not quite as intense now, and the Memorial Mass helps us to move forward into the future." Frequently, in the early days of loss, people experience shock and disbelief, and they put one foot in front of the other because that is how it should be. Into the second month the original numbness may disappear, giving way to the extreme pain of the loss. Gustavo clearly signaled that he was not prepared to get out of bed and move into the future.

Current bereavement research speaks of complicated or traumatic grief, which is seen at least in part to involve issues of attachment. Those with early loss and issues with attachment are more vulnerable to complicated grief. Gustavo was securely attached to Luz; we do not know if this attachment helped to soothe wounds from early attachment issues from his family of origin. Those at risk of complicated grief can be identified one month after the death. Gustavo fits the criteria and should be watched carefully to assess whether he is experiencing grief, or a major depression with vegetative symptoms which may require antidepressants.

One of the biggest challenges in dealing with grief is guilt. Is Gustavo feeling guilty that Luz worked so hard? Does he feel that he, as her husband, should have been the one to pick up that there were problems in Luz's health and insist that she go back to the doctor and be sure to take her medications? Would the situation be different today if the caregivers Luz consulted initially had met not only with her, but with the Gustavo and Maria, to stress the importance of Luz taking her medications and making at least some lifestyle changes that could have prolonged her life, and allowed the family to feel that they were all working together for the best possible outcome?

The Ethical Issues

DAVID ALBERT JONES

The first responsibility of health care providers is the health and life of their patients. Nevertheless, health care professionals' responsibilities do not come to an end when a patient dies. They have an ongoing responsibility for the care of those close to the patient, and a more specific duty to show respect to the human remains and to enable the relatives to grieve appropriately and to lay the body to rest.

The death of Luz has had a devastating impact on the health and well-being of her husband Gustavo. One key ethical concern is whether this reaction could have been mitigated by better medical and chaplaincy support before and after her death.

In many such cases, an important ethical issue is whether insensitive actions of health care staff prior to death might have exacerbated the pain of loss. However, Gustavo is not said to be angry at the standard of care that Luz received, nor at the circumstances in which she died. Her death "on the wards" has not inhibited the family from showing respect for her by bringing the body into the house the day after the death and undertaking their customary rituals of grief.

What does seem to have gone wrong in this case is the transition or continuity of care from Luz to Gustavo. It is clear who had responsibility for the medical care of Luz. It is much less clear who has medical responsibility for Gustavo.

Even before her death, it seems that there was some problem of communication between the health care team and Luz's family. Despite having a supportive family, Luz stopped taking her medication because "she didn't have the time or energy to go to the doctor's office." It does not seem that the doctor engaged the help of the family in helping Luz to control her blood pressure. Nor is it clear what support was sought or obtained from the chaplaincy team at the time of Luz's death or thereafter.

In some cases, the duties of health and social care professionals will be clearer because the bereaved relative will have immediate practical needs and may even need help in arranging the funeral. This was not the case with Gustavo. Gustavo has a strong support network, and the rituals of grief seem to have been cathartic as much as such rituals can be. His further needs were not obvious. Nevertheless, he has not coped with the loss of the love of his life.

A deeper question is whether Gustavo's problems, real as they are, are medical rather than existential or religious. Medication might help to make his suffering easier to bear; but if someone is deprived of what gave life meaning in his eyes, then what he needs is surely to recover such a sense of meaning. A therapist or counsellor could support a patient in this process, but it seems beyond the scope of medicine as such and more the remit of the chaplain or family pastor.

The African Independent and Pentecostal Churches Response

JAMES AMANZE

A death like that of Luz is always a heavy blow to the bereaved. The death of a wife, husband, or child is a real loss in one's life. In many parts of Africa, when death occurs, there is a great deal of wailing, especially among women. The wailing may last for many hours before and even after the burial. In Africa, death is a community affair in which the loss of a member of a family is shouldered by the entire community, starting with the nuclear family, but also including the extended family and the community at large. Death is considered the dismemberment of the community as a whole, and it is the responsibility of everyone to make sure that the pain and the void created by the deceased is shared by the entire community.

African Independent Churches follow African ways of mourning the dead with minor variations. They gather around the bereaved, pray for them and for the repose of the departed, committing them into the hands of Jesus Christ in heaven. In some African Independent Churches, where belief in ancestors is still upheld, the deceased are considered to have joined the company of the ancestors to eventually become members of the church triumphant through whom people can channel their prayers to God. By and large, the living dead (the dead who continue to live in the afterlife) are considered to have moral superiority over the living, and their duty is to offer intercessions to God on behalf of the living. They are also considered guardians of public morality. Death unleashes the living dead into a new life free from physical hindrances, and they live in the spirit world with God. In many African communities, funereal rituals are performed in order to send the dead to the spirit world where they live forever.

In many African Independent Churches, when someone dies, people ask many theological questions such as "What has caused this death? Is this the will of God or punishment from the ancestors?" In African Independent Churches, Luz's high blood pressure and diabetes would be attributed to the devil, witchcraft, evil spirits, the anger of the ancestors, or even displeasure from God himself for sins committed against oneself, other members of the community, the ancestors, and God.

It should be noted that, when death takes place, African Independent Churches do not allow their members to give up the will to live, despite the loss of their loved ones. Church members gather to provide moral and material support to the widow or widower. After burial, members of the extended family discuss the manner in which material support will be offered to the widow or widower. Children are generally absorbed into the extended family and the community at large. This is because children in most African societies belong to the community and not just to the biological mother and father. This being the case, a widower like Gustavo would have no reason to succumb to grief and wish to be inactive or to die. This only happens in exceptional cases when the couple is of an advanced age. In such instances, a widow or widower may die shortly after the death of the partner. Prayers are always said in the home of the bereaved or in church in order to boost the morale of the bereaved.

In Pentecostal Churches, death is also perceived as a spiritual journey to eternal rest. It marks the end of all suffering. God is never considered the author of death. Pentecostals believe that death, like sin, is caused by the devil, whose work is to steal, kill, and destroy. At death, the teaching is that the person who has died has accomplished his/her mission. God gives to every individual person a mission to carry out in the world. Once the mission has been accomplished, the person dies. As for those who remain behind, the teaching is that they should continue with their lives carrying out the mission that God has given them. Life is worth living because this is the purpose of God for the living. They cannot wish to die, even though the situation may look hopeless or helpless. People are taught that, if they are still alive, it is because God kept them for the purpose of doing his work in the world—otherwise they would have died already. Prayers are held in order to give the bereaved comfort and strength so that they can sustain their loss. Apart from prayers, people are taught how to increase their faith in order to be strong in the Lord the Giver and Sustainer of life.

As a result of all this, though death brings a sense of hopelessness and helplessness, it does not make people feel that there is no need to live any longer. This is why suicide has no room in Pentecostal Churches. Pentecostals do not perform traditional African after-death rituals. They go on living their normal lives, because at death the dead enter into a new life, the life of living with God.

When death occurs people ask questions such as "Why has God taken my beloved one? Do I suffer as a result of sin? Did my loved one die because of sin?" Although such questions are asked, Pentecostals teach that God should not be interrogated, because God is God. Pentecostals are taught that they should rejoice in Jesus, since those who are dead in him will be raised on the day of the resurrection. Christians who are dead are regarded as "sleeping." Thus, those who remain should have hope in the future and continue to live normal lives.

The Buddhist Response

SORAJ HONGLADAROM

The key issue in this story is focused on Luz and Gustavo, a loving couple who produced a total of eight children, though one died in its infancy. So Luz and Gustavo are no strangers to bereavement. In the case of Luz, perhaps the key ethical issue for her is that her condition could have been prevented. If Luz had taken the high blood pressure medication prescribed her by the doctor, and if she had eaten fewer tortillas, perhaps she could have lived longer. Perhaps Luz and Gustavo could have lived together until a ripe old age and died together in a storybook fashion. However, life is not as easy as one might want it to be.

In fact, the focus of the story is on Gustavo and not his dutiful wife. When Luz died, Gustavo actually found no reason to go on living—it is as if their lives were tied together. The problem is then how to console Gustavo so that he can find a reason to carry on after his wife's death. Here religion can be very useful. One of the key teachings in Buddhism centers upon death and preparation for it. It is not that Buddhism is a death-centered religion, but as death is the inevitable end of every human being, each person should then come to death fully prepared. Buddhist masters usually compare the preparation toward death as a kind of preparation for a long journey. We need a good map in order to navigate the new territory that we have not experienced before with confidence. In the same vein, there are a number of practices in Buddhism that serve to help practitioners become aware of the contours and the terrains of the territory that one will journey into after one's demise. Of course all this cannot be scientifically proven, but approaching death with a sense of confidence and calmness is, in fact, a much better way to face the inevitable end than fear and anger. In Buddhism it is believed that the quality of one's mind at the moment of death is crucial in determining the kind of life that person will encounter in her next life.

Thus, for Gustavo, a Buddhist would recommend to him that loss is a natural condition that befalls everybody. There is no one in the whole world who has not experienced any kind of loss in one way or the other. Things are always changing, and we just cannot hold on to anything for any length of time without that thing slipping away from us. A Buddhist might ask Gustavo to think of his own father and mother. Presumably at least one of them might be dead by now; and, if so, then Gustavo might want to think about them, about the time he spent with them in the past, and how he felt the loss and bereavement then just as he was feeling right now. Since Gustavo got over the loss of his parents, a Buddhist would ask him to consider his sad feeling at the moment and then think ahead five or ten years from now. Life goes on. Somebody dies, but then somebody else is born. Five or ten years from now, perhaps Gustavo will be so busy being a grandfather that he would not feel as intensely for the loss of his wife as he does now. Time can heal everything. Right now, he might be feeling that the whole world is crumbling before his eyes; but if he realizes that his wife has completed her life and has taken on a new life in her journey in samsara, perhaps he will find her again, in her new life, in the near future. Of course there is no way to know this for sure, because Gustavo is not an accomplished Buddhist Master who has clairvoyant abilities; but it is still a fact that Luz will be taking her own journey in samsara. Perhaps he can find her in one of his own granddaughters. One does not need to be clairvoyant to discern the eyes or the look of one's wife in one's own granddaughter. By then, the intense feeling of loss and bereavement will be gone. What is left will be fond memories that Gustavo and Luz have spent together, busily producing children and running the garage together.

The Confucian Response

RUIPING FAN

Luz was a wife, mother, and grandmother. Like a virtuous Confucian woman, she loved her family members more than herself. Now she is dead, and the burial ritual has finished. What should be done next? Confucianism would think that, in remembering her, the relevant health care professionals and close family members should take a moment to reflect on their interactions with Luz during her sick time and figure out if they should have done anything better in taking care of her. Such reflection would be helpful for the health care providers to improve their services in the future. Meanwhile, the family should take seriously the memorial rituals they are religiously committed to conduct in memory of Luz.

The case does not mention whether Luz's husband Gustavo and/or her daughter Maria had accompanied her when she went to the doctor and found out that she had very high blood pressure and too much sugar in her blood. If they did, the doctor should insist—not only to Luz but also to them—that Luz should be made sure to take her medications and go back to the doctor regularly.

The Confucian account of the family takes it for granted that family members assist each other in health care processes and will be complementary to each other in making appropriate medical decisions. When one is ill, one is understandably weak and vulnerable and should be cared for by other family members. Confucians do not think that one should independently undertake the heavy burden of making medical decisions for oneself or bear the major responsibility of taking care of oneself. In Luz's health care context, what was at stake was not so much her "right" to make "autonomous" medical decisions by herself as it was the responsibility of the family to take care of her in her best medical interest. For Confucians, this privileged, special position of the family in health care is warranted by the reality of the family, reflected in the close bonds of family members which appropriately manifest mutual love and protection. Questions such as whether family members should be informed of a patient's illness without explicit consent of the patient or whether family members should have a right to participate in medical decisions are not important in cases like that of Luz. Given the Confucian appreciation of the familial bonds, it would be a mistake to assume that individual patients should be separated from their families in making and implementing health care decisions because, for Confucians, familial interdependence, shared determination, and mutual assistance are intrinsic to human health care and flourishing.

The Confucian virtue of *ren* (as love) requires a proper deep respect (*jing*) directed toward Heaven (*tian*), deities, and humans. In particular, although such reverence towards gods and spirits does not require everyday service so that one may keep one's distance from them (*Analects* 12.20), one's filial love to one's parents must be incarnated in everyday ritual practices to treat them reverently. In addition, the Confucian tradition emphasizes that a virtuous man must respect his wife. This is because, as Confucianism sees it, "the wife was the hostess of the sacrificial ritual to his ancestors—could any husband dare not to respect her?".[1] However, Confucianism does not require that, for a husband to love his wife or a child to love her mother, one should always follow her desires, wishes, or decisions. Instead, what one should always keep in mind is her well-being or best medical interest. In this case, Luz's husband Gustavo and her children failed to reach a good level of care for Luz. They should have encouraged her to lose weight, pushed her to stop eating tortillas, and helped her to go to the doctor's office to get a prescription for more pills after she ran out of them. If they did all these things, Luz would not have died of heart failure so quickly.

Of course, Gustavo and the children might never have had the chance to get these things clear. If that was the fact, Gustavo's sense of guilt should be mitigated. In any case, it must be recognized that Luz is already gone from this world. The most important thing for the living family members is to perform all important memorial rituals for her. For Confucians, memorial rituals must be performed on the anniversary of her death as well as on each of the culturally relevant holidays.

The Evangelical Christian Response

JOHN GRAHAM

This case brings into focus the impact of the lost of a loved one on those who remain alive but are left grieving. Like so many women throughout human history and in every culture on earth, Luz thought only of others, giving everything she had to meet their needs. In the process she thought very little of herself or her own needs. When she became ill near the end of her life, she did not take the medications she needed and died, leaving her large family and husband with broken hearts.

Gustavo, Luz's husband, said she was his light. In fact, she was his "only" light. This is understandable because of the giving nature of his wife. She was a woman who not only attended to every need of her family but also cleaned Gustavo's mechanic shop. Now she was gone and her loved ones were left grieving.

Initially, the family drew strength from the ancient traditions and rituals of their culture in order to give meaning to Luz's life. Her body was brought into their home and her coffin placed in the living room so family and friends could say their last goodbyes in Luz's home. Her daughters cooked food in the kitchen just as she had done in the past. Everyone ate beans and rice, and her favorite, tortillas. They drank beer and chewed cocoa leaves until late in the evening. Her sons carried her coffin into the church for a traditional noon mass in the cathedral. They lowered her body into the grave while her priest said the final sentences. Then, they took Luz's clothes, washed them, and burned them in a bonfire. Symbolically, Luz rose with the smoke into the heavens. She was free. She was with God.

After these rituals ended, Gustavo found himself alone and his "only" light was now gone. Soon, he sank into depression. He stopped going to work, stayed mostly in bed and told his family he had no reason to live with Luz gone. He had only worked to provide for her and her home. Now that she was gone what reason did he have to live?

The process of grieving does not end with the rituals performed at the church, synagogue, mosque, or temple; and this is especially true when we have much invested in the person who has died. Like Gustavo, if that person is your light, your "only" light, then the loss will necessarily be great.

As an Evangelical Christian, what would I say to Gustavo and his family if I were their pastor? First, what I would not say to him at this time is that allowing Luz to be the "only" light in his life is akin to idolatry. God is to be the center of our life, not a human being, even if he or she is altogether wonderful, meets our every need, and loves us incredibly. God is to be the light of our life, not another human being. But, of course, I couldn't say that to Gustavo. I would have to let him discover that on his own with God's help.

So how would I minister to a person in such depths of grief? Most of us know Kubler-Ross' five stages of dying—denial, anger, bargaining, depression, and acceptance. These can be applied to grief as well. Guatavo is clearly in the fourth stage, depression. He has withdrawn from family, coworkers, and friends. It is a serious time because he is already saying he doesn't have anything to live for now that his wife has died. The next step could be him planning to end it all in suicide.

Realizing the urgency of the moment, I would make every effort to be present for Gustavo and encourage his family to do the same. I would also ask men in the church to make frequent visits to his home and to invite him out for breakfast or lunch. Developing relationships will be key to Gustavo's recovery. Just knowing that he will meet with other men a few days hence will awaken him to the reality that other people are in his life and that they care about him. Again, relationships are key to his recovery.

Also, I would encourage Gustavo to attend church services every Sunday and to be present in an Adult Sunday School class. There he will meet men and women who can be a great support system for him. I would encourage him to attend their parties and other gatherings, as well. My church would also have an ongoing Grief Recovery small group, and I would take him there the first time. I would do anything I could to get Gustavo out of the house with people.

And, I would pray about the right time to invite him to a Bible study group or a Men's Life group that can build his faith in God. Fundamentally, I see that what he lacks is deep faith. Human relationships can bridge him over much of his grief; he may even find another woman for his life; but if he hasn't found God, he is still vulnerable to falling in the same trap of putting his whole trust in another human being and not in God.

Falling in love with God, his creator, and placing his future hope in Christ are what I believe he needs. I believe one avenue may to tell him that a relationship with God will mean he will spend eternity with God and be reunited with his beloved wife, Luz, who is now in heaven. That is the Evangelical message—life with God is eternal life with God and the people of God. It can restore hope for Gustavo to know this is his ultimate destiny.

But just as important is that Gustavo needs to know he has much to offer in this life—to his family and loved ones who are alive, to the church, and to his community. Certainly, his children and grandchildren need him. They can be a great joy to him, and he can enrich their lives as well. In the church setting, there are many people who could be blessed by Gustavo being present for them in their hour of great need. From the pain he has suffered in losing his wife, Gustavo can now minister to others. If he is able to get his mind off himself and onto others, he can give comfort to many who are experiencing loss in their lives. Comforting others in their hour of grief can become his ministry in the church.

It also appears Gustavo has not recognized his work as a mechanic as a vocation, a calling from God. If he can discover that his work is a blessing in itself and not merely a means to provide food for the table and a roof over his head, Gustavo may be able to find meaning and purpose in the remaining years of his life. As a mechanic, he can use the mind and hands that God has given him to bless others. When that happens, he will want to get out of bed in the morning and be in his shop where he can serve others.

Grief from the loss of a loved one does not end with the service in the church and the responsibility of a pastor and church continues long after that. A phone call a week is one way to be present, but the best is to be there in person. In doing so, we represent Christ to one who is deeply hurting. There may be no greater ministry, for Jesus said, "When I was in prison you came to visit me" (Matthew 25:36 NKJV). And, when they protested asking, "Lord, when did we see you in prison and visit you?" Jesus responded, "If you have done it unto the least of these my brethren, you have done it unto me" (Matthew 25:44 NKJV). Truly a person in the grip of grief is in a prison and many have lost all hope. The presence of a loving community of believers can break down those walls and let the light of Christ come in.

The Hindu Response

UMA MYSOREKAR

Following the death of Luz, a dutiful wife and a loving mother to her children, there was a big void in the family—difficult to fill. After the death of a loved one, close family members go through the process of bereavement. Immediately following the death and for sometime thereafter, it is often difficult for those left behind to understand the happenings around them. During this period, the experiences may affect the life of the individual. Bereavement can be mixture of thoughts, emotions, and behaviors. Initially, it is a shock and disbelief, especially if the death of the loved one was sudden and unexpected. Grief, despair, guilt, and self-blame follow in some cases. Once the grieving person adapts to the new circumstances, the individual begins to accept and move on. Family and friends play a great role in comforting the individual.

Among Hindus, scriptures are usually read daily by learned scholars or priests, and hymns are sung in the praise of the Lord to spiritually uplift the bereaved. Most Hindus have intense faith in God and this provides great support needed to go through this difficult time.

Traditionally, during the mourning period, Hindus do not participate in any joyous functions such as weddings or entertain guests. Friends and family visit the bereaved, however, to express their condolences. As the bereaved do not cook at home during this period, family and friends bring food. The initial mourning period is for 13 days. Subsequently, the mourning period varies from three months to one year, depending on various factors such as age of the deceased, etc. Grief and bereavement are interconnected. Grief is the intense mental suffering or sadness caused by the loss of a loved one, and this loss is the bereavement.

The funeral rites of Hindus are based on a very ancient tradition of established practices and core beliefs. Funeral rites have remained the same over the centuries, except for some regional variations, even though Hinduism underwent a great transformation, incorporating many new traditions, beliefs, practices, and divinities. The ceremonies performed are expected to help the further journey of the *jiva*, or *atma*, or *prana* that has left the gross body. When the gross body is burnt, the *prana* is rapidly detached, and the detachment is solemnized by the mantras or prayers at the cremation. Further ceremonies are performed or *shanti* prayers chanted to help the *jiva* to travel from its domain to the domain of ancestors (*pitruloka*).

On the first day, *pashnustapanam* is done. *Pashunam* means the stone, and *pashnustapanam* is the rite in which one stone is placed at the site of *karma* and another on the banks of the nearest river. On the stone kept near the river banks, oil, sesame seeds, and water are poured. *Pinda* (rice balls) are offered on the stone kept at the place of *karma*. This is *Nitya Vidhi* (daily ritual) and is done for 11 days.

The 11th day is the *shraddham*, which is the last rite for appeasement of hunger of the *prethatma*. To fulfill this, a fire ritual (*homam*) is done, signifying it as *prethatma*, and *annam* (rice) and ghee are poured into it.

On the 12th day, *sapindhi karanam* is performed—a rite to mark the transition of the deceased and merging with the ancestors (three generations). This rite therefore includes *shraddham* performed to each of the ancestors of the deceased individual.

For the deceased to reach *pitruloka,* it is believed that he has to cross the river *Vaitharni*. A *Godanam* (gift of a cow) is given by the family to symbolize a safe journey for the deceased. Besides this, there are other items such as sesame seeds, ghee, clothes, silver, gold, etc. depending on the family. With this, the rites for 12 days end and the 13th day is observed as *subasivkarnam*. On this day, offerings and *poojas* are performed to the family Deity or *Ishta Devata*, and family and friends are invited for a feast.

Every year for a human being on earth is comparable to a day for the ancestors. Hence, a *shraddham* is performed yearly. It is a ritual done with the help of a priest by a descendant of the dead ancestors with *sradda* (dedication) and faith. It can be accomplished by giving cooked food or uncooked articles of food (like rice, etc.) and money to priests. Monthly *shraddhas* are generally performed during the first years after death.

The present age has witnessed changes in the method and duration of the mourning period. These are due to time pressures, small families, inadequate facilities, other commitments, and so on. Many would do *"Annadana"*—feeding the poor in the name of the deceased.

The Indigenous Response

IRENE TAAFAKI

According to the Ri-Majōl of the Marshall Islands, after death, the *emmej* begins. This "period of wakefulness" is the first of several key events organized by the family following the death. All combine to provide comfort to the grieving and rebind the ties of family and community.

Great importance is given to preparing the home to which the body returns. This will involve repainting it inside and out, laying fresh mats on inside floors, and covering the outside with fresh small stones and pebbles from the beach. Food is prepared for the visitors to come, while others attend to the practical arrangements for the burial. The casket is placed on a fine sleeping mat in an elaborately decorated room. The mat underneath the coffin will be face down and the body will lie perpendicular to the fold at the center of the mat. This contrasts with the sleeping mat of the living—which always faces upward with the person sleeping across the fold at the center of the mat. Over the next several days, streams of visitors will demonstrate their respect(*ilomej*). Distant relatives, friends, and coworkers, organized in groups, will pray and sing beside the coffin and offer the family small financial contributions toward the expense of the funeral. Each group will designate a spokesperson who, as well as expressing comfort and support, will describe the lineage connection and relationship between the family and the deceased. In response, the family spokesperson will appreciate the condolences and confirm the relationship.

Ri-Majōl have an uneasy relationship with the spirits of the dead. They grieve for the loss of a loved one, yet fear that this recently departed spirit will either haunt their lives or take others from them, particularly the vulnerable younger children of a dead parent. Practices to deceive the spirit into believing that it has already entered the spirit world include lifting up the coffin and having the children and pregnant women pass beneath it, and placing a coconut wrapped in children's clothes into the grave before the coffin enters it. Another practice is the placing of the property of a twin who has died into the grave in order to protect the living one. The clothes, sheets, towels, and utensils used by the deceased during the time of sickness, immediately before death or used in the preparation of the body, will generally also be placed in the grave. For these to be worn or used by others would be *bwijerro*, and hasten their own demise.

The varied ways of expressing grief are accommodated by Marshallese. Wailing, fainting, and the chanting of *roro* are acceptable and particularly common at the death of a chief. Many feel that the prolonged *emmej* made possible by refrigerated morgues and chemical embalming has extended and intensified bereavement both before the burial and afterwards.

One of two spirits can affect the bereaved. *Ledrik ran remman* is positive, and enables the next of kin, particularly the spouse, to cope and recover cheerfully from the loss. *Ledrik ran renana* is negative and causes such deep grieving that the spouse is easily lured onto the *waan kabool ḷal* him- or herself. Treatments exist to relieve the anguish and prevent this from happening. A traditional healer will be called to prepare *uno in būromōj*—an herbal medicine administered with an incantation (*allōk*) to numb grief and cause forgetfulness. In addition the grief-stricken may be wrapped securely (*kilbur*) in a fine mat and pounded on the upper chest or throat, which is believed to be the seat of emotion.

After the *emmej and burial* (*kalep*), the next rite is the *erreak* (to spread and smooth over). The extended family and friends gather with the close relatives to celebrate, and speeches are delivered to set aside differences and express forgiveness to the living and the dead. Baskets of small white rocks, gathered from the beach, are given to mourners who scatter these around the grave. Past disputes and animosities between family members are resolved in this symbolic act of purification, and the unity of this closely related community is restored.

Ri-Majōl acknowledge that grieving often continues long after burial and the term *añak* refers to the combined practice of accompaniment (*kōrwane*) and distraction (*kōmade*) given freely until the melancholy of bereavement has lifted. Family members will stay close by for as long as six months or a year if necessary, offering the care for the living that was once provided to the sick and dying, administering traditional medicine and massage, telling stories, and humoring until balance in life is restored.

The Jewish Response

HERBERT BROCKMAN

In Jewish tradition, it is said that under the wedding canopy, a couple becomes "two bodies with a single soul." It is therefore not surprising that Gustavo feels he has lost his own will to live when Luz dies, for part of his essential being has been lost; and as a survivor, he feels totally bereft and alone in his loss. It is for this reason that Judaism prescribes the obligation of the community to accompany a mourner on his or her journey. From the very beginning of the mourning process, the presence of community plays a very significant role.

The first few days following a loss are particularly difficult. It becomes incumbent upon the community to visit the home of the mourner for seven (shiva) days in order to provide the opportunity for public expression of grief. The mourner is permitted to recite the traditional prayer of memorial only in the presence of community. A minimum of 10 adult worshippers (a minyan) must be gathered together for grief to be expressed, for in the company of others, no one is truly alone. The minyan also begins to provide the opportunity to expand those relationships that had been more intimate earlier.

To further underscore this notion, a rabbinic commentary suggests that a visit to someone who is ill "removes 1/60 of the illness." This was not to be taken as a quantifiable amount, but to suggest that by one's very presence, one can, in some small measure, help to remove part of the pain another is experiencing. The power of presence is essential in Judaism. Nowhere is this more clear than when visiting and comforting a mourner. It has an added benefit for the community as well, for as members become more attuned to their own spiritual natures, they come to see themselves as agents of healing.

As time goes on, the mourner slowly moves out from the most intense pain. The community slowly steps back. Rather than friends visiting the home, the obligation is on the mourner to go to the synagogue to recite the mourner's prayer. The quorum of 10 is still required. For the first 30 days (sheloshim) the mourner is not to visit the cemetery. One is to refrain from frivolous activities during this period but should attend to necessary activities.

As I read the case of Gustavo and Luz, especially how the sons "had to pick up the slack," I had hoped that they would not enable their father in this way. Surely they saw it as an act of caring for their father, but what Gustavo needed more was to feel needed now by his children, to continue to do for them what he and his wife had done over the years. He was still needed. That had not and would not change.

After this period, the mourning period continues for 11 more months, with the mourners reciting the special prayer. Now they may attend parties and begin the long hard journey back to healing. On the anniversary of death, families often gather at the gravesite. Following the custom of the patriarch Jacob, who "set up a pillar on (Rachel's) grave" (Genesis 35:20), the family "unveils" the monument/marker, thus bringing to an end the formal period of mourning.

Each year then, on the anniversary (yahrtzeit) the family gathers in the synagogue, the name of the loved one is read, and the family rises and recites the mourner's prayer.

It is important to note that the prayer recited throughout the year is a doxology, a prayer that does not mention death, but rather praises God. It suggests that the rabbis, in the face of our fears, doubts and loneliness, wanted to emphasize creation, forgiveness, goodness, and life. In these were the hopes for healing.

The Mainline Protestant
Christian Response

JAN HOLTON

Self-sacrifice and love provide the backdrop for Luz's life and are reflected in the rituals after her death. Scripture and the mainline Protestant tradition create a tension between self-sacrifice and self-care. Second only to loving God is the commandment to love neighbor AND self in equal regard (Matthew 22:39 NRSV). Yet, at the heart of the Gospel message is servanthood, self-sacrifice in the service of God's purpose. This is seen most clearly in the form of Jesus' death and resurrection—a sacrifice of the highest degree. It is not surprising that in historical Christian tradition, self-sacrifice, even to death, is often misunderstood to be the highest mark of a Christian that models the love and sacrifice of Jesus Christ. For women, notions of self-sacrifice are particularly complicated by gender norms in many cultures. Nonetheless, mainline Protestantism recognizes that God's love for us encourages care of the self *as well as* love of the other—even in families.

Like those of the Luz family, rituals at the time of death in the mainline Protestant tradition are deeply embedded practices expressed in and through the community. These practices center on personal witness to love and loss and very often take place around a shared meal. They include both familial and religious rituals such as wakes, viewings, funerals, memorials, and services of interment.

Indeed, community is key to the life of the church that is extended to the home of the deceased in times of loss and tragedy. At the news of a death, a pastor or other spiritual caregiver, especially if not already tending to spiritual needs at the time of death, will visit the home and offer support to loved ones. Congregations join neighbors in bringing food to the home of the deceased's family. This is a regular ministry of all congregations.

Community care at the time of death not only pays attention to practical needs but participates in the witness and love for the departed and family through a wake or viewing followed by a funeral or memorial service. A viewing is commonly held in a funeral home the day or evening prior to the funeral, though in some cases the older custom of viewing the body at the church is still observed. There are some indications of a resurgence in the United States of the once common practice of holding a wake in the home, but it is not a common practice in the mainline tradition. A pastor or spiritual caregiver should attend a viewing, even if only for a short time, to offer spiritual and emotional support. This is generally not a time for formal practices of worship, though a brief liturgy may certainly be offered if the family wishes.

Both burial and cremation are accepted in mainline traditions. Though burial remains the most common choice for the disposition of remains, high funeral costs and environmental concerns are making cremation an increasingly popular alternative. The formal worship practices of the protestant church at the time of death include a public funeral preferably held in a church, usually within a week of death with a closed casket present. In the mainline protestant tradition the funeral is primarily a religious service that celebrates Jesus' resurrection and the ministry of the Church. It is also a celebration of the deceased's life but this should not overshadow its religious purpose. This is typically followed by a short graveside service during which the body is interred. Alternately, in cases of cremation, a memorial service may be held at a time of the family's choosing. A service for the interment or scattering of ashes may be held before or after the memorial but is generally attended by a smaller circle of loved ones.

Most mainline denominations embrace cultural traditions such as those demonstrated by Luz's family and encourage these practices that bring comfort during times of grief. For example, the lovely act of cleansing Luz's clothes in the flowing waters of the river and lifting them to heaven by burning has much symbolism. Water, in the Christian tradition, is symbolic of rebirth or new life and is used in the sacrament of Baptism as a symbol of God's grace at work in one's life. The burning of clothes may symbolize the act of letting go of our earthly shell—the human body. This act of love sets Luz's beloved spirit free to lift toward God and its heavenly home.

The Shi'a Muslim Response

NAJMEH JAFARI

Luz and Gustavo lived a great life together. They had an impact on each other's lives. They shared the emotional, physical, and financial aspects of their lives. Gustavo's friend, partner, and soul mate is now gone, and he feels as if a part of him has died as well. He has missed the way Luz's eyes would smile whenever he ate one of her tortillas. He has lost his only light, Luz.

And now, Gustavo is experiencing the pain of grief. After one month, the death of his beloved wife seems more real, and he withdraws from his usual activities. He may ask himself "How can I possibly survive without my Luz?"

It seems that Gustavo needs spiritual therapy to recreate his meaning in life.

Muslims believe that the entirety of life—life's pleasure, joy, suffering, and loss—are from God, who gives us the patience and strength to survive. "All things are from Allah" (Qur'an 4:78), and the entirety of life is a test from God.

> Be sure we shall test you with something of fear and hunger, some loss in goods or lives or the fruits (of your toil), but give glad tidings to those who patiently persevere, Who say, when afflicted with calamity: "To God We belong, and to Him is our return." They are those on whom (Descend) blessings from God, and Mercy, and they are the ones that receive guidance (Qur'an 2:155–157).

Muslims are encouraged to be patient (*sabr*) when they face grief and loss, and they will be rewarded for this patience in paradise.

A spiritual healer should encourage Gustavo to be patient and turn to God and pray for Luz as well as himself, for relieve from this grief: "Those who believe, and whose hearts find satisfaction in the remembrance of Allah for without doubt in the remembrance of Allah do hearts find satisfaction" (Qur'an 13:28). Recalling the biography of the Prophet Muhammad and the multiple losses of his loved ones, Imam Hussein and the Battle of Karbala, are all beneficial when dealing with grief. As a true believer, Gustavo should turn his attention to God, pray, and supplicate, and God will give him the strength to endure the loss and pain. Also, praying on behalf of his dead wife will benefit her. God admires the believers who pray for those who have passed away (Qur'an 59:10).

There are different rituals and anniversaries in the different cultures of the Islamic world. Loved ones and relatives are to observe a three-day mourning period. In this period they receive visitors and condolences and avoid decorative clothing and jewelry. In some cultures, such as among Iranian people, family members will also gather on the seventh day, the 40th day, and one year after death. Family members and friends gather on the gravesite on these occasions, and they will place flowers on the grave and sprinkle the site with rose water. Family members also can pray for Luz and express their feelings and share their loss with each other. These gatherings provide a support system for family members, neighborhoods, and friends.

Luz was a gift from God, and her loss was also God's decree. She loved her husband and wanted him to be happy in his life. So, if Gustavo feels sad, withdraws from his work, and does not care for himself, she will suffer in the other world. When she died, everything in this earthly life was left behind, and there are no more opportunities to perform acts of righteousness and faith. Giving alms with the intention that their reward should go to Luz's soul may be regarded as a gift to her in the afterlife and a healing for Gustavo's pain.

Seeking religious support, going to the mosque and talking to the Imam provide comfort for Gustavo and turn him toward spiritual and religious beliefs to find comfort and meaning in the death of his loved one. This brings him the invaluable awareness of how precious life really is.

The Sunni Muslim Response

TARIQ RAMADAN

The story of Luz and Gustavo is at the same time both beautiful and sad. Marrying as teenagers, being entirely devoted to one another throughout their entire lives, they built a future and raised a family together, based on their particular cultural traditions and beliefs. Each led quite a simple way of life, but it was entirely satisfying for both. In his grief for Luz's death, Gustavo is unable to see the point of his life. He shuts down and disengages. In Islam, it is at this crucial time that Gustavo now needs the support of his family, his faith community, and the care of professionals to enable him to cope with his bereavement, to find relief, and perhaps even a new source of hope.

There are two people in this story—Luz and Gustavo—and each brings to the fore interesting points for consideration. Throughout her entire adult life, Luz gave everything to her husband and her family. She was able to cope with many experiences over the years, but all this was at the price of her own health. Although this is touching, it seems that she was so devoted to caring for her husband and family that she did not care enough about her own health. For example, she did not make time to visit the doctor regularly to have her blood pressure checked as the doctor asked of her, or to go to the doctor's office to get a prescription for more medication. Yet this medicine was essential towards maintaining a safe level of blood pressure, and without it, her body was put under intense physical stress. Yet with correct, well-monitored medication, her symptoms could have been treated.

From the ethical perspective in Islam, the concept of serving is critical. It is entirely correct to serve one's wife, husband, and children but one should not serve them "blindly" without taking care of one's self and one's own needs. So, according to the teachings of Islam, it was indeed an ethical responsibility for Luz, when necessary, to put her own health first before the needs of her family. It is important to understand that, although serving others is good in the eyes of God, one should not forget one's self at the price of one's own health or psychological and physical stability—this is not the right way for a Muslim. One might think here of the analogy of the aircraft safety announcement that is broadcast to passengers before takeoff: passengers are reminded that, if an emergency were to occur, they should fit their own life jackets or oxygen masks first before helping those around them, even their children. This is because protecting oneself first is the best way to be most useful to one's relatives. Tragically, Luz did not perhaps recognize this until it was too late, by which time she was too debilitated to be able to seek help or to want to let those she loved know about how ill she was. In her stoic manner, she may even have felt that she was letting her husband and family down in some way by asking for help.

We also see the other side of the story, that when Luz passed away how much her equally giving and loyal husband Gustavo was affected—simply that his raison d'être was no more. This is the romantic side of the story. Within the Islamic tradition, although it is important to invest oneself emotionally in one's family wholly, with both heart and mind, one should always remember the end and the reason for one's life in this world. One is here in this life now, but at the end one will return alone to God. So, whatever the beauty of love, without doubt, a love story can only ever end in sadness, because predictably someone will always leave first—whether this be through divorce or death. Either way, the person remaining behind must find a way to accept and deal with this, for the sake of his or her own well-being and for the others in the family. So, one should serve one's beloved relatives without worshiping them, without investing all one's life in them. In Islam, this is important and is connected to the very meaning of worshiping only one entity, God.

In the Islamic tradition, what happens after death is also important. Although someone one loved has passed away and it is an important part of the grieving process to celebrate that loved one's life, at some point one must deal with one's own life. This is the case for Gustavo; and although we can understand his intense sadness and suffering, in ethical terms and from a religious viewpoint it is critical for him to face his new life. In Islam, as indeed with other faiths, the best way for Gustavo to celebrate the memory of Luz is to take care of himself and to look after his family. This could be a way to help Gustavo find meaning for his love and the loss of Luz. This is where a religious expert or counselor could help guide and support Gustavo in finding his way through.

Sometimes, in ethical terms, we need to know how to love in the right way. In Islam, to love in the right way is not to love blindly but instead to love with a sense of responsibility and with an ethical understanding of the values that help one to love and carry on serving the other people in one's life. Grieving a loss is important, but it is important to acknowledge that it is part of a "recovery" process and to understand that this is the way of life. Life needs not only to be dealt with by suffering to show how much we love, but with values and principles to show how much our love is nurtured with our consciousness, our sense of responsibility, and with the way we serve. Ultimately, this is a story that highlights the quintessentials of life—we need to learn how to love properly—not blindly or as if we were in prison, but with a sense of detachment. The best love is that which is deep and intense yet protects our autonomy, our freedom—detached love, intense love, ethical love.

This is embodied in the way we should be after death. Muslims pray for the dead in a very simple way. The grave should be simple. One can visit the grave and pray for one's loved one and ponder over one's own life at any time. Lost love should be a reconciliation of human dignity within the protection of God's everlasting love.

The Roman Catholic Response

CAROL TAYLOR

One can only read about Luz and Gustavo and rejoice for the sheer delight and strength of their passion for one another and the life it created for their family. I am trying to picture myself cleaning my husband's mechanic shop with love! When congestive heart failure robs Gustavo of his beloved Luz, Gustavo is understandably bereft and inconsolable. The family and community surrounding Gustavo observe all the religious and cultural rituals related to death and burial and celebrate that Luz—wife, mother, and grandmother—is now in heaven with God. Anniversary Masses would be offered for Luz in the local church, and votive candles could be lit for her happy repose. Gustavo's family fully supports him. One cannot underestimate the importance of family. We need only remember Jesus in the hour of His death on the cross saying to His beloved mother and disciple, "'Woman, behold, your son!' Then he said to the disciple, 'Behold, your mother!'" (John 19:26–27 Revised Standard Version). Although these passages speak to a new relationship between Mary and Christians, they also speak to our need to care for one another in times of sorrow and need. Gustavos's daughters take turns cooking for him and doing his laundry and his sons pick up the slack in the mechanic shop. Gustavo, however, finds himself one month after Luz's death suffering profound loss, meaninglessness, and hopelessness.

Everyone teaches that grief is normal, natural, and necessary. It was Rabbi Earl Grollman who taught that grief is the other side of the coin of love. I remember my mother sharing after my dad's death that if we hadn't loved my dad so much, we wouldn't be grieving so terribly. Time generally heals grief—if we are patient and supported. If Gustavo chooses to go to bed and not get up, to die of a broken heart in spite of the best efforts of his family and friends, they will have no choice but to entrust him to the loving hands of a God who knows, loves, cares for him, and saves him. Before accepting this reality, however, one hopes that his pastor, family, and faith community might help him to explore fuller sources of meaning and worth for his life than his beloved Luz. There is a bit of tragedy in the statement that "Luz was his light—*his only light*" (emphasis added). There seems to be so much more that could give Gustavo a reason to get up in the morning and embrace life in spite of his loss and suffering: his family and community, his work, his Church, and God. I would hope for conversations about what he believes his dear Luz would want for him. He might be engaged with imagining what type of memorial he would want to create to honor the life and memory of Luz. To the extent that Luz is alive in the family they created with their love, might continuing to care for this family be an expression of love for Luz? One web-based guide for companioning the bereaved cites the importance of the five L's: Love, Laugh, Live, Learn, and Listen. "It is important for companions of the bereaved to model an 'attitude of gratitude' towards the gift that is life. In so doing, we honor not the death, but rather the life that was lived."[2]

And what about trying to discern in Gustavo's loss his personal incarnation of the Paschal mystery? Joseph Cardinal Bernardin, in his pastoral letter on health care, *A Sign of Hope,* wrote:[3]

> As Christians, we are called, indeed empowered, to comfort others in the midst of their suffering by giving them a reason to hope....We are to do for one another what Jesus did: comfort others by inspiring in them hope and confidence in life. As God's ongoing, creative activity in the world and the love of Christ make it possible for us to continue to live despite the chaos of illness, so too our work in the world must also give hope to those for whom we care. Our distinctive vocation in Christian health care is not so much to heal better or more efficiently than anyone else; it is to bring comfort to people by giving them an experience that will strengthen their confidence in life. The ultimate goal of our care is to give to those who are ill, through our care, a reason to hope.

Finally, I was struck when preparing this essay by the number of resources available to bereaved Catholics, many on Diocesan websites. The Catholic Memorials website would be a helpful place to start.[4,5] I would also recommend Peter Kreeft's book, *Love is stronger than death.*[6]

The Sikh Response

SURJEET KAUR CHAHAL

Luz loved her family, loved them more than she loved her own life. She loved them even at the cost of neglecting her own health. She did not even take her prescribed medicines regularly. Here one point comes to light—in the Sikh tradition, children have an important responsibility towards their aging parents. This is considered as service (*Sewa*) which begins at home. It was the responsibility of Luz's children and husband to reciprocate her love and service to them. When she was sick, giving her timely medical care was one of their primary duties. In Sikhism, duty or service to the community and to the elderly is considered to be of prime importance. Luz could have been saved if she were given timely care.

Now that Luz is no more, as per the Sikh customs, the family members, the neighboring families, and the members of the religious congregation go to the house of the deceased, offer prayers for deceased, and console the family members. Acceptance of the Will of God, acceptance of the fact that we all have to die one day, and that this human body is just one of the forms that the soul takes, are emphasized by the members of the congregation. This is done in various ways: first, by consoling the family members personally; and second, by singing and reciting prayers, which stress acceptance of the Will of God and the ephemeral nature of this human body. Such prayers and emotional support by members of the community help the family to cope with this stressful situation.

After reciting the prayers, the members of the community prepare for the funeral rituals for the deceased. The body of the deceased is cremated as per Sikh rites. After cremation, a sweet is prepared by the priest or some friend at the nearby *Gurdwara* (Sikh places of worship) and distributed among relatives and members of the congregation. After this, every evening for seven days, female family members, friends, and members of the religious congregation gather at the deceased's house and recite prayers to help the family of the deceased cope with the loss. This is followed by tea and biscuits served to all the people present. During these seven days, at night, both men and women (family members, friends, and members of the religious congregation) gather, and once again, the priests come and sing the prayer for an hour. After this, food brought in by friends is served. On the eighth day, continuous recitation of the holy text of the Sikhs (i.e., *Sri Guru Granth Sahib*) is undertaken at the residence of the departed for 48 hours. This is done by priests and members of the congregation, taking turns. After this, at a nearby *Gurdwara* that the departed frequented, a larger congregation of all relatives and friends gather for the last prayer for the deceased as well as for the emotional stability of the family members. After this prayer, an elaborate meal is arranged by the close relatives of the deceased for all present.

Thus, to combat the emotional loss, for ten days, continuous prayers are performed in the house of the deceased. Every month at least for a year, members of the community gather at the house where the tragedy took place to offer prayers for the one who left this world. One day is chosen in the month to remember the loved one who is gone, and prayers are performed. Usually, it is on the day of the month when the family member died. After 11 months, once again continuous recitation of *Sri Guru Granth Sahib* is arranged, and, in a congregation, prayers are sung in celebration of the death anniversary of the departed soul. All this helps the near and dear ones of the deceased to accept the Will of God and cope with the emotional burden.

The Unitarian Universalist Response

JAN K. NIELSEN

G ustavo is grieving the loss of Luz—his beloved wife. Luz's death was sudden and, even though she had problems with high blood pressure and high blood sugar, unexpected. Gustavo had no chance to say good-bye to the love and the light of his life.

Gustavo was not left to grieve alone. Family and friends surrounded Gustavo with support as they shared food and stories and sat by Luz's coffin laid out in the couple's living room. After the funeral mass, their sons carried Luz's coffin to the cemetery and, when they lowered her into the ground themselves, Gustavo doubled over in sobs. Afterward, the family gathered at the river to wash and then burn her clothes. Together, they watched the smoke carry Luz's soul into the heavens.

Gustavo and his family have engaged in beautiful and deeply meaningful rituals of mourning. He let flow his tears of deep grief. A month after Luz's death, though, Gustavo cannot pull himself out of bed. He cannot seem to find the will to live a life without Luz.

Since everyone's grief experience is unique, not all people will grieve in the same way or on the same schedule. In some situations, it is unrealistic and even insensitive to expect people to "get over" their grief and to put their losses behind them by any certain culturally or medically prescribed time. Although contemporary North American culture tends to make minimal room for people to grieve, it may be healthier to make room for grieving that follows cultural and familial patterns outside whatever may be considered the norm.

Gustavo has good reason to feel heartbroken. His life-long love died suddenly, leaving him no chance to say good-bye. A Unitarian Universalist spiritual caregiver called to respond to concerns that Gustavo may not be coping with his wife's death might caution against being too quick to label Gustavo's grief as "complicated grief." Sudden loss is always hard and can be complicated, but that does not mean that deep grief a month past a loss is abnormal or that it amounts to a condition requiring medication or psychotherapy. Even so, a Unitarian Universalist spiritual caregiver would see to it that Gustavo be screened for depression or another condition requiring medical treatment but would then help to make room for Gustavo to grieve fully the loss of his wife.

A spiritual caregiver might first invite Gustavo to talk about Luz and to share his memories of their years together. The spiritual caregiver might then arrange regular visits from a compassionate listener who could help Gustavo continue his grieving process by allowing him the structure and predictability of a caring presence who could help hold his grief.

A spiritual caregiver could help Gustavo find reasons to go on living. The spiritual caregiver could encourage Gustavo to imagine something he could do to honor her life—perhaps plant a tree or a garden. A spiritual caregiver might help Gustavo create a calendar noting future plans to spend special time with the children and grandchildren. Or a spiritual caregiver might help him begin collecting family photos for a book that tells in both pictures and words the story of his life with Luz, as a gift from Gustavo to the grandchildren of the family he and Luz created together. Gustavo should continue to be held in the caring embrace of family and community so that he can make safe passage through deep grief.

REFERENCES

1. Li Chi. *Book of Rites*. James Legge, trans. New York: University Books, Inc; 1967;266.
2. The five L's for companioning the bereaved: Love, laugh, live, learn, listen. Grief/Bereavement. Web site. http://www.cemeteries.org/services0004.asp. Updated 2012. Accessed July 17, 2013.
3. Bernardin J. *A sign of hope: A pastoral letter on health care*. Office of Communications, Archdiocese of Chicago; 1995.
4. The three N's for grief, grief is normal, natural, and necessary. Grief/Bereavement. Web site. http://www.cemeteries.org/services0003.asp. Updated 2012. Accessed on July 17, 2013.
5. Eterna Link Communications Inc. Grief resources. Catholic Memorials Web site. http://www.catholicmemorials.com/grief-resources.asp. Updated 2012. Accessed on July 17, 2013.
6. Kreeft P. *Love is stronger than death*. San Fransciso: Ignatius Press; 1992.

IV
Coda

MARK LAZENBY, RUTH McCORKLE, DANIEL P. SULMASY

The waters of death are treacherous, and navigation is perilous. Clinical, psychological, social, economic, political, and spiritual currents all converge on death. The time and the place of death, whenever or wherever it is encountered, may be turbulent. The waters may churn furiously when we come to the end of the world as we know it. For some, the waters of death may be calm and peaceful. But for all who remain, life must be navigated without the loved ones who have passed on. Assuring safe passage, for those at the end of life and for their loved ones, is therefore no easy task.

These are not, however, uncharted waters. Religious and spiritual traditions have amassed wisdom and experience in helping patients and those who care for them to navigate these waters over the course of human history. That wisdom and experience is still relevant today. Skeptics might suggest that religion and spiritual traditions have little to say about dying in the 21st century, given all the advances in our technology and knowledge about illness and death. Patients, their families, clergy, and hospice and palliative care clinicians know better. Technology cannot "solve" the riddle of death. Morphine may control somatic pain, but it cannot begin to touch spiritual pain. Now, more than ever, the world needs a form of health care that can integrate the biomedical and the spiritual, particularly at the close of life.

This book has explored how to provide safe passage for a good death. In the first part of the book, we explored safe passage by describing the palliative and hospice care available in a global context, paying special attention to the spiritual and existential aspects of care at the end of life. In the second part, clinicians, ethicists, and spiritual thinkers from diverse traditions provided insightful responses to five cases that provoked serious, pressing questions arising during the time before death, at death, and after death. These cases provided "thick" descriptions, filled with rich details from the personal narratives of the dying and those who cared for them.[1] Sadly, these are not the sorts of case descriptions one finds in textbooks of the professional disciplines—textbooks of health care chaplaincy, medicine, nursing, or even palliative care. These textbooks may teach one how to interview patients at the end of life, how to control ventilator setting and potassium levels, how to use medications and blowing fans to ease the struggle to breathe, how to ease pain and control nausea, and how to encourage families to be present. Yet rarely do these textbooks address the whole patient—the embodied spiritual patient. Human beings only live as embodied spiritual beings, only die as embodied spiritual beings, and can only be cared for as embodied spiritual beings. To care for the dying in soul as well as in body requires understanding them as persons enmeshed in particular cultural, spiritual, and familial contexts and relating to them as unique individuals who have lived particular personal narratives. This book is a step in that direction.

Our authors have touched on themes that are both universal and particular. Obviously, human biology is shared globally with only minor variations. We are one species. We share a common physiology and pathophysiology. We are all susceptible to illness, injury, and death. Less obviously to some, however, we also share the same spiritual questions in the face of illness, injury, and death. These are the questions of ultimate concern—questions of meaning, value, and relationship.[2] These questions are often the most obvious questions at issue in caring for patients who are dying and their loved ones, but they are rarely addressed by clinicians. Our cases illustrate these universal questions. Questions of meaning often arise with anguished cries. Why did the bus hit Huang-Fu? Why did Eman contract breast cancer at such a young age? Questions of value arise in our attitudes and in the decisions we must make regarding the care of the dying and their families. Was there any dignity in Mosupi's death that might transcend the poverty and chaos of health care in sub-Saharan Africa? Would euthanasia ever be permissible for Martha? Questions of relationship arise as a matter of course as the dying seek reconciliation with those who will survive them, and as those who love them anticipate the loss. The spiritual issues in the case of Luz arise precisely in the context of her relational status as *esposa*, *mamita*, and *abuelita*. Across all the five cases looms the question of whether the health care professionals who attended all these patients and families were able to see the transcendent aspects of their own relationships with these dying individuals. These are spiritual questions. They cannot be addressed with drugs or surgery, nor ever eradicated by human progress. It is the central theme of this book, however, that the world's great spiritual traditions have deep wisdom to share with dying persons, their families, their congregations, their communities, and their caregivers as they all struggle with these universal questions.

The answers given to these universal questions share common features but are, at the same time, quite particular. Indigenous, Hindu, Buddhist, Sikh, Confucian, Jewish, Evangelical, Mainline Protestant, Roman Catholic, African Pentecostal, Sunni Muslim, Shi'a Muslim, and nontraditional spiritual responses also differ in important ways in how they would care for those who share their beliefs and how health care professionals from their traditions ought to care for those of different faiths. These traditions differ in their creeds, texts, rituals, prayers, and moral duties. The answers they give are also context specific. Health care in sub-Saharan Africa differs radically from health care in North America. Finally, the cases and the responses all remind us that each case is unique. The issues differ according to the clinical circumstances, such as whether the patient suffers from acute traumatic brain injury, cancer, Alzheimer's disease, HIV/AIDS, or congestive heart failure. The issues differ according to their personal biographies—whom they love and who loves them. Spirituality is always particular.

What we learned from the introductory overviews about hospice in a global context and from the clinical, ethical, and interfaith commentaries on these cases is that safe passage is about creating the right environment—the right clinical or home environment in all the phases of death.

BEFORE DEATH

Sudden deaths. We learned in these pages that in cases of sudden death, especially deaths after traumatic brain injury, trauma surgeons, neurosurgeons, and critical care specialists strive to save patients, not to let them die. But safe passage for families includes these very clinicians explaining, in clear terms, the truth about survival. Importantly, it includes putting families in touch with their spiritual advisors, who can help them navigate through the waters. These waters may be especially dark and foreboding. Such is unexpected death. But clarity of prognosis and spiritual advice on the kind of care to provide can help calm the choppy seas of the unknown.

Disease progression. Sometimes we countenance death when what we thought was a curable disease turns into a life-limiting disease. We learned that clinicians must be honest, yet must also nurture hope among patients and families who now have to contemplate death. One way to accomplish this is to work with patients and families on decision making that focuses on how to define and focus on what they want for the rest of the time they have, and on how to sustain life and its quality for as long as patients have to live. Treatment choices, although they need to focus on six-month, one-year, and five-year survival, also must focus on living life one day after the other—and on what matters to patients. The moral task of clinicians in these circumstances is to support patients and families, with gentleness and compassion, in making decisions about their care based on the criteria of what matters most to them—not what matters most to clinicians. Time and again, the authors in this book brought our attention back to the notion of creating the spiritual space for patients and families to find within themselves inner strength. Creating this space is just how we can nurture hope among patients who once thought they would be cured or live indefinitely with a chronic disease but must now face impending death. Creating this space is also how we can nurture hope among families and friends who once thought their loved ones would be in their lives for life's big events—births, marriages, graduations, and holidays.

Prolonged death. Ideally, when death may be prolonged, clinicians will sit down with patients and families to discuss their wishes for care at the end of life before the patients lose decision-making capacity. One part of such advance care planning includes advance directives, such as living wills and durable powers of attorney for health care. These plans might include whether or not the patient will want artificial nutrition or hydration, and what to do if the patient should pass into a persistent vegetative state. These are not simple issues, and spiritual traditions differ on what to do about them. A recurrent theme across all these traditions, however, is a mandate to care—simply, to care. So, amid all the clinical difficulties, the uncertain questions and answers, the varieties of patients, families, cultures, socioeconomic conditions, and religious and spiritual traditions, clinicians can care. This care may not include direct intervention, but it always includes providing moral and spiritual support to families as they navigate prolonged deaths according to the map of their spiritual beliefs and practices.

AT THE TIME OF DEATH

Whether sudden or expected, death always comes as a shock. Clinicians can mitigate the effects of the shock, however, by giving families a private place to hear the news and to sit with its emotional impact. Clinicians can help them to work out the practical issues, such as care for the body. Clinicians ought to allow loved ones time to sit with the body. Some spiritual traditions have clear guidelines for all these practical issues. Clinicians need to respect these guidelines and encourage families to carry through on their traditions surrounding death. Clinicians need to enable a home death for those whose culture and spiritual traditions value it. If a home death is not possible or desired, clinicians may need to "stretch" hospital policies to make room for families to practice spiritual rituals at the time of death. In essay after essay, we learned from spiritual thinkers the importance of this moment—the moment of death. Safe passage includes careful attention to the time of death, and clinicians can aid safe passage by enabling families to engage in the spiritual practices that support them at this time of ultimate liminality.

AFTER DEATH

Grief strikes us all when we lose someone near and dear to us. When we care for a patient who is about to die, we can at least avoid compounding their loved ones' impending grief by being sensitive. Speaking kind words, moving in and out of the patient's room gently and quietly, not voicing strong disagreements with the family—these are simple strategies to avert exacerbating the pain of loss. Clinicians can also help families by putting them and their dying loved ones in touch with leaders from their spiritual communities who can help them prepare for death. Spiritual leaders will help families navigate the waters of death so that, after death, grief may not overwhelm. When families have trouble coping with the loss of a loved one, grief counselors can provide support. Grieving families also need to be in touch with their spiritual communities, however, who can be present for families stuck in the waters of complicated grief, helping them to find their way. Most religious communities have rituals after death that help families remember and honor their loved ones who have passed on. Clinicians themselves can also punctuate the period after death with regular times or rituals of remembrance, thereby helping themselves to cope with the "mini-griefs" they sustain in the course of their work.[3]

SAFE PASSAGE

There is no guarantee of safe passage for anyone. Clinicians especially ought to avoid falling into the trap of thinking that it is their job to provide a good death for each and every patient.[4] It is equally a mistake, however, for clinicians to avoid addressing the spiritual needs of patients and families or to see it as somehow outside their job descriptions to muster for patients and families the spiritual resources that might help them to make the journey from life to death safely.

To provide safe passage, clinicians need to be present in the way that patients and families need them to be. Patients and families may need clinicians—of whatever stripe; clergy, nurses, physicians, social workers, volunteers, funeral directors—to leave the room, or to stand quietly by; to hold their hands or to knell beside them with bowed heads and honor the sacred moment of passage. Being there for patients and families in the way they need is how clinicians can guide the ship and keep it upright for dying patients and their families on the journey from life to death.

That journey is both universal and particular, but it is a voyage that billions of human beings have made before and billions more will make in the future. Over the many millennia of human reflection on the mystery of death, our great spiritual and religious traditions have learned much about how to prepare us for that journey. Clinicians should be, at the least, prepared to help patients and families access their particular spiritual traditions that can help them navigate these waters safely. As the poet T.S. Eliot has written,

> Fare forward, travellers! Not escaping from the past
> Into indifferent lives, or into any future;
> You are not the same people who left that station
> Or who will arrive at any terminus,
> While the narrowing rails slide together behind you;
> And on the deck of the drumming liner
> Watching the furrow that widens behind you,
> You shall not think 'the past is finished'
> Or 'the future is before us'.
> At nightfall, in the rigging and the aerial,
> Is a voice descanting (though not to the ear,
> The murmuring shell of time, and not in any language)
> Fare forward, you who think that you are voyaging;
> You are not those who saw the harbour
> Receding, or those who will disembark.
> Here between the hither and the farther shore
> While time is withdrawn, consider the future
> And the past with an equal mind.
> At the moment which is not of action or inaction
> You can receive this: "on whatever sphere of being
> The mind of man may be intent
> At the time of death"—that is the one action
> (And the time of death is every moment)
> Which will fructify in the lives of others:
> And do not think of the fruit of action.
> Fare Forward.
>   O voyagers, O seamen,
> You who came to port, and you whose bodies
> Will suffer the trial and judgement of the sea,
> Or whatever event, this is your real destination."
> So Krishna, as when he admonished Arjuna
> On the field of battle.
>   Not fare well,
> But fare forward, voyagers.[5]

To our patients, to their families, to our fellow clinicians, to all of our readers: we bid you fare forward.

REFERENCES

1. Geertz C. 1973. Thick description: toward an interpretive theory of culture. In: *The interpretation of cultures: selected essays*. New York: Basic Books, pp. 3–30.
2. Sulmasy DP. 2006. Spiritual issues in the care of dying patients: "...it's okay between me and God." *Journal of the American Medical Association* 296:1385–1392.
3. Holland JC. 2002. Management of grief and loss: medicine's obligation and challenge. *Journal of the American Medical Women's Association* 57(2):95–6.
4. Sulmasy DP. 2006. *The rebirth of the clinic: an introduction to spirituality in health care*. Washington, DC: Georgetown University Press, pp. 209–210.
5. Eliot TS. 1971. The dry salvages, III. In: *Four quartets*. New York: Harcourt, pp. 29–30.

APPENDIX 1

Case Studies

MOHAMMAD ZAFIR AL-SHAHRI

Case 1. *Mariam is a 30-year-old housewife, with two children. She was diagnosed with breast cancer that was staged at IIB. A curative treatment plan was discussed with the patient and her husband, and they both preferred to postpone consenting for the treatment plan until the next outpatient visit. The next day, Mariam and her husband sought advice from a poorly educated, quack spiritual healer who assertively diagnosed Mariam as a victim of evil eye. He prescribed the patient some amulets and gave her a bottle of olive oil for local use at the site of the breast mass. The quack spiritual healer asked the patient and her husband not to consent to medical treatment. Consequently, Mariam lost follow up with the oncology clinic for seven months, after which she had to see her oncologist for worsening symptoms. Her workup confirmed advanced metastatic disease. This case illustrates the fact that religious beliefs and the commonly strong faith in spiritual healing practices shall be kept in mind while caring for Muslim patients. The case also emphasizes the need for a competent spiritual care provider to be a member of the health care interdisciplinary team.*

Case 2. *Ahmad is a 65-year-old gentleman with prostate cancer widely metastatic to bones. On a routine follow-up outpatient visit accompanied with his wife, he was asked if he had any symptoms or issues that needed to be addressed. "All thanks go to Allah, I am feeling alright," Ahmad said. As the encounter was approaching its end, Ahmad's wife broke down in tears. Empathetic response of the physician encouraged Ahmad's wife to ventilate. She stated that for more than six weeks, Ahmad had hardly been able to enjoy a single hour of uninterrupted sleep. "He is rolling of pain in his bed day and night," she said. "I am begging him all the time to seek medical advice in order to get his pain relieved but he adamantly refuses as he sees this as a sign of dissatisfaction with Allah's will," she added. A spiritual care* *provider was able to convince Ahmad that reporting and treating pain is religiously permissible.*

Case 3. *Ibrahim is a 37-year-old man with advanced non-Hodgkin lymphoma refractory to chemotherapy and extensively involving both lungs, leading to severe dyspnea and cough. Ibrahim's symptoms were severe enough to require admission to a tertiary palliative care unit and to be started on a continuous subcutaneous infusion of morphine and midazolam. A non-Muslim Western nurse called the on-call physician at night to express her concerns about the fact that Ibrahim was refusing the opioid infusion despite his intractable symptoms. The physician arrived shortly at Ibrahim's bedside and realized that Ibrahim was aware that his final hours were approaching and he did not want to be on opioids and sedatives that would disturb his mental capacity and prevent him from performing prayers during this precious time. The physician referred to a religious verdict from leading Muslim scholars supporting the medical use of opioids and sedatives in conditions similar to Ibrahim's. Ibrahim accepted the treatment and died peacefully within a few days.*

INDEX

Bible, identifying ultimate cause of the accident, 124
biopsychosocial spiritual assessment and plan, 111
biopsychosocial-spiritual issues, of clinicians, 112
biopsychosocial-spiritual model, 105
black cumin (Nigella seeds), healing effects, 76
board certification, in palliative care, 14
board-certified chaplains, recognized as the spiritual care experts, 106
bodhisattva, weak tigress story, 127
body
    as a complex machine, 94
    having its parts understood and "fixed," 92
    new one after death, 130
    from one's recent ancestors, 213
    preserving as long as possible, 199
body and the spirit, 93, 94–95
body of the deceased
    attended to by members of the family, 217
    care for the, 260
    cleaning and bathing, 88
    cleansing and shrouding, 87
    cremation of, 216
    family or community members washing, 223
    handled with dignity, 77
    making sacred space around, 229
    respect for at all times, 220
    seeing, 206–207
Bolivia, initiatives in, 62
bomohs, 86
bondage of mind, to matter, 187
The Book of Changes, 128
The Book of History, 127
The Book of Poetry, 127
The Book of Rituals, 127–128
Borobudur, in Java, Indonesia, 81
Bortnowska, Haline, 39
botho. See Ubuntu
Bowlby, John, 38
Bradbury Hospice, in Hong Kong, 83
brain dead, 126
brain death, 138, 191
Brazil, 61, 66
Bright Vision Hospital, 83–84

"the broken heart" syndrome, 233
brotherly love (ti), 183
Buddha, avoiding conflicts, 211–212
Buddhism
    on the Malay Peninsula, 81
    in Nepal, 54
    not addressing political issues directly, 211
    not forbidding curative or palliative choice, 155
    originated from Hinduism, 88
    in Southeast Asia, 89–90
    variants of, 89
Buddhist chanting
    by caregivers, 89
    by monks, 90
Buddhist Lotus Hospice Care Foundation, 83
Buddhist Metta Welfare Services, 83
Buddhist practices, wide variations, 56
Buddhist response
    to Eman's case, 154–155
    to Huang-Fu's case, 126–127
    to Luz's case, 237–238
    to Martha's case, 182–183
    to Mosupi's case, 211–212
Buddhists, substantial variations in ideas, 56
burdens, bringing to God, 131
burial
    accepted in mainline tradition, 248
    choosing over cremation, 220
    in a grave facing to the east, 218
    of Muslims, 87
    rituals, 184
    taking place as soon as possible, 220
    of a whole (intact) body, 137
burial land (uliej), taboos, 218
burial society (chevrah kadisha), of comforting the mourner, 219
burying, bodies of the dead, 227
bwebwenato (stories about the deceased), 133, 218
bwijerro, "is this a death wish for me?," 188

Caja Costarricense de Seguro Social (CCSS), 61
cancer
    cases in Arab League countries, 71

Christian meaning of death, 227
Christian missionaries, nursing care through in India, 51
Christianity, in Africa, 27–28
Christians, in Southeast Asia, 90
chronic care facilities, for the provision of nursing care, 97
chronic disease, increasing prevalence of, 179
church attendance, declining in Western European countries, 44
church community, meeting patients' and families' spiritual needs, 30
churches
    few messages about living with HIV, 31
    members coming to comfort the family, 210
cinerary casket, should be buried in a grave, 213
City of Hope National Medical Center, 106
civil society, development of palliative care driven through, 37
clan's land, buried on, 218
Clinic for Pain and Palliative Care, in Calderón Guardia Hospital, 61
clinical assessment tools, evaluating patients' spiritual concerns, 17
clinical issues
    of Eman's case, 150–151
    of Huang-Fu's case, 121–122
    of Luz's case, 232–234
    of Martha's case, 177–178
    of Mosupi's case, 204–207
clinical pastoral care workers, role of, 17
clinical practice guidelines, for quality palliative care in the United States, 12
clinical question, critical for Eman, 171
clinical settings, implementing spirituality in, 106–107
clinical skills, central to end-of-life care, 99
clinical specialty, maturation of, 40
clinicians, caring for the dying, 3
clothes, burning to carry Luz's soul into the heavens, 232, 240, 248
coffin, plain pine, 220
cognitive and functional decline, future state of, 177

collaborative practice model, 102
collective presence, strengthening spirit of the patient, 133
collectivism, in Africa, 30
colonization, shared history of, 65
colostomies, Muslim patients with, 85
Columbia, initiatives led by psychologists, 61–62
coma, not equating to brain death, 136
comfort, goal of, 178
comforter in death, God of Israel as, 136
comfort-focused care only, 178
comforting
    the afflicted, 143
    others in their hour of grief, 241
communicable diseases, 96
communication, between doctors and the family, 140
communist countries of Eastern Europe and Central Asia, palliative care developments, 37
community
    accompanying mourner on his or her journey, 246
    grieving together, 210
    key to life of the church, 247
    loss shouldered by, 235
    presence at the time of death, 221
Community Based Palliative care, demonstration projects in Sri Lanka, 53
community-based care, focused on terminally ill patients with cancer, 10
compassion
    described, 112–113
    historical aspects, 105–106
    supreme Buddhist virtue, 127
    ultimate expression of spiritual care, 104–105
compassionate listener, regular visits from, 255
compassionate presence, 112–113
    as clinician's tool, 106–107
    of someone willing to listen, 173
complementary medicines, 52
complex spiritual issues, 111
complicated grief, 233, 255
condolences, 78
Confucian classics, five cardinal, 127

ethnospecific needs, in Bangladesh
    community, 53
Eucharist, 198, 226, 227
Europe
    history of palliative care, 36–46
    palliative care and hospice services, 6
European Association for Palliative Care
    (EAPC), 39, 40, 43
European Palliative Care Research Centre
    (PRC), 43
European populations, age of, 43
euthanasia, 178, 179–180, 192
    Buddhism advising against, 183
    Catholic perspective on, 197–198
    considered as unbiblical and unethi-
        cal, 181
    forbidden, 194
    illegal but also immoral, 184
    legalization of, 44
    not accepted, 180
    request for, 196
    strictly prohibited, 77
    those involved in, 188
Evangelical Christian response
    to Eman's case, 157–159
    to Huang-Fu's case, 129–131
    to Luz's case, 240–242
    to Martha's case, 185–186
    to Mosupi's case, 213–215
Evangelical or "born-again" Protestants
    (Evangelistas), 66
Evangelical Pentecostalism, 66
evil spirits, as cause of disease, 153
existential distress, 109
existential suffering, 76
exorcism, 154
extended families
    forming a collective support
        network, 65
    loss shouldered by, 235
    role during bereavement phase, 52

face-to-face interviews, in sub-Saharan
    African nations, 27
facts, acquiring all, 170
"failure" of medical practice, dying
    patient seen as, 38
fainting, acceptable by Marshallese, 245
faith
    accepting the natural reality, 169

as central message, 126
as greatest weapon, 165
having, 174
lacking deep, 241
playing a major role, 153
providing great support during
    bereavement, 242
source of, 158
faith experience, embedded in one's
    relationship with the family, 65
faithful life, expressions of, 165
false hope, 171
familial bonds, Confucian appreciation
    of, 239
families
    spiritual care of, 104–114
    strong spiritual and religious needs of
        in Latin America, 67
    walking with through grief, 134
families and friends, of the dying, 3
familism, Confucian, 128
Familismo, 65
familist way of life, for Confucians, 156
family
    caring for one another in times of
        sorrow and need, 252
    as central concern of the Confucian
        faith, 127
    Confucian symbolism of, 128
    Gustavo needing support of, 250
    help to deal with the reality, 170
    importance of, 8
    scope of, 212
family and friends, encompassing dying
    providing love, 221
family members
    consoling, 254
    looking after one's more than others,
        128
    making shared decisions,
        128, 157
    playing a great role in giving moral
        strength, 161
    resolving past disputes and
        animosities, 245
family network, strong in Hindu
    tradition, 131
family structure, bonds and obligations
    in the Arabic, 77
family unit, emphasis of care on, 10

family-centered care, at the end of life, 205
family-oriented religion, Confucianism as, 212
faring forward, 262
Fatalismo or fatalism, 65
fate, belief in, 65
feeding tubes, 178, 200. *See also* tube feeding
FHSSA (Foundation for Hospices in Sub-Saharan Africa), 22
FICA tool, 108
filial love, 239
filial obligation, 183
filial piety (*xiao*), 183
Final Goal of Nirvana, 212
fine tentacle (aolok), 218
fire ritual (*homan*), 243
fistulas, patients with, 85
five elements, elements of a body reverting back to, 145
five L's (Love, Laugh, Live, Learn, and Listen), 253
five pillars of Islam, 86
five pillars of religion (*Arkan ul Islam*), 74, 75
flat brain wave, 135
food, bringing to home of the deceased's family, 247
formal training, leading to improved end-of-life care, 100
Fornells, Hugo, 62
Foundation for Hospices in Sub-Saharan Africa (FHSSA), 22
four noble truths, 89
Franciscan Missionaries of the Divine Motherhood, 83
fulfillment, prayer road to, 132
full immersion, into the condition of being human, 105
funeral
    Antyeshti or last sacrament, 216
    as a celebration, 186, 214
    having as soon as possible, 135
    promptness allowing family to enter into period of mourning, 220
Funeral Liturgy, 227
funeral rites
    of Hindus, 243
    in Islam, 78

funeral rituals
    for the deceased, 254
    in many African communities, 235
futile medical care, 141

Gautama Buddha, 89
generations, in the scope of a family, 212
generic medicines, making available, 224
gentleman (*junzi*), 183
George Washington Institute for Spirituality and Care, 17
George Washington Institute for Spirituality and Health, 106
Germany, 37, 40
gift receiver, 213
giver in the Confucian way of life, 213
global disease burden, Africa shouldering 68% of, 20
global injustice, clear case of, 211
global poverty, as societal problem, 215
God
    always a victor over the powers of evil, 125
    belief in the power of to restore health, 165
    bestowing upon us what we by ourselves cannot attain, 171
    bringing to life those who are dead, 125
    falling in love with, 241
    goodness and justice is a priori, 134
    as light of our life, 240
    with Mosupi at the time of his death, 214
    never abandoning beloved people, 166
    nothing impossible with, 154
    power to heal regardless of sick person's condition, 181
    putting trust in, 158
    as the real healer, 167
    seeing face to face in heaven, 129
    sovereignty of, 126
God or Heaven (*tian*), 213
Godanam (gift of a cow), 243
God's healing, coming in many forms, 166
God's will. *See* Will of God
good death
    Evangelical Christianity speaking of, 159
    Ghana, 30

good death
    nurse's reflections on, 117
    principles of, 159
    sacrament highly valued as a means
        to, 143
    spiritual beliefs and practices,
        117–119
"A Good Death" (essay), 117
good deeds, of ancestors, 29
Good Samaritan, parable of, 93
grandchildren, needing Gustavo, 241
Greco-Roman medicine, Christian
        Europe adopted, 94
grief
    constellation of overwhelming
        emotions, 222
    expressing, 223
    human reality of, 166
    interconnected with bereavement, 243
    as other side of coin of love, 252
    person in the grip of in a prison, 242
    varied ways of expressing accommo-
        dated by Marshallese, 245
grief counselors, providing support, 261
grief experience, everyone's unique, 255
Grief Recovery small group, 241
grief-stricken, wrapped securely (kilbur)
        in a fine mat and pounded on
        upper chest or throat, 245
grieving
    continuing long after burial, 245
    as part of a "recovery" process, 251
    process of, 240
Grollman, Earl, 252
gross body, burnt, 243
ground of being, as a present reality, 164
Guatemala, 62
Guidelines for Quality Palliative Care, 13
guilt, 182, 233, 239
Gurdwara (Sikh places of worship), 172,
        228, 254
Gurus, regarding suffering as a result of
        a person's karma, 173

hand feeding, 184, 198, 199
Hanuman Chalisa, recitation of, 132
Harding, Richard, 62
hastening death (bwijerro), 162
HAU (Hospice Africa Uganda), 22
Haven of Hope Hospital, 83

HCA (Hospice Care Association), 83
"the Healer" (al-Shafi), 167
healing, 154, 162
health
    caring for own, 250
    Hindu beliefs linked to, 187
    in a particular context, 224
health care
    appropriate access to, 221
    family members assisting each other
        in, 238
    history of, 92–93
    involving much more than treating
        the patient for a medical
        condition, 225
    rights to adequate as proposed by
        World Health Organization, 212
    special position of the family in, 239
health care professionals
    lack of education and knowledge as a
        major barrier, 12
    limited workforce capacity in U.S., 16
    ongoing responsibility for the care of
        those close to the patient, 234
health care providers
    advising patients on treatment
        choice, 151
    considering spiritual needs, 167
health care proxies, 16
health care research, in Latin American
        countries, 63
health care staff, training for the dying,
        98–100
health care systems
    embedding models of care within
        mainstream, 25
    implementing public health
        strategies, 96
    neglect of the dying within, 38
    underfunded in Latin America, 60
health care workers
    learning their art through practice, 101
    thinking of health care as separate
        from religion and spirituality, 94
    wearing lab coats, 93
health concerns, prayers for, 161
health proxy, not popular among
        Hindus, 187
heart, as center of life, 126, 127
heart is rent, sign of, 219

heaven, reward of the kingdom of, 154
heavenly realm, 164
herbal and nonherbal treatments, 133
herbal remedies, often a first resort, 161
heterogeneity, of the Latin American
    populations living in U.S., 63
high blood pressure, Luz's, 235
Hindu, rituals, 88
Hindu concepts, 88
Hindu Dharma. *See* Hinduism
Hindu Krishna temple, 85
Hindu response
    to Eman's case, 160–161
    to Huang-Fu's case, 131–132
    to Luz's case, 242–244
    to Martha's case, 187–188
    to Mosupi's case, 215–217
Hinduism
    in Nepal, 54
    in the Southeast Asian region, 81, 88
    as universal religion, 160
Hindus, customs and rituals for a dying
    person, 55–56
Hinton, John, 38
Hispanic Catholicism, structure of
    organized, 65
historical perspectives on end-of-life care
    Asia Pacific, 80–91
    Europe, 36–46
    globally, 4
    Indian subcontinent, 48–56
    Latin America, 59–67
    Middle East, 71–78
    North Africa, 71–78
    United States, 10–18
HIV
    difficulty of disclosing a positive
        status, 30
    lack of awareness to the danger of, 214
    majority of children in the world
        living with, located in sub-Saharan
        Africa, 25
HIV/AIDS. *See also* AIDS
    considering as any other disease, 211
    patients with as special cases, 208
    persons contracting confessing before
        death, 210
    prolonging the lives of patients
        indefinitely, 219
    response to epidemic, 22

in sub-Saharan Africa, 20
    toll in Africa, 226
HIV-positive new TB cases, in Africa, 20
holistic approach, to care, 105
holistic assessment and treatment
    plan, 111
holistic model, demonstrated by Cicely
    Saunders, 103
holy ash, applied on the forehead, 216
holy oil, applying to the body, 153
holy water
    pouring in the person's mouth, 55
    trickled into the mouth, 216
    use of, 210
home
    Hindus preferring to die at, 215
    preparing for the body, 244
home care, barriers to efficient,
    54–55
home deaths
    emphasis on, 10
    enabling, 260
home-based care, 55
home-based care (HBC) model, 23
Home-based Palliative Care Service, in
    Sri Lanka, 53
honey, healing effects, 76
Hong Kong, first hospice ward, 83
hope, described, 171
hope against hope, always, 131
Hope Institute, in Jamaica, 62
HOPE tool, 108
"hospice," in English, 82
Hospice Africa Uganda (HAU), 22
hospice and palliative care organizations,
    operating in African countries, 21
hospice and palliative care services,
    typology depicting levels of service
    development by country, 23–24
Hospice and Palliative Nurses
    Association (HPNA), 13
hospice care
    current status in the U.S., 15
    delivery of palliative care, 8
    late referral to in the United
        States, 15
    providing, 5
Hospice Care Association (HCA), 83
Hospice Foundation of Taiwan, 83
hospice home care, in Japan, 83

James, William, 4
Japan, 83
Jaramillo, Isa de, 61
Jesus
    healed all manner of disease, 158
    leaving our burden with Him, 131
    perturbed and troubled in the face of
        human suffering, 143
    raised from the dead and ascended
        into heaven, 214
    rejoicing in, 236
    return to Earth, 27
Jewish response
    to Eman's case study, 163–165
    to Huang-Fu's case study, 134–136
    to Luz's case, 245–247
    to Martha's case, 190–191
    to Mosupi's case, 219–330
jia ren (family members), 128
jiva, helping to travel, 243
Joint Commission on Hospital
    Accreditation, 13
joint family systems
    common among Hindus, 161
    making important ethical
        decisions, 187
Judaism
    not finding redemption in suffering
        and death, 134
    in Southeast Asia, 90
"just-ness," value of, 135

kafan, sheets of clean, white cloth, 223
Kaposi's Sarcoma, 205
karma
    accumulating positive, 144
    belief in, 56
    described, 55, 88
    law of, 131, 155, 160
    next life decided by, 188
    place of, 243
karma and rebirth, Hindus believing in,
    216
Kashiwagi, Tetsuo, 83
Katongole, Fr. Emmanuel, 226
Kenya, integrating palliative care into
    public and provincial government
    hospitals, 25
Kerala (southern India), services more
    widespread, 48

Kevorkian, Jack, 185
kiden (Beach Heliotrope), embalming
    using leaves of, 217
killing, strong objection against, 182
King Faisal Specialist Hospital and
    Research Center (KFSHRC), 71–72
Korea, earliest development of hospices
    in Asia, 82
Kornfeld Foundation, 12, 14
Kuan Yin Temple, 85
Kübler-Ross, Elizabeth, 5, 241
kufiya, worn by Eman's father, 148

Lai, Ernest, 83
last-will-and-testament, preparing, 164
Latin America
    countries not meeting need for
        palliative care, 59–60
    current status and areas for
        improvement, 62–63
    historical perspectives on end-of-life
        care, 59–67
    history and current status of
        palliative care, 60–63
    history of palliative care by country,
        61–62
    interaction between spirituality,
        religion, and health care, 66
    palliative and hospice care coming
        to, 6–7
Latin American Association for Palliative
    Care, 62
Latin American Congress of Palliative
    Care, 63
Latin American countries, barriers to
    delivery of palliative care, 60
Latin American Palliative Care
    Congress, 63
Latin American patients, expecting
    physicians to take a more directive
    role, 63
Latino cultural values and daily lives,
    spirituality and religiosity
    enmeshed with, 65
Latino Evangelicals, 66
Latinos
    religion and spirituality, 64–67
    religious diversity of, 65–66
    in the United States, 63
"Law 100," in Columbia, 62

Mackay Hospice, 83
Mainland Southeast Asia, 80
mainline Protestant Christian response
    to Eman's case, 165–166
    to Huang-Fu's case, 136–137
    to Luz's case, 247–248
    to Martha's case, 192–193
    to Mosupi's case, 220–222
mainline Protestant traditions,
    encouraging organ donation, 137
mainstream health care provision,
    palliative care seeking to gain
    recognition within, 39
*Making Health Care Whole: Integrating
    Spirituality into Patient Care*, 106
Malay Peninsula, 80
Malaysia, 80, 84, 86
Mandate of Heaven, 128, 213
mandate to care, 260
mantras or *slokas*, chanting, 216
Mariam's case study, 263
Marshallese people (Ri-Majol)
    belonging to a clan, 217
    continuing curative-oriented treat-
    ment, 161
    life defined as the drawing of breath,
    132–133
Maryknoll Hospital, in Hong Kong, 83
material dimension, of culture, 44
maternal blood line (*bwij*), clan identified
    by, 217
matrilineal society, Marshall Islands
    valuing women, 163
meaning
    as a core concept of spirituality, 108
    recovering a sense of, 235
meaningful life, in the here and now, 145
mechanic, work as a calling from
    God, 242
medical care
    directed towards others who may
    have contracted the HIV/AIDS
    virus, 229
    historically primarily supportive and
    palliative with few options for
    curing disease, 105
Medical Council of India, postgraduate
    course recognized by, 50
medical curricula, integrating spiritual
    care in, 17

medical decision making, family-based
    approach to, 157
medical devices, removing from the
    body, 222
medical evidence, conclusions drawn
    from, 140
medical facts, clear understanding of, 168
medical futility, issue of, 156
medical intervention, patient needing
    increased, 195
medical knowledge, needed to relieve
    suffering and improve end-of-life
    care, 99
medical nutrition, criteria making
    morally optional, 198
medical science, as a good gift from
    God, 192
medical systems, impacted by the
    economic system, 224
medical treatment, encouraging patients
    to accept, 170
medically underserved, issue of, 215
Medicare costs, escalating, 11
Medicare Hospice Benefit, lobbying
    Congress to pass, 10–11
medication
    with intention to facilitate death, 192
    Luz stopped taking, 234
medicine
    gift from God, 165
    keeping people alive, 185
    in a particular context, 224
    prolonging life without attention to
    quality, 165
    situation overall in Africa, 224
    use of traditional and herbal, 29
meditation
    for a harmonious life, 187
    Hindu oriented, 50
    important part of the Buddhist way
    of life, 89
    improving patient outcomes, 54
    sharing in a time of, 174
memorial, creating to honor life and
    memory of Luz, 253
memorial services, for Hindu dead, 89
men, dying of "the broken heart"
    syndrome, 233
Méndez, Eduardo, 62–63
mental illness, as a result of *karma*, 187

National Center for Pain Control and
    Palliative Care, Costa Rica, 61
National Coalition of Hospice and
    Palliative Care Organizations, task
    force of, 12
National Comprehensive Cancer
    Network (NCCN), 111
National Consensus Conference, 106
National Consensus Project for
    Quality Palliative Care (NCP),
    guidelines and domains in
    palliative care, 105
National Consensus Project (NCP), 12
National Framework and Preferred
    Practices for Palliative and Hospice
    Care Quality, 13
National Hospice and Palliative Care
    Organization (NHPCO),
    representing hospice and palliative
    care providers, 15
National Institutes of Health (NIH),
    funding, 14
national palliative care associations, in
    eastern and southern Africa, 23
National Palliative Care Research
    (NPCRC), 13
National Quality Forum, 13
National Radiotherapy Center,
    Nicaragua, 62
national standards, creating in the U.S.,
    12–13
natural body, raised as a spiritual
    body, 130
natural death, 186, 192
necessity, principle of, 77
negative *karmas*, bearing fruit right now,
    155
Neighbourhood Network in Palliative
    Care in Kerala, 53
neo-Pentecostal movement, in Africa, 28
Nepal, 48, 54
New Testament Scriptures, miraculous
    cures in, 142
NGOs, involved in providing supportive
    services for palliative care in
    India, 51
Nicaragua, 62
NIH Summit Meeting, recommendations
    supporting palliative care
    research, 14

nine generations (*jiuzu*), including all
    members of, 212
Nitya Vidhi (daily ritual), 243
Noah, "a righteous man in his
    generation," 135
nokin, morning and evening prayer, 162
non-cancer population, entering hospice
    in U.S., 15
noncurative care, increasing demand for
    HIV-related in Africa, 20
noncurative interventions, need for
    children in Africa, 25
nonreligious patients, similar needs to
    religious counterparts, 45
normalities, setting aside, 219
North Africa, 7, 71–78
Norwegian University of Science
    and Technology at Trondheim
    University Hospital, 43
nurses
    caring for dying patients identifying
        spiritual interventions, 89
    certified in hospice and palliative
        care, 14
    comprehensive training program
        for, 13
nursing and care homes, palliative care
    rarely integrated, 41
nutrition
    artificial, 179, 195, 260
    intravenous, 198, 199
    medical, 198
    whether or not to initiate, 186

obstacles to palliative care and opioid
    usage, in Indian subcontinent, 54
obuntu. See Ubuntu
occupational therapy, in palliative care in
    Europe, 42
Oil of the Sick, anointing with, 143
old age, as a symbol of wisdom, 180
old peoples' homes, not in most African
    societies, 180
old-age dependency ratio, 43
Omega Foundation, 61
oneself, protecting first, 251
opioid drugs, inadequate supply of, 50
opioids, medical prescription of, 77
opioids and sedatives, medical use
    of, 264

opium use, in India, 50
options
  considering all on the basis of plain
    facts, 169
  for Eman, 169
oral morphine
  availability of, 50
  giving of, 97
organ and tissue donation,
    considering, 124
organ donation
  Buddhist approach to, 127
  Catholics supporting, 143–144
  considered a wise choice, 146
  decision on, 142
  for further medical use, 125
  joining two or more families by tragic
    circumstances, 137
  a moot question, 135
  new concept to Ri-Majol, 134
  permitted in Islam, 141
organ donor, registering as, 130
organ transplantation
  Hindu teachings making no direct
    reference to, 132
  issue of, 135
  practice of, 122
  question of, 138
  universally approved among
    Evangelicals, 130
organs
  donating Huang-Fu's, 122, 127
  should be donated, 144
over-medicalization, of death, 10

Pacific Asia, care of the body
    after death, 7
pain. *See also* "total pain"
  from cancer, 50
  dying experiencing, 5
  phenomenon of, 36
  treating as religiously permissible,
    263–264
  trials from God, 194
Pain and Policy Studies Group/WHO
    Collaborating Center, 63
pain medication, always permitted, 191
Pakistan, palliative care services, 51–52
palliative and end-of-life care, region by
    region, 7

palliative care
  1945–1965 phase in Europe, 38
  1965–1985 phase in Europe, 38–39
  1985-Present phase in Europe, 39–40
  African culture and, 27–32
  alternate and unorthodox medicine, 49
  Arabic culture and, 73–78
  areas of improvement in the Indian
    subcontinent, 54–55
  Asia Pacific cultures and, 85–91
  attention to, 163
  attributes of, 43
  better option for Eman from an
    Islamic viewpoint, 170
  for children needing to start at time
    of diagnosis, 11
  countries with the highest
    development of, 40
  cultures of the Indian subcontinent
    and, 55–56
  current status in Asia, 84–85
  current status in the U.S., 15
  defining religious and spiritual
    aspects of in the U.S., 17–18
  desire for, 193
  embracing varieties of cultural and
    spiritual beliefs and practices, 4
  endowed chairs in, 14
  growth in the United States, 16
  guidelines and domains in, 105–106
  history and current status of in
    Africa, 21–26
  history and current status of in Asia,
    82–85
  in the Indian subcontinent, 48–54
  Latin American culture and, 63–66
  in long-term care settings for
    older people, 42
  models of, 55
  need in Africa, 21
  no longer needing a religious
    society, 45
  obstacles in the Indian
    subcontinent, 49
  practiced since ancient times, 48
  rarely integrated into hospital
    departments, 41
  rich and diverse in Europe, 37
  right of every adult and child with a
    life-limiting illness, 22

palliative care (*Cont.*)
  roles of complementary and
    alternative medicine, 49–50
  sense of "vitality" in the European
    context, 42
  thriving in times of declining church
    attendance, 45
  as a Western phenomenon, 48
Palliative Care Certification Manual, 13
palliative care coverage, remaining
  deficient in Africa, 25
palliative care developments
  barriers to, 40
  map of levels across Europe, 42
Palliative Care program, in Sarawak,
  Malaysia, 55
palliative care provision
  current status of in Africa, 23–25
  limited or non-existent in a number
    of states in Asia and the Pacific,
    84–85
palliative care research
  across Europe, 43
  in Africa, 25–26
palliative care services
  extent of in the Indian sub-
    continent, 55
  reducing referrals to hospice care, 16
palliative care staff
  focusing on traditional African beliefs
    as a barrier, 31
  training of, 8
palliative care teams
  focusing on reducing distressing
    symptoms, 178
  in US hospitals, 15
palliative care unit
  in Royal Victoria Hospital in
    Montreal, 6
  staying in a, 183
  transfer to, 186
palliative home care, 49
palliative medicine
  medical subspecialty status in the
    United States, 13–14
  questions about in Pakistan,
    51–52
palliative treatment
  option of, 169
  seeking, 152

Pallium Latino America training
  initiative, 61
Paraguay, 62
parents
  including Dao and Lien's, 129
  taking care of one's own, 182
Parkes, Colin Murray, 38
Paschal mystery
  of the death and resurrection of
    Christ, 227
  personal incarnation of, 253
  source of hope for Huang-Fu's
    parents, 143
pashnustapanam, on the first day, 243
pashunam, meaning stone, 243
passive dying, 164
passive euthanasia, 188, 196
patients
  consenting to conversion to make
    children happy, 90
  desiring and needing continuity, 101
  easily overcome by extreme
    passions, 157
  experiencing pain in the last three
    days of life, 12
  not leaving alone, 162
  providing with food and water, 198
  spiritual care of, 104–114
  use of narratives, 38
  vulnerable end of their lives of, 51
  when facing grief and loss, 249
patient's life, meaning and connection
  in, 108
Peace House Hospice, 83
pediatric hospice services, in the U.S., 11
pediatric palliative care, in Africa, 25
pediatric services, in Africa, 25
"the peer of Heaven and Earth," parents
  as, 184
pekuah nefesh (saving a soul), encouraged
  over any other obligation, 136
Penance, 198, 226
Pentecostal Churches
  believing in healing by God, 153
  continuing to pray for full
    recovery, 181
  death of Mosupi would carry a lot of
    stigma, 210
  death perceived as a spiritual
    journey, 236

prayers (*Cont.*)
    offered for the deceased, 87
    performance of, 228
    proving ineffective, 153
    purpose of, 132
    rituals enhancing spiritual support
        at bedside of those approaching
        death, 221
    sharing in a time of, 174
    singing and reciting, 254
    used to call upon the Divine, 136
predeath phase, 117, 118
preparation, toward death as preparation
    for a long journey, 237
Presbyterian Mackay Memorial Hospital
    in Taipei, 83
presence, helping to remove part of the
    pain, 246
present condition, result of previous
    causes, 155
President's Emergency Plan for AIDS
    Relief (PEPFAR), 22
    targeting HIV/AIDS interventions,
        22–23
presumed consent, 139
prethatma, hunger of, 243
priesthood, Islam acknowledges no, 74
primary caregivers, interviews with
    bereaved from Bangladesh, 53
primary end-of-life care, 98
product champions, shortage of, 40
professional health care, as old a human
    history, 92
professional organizations, supporting
    in the U.S., 15
professions, differentiation toward
    training in, 101
prognosis
    clarity of, 259
    Huang-Fu's uncertainty about, 123
    uncertainty leads to acceptance of
        miracles, 145
Project on Death in America, 12
prolonged death, safe passage for, 260
prophet-healers
    in African Independent Churches, 153
    answering theological questions, 125
    claiming they have power to heal
        HIV/AIDS, 209–210
    consulting a, 124

determining cause of Alzheimer's
    disease, 180
Prophets of Allah, 75
proportionate means, of preserving life,
    171–172
prosperity gospel, Pentecostal movement
    associated with, 28
Protestant anointing, blessings, prayers,
    and liturgies, 137
Protestant Reformation, 93
Protestantism, diverse in sub-Saharan
    Africa, 27
psychological distress, 109
psychospiritual implication, of an acci-
    dent, 136
public, lack of familiarity with the dying
    process and death, 97
public funeral, preferably held in a
    church, 248
public health approach
    in Africa, 23
    as a solution to the challenge of
        coverage, 84
public morality, ancestors guardians of,
    235
punishment, threat of ancestral, 29

Qibla, facing, 223
quality of life
    emphasis towards, 45
    palliative care improving, 95
Quesada, Lizbeth, 63
Qur'an
    every Muslim entitled to read, 74
    holy book for Muslims, 86
    teachings of, 73–74

rabbi, job of, 134
raw opium, traditional use of in Indian
    society, 50
reaping, the fruits of *karmas* or deed,
    173
rebirth and reincarnation, theory of, 173
red paper, at entrance to elevator leading
    to deceased's home, 81
Redemptorist brothers in Singapore,
    Roman Catholic Church run by, 85
reincarnation
    belief in, 29, 54, 55
    described, 88

Robert Wood Johnson Foundation, 11, 12
Rodriguez, Rene, 62
role beyond death, helping the patient
    see, 163–164
roles, of those trained in end-of-life care,
    101
Roman Catholic response
    to Eman's case, 170–172
    to Huang-Fu's case, 142–144
    to Luz's case, 252–253
    to Martha's case, 197–198
    to Mosupi's case, 226–227
Romania, 37–38, 42
Rosas, Gustavo Montejo, 61
round-the-clock care, expense of, 176
routinization, of hospice and palliative
    care, 46

Sacrament of the Anointing of the Sick,
    143
sacred duty, to look after old people, 180
sacred water, contact of the ashes with,
    217
sacrificial rituals, 184
safe environment, creating, 5, 8
safe passage
    about creating right environment,
        259
    beginning early in diagnosis of a
        life-limiting disease, 6
    described, 118
    for a good death, 257
    palliative and end-of-life care for, 3–9
    providing, 5, 261–262
Samsara (worldly life), 88, 238
Sanatana Dharma, 160. See also
    Hinduism
sandalwood paste, applied on the
    forehead, 216
Sangha, order of Buddhist monks, 89
Santa Cruz de la Sierra, palliative care
    unit, 62
sapindhi karanam, performed on the
    12th day, 243
Saudi Arabia, palliative care most
    developed in, 71–72
Saunders, Cicely, 9, 36–37, 39, 82, 83, 97
    concept of "total pain," 105
    efforts firmly within Christian
        tradition, 46

holistic model demonstrated by, 103
legacy of, 5
new philosophy and practice for care
    at the end of life, 38
principles of care described by, 10
Schulweis, Harold, 190, 191
science, gift from God, 165
Scripture (the Bible), Evangelical
    Christianity basing understanding
    upon, 129
secondary levels, requiring specialist
    skills, 98
secularization, 44, 45
self, taking care of one's, 250
self-realization, prayers leading do, 132
self-sacrifice, tension with self-care, 247
sensitivity, averting exacerbating pain of
    loss, 261
servanthood, at heart of the Gospel
    message, 247
service
    concept of, 250
    to humanity, 144
    living a life of, 232–233
service (Sewa), beginning at home, 253
serving rituals, 184
sewacho, holy water mixed with ashes,
    153
sexual behavior, changing, 210
shaddham, performed to each of the
    ancestors, 243
shahadatain, of Islam, 223
shamanic and traditional-healer
    practices, in Latin American
    countries, 67
Shanti Avedana Ashram, in Mumbai, 48
shanti prayers, 243
Shaw, Rosalie, 82
"Shechina" (divine presence), at the
    bedside of the sick, 136
shepherd, leading his flock from the rear,
    134
Shi'a Muslim response
    to Eman's case, 166–167
    to Huang-Fu's case, 138–139
    to Luz's case, 248–250
    to Martha's case, 193–194
    to Mosupi's case, 222–223
shock, death coming as, 260
shraddham, 243

spiritual care (*Cont.*)
    as important as physical care, 102
    monitoring outcomes, 32
    not part of health care, 94
    of patients and families at the
        end-of-life, 104–114
    providing a chance to remember God,
        167
    understanding in a wide sense, 31
spiritual care model, as a relational
    model, 112
spiritual caregivers
    allowing Eman to tell and perhaps
        retell, 173
    encouraging active participation of
        loved ones, 221
    helping the family clarify whether or
        not Haung-Fa is clinically dead,
        137
    inviting Gustavo to talk about Luz, 255
    offer to pray with Dao and Lien, 146
spiritual concerns, potential, 76–77
spiritual counseling
    by an expert spiritual healer, 139
    Huang-Fu's parents needing, 145
spiritual diagnoses
    notion of, 107
    potential, 109–110
spiritual discipline, compassionate care
    as, 112–113
spiritual distress
    creating taxonomy of, 111
    detrimental effect in sub-Saharan
        context, 30
    presenting in different ways, 109
    process of identifying, 109
    as significant source of suffering for
        patients, 107
    tools identifying, 108
spiritual domain, a part of the care of the
    dying, 8
spiritual experiences, exploring death
    from within, 4
spiritual force or power (*Anij*), deep
    conviction in, 133
spiritual healers
    encouraging Gustavo to be patient,
        249
    quack, 263
    ri-allok, 162

taking patients to, 85
spiritual healing
    African Independent Churches
        resorting to, 124
    as faith healing, 161
    Pentecostals believing in, 153
    practices, 76
spiritual leaders, helping families
    navigate waters of death, 261
spiritual legacy, passing on to children,
    174
"spiritual lung for humanity," Africa as,
    226
spiritual medical practices, 76
spiritual needs
    assessment of, 31
    of patients, 8
spiritual perspectives, sharing, 146
spiritual practice, compassion as, 112
spiritual questions, sharing, 258
spiritual resources
    in a safe environment, 8
    tools identifying, 108
spiritual screening, 108
spiritual space, creating for patients and
    families, 260
spiritual therapy, Gustavo needing, 249
spiritual traditions, 258, 262
"the spiritual turn," within palliative
    care, 45
spiritual well-being, in Africa, 30
"the spiritual works of mercy," 143
spirituality
    always particular, 259
    among Latinos, 64–67
    definition of, 108
    as an essential element of palliative
        care, 105
    implementing clinical settings,
        106–107
    intersecting with other domains of
        personhood, 107
    more encompassing concept of, 45
    not universally positive, 31
    in palliative care, 105
    responding to need to find meaning
        in death, 205
    in South Asian countries, 48
spirituality (*la espiritualidad*), powerful
    influence on many Latinos, 65